'What a joy of a book, plunging you straight away into the very body, bosom and blood of America . . . makes me cry with pleasure, enfolding me, as it does, with the sheer magic of being able to be back on the road in America . . .'

Lucinda Lambton, *The Oldie*

'. . . an astute observer and a careful listener, who writes like a dream. America's vitality and variety, its comedy and its sadness, and the spirit of the common man and woman has seldom been more vividly captured.'

Mick Brown

'Bloody gorgeous . . . and *so* needed right now . . . What a generous, empathetic book it is.'

Stella Duffy

'. . . hugely enjoyable travelogue. If, like me, you are never likely to cross America at this leisurely pace, this is the next best thing.'

David Allan, *Country Music People*

'. . . his genuine love for travel, history, and a general sense of curiosity shine through . . . traveling along with him in this highly readable book, will leave readers hopeful for a better future.'

J. R. Patterson, *Travel Writing World*

'. . . an absolute joy . . . Like all the best road-trips, I didn't want this ride to end.'

Joanne Owen, *LoveReading* ★★★★★ A Book of the Month

T0018391

SLOW ROAD TO SAN FRANCISCO

Across the USA from Ocean to Ocean

David Reynolds

MUSWELL
PRESS

First published by Muswell Press in 2020
This edition published 2021

Copyright © David Reynolds 2020
Map by Roy Williams

Lines from 'I Am Waiting' by Lawrence Ferlinghetti (p. 287–88) from
A Coney Island of the Mind © 1958 Lawrence Ferlinghetti, reprinted
by permission of New Directions Publishing Corp.

Typeset in Bembo by M Rules
Printed and bound by CPI Group (UK) Ltd, Croydon CR0 4YY

David Reynolds has asserted his right
to be identified as the author of this work in accordance
with the Copyright, Designs and Patents Act, 1988

A CIP catalogue record for this book
is available from the British Library

ISBN: 9781838340162
eISBN: 9781999313586

Muswell Press
London N6 5HQ
www.muswell-press.co.uk

For
Freddie, Florence, Rocco, Albert, Archie and Margot

'You know, travel helps people to learn, and you learn most if you have no plan, no itinerary.'

Robert, motel receptionist, Pueblo, Colorado

'I like the pretty things. I think they say more, and the important thing is being able to feel them.'

Ben Webster, saxophonist

Contents

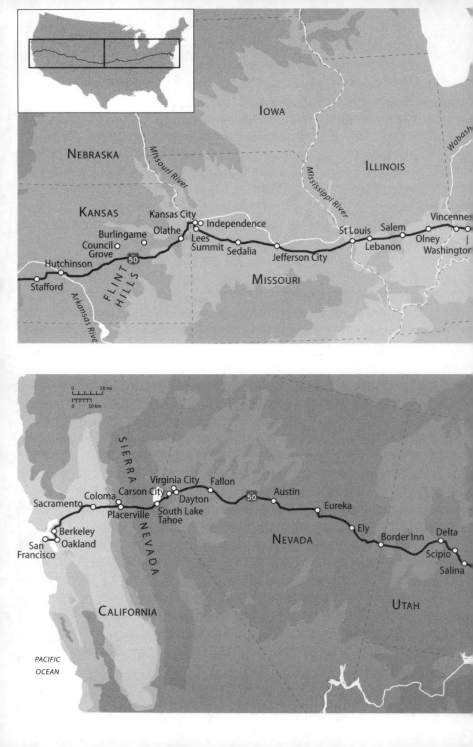

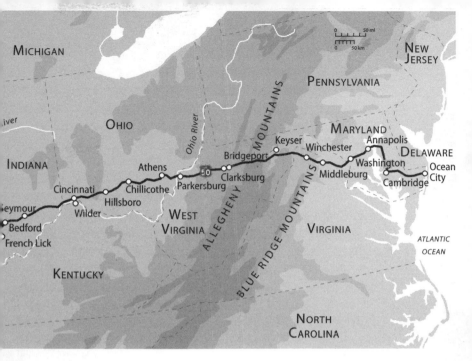

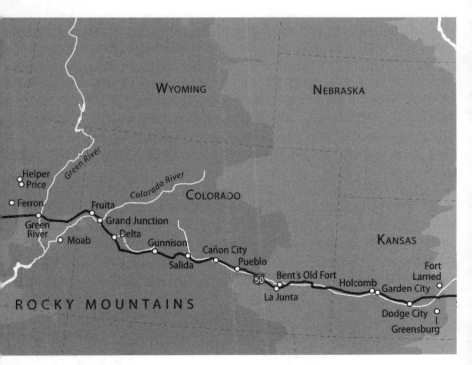

Introduction to 2021 edition

Curious readers have asked me how, since I don't live there, I got to Ocean City Beach – the setting-off point for my 3000-mile drive to San Francisco.

The literal answer is that I walked out of my house in London as if I were going to the corner shop for a pint of milk but, unusually, kissed and hugged my wife fulsomely in the doorway, pulled a suitcase along the pavement behind me and walked past the corner shop to a bus stop. And there I stood, three minutes from home, feeling lonely; I wouldn't be returning to this familiar, comfortable place – from which, going the other way, red buses could take me into central London – for seven weeks: a short time sometimes, but a long time then.

A bus took me to Hammersmith, the tube took me to Heathrow Airport and a plane lumbered across the Atlantic to Washington Dulles International Airport with me onboard. At Dulles I went to a portacabin to collect a prebooked hire car. And there something fateful happened, something that affected the course of the next 46 days. As I waited in a short queue, loud shouting and cursing broke out at the front. A group of seven had come to collect a large car called a Ford Explorer only to find that there was none available, despite their having booking ahead. Both men behind the desk had to focus on pacifying a small angry mob.

Meanwhile I got chatting to the man who was waiting behind me. He picked up on my accent and asked where I was going.

'Ocean City, Maryland. Then I'm going to drive from there to San Francisco.'

He looked puzzled, so I explained that I wanted to cross the US on a single road and that Highway 50 went all the way, ocean to ocean.

He smiled. 'OK. I get it. Didn't know 50 went all the way across. That'll be fun. You'll see much more than you would on interstates.' He ran a hand through thick curly hair. 'What car are you getting?'

'I don't know what make. I just booked a midsize. I thought for that distance, I should have a bit of space.'

'Get a Chevy Cruze. That's best for longer distances. I rent cars here all the time. I get a Toyota Corolla to go to, say, New York. Further than that, Chevy Cruze.'

The tantrums up at the desk subsided; the group of seven were given two cars for the price of one. And soon it was my turn. I signed pieces of paper and said I'd like a Chevy Cruze.

'You can have any car you want from Lane 3.' The man pointed through the window to the car park. 'Should be some Chevy Cruzes there, but I'm not sure.'

I went outside and walked along Lane 3. There was just one Chevy Cruze – white and gleaming in hot, afternoon sun. I opened the driver's door. The key was in the ignition. My curly-haired friend appeared. 'So you got the only Cruze, darn it!' He grinned. 'That's OK. I'll take a Corolla.' He went down the row and climbed into a red one.

Meanwhile I couldn't work out how to open the boot. I ran over to my friend. 'Can you tell me how to open the ... trunk?'

He came and pointed to a lever beside the driver's seat. 'Pull that.'

I pulled it and the boot sprang open. 'Thanks. Sorry to hold you up.'

'It's OK. Good luck,' he said. 'Have a wonderful trip.'

And thanks to that friendly, knowledgeable man, whose name I don't know, I acquired the car that was my companion for the next forty-six days. Soon I gave my Chevy Cruze a name derived from its licence plate – and when the view from a hill was beautiful or gasp-inducing, or when I felt lonely or was literally lost, or when it surged uphill past a crawling truck, I spoke to it.

With some difficulty, and with the help of a road atlas and the advice of groups of kind and patient Americans in two gas stations, I drove the thirty-five miles into DC and found myself passing the White House on Constitution Avenue. I waved in sympathy to Melania and, stretching my imagination, gave Jon Sopel of the BBC a lift for about a mile and around a couple of shallow bends in the road to the Capitol Building which looks a little like St Paul's Cathedral coated in thick white paint.

Eventually I managed to leave DC and press on towards Ocean City, 135 miles to the east. When it grew dark I stopped for the night at a motel in Cambridge, Maryland, and reached Ocean City in a rainstorm the next day.

The longer, more fundamental explanation of how I came to be on the beach in Ocean City that day begins, perhaps, with my being given an Indian head-dress when I was five years old. Not long after that I was given two toy Colt revolvers that fired caps.

Around this time my father brought home our first television: a wooden box fronted by a small screen which showed the only available channel, BBC, in black and white. Half-hour western series were on children's television in the early evenings, and I grew used to eating my kiddie-size rissoles while watching the Cisco Kid or Hopalong Cassidy. I kept my revolvers loaded with caps beside my plate, and would drop my knife and fork to pick them up, so that I could help out Cisco and his sidekick, Pancho, by shooting at the baddies.

The guns were followed by a cowboy outfit with a hat and colourful waistcoat, then a teepee in which I could sit with my friend Richard, wearing my feathered head-dress. Richard and I began to spend our pocket money on plastic model Indians and invented a game in which his Indians, the Apaches, fought my Indians, the Comanches, on his living-room carpet. We bought and swapped cowboy comics; Cowboy Picture Library published four every month with 64 pages of high drama exuding the arousing aroma of ink and newsprint, featuring Kit Carson, Buck Jones, the Kansas Kid and Davy Crockett. We watched westerns at our local cinema, and John Wayne became my favourite actor and perhaps – forgive me! – role model.

The wild west, which I began to understand wasn't in another part of England but across the sea in America, was a huge source of entertainment for British kids in the 1950s and '60s – and for me, in small-town England, it seemed to be an idyll – a place where there was space and freedom and excitement.

When I was ten my parents separated and my mother and I went to live with her uncle, a genial old man who liked to sip whisky and soda while watching westerns on television – *Rawhide, Bonanza, Wagon Train* – in hour-long episodes. I loved those series and, by then, understood that they were set about 100 years earlier. At the same time, I grew to love other American television series that my great-uncle watched, and I realised that they reflected the US as it was then: *Perry Mason, 77 Sunset Strip* and my favourite, *Highway Patrol*, in which a grizzled cop called Dan Matthews drove on long empty roads, searching for and chasing gangsters, while shouting 'ten-four' into his walkie-talkie. The freedom and excitement of the westerns seemed to have arrived on city streets and country roads in this wonderful country called America.

As I got older, my enthusiasm for American culture grew. I moved on from western novels by Zane Grey and Louis L'Amour, through Mark Twain to the twentieth-century maestros Fitzgerald, Hemingway, Faulkner and Steinbeck; and on to the beat writers and others, including Joan Didion, William Styron, Cormac MacCarthy, Annie Proulx, Stephen King and Richard Ford; and now to younger writers like Colson Whitehead and Yaa Gyasi.

When I was thirteen my great uncle took me to a Classic Cinema to see *They Drive by Night*, a 1940 movie starring Humphrey Bogart and George Raft. I've been lit up by road movies ever since – perhaps most of all by those that were made in the late '60s and early '70s, *Easy Rider, Five Easy Pieces, Two-Lane Blacktop, Scarecrow* and *Midnight Cowboy* – and by the music that came from California, along with the hippies, at that time, particularly Jefferson Airplane, CSNY, Jackson Browne and the Eagles.

In my thirties and forties, I had jobs that meant I visited New York often, and Boston occasionally. I discovered jazz and went on holiday to New Orleans. Then I learned about the old roads that were there before the interstates, roads that ran north–south and east–west forming a grid across the country. Some of these, like Route 66, are no longer there, but others survive. So I took a slow road trip, from north to south on a single two-lane road that crosses the prairies – where there are still some cowboys and Indians – from way up in Canada to the Mexican border at Brownsville, Texas.

After that: what to do? I decided to drive an east–west route. Find a single road that goes right across. Visit California for the first time. And follow the history of this huge inspiring, flawed country, across which European immigrants spread slowly from east to west.

And that, in brief, is the full story of how I came to be on the beach in Ocean City, Maryland.

I drove along Route 50 before the pandemic, before the murder of George Floyd, before Biden and Harris. Black Lives Matter was there – and, of course, the history: the Indians, the early immigrants, the slaves, the settlers, the founding fathers, the railroad builders, the homesteaders, the cowboys, industrialists, tycoons, architects, writers, musicians, artists, movie-makers, politicians, gangsters, crooks and rebels. Along the road I met the descendants of Indians, immigrants, settlers and slaves: bartenders, waiters, engineers, librarians, farmers, shop workers, business people, lawyers, teachers, students. Ordinary people who gave generously of their rich history.

I made the trip, came home and wrote this book. I hope you enjoy it. You don't have to start at the beginning. A friend started at chapter 29 because its title intrigued him; he read from there to the end and went back to the beginning. Currently my favourite chapter is chapter 63.

DR 2021

1

On the Beach

A lifeguard in red shorts climbs up to his chair. Still standing, he looks both ways and waves to other lifeguards; they are all along the beach, sitting in their high, white-painted chairs, spaced about a hundred yards apart. Yet no one is swimming, and I *have* to swim here – from this beach. I promised myself and others that I would, before I set off from England on this odd escapade. An hour ago, as I drove in creeping traffic through thunder, lightning and blinding rain, it seemed even crazier. Why was I doing this, and why was I doing it on my own?

Now it seems a little less mad. I've reached the beach. I can see the sea, the Atlantic Ocean, the place where the journey begins! Now all I have to do is swim here, dry myself, walk back to my rented car, change out of my swimming shorts and drive west for more than 3,000 miles until I reach the Pacific at San Francisco.

Black-headed gulls poke in the sand and squawk. A couple are playing baseball with a small boy who is waving a red plastic bat above his head, like a real batter. The sand is grey, wet and receptive.

My bare feet – I'm carrying my shoes – sink in as I clomp down the beach towards the lifeguard. There aren't many people here, perhaps because of the storm. A few children play in the sand. Some grown-ups stroll alone or in pairs; others sit on chairs under bright umbrellas which they have brought with them. Seagulls, larger than the black-headed ones, circle and swoop. The scene reminds me of those French beach scenes painted by Eugène Boudin and Claude Monet: happy, old-fashioned leisure and fun. There are no speedboats, no boats of any kind, and no surfers – just small waves.

The lifeguard has short dark hair and isn't especially tall. Otherwise he's a cliché of a lifeguard: good-looking, tanned and fit. He is wearing a red T-shirt and red shorts and has two red ping-pong bats, which he uses to signal to his fellow lifeguards. He looks down at me from his perch and says that swimming isn't permitted right now because of the recent storm; they want to be certain that there will be no more lightning. 'Lightning can strike swimmers,' he says and shrugs as if he thinks it is unlikely. 'My guess is we'll get an all-clear in about fifteen minutes.'

Fifteen minutes later – he was right about the all-clear – he says I can leave my towel, trousers and shirt hanging on the lower rungs of his chair, and he'll keep my bag with my phone and car keys up there beside him while I swim.

Grey clouds linger; it's not warm on this August day. The water is cold but not too cold. I step into the sea and advance slowly, letting the water rise up my legs an inch at a time – I've never been able to charge in with a lot of splashing. Eventually, when the water reaches my waist, I take courage and a breath, plunge and go right under. It feels great! Refreshing! Clean water, no seaweed, no stones. Just sand and gentle waves. I dive and go under, swim a few strokes, turn on my back, float and gaze at the sky, at the streaks of silver and even blue in the grey that marked the storm. The lifeguard has said that he is not allowed to use anyone's phone or camera. I fetch my phone from him and ask a man who is standing nearby with a child to take my photo, and run back into the shallows. The man looks glum, but he takes two pictures. They're not great but they're mementoes, proof of something significant – of me in the Atlantic Ocean at Ocean City, Maryland – and if all goes well, they will be complemented in seven weeks' time by photos of me in the Pacific at San Francisco.

Ocean City is a strange string bean of a city, with water on both sides of the bean. It is nine miles long and three blocks, perhaps a quarter of a mile, wide, and covers the southerly end of a long peninsula, or spit, which stretches north into the state of Delaware. On its eastern edge the Atlantic Ocean washes up on nine miles of sandy beach; to the west, between the city and the mainland of Maryland, lies a calm lagoon where people fish, sail and watch birds.

This strip of land has been a popular resort since the 1870s. Nowadays Americans crowd in for holidays, weekends and day trips – 330,000 of them over any weekend in the summer – attracted not only by the beach and its boardwalk, but by old-fashioned fun-fairs with roller-coasters, ferris wheels, carousels and ghost trains; and by shops, bars, clubs, restaurants, fast food, pleasure cruises, sea fishing, and hotels and holiday apartments at every price point. Close to where I found a free parking space, I also found: the pink-fronted Candy Kitchen ('since 1937'); a concrete block of balconied vacation apartments labelled 'Constellation House South 12'; another, more appealing wood-faced block with white-painted balconies and exterior staircases, with the lettering of its name, Siesta Villas, decorated with a woman hidden beneath a straw hat leaning against a palm tree; and a strip mall containing Johnny's Pizza Pub, the 56th Street Beer and Wine Market, Dunkin' Donuts, and, next to it, Fractured Prune Donut Shoppe (might this be a misspelled doughnut too many, on sale inside an anachronism?).

It's 2.30 p.m. I've managed to wriggle discreetly into dry clothes behind my car with the boot open. I'm hungry but I don't want to spend long eating. I head for Johnny's Pizza Pub. Inside it's warm and crowded. I slide onto a stool at the bar and order Johnny's Pizza Margarita and a Coke. Everyone else seems to be drinking beer, but that's OK; I have some driving ahead. A small man comes in from the street and begins talking very loudly to a group of people further along the bar. The bartender brings the Coke and the pizza soon afterwards; he slaps down two large paper napkins and rushes off to serve some drinks. The topping covers the whole pizza – the cheese is thick, melted and sliding off on every side. There is no bread to grip it with, nor do I have a knife or a fork. But it is cut into triangles, so the form here at Johnny's must be to eat pizza with your fingers using the huge absorbent napkins to mop up your hands. I can't see anyone else along the bar doing this, but no one else is eating.

I start eating, and cheese and oil ooze and drip all over my hands and chin. But I persevere until I am interrupted by the small loud man. He wants me to move to the empty stool to my right; I am sitting where he always sits. 'I've been sitting on this stool for nine years,' he says. 'I'm Jay.'

Of course I move along to the next stool, sliding my Coke and my pizza along the bar, and once I am out of his way Jay ignores me. Close up, I see that he is extremely skinny with little legs and bony knees inside worn blue jeans; his hair is grey and tied back in a ponytail and his face has the lines of a keen smoker. With his bare feet inside deck shoes, could he be some kind of beach bum? A bartender brings him a beer and turns away to make a drink for someone else. Jay addresses the bartender's back and tells him that he has had a row with his sister; he can't go on working with her – and I learn that he works for his sister as a chef. The bartender, a tall man with close-cropped blond hair, shakes his head, looks over his shoulder at Jay, smiles and grunts.

I notice unusually thick dark hair on Jay's forearms, and wonder whether he is a sous chef or a burger flipper. I turn away and face forwards, and study the spirits on the shelf behind the bar and keep on eating my pizza, all the time wiping oil from my chin and wondering whether to try to start a conversation. But what can I say? He has shown no interest in me since I climbed off his stool. That stool is one away from the end of the bar – the end further from the door onto the street.

Jay orders another beer and mutters something to himself.

And I hear myself say, 'Why did you choose that stool nine years ago?'

I'm looking at him. He turns to me. 'I like to be at the end – you know?' He pauses. 'Facing the door.'

'What about that one?' I point at the stool that is beyond him, the one that really is at the end of the bar.

He twists round to look at it: a stool with a padded seat covered in brown fake velvet, like all the others. 'No one sits there. You can't put your drink down. That stuff is in the way.' He gestures sideways with his head towards an ice bucket, a jug with a pair of tongs in it and a pot plant with orange flowers. 'My friend usually sits there,' he nods towards my stool, 'but he can't come in today; he's too drunk.'

It wasn't much of a conversation but it was better than nothing. Soon Jay gets off his stool and slowly walks towards the back of the room, pulling a red pack of Marlboro from his pocket as he goes. He opens a door and walks towards some bins. And the door swings shut.

I pay my bill and leave before Jay returns and, as I leave, I see a man sitting further up the bar eating a pizza with a knife and fork.

The US Highways, also known as US Routes, were planned and built in the 1920s and early 1930s, because cars had become commonplace and because, in the Great Depression, men needed work. They formed a grid of more than a hundred two-lane roads, which crossed the country from east to west and north to south. Beginning in the 1950s, they were gradually superseded by multi-lane Interstate Highways, which, with central reservations and slip roads for entering and leaving, encouraged speed, filled up with trucks and bypassed towns. William Least Heat-Moon, author of what is perhaps the best American road book, *Blue Highways*, wrote sagely, 'Life doesn't happen along interstates. It's against the law.'

Many of the old US Highways, including Route 66, have been decommissioned; parts of them lie buried under interstates or have been allowed to grass over, and, even where a stretch of road survives, their distinctive shield-shaped signs, with the highway's number, have been removed because short lengths of road are not US Highways. But US Highway 50 is still a US Highway. It does what it was designed to do; it crosses the country, is still pretty much intact and has shields beside it all the way.

I am waiting at traffic lights at the southern end of Ocean City, waiting to drive onto the bridge where Highway 50 begins or ends, depending on where you start from. I'm starting here, at the eastern end of the bridge at Ocean City, because Europeans landed on the east coast of the landmass that they named America, and moved slowly west until they reached the other side, the ocean that they called the Pacific – and I want to do the same. It's a matter of following history, which, in one sense, is going to be easy for me because all I have to do is start here and keep driving.

2

Slavery and Bravery

I leave Ocean City at around 4 p.m. and, for the first time since the storm broke that morning, the sun comes out. Soon I sense heat and see that there are just a few clouds floating in a clear blue sky. The land is flat, green and lush. I pass through pine woods and emerge among fields of low, deep green plants which I am pretty sure are soybeans.

I am driving across the wonderfully named and pendulous Delmarva Peninsula, a thick slab of land – 170 miles long and up to seventy miles across – that dangles south into the Atlantic. Delmarva is an acronym for Delaware, Maryland, Virginia; the peninsula comprises almost all of Delaware and bits of the others. The string-bean peninsula that contains Ocean City is a peninsula within a peninsula, a teeny appendage to the Delmarva. Delaware Bay and the Atlantic lie to the east of the Delmarva, while to the west is Chesapeake Bay, a vast waterway that runs north to Baltimore and into which flows the Potomac River, beside which Washington DC was built.

An old wooden house with a well-kept garden sits in a grassy pasture like a child's toy on a green carpet. Fields of tall, yellowing corn alternate with the expanses of soybeans. Here and there trailer parks are in sight of, but away from, the road. I turn off and drive past one. People sit outside their trailers on haphazardly arranged canvas seats; many look tired, some look worried. A man who I guess is from the Indian sub-continent stares blankly at what might be a chequebook, while a small child tries vainly to attract his attention. I notice a car that looks new parked beside a smart, shiny pick-up truck outside a neighbouring trailer. Are these people poor? I am a long way from the sea now, and these don't look like holiday homes. I remember, when I taught creative writing at a secondary school in a deprived part of London, a teacher telling me that the more televisions a family had, the poorer they were; they couldn't afford to go out, and would buy televisions on credit. New cars can be bought on credit; old ones more often with cash.

I return to Route 50 and carry on driving towards Cambridge, a fishing port on the west side of the Delmarva Peninsula. I'm perhaps ten miles from Cambridge and driving on a stretch of dual carriageway when I see a small brown sign: Harriet Tubman birth-place – next left.

I've heard of Harriet Tubman, but all I know is that she was a slave who somehow acted heroically, and that the Obama administration planned to put her face on the $20 bill (in place of President Andrew Jackson, who signed the infamous, genocidal Indian Removal Act of 1830, whereby all tribes east of the Mississippi were to be moved west of that river, a forced migration which, for the Cherokee, came to be known as the Trail of Tears). At the time of writing, the Trump government is shilly-shallying on this excellent idea.

I turn off and find myself on narrow country lanes where there are forks in the road with no signs that mention Tubman or her birthplace. At each junction I take the widest road, or the one whose hardtop matches the road I am on, or simply the road that looks most travelled. After a while I decide that I have taken a wrong turn; I have driven three miles or so down a wild and pretty lane with pine woods crowding the verges on both sides, with no houses, no sign of humanity, no traffic. The road is so narrow that turning the car would take several minutes of huffing and puffing backwards and forwards. Eventually a stony space appears to my right, and I drive into a derelict rubbish dump where the fridges and washing machines are rusty and a hoover is coated in verdigris. I turn the car and drive back towards the lane. A young man driving a huge four-wheel-drive and towing a boat slows as he drives past, stares relentlessly and frowns. By comparison, my pristine white Chevrolet Cruze feels small and dainty.

I drive back the way I came, take the other fork and soon come to a junction where there is a cluster of old clapboard buildings – six or seven of them, mostly well preserved and painted. (Clapboard, usually pronounced 'clabbered', is used to describe outer walls covered with wooden boards placed horizontally, often overlapping. Clapboard is usually painted, most commonly white.) At first, I wonder if this is some sort of museum – and it is, although I can see people live in some of the houses – in particular a three-storey house, painted a delightful blue-green with white-painted Georgian window frames, two dormers in the roof, and a veranda with slim, elegant pillars and wicker chairs out front.

I park on the grass verge. Another car is parked further up and three black people, an elderly couple – the woman walking with a stick – and a teenage girl, are staring at a notice on the side of a small cream-painted building. An old sign on the front gable of this building reads GENERAL STORE, and underneath, in smaller letters, BUCKTOWN MD T. MEREDITH PROPRIETOR. I walk round the side to read the notice – the group of three have moved off – and learn that 'The famed Underground Railroad conductor Harriet Tubman grew up here in Bucktown,' and that in this building – this tiny, now empty, general store – when she was thirteen, Harriet 'made her first stand against the injustice of slavery', by refusing to help a white overseer tie down a young male slave he was trying to discipline. The slave broke free. The overseer threw a two-pound weight at him, missed and instead hit Harriet on the head, almost killing her. As an adult she suffered frequent seizures, which some historians say were caused by this event.

The elderly black couple are looking at a small, unpainted building nearby. I wander over and see that much of it is rotting and many boards are missing. A notice explains, 'Anthony Thompson Smokehouse Circa 1810 Restoration Efforts Underway!!' I get talking to the elderly couple. They are from Baltimore and have been here twice before; this time they have brought their granddaughter, because they think she should see this place and be aware of the Underground Railroad and Harriet Tubman. They tell me that Harriet's birthplace is further up a road off to the right. 'You should drive. It's too far to walk,' they say.

I find it, a small gravel lay-by beside a plaque set on a post. It faces a broad field planted with soybeans, surrounded by thick woods. The only building in sight is about a quarter of a mile away, connected to the road by a line of weathered telegraph poles; it is painted cream and has a slate roof. Can that be Harriet Tubman's birthplace?

The plaque is metal, designed in what might be called formal-commemorative style, its top edge curved and featuring black-painted embossed curlicues. It gives Harriet's name and her dates, 1820–1913, and describes her as 'the Moses of her people' who 'found freedom for herself and some three hundred other slaves whom she led north. In the Civil War she served the Union Army as a nurse, scout and spy.'

Beside this formal plaque, a smaller board stands waist high at an angle to the ground. It gives more information and includes a map, copies of old documents and a sepia photograph of Harriet wearing a long Victorian skirt and a matching high-necked jacket with a white neckpiece; she stands with her hands resting on a chair in what must be a photographer's studio, and has the stern expression of someone who is trying not to move during the long exposure of a sheet of film. Or is it the expression of someone who was once a slave, is now free and is taking great risks to free others?

The board tells me that Tubman's mother was owned by a farmer named Edward Brodess. His farm was close to this spot and Harriet was probably born there. I also learn that in the mid-nineteenth century 8,000 African Americans lived in this region, Dorchester County, an area of almost 1,000 square miles with a total population of 19,000. Half of the African Americans were slaves; most of the rest were free and worked as labourers. 'Enslaved blacks, free blacks, and abolitionist whites' – the board says – 'worked together to operate the Underground Railroad, a secret network of "stations" and "conductors" that led hundreds of enslaved people to freedom and became a powerful national symbol of resistance to slavery.'

I have recently read two novels that take their readers deep into the lives of slaves and make the callousness and cruelty palpable and infuriating: *Homegoing* by Yaa Gyasi, and *The Underground Railroad* by Colson Whitehead. Longer ago I read William Styron's *The Confessions of Nat Turner*, a fictionalised telling of the true story of Nat Turner, a slave who led a bloody and murderous revolt against slave owners in Virginia in 1831. The scene in front of me is green, pastoral and peaceful, yet it is not hard, although deeply distressing, to imagine, as these three writers do, a comfortable house where a white family is waited on by black staff, with slaves – men, women and children – living in shacks, working long hours in fields and enduring the constant threat of violence, humiliation and, worse still, of being sold to another owner and separated for ever from loved ones.

3

Muskrats and Linguine

I get in the car and drive on, rather than back towards US 50. It's 6 p.m., there's plenty of light, and I feel like seeing what is round the next corner. The road emerges from woods and crosses low-lying marshland without trees; lakes and ponds close in on the road and I come to a stretch that is flooded. A car, some way behind me, stops and turns back. I keep going, driving slowly. Water surges from the wheels, but it isn't deep and I can see grey tarmac ahead. The place is flat, empty and beautiful with a big silvery sky overhead; a lone gull flies across in front of me, and I sense I am close to the sea – but not the Atlantic with its waves. My sense of direction and the landscape itself suggest Chesapeake Bay, where I guess the water is more estuary than ocean.

The road rounds a bend and begins to follow a wide, slow-moving stream. Soon I come to a bridge: flat, wooden, about thirty yards across. A man in a straw hat is standing at the near end leaning on a thick wooden beam that forms the bridge's side. I drive past him across the bridge and pull into a small car park on the other side where a small red car is parked and a blue plastic toilet is set back from the water. I leave the car, walk to the edge of the water, stand and stare; the stream meanders between grassy banks, under a beautiful, post-storm evening sky. There is one small house on this side of the river; otherwise there is just marsh, water, bridge, sky and the man in a straw hat. I walk slowly back over the bridge, gazing down at the sunlight shimmering on the water. I pass the man, who is drawing with a pencil in a sketchbook. I walk a little way, come back and somehow we start talking.

He tells me that when he was a child his grandfather lived close to here. He visited often and came to love the place. Now he comes back from time to time, though he lives a hundred miles away. 'I come for inspiration: the smell of the creosote and the water.' He's right about the creosote; except for the tarmac road surface, the bridge is built entirely of wood coated in the stuff, and stands on wooden piles driven into the water. He leans over his sketchbook and uses his thumb to smudge some pencil marks; on the page there are three or four rough sketches. 'These are nothing,' he says, waving his pencil. 'I'll maybe work up a painting from them, though.'

I ask if he's a professional artist.

'No, no,' he says and shrugs. 'I do it because I like doing it – to relax. Occasionally sell a painting.' He's a big man, with a neat beard and moustache. He tells me that this area of marsh and wetland is the Blackwater Wildlife Refuge and this bridge is Shorter's Wharf Bridge; the wharf itself, from which people sometimes launch boats, is where our cars are parked.

Then he tells me about muskrats: they live here in the marshes and reeds. Some people eat them, but they are valued much more for their fur, which fetches big money. People make a living from trapping them; his grandfather did. Slaves used to trap them and skin them so their masters could sell the pelts.

'Harriet Tubman ...'

'Yeah ... she would have had to do that.' He looks away. 'Don't like thinking about slaves. I'm sure my ancestors had something to do with that.' He shakes his head. A puff of wind blows up from the river. 'The breeze is keeping the insects away,' he says, 'and cooling the hot humidity.'

It's time for me to move on. If I want to get to Cambridge, I should go back the way I came, he says.

I find Cambridge, check into a motel called America's Best Value Inn, and head out for a restaurant I had driven past, Carmela's Cucina: a small, colourfully painted detached building, alone on a plot of land beside a major road junction near the middle of Cambridge.

It's warm in Carmela's, low-ceilinged, a little steamy, busy. I am given a table close to the door with a view of the kitchen and of a host of happy Italians, old and young – a family, I guess – cooking, waiting, greeting and smiling. The place is crowded, but I am brought a menu – and about a minute later get what I most want, a beer. Then comes a free plate of garlic bread with salsa. This is a great place; they don't waste time and they smile before they rush off to serve someone else. I glug cold beer and look around: yellow walls, green doors with yellow panels, green dado rails, framed jokey messages on the walls, 'All our visitors bring happiness, some by coming, some by going.' Nearby sits a noisy family of eight; close to them a middle-aged couple seem to be flirting as he tops up her wine. The outside door opens and three men, two of whom have striking red hair, come in – and are soon seated behind me to my left.

I slowly suck in a huge plate of linguine marinara, and pile mussel and clam shells in a bowl, breaking off from time to time to write in my notebook.

A thin woman aged about forty comes in to collect a takeaway. She has come too soon, she is told by the no-nonsense, dark-haired woman by the till, who I'm sure by now is Carmela; but would she like a glass of wine?

· Yes, she would.

Carmela tells her that they don't have Chianti tonight.

The woman seems put out, but agrees to have a glass of Valpolicella.

She sits down on a bench against the wall, sips wine, and says to

Carmela, 'I've got a new job. I'm working in Baltimore. It's a bit of a drive, but I'm going to give it a go.'

Carmela mutters something I don't catch. A boy aged about eight crosses from the kitchen area, followed by a handsome, grey-haired man with a moustache and a big belly. They sit down on the bench beyond the woman with the wine, and the man hugs the boy to him with an arm round his shoulder. I guess this is Carmela's husband. Is the boy their son or their grandson? There are plenty of younger adults around who could be his parents.

I take a gulp of my second beer. And I hear the woman with the wine say very clearly, 'They look a bit gay.'

I look up and see Carmela by the till frowning and wagging her finger at the woman, subtly, from side to side. Then she puts her finger to her lips.

'Oh! Did I say that out loud? I was just thinking it.'

Carmela nods her head, and then shakes it.

Soon the woman's food is ready. She pays and leaves. As soon as the door shuts, there is an outburst of chuckling. Carmela has her hand in front of her mouth. Her husband pulls a face and shrugs, arms out, palms up. Both are looking towards the red-haired men and their friend, who just laugh and call out: 'Woo-oo!' 'Way to go!' 'Smart ass!'

The three men leave before me. I'm feeling mellow, and have been persuaded to have a dessert, which turns out to be the largest tiramisu in the state of Maryland.

When I go up to pay, Carmela says, 'That woman, she comes in about three times a week, usually a little drunk, and always she comes early and has a glass of Chianti while she waits. Tonight we didn't have any Chianti. She had to have Valpolicella.'

'Oh dear,' I say.

'Well, those guys didn't mind. We know them. They thought it was funny.'

I get lost driving the mile or so back to America's Best Value Inn in the dark streets of a small town that seem to stretch in every direction except towards US 50 where the motel is. Four or five times I decide I have to turn around and try again, but can find no easy place to turn and am hampered by the headlights in my mirror of a driver who surely would like to pass this idiot who has no idea where he is. After a while, a mild sense of panic takes hold of me. It's getting late. I am tired. I want to get to my motel room. Will I ever get there? The streets are dark. There are no people on the pavements. Nor is there a shop or gas station to stop at and ask for directions.

I find it, of course – and am greeted warmly by the young night manager, Deepak. I sit close to the floor in a revolving desk chair, which someone has wound low, flip through the TV stations and find a satire programme called *Late Night with Seth Meyers*. Seth is telling us about a man who will be in the news throughout my journey across America: Brett Kavanaugh, 'The first white man nominated to the Supreme Court in at least a year ... He has a habeas tattoo somewhere on his corpus ... His handshakes can best be described as moist.' At this last the audience groans.

I go to the bathroom, where I gaze at and appreciate a large, beautifully framed photograph of a mountain stream with ferns and maple leaves, which is hanging above the cistern. Beneath it, on top of the cistern, half a loo roll stands upright and a little unrolled. As I clean my teeth, I silently applaud the priorities of America's Best Value Inn. Who needs a loo-roll holder?

4

The Harriet Tubman Underground Railroad

I'm in the Cambridge Hospital car park, standing beside the car, eating my breakfast – banana, blueberry muffin and coffee – from the Walmart nearby. There aren't many cars here, but there are a lot of trees; I have a large space and several trees to myself. Every five minutes or so a skinny man of Asian origin, dressed in the flimsy blue pyjamas worn by surgeons, jogs past, carrying a phone that emits unrecognisable, tinny music. He doesn't look at all well. He seems exhausted. His jog is barely a jog, more a slow shuffle. In my opinion, he should stop, go indoors, have a shower and collapse into the arms of the nearest doctor, even if he is himself a doctor. But perhaps he is a patient, determined to run even if it kills him.

Last night, as I searched for US 50 and my motel, I saw a sign to the Harriet Tubman Underground Railroad Visitor Center. (In the US, 'visitor centre' means 'museum', perhaps because a visitor centre sounds less frightening.) I didn't know there was such a place but, now that I do, I want to see it before I drive away west.

I drive east down 50, thinking the Tubman Center will be signed to the right. I see no sign and, after twenty miles, I drive back towards Cambridge. I pass a field in which stands an old peeling billboard with the words Van Go in large letters. I noticed this yesterday and wondered what it meant. Now I slow up, look harder and see that it is advertising a bus company with facilities for disabled people.

When I reach Cambridge, I turn round and start east again. It all seems boringly familiar. Can I really have missed a sign to the Tubman Center? I see a Days Inn motel ahead – maybe someone in there can help me. I stop and go inside. There is no one in reception. A notice on the counter says: Use lobby phone for assistance.

There is a phone on a table on the other side of the room. I pick it up and put it to my ear.

Immediately a phone rings behind the counter I have just left and a woman's voice says, 'Days Inn.'

'Hello. I'm in reception,' I say.

'So am I.'

I turn. A young black woman is smiling at me from behind the counter. 'Sorry,' she says. 'I was here' – she points down to her left – 'reading. You didn't see me?'

'No,' I say.

She has a pleasing round face and hair arranged in long cornrows, each with a shiny silver band around it. She knows everything about Harriet Tubman museums. There are two, she says, one in a former shop in Cambridge, and the other, newer one – the one called a visitor centre – is bigger and better and is on a country road. She writes down the address and tells me to drive back up 50 into Cambridge and turn left onto Route 16.

I find the Harriet Tubman Underground Railroad Visitor Center beside a narrow road surrounded by green fields, woods, ponds and marshland – just a few miles from Bucktown and Harriet's birthplace. It is a handsome, low, modern building, opened in 2017, funded and run jointly by the National Park Service and the State of

Maryland, and set within another tribute to Tubman, the seventeen-acre Harriet Tubman Underground Railroad State Park. On this sunny afternoon, the setting is idyllic, and again hard to square with the evil of slavery. Inside the Center I learn that, when Tubman lived nearby as a girl, as well as doing farm work and standing for hours in freezing water trapping muskrats for their thick winter fur, she worked with her father cutting down trees, turning them into timber and hauling it to local wharves. That work gave her the knowledge and contacts that later enabled her to set up escape routes from here in eastern Maryland to, initially, the free state of Pennsylvania.

It is also hard to accept that this slave system held sway so recently. Slavery was abolished in 1865. Tubman herself escaped to freedom in Philadelphia in Pennsylvania in 1849. Between then and the beginning of the Civil War in 1861, she made thirteen trips during which she led seventy slaves from her old homeland to freedom, many of them to Canada, where they were safer than in the free states of the United States, from which they could be returned to slavery. She also helped another fifty slaves to escape by advising them where to go, how to hide and so on. Many years later she said, 'I never ran my train off the track and I never lost a passenger.'

I gaze at a cradle made from a hollowed-out tree and imagine it lying on an earth floor in a flimsy shack, a baby asleep, a young mother nearby and a tired father rocking the cradle with his foot. The Center is designed with reverence – is almost a shrine, dimly lit in places, with modern brass sculptures, some of Tubman herself, and a movie that shows a succession of eminent people paying tribute to her character and achievements. Another movie re-enacts some of her great escapes, including cliff-hanging moments when she and those she is leading came close to being discovered. Old photographs, documents and objects are mixed in with huge modern colour illustrations, some of which have a three-dimensional element – a wooden gate or the prow of ship jutting from them.

The civil war between the northern and southern states, the

Union and the Confederacy, was fought on the issue of slavery. Harriet Tubman moved south with the Union troops, working first as a nurse and a cook and then as an armed scout and spy. A sculpture here shows her leading the famous Raid on Combahee Ferry, an action that defeated a detachment of the Confederate Army and freed 750 slaves, many of whom joined the Union Army.

I spend an hour wandering around and visiting the shop, which has a wall filled with serious books about slavery and the Civil War, alongside Harriet Tubman finger puppets, key rings and rulers. Then I walk across lush grass to a picnic building with tables and a sink with running water. I look out towards a still lake in which clouds and sky are reflected; beyond is a field bordered by trees: 'Countryside preserved,' as the woman who ran the shop put it, 'as it would have been back in the slave days.'

5

Tailgating on the Delmarva

That woman, the one who ran the shop, said that there would be a lot of traffic on 50 heading west towards Annapolis. 'There always is on Sunday evenings in summer,' she said. 'People driving home to DC, Annapolis, Baltimore, from Ocean City and the coast.'

She was right. I sit in slow-moving traffic and stare at wooden houses, large, small, old and new. They look as if they have arrived from somewhere else and been plonked on a patch of grass – which is usually green and well watered. Some of these houses may have been bought by mail order from retailers like Sears Roebuck, who advertised 370 different designs as kits for self-assembly in their catalogues between 1908 and 1940. In the towns, although houses are closer together, there is a similar sense of buildings that have arrived ready-made from somewhere else. 207 High Street, Cambridge, was built in Annapolis around 1750, moved the sixty miles to Cambridge ten years later, and moved again within Cambridge in 1772 when the removal men put it down sideways on its new plot and then didn't have room to turn it round to face the street; it still looks slightly odd.

This stretch of 50 is a four-lane divided highway. Sometimes the traffic almost stops. I study the cars and feel warm towards the few old ones on view, in particular a low-slung blue four-door saloon carrying six people; I can count the people inside because, unlike most cars, including mine, its windows are open, which suggests it doesn't have air-conditioning.

I'm in the inside lane when a swanky black SUV pick-up swerves across in front of me and then swings back out into the fast lane and tailgates the car in front. We're moving so slowly that it makes little difference which lane any of us are in. There is a sticker on the back of this arriviste pick-up. It says simply Mike Evans. I've seen plenty of election billboards and stickers in my travels on the Delmarva Peninsular. With supporters who drive in this arrogant manner, Mike Evans is surely a Republican and a fan of Donald Trump. Does Trump drive, I wonder? Probably not now, but if he did, he would, without thinking, swerve between lanes and bully people by tailgating them. Later I google Mike Evans and find that he is the Republican candidate for sheriff in Calvert County – which is on the other side of Chesapeake Bay. (Much later I discover that Mike Evans had been the sheriff for sixteen years already and was re-elected; he had a good record of reducing crime.)

The road widens to three lanes and we move a little more quickly. Big spots of rain splat on to the windscreen. We slow again as we approach the Bay Bridge. At first there is nothing special about this bridge; it's just a load of concrete. But it turns out to be long – more than four miles long – and then I see that there are two bridges, parallel, similar but not identical, westbound and eastbound. After a while the bridge steepens, then flattens out and I see that both bridges are now suspension bridges with elegant towers at either end. I'm in the middle of the bay, high above the water and can see the shore a long way ahead. This section must have been built high to allow tall boats to sail underneath.

As I come down from the bridge, the rain thickens. The traffic speeds up and driving is more difficult. Annapolis is still some miles ahead. I have no idea what to expect – nor where I will sleep tonight – and I am having trouble seeing anything other than the tail lights of the car in front.

The world is a blur. I have the windscreen wipers going full tilt. I'm in the slow lane driving at seventy simply because everyone else is. I feel that, if I drove more slowly, as I would if I weren't on this crazy conveyor belt, there would be much changing of lanes to get past me, and that would endanger the cascade of dripping cars – and me in particular.

I career on and, from time to time, manage to read road signs or bits of them through the murk. By now I must be either in or bypassing Annapolis, although I haven't seen that Greek-sounding word anywhere, just signs to named streets. I glimpse a sign that includes mention of motels, and at the last second see the words 'Best Western'. I've stayed in Best Westerns before. But too late: I've missed the turn-off. A mile on, I take the next turn and battle through rain, growing darkness, and the glare of headlights coming towards me and reflecting into my eyes from the mirror. I manage to get back on 50 going the other way, and to get off again at another sign mentioning Best Western, among other motels.

I drive around and see no motels – just a large car park in front of a giant DIY store. I turn back and go a different way. Again no motels. I turn back again, find the DIY store, park and run in through teeming rain. I ask a woman sitting at a till whether she knows where the Best Western is. She calls another woman, a striking black woman with straight blonde hair and emphatic, carefully applied make-up. She knows exactly how to get from here to Best Western. I try desperately to remember everything she says. It's not far but sounds complicated; there are one-way systems, overpasses and underpasses. A security man wearing a peaked cap joins us and runs over the same directions. He takes me outside, where we stand under the porch. He points to some traffic lights and swerves his hands around imaginary corners while explaining once more where I should go. Once again, I try to take in and remember what is clearly, to him, perfectly straightforward.

I drive off, trying to follow the route that these helpful people have given me. Some awkward lane-changing is needed – and I'm soon sure I have gone the wrong way because I failed to change lane and was forced to turn right. I drive alongside a group of buildings, more than one of which could be the Best Western, but I can't get in there because a pavement and a low wall are in the way. I slow down. There is a way in. I find myself among red-brick buildings and a series of car parks. There is a bank, a supermarket, a Mexican restaurant, a huge Burger King, a sports bar called the Greene Turtle, and a hotel called the Crowne Plaza. There is no Best Western and the rain continues. The Crowne Plaza looks new, swanky and expensive – with the kind of postmodern architecture that is all brown bricks and outsized plaster pediments. It has an enormous covered entrance portico with room for several cars. I'm fed up with being lost in the rain and dark, so I park and go in.

6

Trump, Putin and Bote

Marble floors, mirrors, low-slung sofas, coffee tables – space, plenty of space: a bar way off to the left, grey, beige, subtly lit; long, marble-topped reception desk to the right. The receptionist is tall and dark, with long, wavy, shiny hair hanging down in front of her left shoulder. She gushes, even though I am a damp, harassed, scruffy man who isn't sure he really wants to be here – especially after he's learned the price of a room: almost twice the price of America's Best Value Inn in Cambridge, breakfast *not* included. The room is at least four times as plush as good old America's Best Value: a grey-and-white look, soft carpet with an abstract pattern in black and white; two beds, eight pillows, a comfy armchair, desk and so on. I go into the bathroom and – horrors! – there has been a flood. I look more closely and see that the flood is a mirage brought about by the ultra-shiny marble floor. Of course there is a loo-roll holder and, predictably, the end of the loo roll has been firmly folded into a point.

I want to eat something and drink a beer. The receptionist

smiles as I walk past. I ask if she recommends anywhere to eat. She wouldn't eat at the Greene Turtle, which – she gestures – is next door. She recommends an Italian restaurant. 'It's very close but you will have to drive.' She gives directions. It's about fifty yards away on the other side of a four-lane freeway, or perhaps it's a beltway; it's certainly four lanes with cars all going the same way fast.

So I would have to drive, but I've had enough of driving – and the rain has stopped. I walk over to the Mexican restaurant, which looks smart and about half full. Do I want to sit in there at a table for one? I walk back to the Greene Turtle, which is subtitled Sports Bar and Grille (isn't a grille something you find in the door of prison?). There aren't many people there, but there's a bar, where I could sit and perhaps talk to someone, and loads of large screens showing sport. There's also a perverse satisfaction in going to a place that the receptionist actively didn't recommend.

At the Greene Turtle, I meet a bartender called Emily, who has glasses and a serious look and a great sense of humour; she wears a Greene Turtle T-shirt and sawn-off black jeans from which dangle strands of cotton, and she has a small silver nose ring. She talks to me and, at the same time, to two black guys who are sitting at the corner of the bar at right angles to me behind a pillar; occasionally I glimpse one of them when he leans forward; the other is hidden by the pillar. It's a curious conversation in that Emily speaks to the three of us, turning her head frequently – but we don't speak to each other. It's hard, after all, to speak to a stranger you can't see.

We learn that Emily recently broke up with a boyfriend, even though she had kindly moved to Baltimore to be with him. 'He got this big corporate job, and I'm still serving,' she says. She shrugs. But now she's met another guy 'who is very respectful'. She nods and smiles as she pours drinks for the men behind the pillar. 'So I'm very happy.'

And so am I. I didn't like the sound of this big corporate guy who dumped her because she wasn't corporate. But I didn't expect this happy ending.

I drink two pale ales and eat Cajun pasta with shrimp. Emily tells us that her grandmother came from Manchester and her grandfather from Jamaica, and they live in New Brunswick. Her mother also lives in Canada and has four tattoos while Emily has seven, one of which, on her shoulder, is the same as one of her mother's. She shows us a perfectly symmetrical black lotus flower on her right arm.

After I've eaten, Emily easily persuades me to order a slug of Maker's Mark bourbon. She turns the bottle upside down above the glass, releases a stream of clear brown fluid from a great height, and goes off to serve some new customers. A baseball game has been on the screen above the bar ever since I arrived, and the score – 3–0 to the Washington Nats against the Chicago Cubs – hasn't changed, despite a good hour of knee-raising and bat-twirling. I watch this game now and read the subtitled commentary. Batters come and go. Nothing much happens, except that the Cubs manage to get a man on each of the three bases. This is their ninth innings, and they are the home side, which means that the Nats will not bat again and the game will soon be over – and, judging by the Cubs' feeble efforts of the last hour or so, the Nats are about to win. The Cubs need to score four runs to win, which is almost – but not quite – impossible.

Soon the last batsman for Chicago, who is called David Bote (rhymes with Boaty, as in Boaty McBoatface), steps up to the plate. The Cubs are in the last-chance saloon, and Bote is on his own in there, trying to vault over the bar. I pick up from the subtitles that he is what in English football would be called a tactical substitute. The coach thinks that if anyone can rescue the Cubs at this late hour, it is him. The implication is that he is a good batter, but not quite good enough to be in the original line-up; I guess that he is what in cricket would be called a slogger, a man who, *if* he hits the ball, hits it hard, but is liable to miss the ball altogether.

My knowledge of baseball, gleaned from watching the game in bars and trying to work out what is going on, is almost nil. I do know that if a batter gets three strikes (which, curiously to fans of soccer, means missing the ball), he is out. However, the pitcher has to throw the ball into the zone where the batter has a chance of being able to hit it, otherwise the pitch doesn't count. This is judged by the umpire, who stands behind the catcher, who is squatting on the ground behind the batter. I take a sip of bourbon and watch Bote miss the first pitch – one strike. There follow some pitches that Bote misses, but they are judged invalid by the umpire. Bote then misses the second correctly pitched ball. Two strikes.

Bote has one more chance. To win the game he has to hit a home run (hit the ball out of the ground into the crowd or even into the street outside). Home runs are not uncommon, although many games go through their eighteen innings without anyone scoring one. However, if Bote can hit a home run off this next pitch, which is the last ball of the game, he won't score just one run, he will score four, because there is a Cubs batter waiting at each base and they will all, along with Bote himself, run from their bases around to the plate. That means that Bote will score a grand slam, four runs, and the Cubs will win the game 4–3. If this happens, it will be not just a grand slam, but a 'walk-off grand slam', because the players will walk off the pitch and that will be the end of the game.

I know all this only because it actually happened before my eyes as I casually sipped at my bourbon. The commentators didn't antic-ipate it, didn't even mention a walk-off grand slam as a possibility. The players and coaches on both sides looked bored; the game was drawing to a dull end – and the Washington Nats were going to win 3–0.

Well, as you must have guessed, Bote walloped that ball so hard and so high that he is now in the history books. Part of the crowd shot into the air. Bote threw his bat on the ground and ran round the bases and back to the plate, a necessary formality, and disappeared beneath a pile of his teammates, who tore off his number 13 shirt. The Washington players walked slowly away, wide-eyed, not even shaking their heads.

The two black guys have gone. No one else in the Greene Turtle has seen this. They are chatting away, all unaware.

I drink my bourbon, watch the screen, read the subtitles and appreciate the full story of, and the history behind, what I have just seen. I learn that a walk-off grand slam that erases a three-run lead is called an 'ultimate grand slam'; there have been twenty-nine of these in major-league baseball history, which began in 1903. The first ever player to hit an ultimate grand slam for a team who were 3–0 behind was Sammy Byrd for the Cincinnati Reds in 1936. But since then it has never happened again – until tonight.

I try to tell Emily about this as I pay the bill. She nods and smiles, but I don't think she quite gets it.

Later, in my room, I watch the news headlines. Trump, Putin – and Bote.

7

Hugging George Washington

I know that I am close to the historic centre of Annapolis because five minutes ago I saw a sign to the visitor information centre, and I followed it. However, I am in a street lined with old houses that are clearly people's homes – reasonably wealthy people, I guess – and I can't see an information centre. The street ends at the sea, or at least at an inlet from Chesapeake Bay, where boats are moored and a couple of men are fishing.

I leave the car and approach an elderly man who is walking slowly with a stick. He is wearing mirror shades, but even though I can't see his eyes, I ask him if he knows where the visitor information centre is.

He is tall, looking down at me. 'I live here. I didn't know there was a visitor information centre.' He smiles. 'I suppose I wouldn't.'

'The visitor centre is at the harbour. Is this the harbour?' I point to the water and the boats.

'No. This isn't the harbour, but you're close. Five minutes.' He gives me directions. The harbour is on the other side of a bridge.

He is keen to help me – a clueless man with a funny accent. He runs over the directions again, and is very precise.

I find the harbour and the visitor centre. I get a free copy of the Annapolis Discovery Map, a colourful, easy-to-read map with cartoonish drawings of buildings, boats, people. Then I wander about in the picturesque, tourist-oriented district that the map calls 'Historic Annapolis', and reflect that getting lost is becoming a feature of this trip. It's only the third day and I've been lost at least four times. I've never had satnav – have never felt I needed it – in London, England, Scotland, Europe or the USA. I could get it on my mobile phone right now, but I would have to pay the exorbitant cost of data roaming. I rely on sense of direction, signposts and maps. I have the *Michelin Road Atlas of the USA, Canada and Mexico,* which has maps of cities, including Annapolis, but it doesn't show the visitor centre. And when I'm online, at a motel, café, bar or wherever, I can look at maps – but I can't study a map *while* I'm driving. That would be the beauty of satnav, but I've never used it and I'm too stubborn to start now.

Historic Annapolis is stuffed with history and tourists. Around the harbour and on the streets that climb the hill above it, no one is moving very fast. People are lolling, arms outstretched along the backs of benches. Others sit with children at pavement cafés. A man with slicked-back hair smokes the stub of a fat cigar, the label between his fingers. I walk uphill on Main Street, looking in shop windows. Even to my English eyes, many of these buildings – homes, small and large, terraced and detached; shops, bars, restaurants, churches – are old; many date from the eighteenth century.

The Maryland State House stands close to the top of the hill. At a glance it looks like an imposing, classically proportioned red-brick Georgian building with a lighthouse on its roof. In fact, it is topped with an elaborate series of domes and octagonal rotundas, which from some angles add to its grandeur. It was built between 1772 and 1779 and has housed the Maryland General Assembly ever since, making it the oldest state capitol, or parliament building, in the United States.

Inside I find marble columns, porticoes and balustrades, beige- and grey-painted walls, and plenty of old portraits in oils of great and good Americans. The Maryland Senate Chamber is protected by a rope, but I can see red leather seats and polished dark-wood desks; the Maryland House of Delegates Chamber has green seats.

From November 1783 to August 1784 Annapolis was the capital of the newly independent United States, and the US Congress, which included Washington, Jefferson, Madison, Hamilton and Franklin, met here. I walk into the Old House of Delegates Chamber, which has been restored to how it was in 1783. There, I come across a tall, grey-haired, patrician American with two small girls, aged perhaps eight and ten, wearing pretty floral dresses; he is telling them about the War of Independence and how the United States wanted to be freed from paying taxes to the English and their king. I find myself congratulating him on his clear explanation of what happened, and I say to the girls, 'I'm from England, the place you got independence from.'

'Ooh,' the older girl says. 'Was that long ago?'

'About 250 years ago,' I say.

'Are you that old? You look old. How old are you?'

'I'm not *that* old. I wasn't *alive* then. I just know that your country ganed independence from mine all that time ago.'

The girls look puzzled. Grandfather and I laugh. Bonhomie breaks out. The girls spin around in their shiny shoes, and I tell grandfather that I think it is a good thing that America gained independence from Britain. 'We wouldn't want to be one country now, what with one thing and another.' I don't use the Trump or Brexit words but, from grandfather's chuckle, I sense that I guessed correctly that he is no fan of Trump and is as puzzled as I am by Brexit. I'm no expert, but I think this smiley man is an East Coast Democrat, a member of what some now call the elite.

I say goodbye to them and cross the hall to the Old Senate Chamber, an airy room where a life-size bronze statue of George Washington stands on the very spot where historians have decided that the man himself stood on 23 December 1783, when he made a short speech resigning his commission as Commander-in-Chief of the Continental Army; Washington had just won the War of Independence and had overseen the withdrawal of the last British troops from New York. This was an emotional moment for the wise and modest Washington, who had commanded the army since the beginning of the war in June 1775. He resigned because he longed to get back to what he saw as his normal life as a farmer in his home state of Virginia and because he wanted to make clear that he did not want political power. Throughout the war, Congress had given him the power of a dictator, and he could have continued to rule the newly independent country – indeed some groups wanted him to be their king – but power did not corrupt him. He had fought for the independence of his country, but also to bring about a revolution: a republic and a people's democracy.

Washington's resigning his commission is seen as a pivotal event in American history. The ceremony has been painted numerous times – one huge canvas, by John Trumbull in 1824 – hangs in the Capitol Building in Washington DC. Trumbull described Washington's resignation as 'one of the highest moral lessons ever given to the world'. Gordon S. Wood, winner of the Pulitzer Prize for History in 1993, described the resignation as 'the greatest act of his life, the one that gave him his greatest fame', and the historian Thomas Fleming wrote: 'This was – is – the most important moment in American history. The man who could have dispersed a feckless Congress and obtained for himself and his officers riches worthy of their courage was renouncing absolute power to become a private citizen. He was putting himself at the mercy of politicians over whom he had no control and in whom he had little confidence.'

Back then there were only thirteen states, so this room, which was designed to house the Senate of Maryland rather than that of the United States, is not especially large, but is elegant, painted cream and white, with a balcony and balustrade above the door supported by Ionic columns. Like the Delegates Chamber, it has been restored to how it was in 1783, with old wooden chairs for the senators and a

33

dais on which the president of Congress sat between two windows at the far end.

I walk towards George Washington and find that I'm looking up at him; he was tall, about six feet six inches. A young couple come into the room and ask me to take their photograph. They stand next to Washington; the young man puts his arm round his girlfriend's waist and she brushes her cheek against the bronze epaulette on Washington's shoulder. They smile. Click – and I ask them to take my photo. I look up at Washington, put my hand on the small of his back and try to grin. In the resulting picture I look unequivocally asinine: a short, scruffy man in trainers and blue shorts holding on to a tall, imperious fellow in eighteenth-century formal dress who is making an emotional speech to Congress while cast in bronze.

In 1787 Washington's friend James Madison persuaded him to attend the newly set up Constitutional Convention, telling him that only his involvement would convince all the states to send delegates. Reluctantly, Washington showed up at the convention and played a vital but characteristically low-key role in uniting the states and persuading them to agree a constitution, without which he thought anarchy would ensue. Two years later, under that constitution, he was unanimously elected the first President of the United States.

8

Martin Luther King and the Founding Fathers

I wander out into the ninety-degree heat. As I stroll among the trees in the State House garden, my head is filled with Washington and what a good bloke he was. Then I come across an oak dedicated to Martin Luther King. The inscription quotes the great civil rights leader: 'Freedom must ring from every mountainside . . . and when this happens, all . . . will be able to stand together . . . and sing a new song . . . Free at last, free at last, great God Almighty, we are free at last.'

One fight for freedom followed another. What would Washington make of Martin Luther King and the Civil Rights Movement, and now Black Lives Matter? Surely he would be horrified to find that the colour of someone's skin is still an issue almost 250 years after the signing of the Declaration of Independence, the famous second sentence of which was: 'We hold these truths to be self-evident, that all men are created equal, that they are endowed by their Creator with certain unalienable Rights, that among these are Life, Liberty and the pursuit of Happiness.'

Critics of the Declaration of Independence, both in America and in the British Parliament, asked how a nation that condoned slavery could adopt a declaration stating that all men are equal and should enjoy certain inalienable rights. The same question might well be asked now, when black people, the descendants of slaves, are still not treated equally, and when many fear for their lives in the wake of the killings by police of Trayvon Martin, Michael Brown, Tanisha Anderson, Sandra Bland and others.

And wouldn't George Washington find it strange that, in the twenty-first century, football players, led by a star quarterback, Colin Kaepernick, are kneeling down in protest against racial injustice and police brutality during the playing of the anthem of the nation whose freedom he did so much to win? And how would the first president react to the forty-fifth president saying that if football players refused to stand for the anthem, owners of their team should 'get that son of a bitch off the field right now'.

I walk away from Martin Luther King's tree and soon come to a long, beaten-up cannon pointing out to sea over the rooftops and harbour of Annapolis. A notice says that it was brought from England 'by the first settlers March 25, 1634'.

I'm still thinking about Washington: in particular that he owned slaves, several hundred of them; as did Thomas Jefferson, the author of the Declaration of Independence and the third president; as did James Madison, the fourth president. (A point that is perhaps important is that they inherited their slaves from their fathers and, because slaves had children who became slaves of their parents' owners, they tended to gain, rather than lose, slaves over time. An unimportant point – in fact, pure gossip – is that, after the early death of his wife, Jefferson had a secret, long-lasting relationship with a slave called Sally Hemings, who bore six children, all of whom are now thought to have been Jefferson's.)

The seven Founding Fathers of the United States – Washington,

Jefferson, Madison, John Adams (the second president, who never owned a single slave on principle), Alexander Hamilton, John Jay and Benjamin Franklin – believed ultimately in the abolition of slavery. Jefferson called slavery 'an execrable commerce ... this assemblage of horrors', Madison dubbed it 'a deep-rooted abuse', and Washington's slaves were freed when he died in 1799, as directed in his will. Yet neither the Declaration of Independence nor the Constitution, which was written in 1787, condemned slavery or called for abolition. The Founding Fathers had two practical problems with abolition. They feared chaos, even a race war, if the slaves were suddenly freed: in 1790 there were 700,000 slaves out of a total population of 3.9 million. Secondly, they believed that the thirteen states must unite in order to survive and to trade effectively in a world dominated by the British, the Spanish and the French. Delegates to the Constitutional Conference from three states, Georgia and the two Carolinas, would not sign if abolition were included in the Constitution – and some delegates from other states would also back off.

It would take eighty years and a civil war before slavery was abolished in 1865, by Abraham Lincoln – and that great man was then murdered as a result. And abolition, as we know, had little or no effect on racial prejudice. The constitution allowed the individual state governments to make many of their own laws. So, despite the freeing of the slaves, the Jim Crow laws, enforcing segregation, were enacted in the southern states in the 1870s and 1880s, ratified by the US Supreme Court in 1896, and enforced until 1965.

Martin Luther King and the Civil Rights Movement were fighting segregation and discrimination – and they succeeded in the sense that a Civil Rights Act, making discrimination based on race, colour, religion, sex or national origin illegal, was proposed by President John F. Kennedy and, after his assassination, was pushed through Congress and signed into law by President Lyndon B. Johnson in 1964. Yet discrimination smoulders on to this day (some might say that it has been practised by the forty-fifth president). The average black family has one tenth of the wealth of the average white family. Twelve per cent of adults in the United States are black, yet black people make up 33 per cent of the prison population. And, most noticeable: white policemen and vigilantes have sometimes evaded punishment for killing black people – particularly young black men.

Would Washington have been surprised? He seems to have been a realist with a streak of pessimism, so perhaps not, once he had got over the shock of the demise of the buffalo, women wearing short skirts, hip-hop and other developments since his death in 1799. Jefferson was different; he had a great and eclectic mind. As John F. Kennedy remarked to a group of forty-nine Nobel Prize winners, whom he had invited to dinner: '. . . this is the most extraordinary collection of talent, of human knowledge, that has ever been gathered together at the White House, with the possible exception of when Jefferson dined alone.' Jefferson was an optimist who sought out solutions to problems: he thought that the slaves could eventually be returned to their homelands in Africa, and that the Indians could be taught to settle down and become farmers. I think Jefferson would be startled at the state of the United States in the twenty-first century. But he would quickly grasp why young black men in funny clothes are kneeling down on rectangles of grass watched by thousands of people standing in the bleachers while 'The Star Spangled Banner' is sung – and he might recognise the song, which existed in his lifetime but didn't become the official national anthem until 1931, when Congress passed a bill adopting it and President Hoover signed it into law.

I tilt my head back, take a swig from my water bottle and look down at the old English cannon. There aren't many people in the State House garden. Those that are here are wearing shorts – *all* of them. It's hot, even in the shade. I straighten my sun hat and walk towards the gate. The young man who took my photograph with George Washington looks up from a shady bench and calls out, 'Go Washington!'.

'Go Jefferson!' I call back.

He and his partner smile. They are both white – or perhaps Hispanic, or perhaps one-eighth black like the children of Sally Hemings and Thomas Jefferson.

9

Pointless in Annapolis

I walk east and gaze down on the US Naval Academy – a sweep of majestic stone buildings, set off by a couple of domes, where naval officers have been trained since 1845. I keep walking on brick pavements under hot sun and blue sky; I stretch my arms and somehow feel good, and the place feels old, beautiful and romantic. I pass a low, red-brick church, St Anne's Episcopal, standing on an island in the middle of the street, and come to another old building, where Georgian windows sprout Union flags, pots filled with flowering plants stand outside, and a veranda with columns topped by a portico leads to the front door. A sign hangs over the pavement: 'Reynolds Tavern, Food and Spirits since 1747'.

It's 4 p.m. It would be good to sit down and drink something other than water, though it's too early for alcohol – and, of course, I want to know about this Reynolds. Through the window the place looks dark, but around the side a gate leads to a garden with tables and umbrellas.

I am the only customer and I get a big welcome from a red-faced, white-haired man who is standing behind a roofed-over, well-stocked bar at the farther side of the garden under some trees. His name is Tim. He is friendly and garrulous, and interested in me. What am I, an Englishman, doing here?

I tell him: driving from Ocean City, Maryland, to San Francisco along Route 50. At first he is startled, and then full of suggestions. As he fixes me an orange juice with soda water, he tells me where to find cheap hotels in Washington DC (which is only about thirty miles away). Tim has lived most of his life there, and he has travelled a lot within the states. 'I spent three years at the University of Texas. Got a degree in western history.' He laughs. 'That means cowboys and Indians.' He plonks a large glass of frothing orange liquid in front of me. Then he asks which towns I will be going through after DC.

I name a few small places and then mention 'Cincinnati, St Louis, Kansas City. They're on Route 50.' I suck fizzy orange juice through a straw and feel a light rain falling on my shoulders. I pull my stool closer to the bar.

Tim is frowning. 'Route 50? I know Route 50. It goes through DC.'

'Yes. That's why I'm going there.'

'So where does it go? I should *know* this.' He frowns again and pulls out his phone. He stabs at the screen and strokes it with his forefinger. He sighs and keeps frowning ... until, suddenly, his face relaxes. 'Oh I see!' He looks over at me. 'Yeah! I didn't know 50 went right over there. You got such a lot' – he looks back at his phone – 'Ohio, Indiana, Illinois, Missouri – that's great, Missouri, a lot went on there. Boy! Missouri and Kansas, they're fascinating.'

'Very flat,' I say.

'Well, no. There's some hills,' he says. 'Oh, it says here – wow! Route 50 is "the Loneliest Road in America".'

I've read this too, and tell him I think it refers principally to 50 in Nevada, where there are no towns for long stretches – eighty or a hundred miles.

It's now raining heavily and I'm getting wet. Tim and I run across the garden and through a basement door. He leads me along a passage and into a cellar bar: two little rooms with brick floors, low ceilings, off-white walls, dark beams and high windows. There are no customers, just a young, studious-looking bartender with short hair and glasses. I say something about these rooms seeming very old.

The young bartender nods and smiles and says that there are rumours that the place is haunted. The building was constructed in 1737, he says, but didn't become a tavern until ten years later when the first publican was William Reynolds. 'Washington, Jefferson, their French friend Lafayette and those guys from Congress used to drink here,' he says.

'Really! Good heavens.'

'Well, that's the rumour, you might say. But those men did drink together – they were known for it – and the bar was here then, nearly forty years before Congress arrived at the State House – just two minutes away.'

I rest my hand on the dark surface of the bar. 'Was this bar here in 1783? Did Washington stand here?'

'He might well have. But the bar is newer than that. The windows were here, and the beams.' I gaze at the beams and the windows. Did Washington and Jefferson look through these windows? There isn't much to look at: just the leaves of a tree in the street. 'William Reynolds had a wife called Mary, and there's a story that William threw George Washington out of here one night for flirting with Mary.' He smiles. 'There's some documentation of that; I think it's true.'

I wonder whether to tell him that my name is Reynolds and my mother was called Mary – and my father was the kind of man who might have tried, and would certainly have failed, to throw a flirtatious customer out of a pub. There doesn't seem to be much point. Tim has returned. I've finished my orange juice. I stand up and thank them for all the chat.

*

This morning I dared to ask the tall, dark receptionist at the Crowne Plaza where the Best Western was. With much sighing she told me – around a beltway and off a freeway – and made sure that I knew that Best Western pretends to be a hotel when, of course, it isn't. No, it isn't, but the even more charming receptionist over at Best Western did let me check in at 10.30 a.m. at no extra cost – and I unloaded the car outside my own front door; the bill was half that at the Crowne Plaza and breakfast was thrown in. (I prefer hotels – unless they are part of a pretentious chain – to motels because I have met more people – I mean interesting strangers – in hotels than in motels; hotels have bars and, often, leisurely breakfast rooms where people linger. William Least Heat-Moon made the distinction neatly in his great American road book, *Blue Highways*: 'The hotel was once where things coalesced, where you could meet townspeople and travelers. Not so in a motel. No matter how you build it, the motel remains a haunt of the quick and dirty, where the only locals are Chamber of Commerce boys every fourth Thursday.')

So now I return to my room at Best Western, google nearby bars and restaurants and head for the West End Grill, which turns out, after an easy five-minute drive, to be a laid-back, old-style place with great food, sport on screens, booths, a jazz playlist, and a friendly waiter called Matt. I eat tuna, drink some beer and surreptitiously examine the other customers: three or four couples, black and white, in their thirties or forties, and small groups of middle-aged white men spread around the room and at the bar. Most of the men, including Matt, are wearing those long shorts with side pockets, clean and pressed; it's still hot outside at 9 p.m.

Matt and I discuss David Bote's terrific home run. 'Home runs are quite common,' he says, 'but the interesting and unusual thing about it was that it was a grand slam close-out. Four runs, and they won the game, 4–3 with the last hit!'

Close to my table a chic black woman, about forty years old, plays a game that looks like Space Invaders. She wears a red turban, blue jeans with glitter on the pockets and a dark blue T-shirt with

'Harper 34' on the back. She pumps her right forefinger on the firing button and swivels a joystick with her left. Her partner, a slim black man with grey hair and a white moustache, hugs her round her waist and stares lovingly over her shoulder at the screen.

I leave at 10.15 and take one and a quarter hours to get back to Best Western, which is less than two miles away. I miss the turning left onto Riva Road and take the next left which, instead of offering a turn back, leads straight onto I-97, the interstate to Baltimore. After minutes of cursing myself for getting lost in the dark *again*, I calm down and realise that I'm not lost. I know where I am – I'm on I-97 between Annapolis and Baltimore; it's just not where I want to be. But that's OK. I drive for some twelve miles to the first turn-off, but the bridge across the interstate, which I'd hoped to cross so that I could drive sedately back to Annapolis while listening to Emmylou Harris on the sound system, isn't there. Instead I am really lost, in dark countryside. I career around on a two-lane road for long exasperated minutes through woods and past isolated houses, desperately trying to retain some sense of direction. Eventually, I come to a crossroads where a sign points left to somewhere called Odenton and – hurray! – Annapolis. After ten more minutes of bends, trees and a horse showing up in the headlights, I come to a dual carriageway and I glide back into town, tired and irritated.

I find Riva Road, but I cannot find the little side road, Hearne Road, that leads to the Best Western. I end up by the Crowne Plaza having a desperate pee in the car park. From there I know the way and make no more mistakes.

Tomorrow I will go to Washington. My *Michelin Road Atlas* suggests that, some way beyond that great conurbation, Route 50 becomes a two-lane country road and passes through small towns in West Virginia, Virginia and Ohio for something like 450 miles. What bliss!

The tiredness and irritation fade and I remember the West End Grill, the warmth, the music, the food. I google 'Harper 34' on my laptop. Bryce Harper is a star player for the Washington

Nationals baseball team and wears the number 34 in red on his dark blue shirt.

I go into the bathroom and smile at the loo-roll holder – and at the loo roll, which is pointless.

10

Where's Melania?

I get on the Metro in a suburb to the east of DC called Cheverly. The carriage seems new, as if straight from the factory, with stainless-steel poles and pastel-coloured seats – grey, blue, pink, apricot – and is strangely clean: no litter, no gum, no graffiti. A young black woman with luscious cornrows, tattoos and a nose ring lies across a seat with her back to the window. She talks on her phone through-out the seven-stop journey, her tone that of someone complaining about some malfeasance to a faceless corporation or government department. I can't hear her words, but find that I sympathise. Further up, a white man wearing a black pork-pie hat with a white rim rests his head against the window.

At Capitol South an escalator takes me to the street for my first view of DC: grey government buildings, leafy trees and parked cars. It is already noon; the sky is blue and the air is hot. A sign points towards the Capitol and I am soon walking across grass between trees towards it. It is familiar from television: a well-proportioned domed building, white and glossy with masses of pillars. It is more striking in reality and up close – imposing, pleasing – and at the same time mundane, with four parked cars, one of which looks like a hearse, piles of plastic crush barriers, a solitary blue plastic bin, and a few small groups of people standing around wondering what to do next. I look up, shade my eyes and see, on the top of the dome, a statue of a figure in classical robes with a bird sitting on its head. (I discover later that the bird wasn't just passing by; it had been there since 1863 and is an integral part of the *Statue of Freedom*, a sculpture of a woman holding a sword and a wreath of olive leaves.)

I sit down on a stone seat at the edge of a vast paved terrace, and reckon that I am looking at the north side of the building. About fifty teenagers, girls and boys, dressed in identical green T-shirts and dun-coloured shorts walk across from my left; their teacher, a short, sweating, bearded man, dressed like them, is at the back. They must be going somewhere interesting. I follow them down a wide path through trees and round to the back, or front, of the Capitol. I'm hoping to find that huge space that we see on television, where people gather for presidential inaugurations, Independence Day celebrations and protest marches; the long – two miles long – stretch of grass, photographs of which proved the absurdity of President Trump's claim that more people watched his inauguration than Obama's. And suddenly I realise that I'm there: the west front of the Capitol rises behind me and the tree-lined space, all two miles of the National Mall, is in front of me.

I sit on another stone bench and stare out over patchy grass at the mighty needle of the (George) Washington Monument shooting up into the blue. I remember watching the Women's March on television on the day after Trump's inauguration in 2017, and try to imagine this long vista crammed to the trees at its edges with women wearing pink 'pussy hats', a witty, 'fuck-you' response to the pervy Trump's boast that women would let him 'grab them by the pussy'. I find myself smiling, and mouthing, 'As if.'

A woman's voice interrupts my thoughts. 'You do that,' she is saying, perhaps a little angrily. A young white couple are walking past. The woman sits down at the other end of my bench.

'OK. I will,' the man says, and keeps walking.

I carry on staring around and wonder whether to ask the young woman if she knows where the White House is. I glance at her. She is well turned out, possibly even what Americans call 'upscale', though the man who walked off didn't seem upscale: small and hairy with a black beard – though he could be a famous film director for all I know – while she is chic, pretty, mid-twenties with a pink leather clutch bag,

'Excuse me,' I say. 'I've not been here before. Do you know where the White House is?'

'I think it's up there to the right.' She points straight ahead towards the Washington Memorial.

'OK. Thanks.' And then I say something about Trump's inauguration happening right here, and how he said, wrongly, that more people were here than were at Obama's inauguration. She doesn't seem to know about that – and she doesn't even wrinkle her nose at the mention of Trump. She has a strange, non-American accent. I decide that she is Swedish.

A haze of cloud smudges the horizon beyond the Washington Monument, but I think I can see the columns of the Lincoln Memorial, two miles away.

I set off for the Washington Monument, and hope that from there I will be able to see the White House. Will Melania be there? Will I be able to rescue her? I haven't gone far before I see the National Gallery of Art off to my right. I dodge in to have a pee, but my schedule is reset by a charming, elderly woman with pearl earrings, who approaches me inside the entrance and asks if I need any help. Am I looking for anything in particular? A badge pinned to her jacket says that she is a volunteer helper.

I don't like to ask her where the men's restroom is, so I say I want to look at American art. She whips out a two-sided, colour-printed, diagrammatic map of the place, which shows 122 galleries. Galleries 60 to 71 contain American artists. This excellent woman then asks if I like Degas. It's hard to say 'no', so I say 'yes' – and she writes Degas on the map over the appropriate gallery. We move on to da

Vinci, and then nineteenth-century French and, perhaps a favourite of hers, seventeenth-century Dutch and Flemish. Before we part, she suggests that I have lunch – it is approaching 12.30 p.m. – in the Cascade Café in the basement. 'It's a cafeteria,' she says, 'not expensive, but very good.' I wander away and look closely at the map. There are plenty of restrooms.

Soon I am gazing at *Green River Cliffs, Wyoming* (1881), by Thomas Moran, a wild landscape in which red cliffs, their redness intensified by the sunset, tower above a pale river as a party of twenty or so chattering Indians ride idly by on assorted horses: black, brown, white, piebald. The painting arouses in me a memory of the fondness I felt, as a child, for the American Indians I saw in cowboy comics, on television and at the local Odeon. As an adult, I discovered the reality that overlaid the romance of the lives of Indians, and was devastated by Dee Brown's book *Bury My Heart at Wounded Knee* with its grim details of the often heroic but, in the end, hopeless struggle by the Indians of the west to preserve their lives, communities and ancestral lands.

Thomas Moran's painting shows what he wanted to see – happy Indians in a beautiful and unblemished landscape – rather than what he actually saw. Green River was a railroad boomtown when Moran first visited it in 1871. In this painting, made ten years later, he left out the town – its houses, hotel, brewery and school – and the railroad itself. It seems that he wanted to celebrate the pristine landscape, unchanged by the progress of white men across the continent, and to immortalise the local, probably Shoshone, Indians, who by the time he was painting had been moved on.

Albert Bierstadt's *Buffalo Trail: The Impending Storm* (1869), a moody painting in which black clouds close over a silver sky as a line of buffalo plods across a stream, reminds me how close the buffalo came to extinction – as did the Indians, who depended on them for food, clothing and tepees for shelter. At the end of the eighteenth century, 20 to 30 million buffalo lived on the plains between Alaska and the Gulf of Mexico. In 1889 just 1,091 survived. The Indians had lived off sustainable numbers for centuries, but these great beasts

49

were laid low to enrich and amuse hunters like General Custer and Buffalo Bill Cody, and by disease brought by cattle from Europe.

I drift past mournful paintings of old Dutch boats, then wander through a homesick bunch of Turners and Constables, including the latter's *Salisbury Cathedral from Lower Marsh Close*, in which there are hints of people loitering beneath trees.

Down in the basement, I slide a tray along stainless-steel rails at the Cascade Café and emerge with the chef's special, spaghetti with meatballs with a side order of roasted vegetables. The café is spacious and cool with tables set far apart. I sit with my fork loaded and stare blankly at the long glass wall in front of me. Behind it water cascades down a corrugated surface, frothing prettily in sunlight – even though we are in a basement – before falling off an edge that runs diagonally from top left to bottom right. I walk up to the glass and look up. There, on street level, a line of fountains reaches up into the blue, like a row of windswept poplars. Only now does it occur to me how this café got its name.

Two men, who might be father and son, laugh loudly – perhaps excessively loudly. Somehow I feel they are faking it, pretending to each other – there's no one else – that they are having a good time. A young couple with East Asian features, clearly well heeled, wear perfectly clean, perfectly ironed matelot shirts, obviously (to me, anyway – but what do I know of such things?) from the same label. His has blue stripes, hers pink. Did they plan this? Or did they arrive here from separate homes and hoot at the coincidence?

If you lived in Washington, this would be a great place to meet your friends for lunch. I bet Melania comes here and hides behind a pillar and a pair of shades. I feel sure she is a secret culture vulture – which must make it difficult to hang out with a man who, according to Michael Wolff in his book *Fire and Fury*, eats cheeseburgers in bed while watching three televisions and tweeting mean-spirited nonsense. I feel sorry for her and her boy, Barron. Am I crazy? Is this misplaced chivalry? Is it, incidentally, possible that Barron is named after Kenny Barron, one of the greatest living jazz pianists, who has played with everyone from Dizzy Gillespie and Stan Getz to Charlie Haden and Dave Holland? Perhaps Melania likes jazz? It seems unlikely that Donald J. does. If Melania and Barron visit London, I would be delighted to take them to Ronnie Scott's, ideally when Barron's namesake is performing. (She can contact me via my publisher.)

11

Ice-Cream Music

My curiosity about, and sympathy for, the Indians, as well as my indignation at the way they were, and many still are, treated – leads me back across the National Mall to the National Museum of the American Indian, following a map given to me by the elderly woman with pearl earrings. From the outside it is a delightful building with curving, swerving, yellowish stone walls, and upper floors that overhang in irregular layered shapes. Despite its strangeness, it has a peaceful air. It doesn't look governmental, nor is it an elegant repository of stuff, with columns at its entrance, like many of the other buildings along the Mall.

Inside it is a place of high curving walls, long curving staircases, circles, semicircles, ovals and ellipses; an exciting place in which I will learn much, I hope, about the history and contemporary life of North American Indians. But, as I move down through the building from the fourth floor, as recommended by the authorities, I don't find what I hoped for. First of all, I'm faced with vast swathes of dispiriting emptiness: landings, halls, corridors that contain nothing but a few benches. Then, between bending, looping walls, I see photographs, short films and objects – pottery, teepees, costumes, rugs, snowshoes, drums, moccasins, wampums, arrowheads, spears, baskets, carved and sculpted animals. One of these spaces celebrates the survival of American Indians in the modern world; another focuses on the traditional beliefs of a handful of tribes. But I find no coherence, no story, within these oval areas. The spaces that are easiest to understand are the least interesting: the shop and the café. Back on the ground floor, I find a huge circular space where tired tourists sit on benches contemplating three or four wooden canoes. It is as if the swerves and curves – there is hardly an angle in this building, with the exception, in my brief experience, of the men's restroom – have fuddled the thinking of the organisers, though I suspect that committees and competing interests are the prime culprits.

In the middle of the morass there is an exhibit that defies the trend, and it is perhaps significant that this exhibit was installed in 2015, while the rest of the museum has been there since it opened in 2004. It tells the story of the Native American peoples from first contact with Europeans to the present day, through three phases of treaties. In the early days of independence, optimistic treaties were agreed that genuinely intended to promote peace. Later followed the cynical, always broken, land-grabbing treaties of the nineteenth century, which tricked the Indians in the name of the repugnant doctrine of 'manifest destiny' – the belief that God required the white man to own the entire continent and either eradicate the natives or convert them to Christianity. Then – and not until the second half of the twentieth century – came the legal implementation of old treaties and land grants, under pressure from Native American leaders and aided by a belated stirring of liberal conscience.

I go out into the heat and sunlight and head for the shade under the trees on the south side of the Mall. My head is filled with the evidence of the cruel treatment of the Indians. I already knew about the Cherokee 'Trail of Tears', the forced trek from their homeland in Georgia to Indian Territory, west of the Mississippi, during which 4,000 Cherokee died, a tragedy brought about by the Indian Removal Act of 1830, pushed through Congress by President Andrew Jackson – the man whom the historian Simon Schama described as 'the ethnic cleanser of the first democratic age'. The Act effectively cancelled previous treaties and, I had just learned, led to other atrocities. In particular, the exhibit noted the fate of the Potawatomi, a tribe from the Great Lakes region whose leaders had signed numerous treaties guaranteeing them ever smaller tracts of land, and who were eventually, in 1838, forced off their land at gunpoint into what became known as the Potawatomi 'Trail of Death'.

Years ago, a friend who knew more history than I did, said of the United States: 'Of course, it was founded on genocide and grew rich on slavery.' Back then, this seemed a harsh assessment, but America's evil history – like that of other countries – cannot be forgotten, least of all among its capital's monuments to freedom and democracy.

I walk under the trees towards the thin spire of the Washington Monument and, as I walk, I hear music – tinkly renditions of traditional tunes: 'I Wish I Was in Dixie', 'Oh Shenandoah', 'Danny Boy'. It is as if someone is playing a xylophone under a distant tree. Or could it be coming from hidden speakers? I'm reminded of walking on Main Street in Garden City, Kansas, where Beatles music snuck subtly out of speakers tied to lamp posts. I walk on and the music recedes – and returns, as I approach a road junction. It gets louder, but not loud. A low white van is parked on the corner – a discreet sign says 'ice-cream'. The music is coming from the van. I look across the grass to the north side of the Mall, and back towards the Capitol: white vans on each corner, six of them. It's ice-cream music, tinkly, subtle, discreet – like the vans. Nothing garish or vulgar or loud here. No litter, no reminders of our earthiness, such as signs announcing Toilets, or even Restrooms. All is fitting, for this is the heart of the capital city of the most powerful country on earth, this two-mile-long strip of grass with a pool at each end reflecting the Capitol in the east and the Lincoln Memorial in the west, lined with museums and mature trees, and adorned with monuments to great leaders – from east to west: Ulysses S. Grant, George Washington and Abraham Lincoln, with Thomas Jefferson, Franklin Delano Roosevelt and Martin Luther King Jr off to the side – and with memorials to World War II, Korean War Veterans, Vietnam Veterans and the Holocaust.

I reach the Washington Monument, a dull needle standing sharp against the evening sky. I sit on a wall beside children licking ice creams and look north towards the White House, at the familiar curve of columns that mark the south side of the building. I walk downhill and cross Constitution Avenue to get a closer look. Guards in a line check cars, and I walk past unhindered. A fountain gushes on the lawn. Two marksmen dressed in black stand on the roof, machine guns ready. And I stare from behind a fence.

This is where Jefferson dined alone – and where, in 1803, having obtained funding from Congress, he instructed his private secretary, Captain Meriwether Lewis, to lead an expedition to the Pacific Ocean; Lewis, his fellow army officer and co-leader of the expedition William Clark, and thirty men became the first white men to cross the continent when they reached the coast of what is now Oregon in November 1805; they were greatly assisted by Clark's personal slave, Yorke, and by a young Indian woman called Sacagawea.

And this is where Trump lies in bed eating cheeseburgers.

Constitution Avenue is also US Highway 50, *my road*, which leads to San Francisco. I walk east along it towards Federal Triangle Metro station – and an hour later I am driving, inching, crawling, west on the same strip of road between the Washington Monument and the White House. It's rush hour in downtown Washington; there are numerous traffic lights and a frequent,

55

panic-inducing necessity to switch between the two lanes heading west. In the faster left lane I come up against signs saying LEFT LANE MUST TURN LEFT, but I don't want to turn left, so I switch to the slower right lane, and before long come to a sign, RIGHT LANE MUST TURN RIGHT, which I don't want to do either. Everyone, especially the drivers of huge trucks, is changing lanes – and they are all quicker, niftier, than I am.

I lose Highway 50 sometime after crossing the Theodore Roosevelt Memorial Bridge over the Potomac. I keep hoping, but there are no more of those shields framing a '50' beside the road. I plunge on, and talk to Harpo.

Harpo is my car, the white Chevy Cruze. His registration is HRP 4099. I'm not usually keen on cars with names, but I feel an attachment to Harpo, perhaps because I am alone with him and will be for many weeks – so giving him a name, let alone a gender, particularly of my favourite Marx brother, doesn't seem any more crazy than talking to him, which I do from time to time: 'Go for it, Harpo'; 'Nice one, Harpo'; 'That was hairy! Well done, Harp'; 'Harpo, my man! Where the fuck are we?' After all, we are in the era of Alexa and her peers, and many people's cars – not mine – talk to their drivers.

I stop at a gas station at the bottom of a hill and ask the guy behind the till if he knows the way to Highway 50. He smiles in a mix of apology and incomprehension. A white van pulls up. I ask the driver, a small, highly intelligent, knowledgeable, Mexican-looking man. He tells me exactly how to get to Route 50 and, after filling his tank, leads me part of the way.

Here 50 is a dual carriageway packed with cars going fast, changing lanes, desperate to get home, and constantly frustrated by traffic lights. This speeding from a green light to the next red light goes on and on and on through interminable suburbs until, eventually, the street lights end. There are no more traffic lights. The cars thin out. Then, holy of holies, 50 narrows to two lanes, one each way. It's dark, but I sense countryside: 50 curves among fields and woods, climbs hills and glides down

56

the sides of valleys. The traffic falls away – until there is just one car in front of me. I am busting for a pee, stop and stand by a gate. The air is cool, a solitary car hurtles past, and a bird drifts across the night sky.

12

In the Blue Ridge Mountains of Virginia

In the morning, after an uneventful night at the Super 8 in Winchester, I drive back east along Route 50. I want to see the countryside and the towns out here in Virginia in daylight. After a long slope down to the brown waters of the Shenandoah River, the road rises to Ashby's Gap in the Blue Ridge Mountains where, below me, to the south-east, ridge after ridge – first green, then blue, then paler and paler blue – recedes into the distance. These mountains rise north of here, in Pennsylvania, cross Virginia and flow on down into the Carolinas, Tennessee and Georgia.

From the summit of Ashby's Gap, I look east, half close my eyes and imagine the precursor of the smooth, wide US 50: a dusty trail that was used by Indians for hundreds, probably thousands of years following its creation millennia ago by the hooves of migrating buffalo. Until the 1750s, when they moved west to get away from European settlers, Shawnee Indians – and their predecessors, the

Iroquois and others – would have been up and down this trail hunting for deer and turkey in the woods that still line Route 50; and with them would have been the dogs they used as pack animals. (After horses became extinct on the American continent 12,000 years ago, there were none until the Spanish coloniser Hernán Cortés brought just sixteen to the region that became Mexico in 1519; from there they slowly spread across the continent.)

As I drive on east, Route 50 dips and bends between old woods, meadows and paddocks, four-bar fences, dry-stone walls and mown grass verges. Old stone houses hide among trees, and neat, white clapboard homes stand behind white-painted fences; occasionally, but not often, the Stars and Stripes flutters on a perfect lawn. It's a beautiful, easy-to-drive road, with little traffic. I roll slowly down-hill through Upperville, a linear, grey-stone town with a discreet restaurant or two but no overt shops, old and clean, and clearly lived in by some form of that hot concept, an elite.

A few miles on, Route 50, labelled East and West Washington Street, becomes the main street of Middleburg, a larger, tidy, upscale kind of place with no dirt and plenty of trees and flowers.

In his book *Roads: Driving America's Great Highways* the novelist and screenwriter Larry McMurtry describes this area as 'one of the great old-money country-house enclaves still left in America ... In most parts of America some deference is paid to landed wealth, but exceptional deference is shown the horse farm set in Virginia – after all, the horse farm set has been there ever since there was a Virginia [1607] ... In Loudoun and Fauquier Counties the squirearchical habits of the English gentry, including shoots and riding to hounds, have come down intact through the centuries.' Upperville and Middleburg are on the border of Loudoun and Fauquier counties.

I park and dawdle along a faded red-brick pavement. It's hot, at least ninety degrees; the sun bears down from a sky with just a few sheep-like clouds, and I wear my floppy, agricultural sun hat. I pass antique shops, clothes shops and restaurants, a small and beautiful red-brick church with gothic windows, founded, a plaque says, in 1842, and an old Georgian house with a white-columned veranda.

Across the road is Les Jardins de Bagatelle: Magazin Français, A French Store. Straw hats on a stand outside Lou Lou Too have messages written on their brims in looping cursive script: 'just chillin', 'always on vacay'. A survey of a realtor's window confirms that this is a horsey place and that there are vineyards nearby.

Two young white men wearing open-neck shirts and dark trousers walk past, carrying their suit jackets folded over their arms. They are not fat, but are a little sweaty and both have large bottoms.

One young man says, 'I think he's OK. He's fair and he listens and seems to be to the left.'

'Yeah. That's right,' the second man says. 'I like him.'

Five more young men come past in a group. All are tieless and carrying their jackets; some have regular bottoms, while a couple have a degree of podge.

Could they be on a break from some kind of political gathering? The word 'left' suggests Democrats, or even supporters of Bernie Sanders.

Middleburg Visitor Information Center is housed in a tiny old building called the Pink Box. I open the door and startle a white woman with permed hair, who recovers sufficiently to give me a map of the town with, on its front, a photograph of two beautiful horses leaning out of a stable door.

I go into Second Chapter Books, a small shop with a lot of books and two customers, a woman and her young daughter. I pick up a local guide book and gaze at photographs of what I have just seen: horses grazing, horses with riders, horses poking their heads out of stables, the Shenandoah River and the Blue Ridge Mountains. While the woman and her daughter discuss which book to buy as a birthday present for another child, I come across a small booklet, *The Constitution of the United States*. Its fifty-two pages contain the full texts of the Constitution, the twenty-seven amendments and the Declaration of Independence; there are plentiful quotes from the Founding Fathers and a handy index. A note at the front says that this version was proofed 'against the original constitution, housed in the Archives in Washington, DC. It is identical in spelling, capitalization and punctuation' and is the same size as 'one produced by President Thomas Jefferson'. Another note states that 16 million copies of this edition have been distributed.

Mother and daughter buy *Tell Me Three Things* by Julie Buxbaum. And then I pay $1.95 for *The Constitution of the United States*. And I ask the businesslike woman at the till if it is up to date – and explain that I'm from England. 'Have there been any new amendments?' I'd noticed that the most recent amendment listed was ratified in 1992.

'Amendments take a long time,' she says, 'many years. The people have to vote on an amendment. So' – she thumbed the little book – 'this is up to date.'

'I guess Trump would like an amendment to make him president for life.'

'I think he just might.' She sighs. She has taken me more seriously than I'd expected. 'I have to say I'm not a Trump supporter.'

'Perhaps I was probing,' I say. 'But I kind of guessed that.'

'How about Brexit? I was really surprised that you people did that.'

'Surprised me, surprised a lot of us.' I grimaced. 'So you know about that?'

'Of course.' She smiles for the first time. 'It's on TV, in newspapers, all the media.'

'It's a total nightmare. People didn't know what they were voting for.'

She nods. 'Misinformation was distributed, I think.'

I tell her about the infamous bus and its claim that leaving the EU would give the NHS £350 million every week. And we talk about Trump, his attitude to women, his mockery of a disabled journalist, his promise to prosecute Hillary Clinton, his proposed wall along the Mexican border, and more – until some new customers claim her attention, and I leave carrying *The Constitution of the United States*.

I drive back towards Winchester – and remember the young men with large bottoms. Would supporters of Bernie Sanders wear suits to a meeting of local Democrats on a Wednesday morning in Middleburg? Maybe – but it seems more likely, now I think about it, that they are wine merchants, stable manufacturers, agronomists, or just boring old realtors. This time, as I cross Ashby's Gap and drop downhill into the Shenandoah Valley, I try to imagine the old trail, wider and paved, and the hills and ridges on either side as a battleground, as they were during the Civil War. Though, to me, Virginia doesn't seem very far south, it is a southern state and was a slave state. In 1862, the Confederate General Thomas 'Stonewall' Jackson was in command of three divisions, which means 30,000 men. Right here, in the Shenandoah Valley, he fought and defeated Union armies three times, preventing them from joining the main Union army, which was trying to take Richmond – the capital of Virginia and, during the Civil War, of the Confederacy – from General Robert E. Lee.

Then an image from an earlier era comes into my mind: the eighteen-year-old George Washington, tall and skinny, working here as a surveyor with two men helping him by holding up poles and stretching out chains so he can take measurements. Washington was here, surveying and drawing maps of the Shenandoah Valley, in 1749 and 1750.

The air is warm, the sky is blue; I drive a little faster than usual. This is the third time I have driven through this pastoral scene, and there is somewhere I want to visit in Winchester this afternoon.

13

On the Trail of the Patsy Cline

Back in Winchester, I follow a sign to the old downtown, fail to find it and fetch up in the car park of Apple Blossom Mall, a building that contains more than eighty shops. I cross the car park, intending to go into this huge building, find someone who looks knowledgeable and ask the way to Patsy Cline's house. Before I get there, I pass a middle-aged white woman with wild hair, who is lifting a book from the boot of her car. I can't see the book's title, but it is by Susan Sontag. People who read Susan Sontag are likely to know a thing or two.

'Excuse me,' I say in my best English voice. 'Do you know where Patsy Cline's house is?'

She clutches the book to her chest, sighs, twiddles a strand of her hair and looks me in the eye. It's in the old town, but I can't tell you how to get there. I have very poor spatial awareness.' She turns away, shrugging and closes her boot.

This not unfriendly but useless encounter reminds me of a similar but more succinct response I got when I asked a woman behind the counter of a post office in Cheverly for directions to Cheverly Metro station. She smiled, shook her head and said, 'I know where it is, but I can't explain how to get there.' There's something Zen-like – worthy, perhaps, of Susan Sontag – about this.

I go into Apple Blossom Mall and find a tired place – though it was built not that long ago, 1982 – with several closed shops and few people, most of whom are children. I leave without asking anyone for directions, and decide that I must, at least, be able to find the old town; Winchester isn't *that* big.

Ten minutes later I pull up in a different kind of shopping mall: the outdoor type, where an enormous car park, dotted with trees, is surrounded by shops, most of them chain stores. I open up my laptop. I've remembered that someone in England emailed me about Patsy Cline in Winchester. Maybe that email includes its address. It doesn't, but the screen is showing a long dropdown list of wifi connections provided by the shops that surround me. All but one display a locked padlock. The exception is a store called Famous Footwear. I can see it fifty yards away to my right. I click on its wifi, fill in my name and email address and get online.

I can't see Patsy Cline's house on Google's map of Winchester, but there is a visitor centre and it's not far away; I find it easily with my laptop open on the seat beside me. There, a charming, almost elderly, white woman gives me a map which actually marks 'Home of Patsy Cline' – on Kent Street; this sweet woman takes a purple felt-tip and traces the route from here to there, less than a mile. 'And,' she says, 'we have our own Patsy Cline exhibit right here. You're more than welcome to look. It's free.' She is pointing down the room, past racks of leaflets and tables of souvenirs. 'We call it "Becoming Patsy Cline",' she says, 'because it's about when she was younger. You'll see.'

A small space is filled with photographs, posters, fanzines, badges, sheet music and some of the clothes that Patsy wore on stage, including a fringed cowgirl outfit made by her mother, Hilda, who was a dressmaker.

I'm not a fan of Patsy Cline in the obsessed sense, but I liked her hits, which I heard on the radio when I was a kid, realised she had a sensational voice when I grew up, and discovered more recently than she was a brilliant self-taught pianist who couldn't read music because the piano teacher to whom her mother sent her said she didn't need lessons; they would spoil her natural way of playing – she had perfect pitch and should continue as she was, playing by ear. Now, fifty-six years after she died in a plane crash at the age of thirty, I am looking at the piano she first played when she was fourteen with a band called Joltin' Jim McCoy and the Melody Playboys – and continued to play on Saturday mornings at WINC AM, the local Winchester radio station. A notice invites me to sit down and play a tune and have my photograph taken. There aren't many people around, so I sit down and press middle C twice. That's enough. I've pressed a key that Patsy Cline pressed.

I drive with ease to 608 South Kent Street, a small, white-painted clapboard house which, viewed from the street, looks like a child's drawing of a typical house: two windows and a door downstairs; three windows upstairs. A porch, level with the pavement and the street, runs the width of the building, its roof supported on four narrow columns.

Houses nearby are similar but different: small, well-maintained, tidy – so I guess that the street is now 'respectable', which it wasn't when sixteen-year-old Virginia ('Ginny') Hensley – soon to become Patsy Cline – moved here with her mother and her younger brother and sister in 1948. At that time poor white people lived here, so the street wasn't considered respectable – at least, not by respectable people. (The snobs of Winchester didn't rate *North* Kent Street either, because black people lived there.) Even when Patsy Cline had made hit records and had a big reputation as a live entertainer, many locals looked down on her; in 1961 honking car horns drowned out clapping when she performed on the roof of the refreshment stand at the Winchester Drive-In Theater. As late as 1986, by which time Cline was long dead and a worldwide legend, the local council voted 11:1 against renaming a local street Patsy Cline Boulevard.

However, in 2009, Winchester's John Handley High School built a new theatre and named it the Patsy Cline Theater; ironically, Ginny Hensley enrolled at this school but never attended because, not long before they moved to South Kent Street, her father left the family and Ginny felt she had to get a job and help her mother with the younger children.

There's a notice on the door: 'If door locked, tour is in progress. Tours last 30 minutes. Please wait.'

I hesitate. Do I want to go on a thirty-minute tour? I hate guided tours; I like to wander around on my own. I decide that if it's locked, I'll go away; I want to move on west along Route 50. I try the door. It opens and a woman's voice says 'hello'. I step into the Hensley family's living room and into the 1950s – and begin chatting to a woman called Teresa who knows everything about Ginny Hensley and this house. As she talks, I can't help glancing round the room at an old sofa, an upright piano, a tiny black-and-white television, a rack of 45 rpm singles, framed family photos and portraits of Patsy. On a table beside me three cigarettes, two of them smeared red with lipstick, sit in an ashtray – a reference, I realise later, to one of her lesser-known songs, 'Three Cigarettes in an Ashtray'.

Ginny lived here from 1948 until 1953 when, aged twenty-one, she married Gerald Cline. In those years she worked in a meat-processing plant cutting up chickens, as a waitress in a diner and as a soda jerk in a drug store, while building a reputation as a singer locally – in Virginia, Washington DC and the nearer parts of Maryland. She moved back to this house to live with her mother, Hilda, after divorcing Cline in 1957. 'Cline was a good man, and wealthy,' Teresa says, 'but he wanted a wife to cook, run the home and all that – and Patsy wouldn't do that; she wanted to sing, perform.'

In January that same year, with Hilda's help, Patsy appeared on *Arthur Godfrey's Talent Scouts*, a popular CBS television show, broadcast from New York and watched all over the United States. Each week three performers competed, and the winner was chosen by a clapometer, a device that measured the noise generated by applause.

As Teresa tells me this, a sultry voice fills the room – indeed, fills the little house. Patsy Cline is singing 'Walkin' After Midnight'. 'That's the song that won on the Arthur Godfrey talent show,' Teresa says, 'and it changed her life. It was played on radio stations across the country, became a hit on the country music charts and then on the pop charts too.'

Later in 1957, Patsy married Charlie Dick, a linotype operator whom she described as 'the love of my life'. They moved to Nashville, had two children, and Dick became Patsy's road manager. Patsy died in 1963; her husband lived until 2015 – and was buried next to her in Shenandoah Park cemetery in Winchester.

Teresa talks about the house itself. When the family moved in, there was no indoor plumbing or electricity, both of which Hilda was eventually able to install. The building was originally a log cabin; a rectangle of plaster has been taken from the wall near the front door to show the logs below. Beautiful, wide, Virginia-pine floorboards are now polished to a chestnut brown, but one board in the living room is darker, preserved as they all would have been in Patsy's time. Hilda's wallpaper choices have been uncovered and are displayed in small, framed patches on walls now painted in whites, creams, and greys.

Teresa leads me up the narrow stairs and into a fully furnished bedroom with three beds. 'All four of them slept in here: Ginny's brother slept behind a curtain to give him privacy.' A doll lies on a crisp white counterpane; she is wearing a long blue print dress with a white collar and lace trimmings. Teresa picks her up and tells me to look at the stitching; the tiny dress is beautifully made. 'Hilda made that. She was a wonderful dressmaker; that's how she supported her family and she made doll's clothes to order as well.'

Hilda worked in the dining room at the back of the house, and there I see her sewing machine and Patsy's sketches in black ink for her stage dresses. Two of those dresses, blue and red with cowgirl fringes, made by Hilda, stand against the wall on headless mannequins. Hilda also made ballgowns for Patsy to wear at venues like New York's Carnegie Hall and the Mint Casino in Las Vegas, where

Patsy was engaged for thirty-five consecutive nights in 1962; one of these featured 3,000 sequins, hand-stitched by the devoted Hilda. My admiration for Hilda, already high, swells further. She was only sixteen years older than Ginny – and they were said to be more like friends than mother and daughter.

An iron sits on an old ironing board with wooden legs. As I look at it, I have a sense for the first time that I'm invading someone's privacy, even though Hilda, like Patsy, is now long dead. The feeling grows when Teresa leads me into the kitchen. Cooker, fridge, sink, work surfaces, cupboards are all in 1950s style, though, like much of the furniture in the house, these actual items weren't there when the Hensleys lived here. However, it's the same room, the same layout. Why didn't I have this guilty sense of gawping at strangers' lives when I was upstairs in a bedroom where four people used to sleep? Familiarity, I think, is the answer. I know more now; I've been in every room in the house. At the end of the kitchen, by a window overlooking the garden, is a little table with two red-painted chairs. Teresa says that Patsy and Hilda often sat there, looking out at their garden. She points to a tall tree to the right and tells me it's a walnut tree, planted by Hilda, who harvested the walnuts and baked walnut cake. A shed now stands where the outhouse was when the Hensleys arrived. At the end of the garden is a wood where the redoubtable Hilda hunted small animals for food when the family first arrived.

Teresa is great; she has described Hilda's and Patsy's lives in this house, and beyond it, without exaggeration or invention. She invites me to sit down, and points to one of the chairs. And then her phone rings. 'Excuse me,' she says, and walks back into the living room.

I sit down and stare out. Patsy Cline and her mother sat here, looking at the same tree – smaller then – and at the woods. Patsy planted herbs, Teresa said. She liked to cook with them. Glimpsing someone else's life when they are not there is a privilege, whether or not they are, or were, famous.

I pay $8 for the tour, buy a pack of Patsy Cline playing cards and a tea towel with Hilda's walnut cake recipe, and say goodbye to Teresa. As I shut the door behind me, I remember half-hoping that it would be locked when I tried it forty minutes ago. Well, I'm just thrilled that it wasn't.

14

Lugubrious in Keyser

On Route 50 out of Winchester, I pass Lynette and Jerri's Diner and can't resist stopping; it's 4 p.m. and I'm hungry. The place is run by two friendly women, has been here in one form or another since 1958, and looks as if it hasn't changed much since then: black-and-white floor tiles, beige plastic-covered seats at the counter and in the booths, and plenty of formica and chrome. There are ten other customers; all except two are over sixty. Some are lean, some are not so lean; one looks like Father Christmas. The least lean are a pair of teenagers, or perhaps young twenties, in a booth; they are colossal. I get many smiles. The two women, Lynette and Jerri, ask where I'm from and call me 'honey', which is nice, but it doesn't go much further than that. I eat a large and sedate chicken salad, drink a holier-than-thou orange juice, pay and move on.

Soon I'm climbing on a smooth, curvy road. There are blue ridges here, too – this evening, anyway. In front of me, a bank of blue rises behind a ridge that is green with trees. A bend in the road brings me closer and the blue begins to fade. I remember listening to a recording of the talent show that made Patsy Cline famous in 1957. Patsy's mother, Hilda, told Arthur Godfrey that she was born in the Blue Ridge Mountains, and in his cuddliest voice, the avuncular Godfrey replied, 'It all looks blue from a distance – and you know what kills me? I never saw a range of mountains yet that didn't look blue from a distance, so I don't know why they're not all named Blue Ridge.' Godfrey was right. These aren't the Blue Ridge Mountains; they are behind me now. These are the Alleghenies.

High up on a grassy plateau, we – Harpo and I – sashay through a gap between mountains and find a scene from *The Sound of Music*: deep valleys, huge hills, cows wandering on lush green grass. Then downhill, with tall trees all around, on what I have learned that Americans call a divided highway (in the UK a dual carriageway) with the eastbound highway somewhere below.

The speed limit is 55 mph. We cross Bat Creek, though I can't see it and imagine it to be a muddy ditch. A small floral arrangement sits outside a house behind a sign saying 'Thank you Jesus' – and the road winds on, more bendy, with hairpins. Coming to Capon Bridge means I've crossed the state line into West Virginia. And I drive for another hour, slowly, obeying speed limits, which are signed before every bend: 45 mph, 35, 25. I learn to judge the bends by the recommended speed. A sign insists: Watch for Fallen Rocks – so I try to do that, and wonder what I will do if I see them. I pass through Hanging Rock, then Shanks and, at the top of a mountain pass, against a backdrop of blue ridges, Sunrise, which has a gas station, a couple of bars, a few small houses and unexpected traffic lights where I join a line of cars.

I follow a black Jeep, with the licence plate DLIVERY, across the south branch of the Potomac River – and drive on into a landscape that becomes increasingly dramatic: vast grey ridges – like the Atlantic on a cloudy day – trees everywhere, a forest. For the first time, miles from a city, America seems wild. But then, sudden serenity: a herd of sleek black cattle, grazing on rich grass in the depths of a valley.

It begins to get dark – and I am sixty miles from the next town of any size. I stop at a gas station and ask if there is a motel to the west on Route 50. A man in a red baseball cap suggests I turn right a few miles on and drive ten miles on Route 220 to Keyser. 'And go to Keyser Inn. You'll see it. It's better and cheaper than the other one.' I thank him at least three times. He smiles and waves a hand. 'No problem. No problem. You're very welcome.'

Keyser sprawls along a road deep in a valley. Keyser Inn is two-storey, stone and clapboard, a clean, newish building. I'm greeted by an enthusiastic woman who wants to know where I'm from and what I'm doing here.

'Driving to San Francisco.'

'Wow! Really! When are you going to get there?'

We discuss my plans for a minute or two, and then she says, 'Well, I'm sure glad you've decided to stop off here.'

I go back to the car to get my suitcase and, when I return, the enthusiastic woman has disappeared, replaced by a tall, grey-haired, lugubrious man who doesn't smile once during the check-in process. But he gets the job done efficiently – and knows how to spell Reynolds.

I return to reception a few minutes later. There is no one there, but I can hear the sound of a television in an office to one side. I slap the bell on the reception desk – something I hate doing: it's aggressive, like shouting out 'Oy!' The lugubrious man appears, his shoulders, cheeks and mouth on full droop.

'Sorry to bother you,' I say. 'Can you tell me the password for the wifi, please?'

He eyes me, as if deciding whether to tell me, whether I deserve to go online. 'Cleaning,' he says.

'Cleaning? That's the password?'
'Yep.' He turns and walks away.
And he's right.

15

Fear and Tranquillity in the Alleghenies

In the morning I see a line of white windmills, the three-sail turbine kind, sprouting from the wavy ridge of the fir-clad hills above the Keyser Inn. They look good up there in the sun, equally spaced and turning slowly against a pale blue sky.

I'm soon back up in the Alleghenies where the road winds on, up and down, up and down, throwing me into an incessant routine of slowing for a bend, turning the wheel and accelerating for a short distance before slowing for the next bend. It takes concentration but isn't difficult; the road is wide, there is little traffic and I have the pleasant sense of moving slowly among the greens and yellows of trees and grass. At the top of a hill, I turn off to a 'Scenic Overlook' where I park on an acre of cracking tarmac and lean on a bent and rusty crash barrier, intended to prevent people and cars from stumbling downhill. From here I look out at distant hazy ridges, rising one behind another like waves viewed from a low cliff. A perfect curve, like a giant's thumbprint, is carved into the nearest and bluest – or perhaps least grey – of these rows of Alleghenies.

A few yards from me, a man and a woman stand in the sun with a small boy, looking, pointing, talking. We chat – at first praising the weather and the view. They are local, out with their grandson for the day – and they want to know where I'm from and where I'm going.

I tell them that I'm from London, England.

The little boy looks up at me, his head to one side.

I smile at him. 'Quite a way from here.'

'Oh, I have an English aunt,' the woman says. 'She's ninety-three and lives in Palm Springs, California. She married my uncle during World War Two.'

'A GI bride,' I say.

'That's right. They met over there someplace.'

Route 50 is below us. I point at it and tell them that I am driving to San Francisco along this road.

The man frowns and says that a few miles on from here the road gets harder to drive: '. . . narrower, steeper, more bendy – it's tough,' he says.

'That's a long way,' his wife says. She turns down the corners of her mouth. 'You take care.'

'I've got plenty of time,' I say, 'more than five weeks.'

Again, we all look out at the landscape. The man tells me that the ridge with the perfect curve is called Saddle Mountain. 'Abraham Lincoln's mother was born over there, just beyond the mountain, in a log cabin. It's still there, but it's not much to look at.'

Before they get back in their car, the man reaches into his pocket and hands me a penny, an American cent. 'Here. I make these for friends. Keep it in your pocket – to keep you safe.' A cross, a Christian cross, has been stamped out of the little coin to make a cross-shaped hole.

I'm not a Christian, but I am touched and I thank him. 'That's so kind.'

He climbs into his car. His wife helps her grandson with his seatbelt. She turns. She looks worried, but looks me in the eye and smiles. 'Stay safe,' she says and climbs in next to her husband.

As I drive on, I think about those kind people. 'Stay safe.' She had said it with meaning, and a look – not as a throwaway postscript to goodbye. And he had given me this customised coin in the hope that it would keep me safe.

I had been wondering over the last two or three days whether this trip was a good idea – not because it might be physically dangerous, but because it now seemed a long haul, longer than I had envisaged – perhaps too long – too long to be heading into the unknown alone.

Did they – she and her husband – mean safety on the road? It had narrowed – one slim lane each way; bends were sharper; hills were steeper; there was no shoulder; in places a crash barrier with the land falling away beyond it was two feet from my front wheel. But that didn't bother me – I've been on similar roads in England, Scotland and Wales. Roads like this are more unusual in this spacious country – and maybe scare some people. What I'm scared by is six-lane beltways with every lane signed to a different place, and every vehicle, including trucks, speeding while changing lanes.

Or did they mean other kinds of safety? Had her thoughtful stare meant watch out, be alert, danger awaits in unexpected places? If I didn't watch out, might I be attacked in a dimly lit street by a gang of deprived youths who sensed an ignorant foreigner with an iPhone and some dollars? Or, if I wasn't alert, could I be hit over the head with a sock full of ball bearings by a lone desperado in a remote place where there were just the two of us – a canyon in Colorado, for example? I am, after all, a middle-class, liberal white man. Plenty of people don't like the likes of me.

So, what to do?

For today: concentrate on the driving, stop to admire the landscape and go for a walk in a wood – which turns out to be Cathedral State Park, a rare tract of virgin forest, a quiet and shady place where Indians lived for centuries, entranced by sudden shafts of sunlight and sheltered by tall, slender trees – conifers called eastern hemlock, some of which have been there for 400 years.

For the rest of the trip: follow the English mantra, keep calm and carry on; and, despite your lack of religious faith, keep the coin with the cross-shaped hole in your pocket.

16

Women Swimming in the Rust Belt

The road flattens out. The bends become curves. I am in the western foothills of the Alleghenies and come to the city of Grafton, where I walk around downtown and am startled by its aura of gloom and dilapidation. On Main Street the few people around are scurrying rather than lingering – except for two women with lined, raddled faces who stand by a wall smoking. Leonard's Grill and the 123 Café are open, a few American flags hang vertically from lamp posts, and the tall, gabled courthouse is functioning but looks worn and uncared for. Further along, an old woman with thick, blotchy calves sits facing an emaciated old man on a square of concrete, surrounded by an offering of junk that surely no one would want. Many buildings are either boarded up or protected by wire fences; the rest are closed.

It takes me a few minutes to think through the decline I see around me. I have reached the Rust Belt, and am among people who voted overwhelmingly for Donald Trump – people whom Hillary Clinton foolishly called 'a basket of deplorables' and labelled 'racist, sexist, homophobic, xenophobic, Islamophobic – you name it'.

During the nineteenth and much of the twentieth century, when West Virginia thrived on coal and steel, Grafton was a major transport hub – where railways met roads and the Tygart River, which flows just south of Main Street. Since the 1980s jobs have been drying up, and they evaporated further during the Obama years with the decision to fight global warming by reducing the use of coal as a fuel for generating power. Trump, who conveniently thinks climate change is a hoax, has reinstated coal; some mines have reopened and jobs have been created – but Grafton doesn't seem to have benefited much, if at all.

On my way out of Grafton I stop at Hometown Hotdogs, a white-painted, clapboard building set high above a bend on Route 50. It is after five o'clock and I've eaten only a few nuts since breakfast. I wait in line at a clean white formica counter, behind a woman with several children, and order a dog with mustard and gravy from a smiley man aged about forty. An elderly man sitting on a high stool points to the back of smiley man's head. 'See that line,' he says.

I can't see anything. Smiley man has normal short-cut brown hair. But I feel I must say something. 'What's it mean?'

'Means he's getting old.' It seems that the elderly man can see some grey hairs that I can't. 'I'm seventy. How old are you?'

'Sixty-nine.'

He doesn't say anything, but I can tell that he is surprised, and I feel a tingle of gratification. Then he says, 'When I go swimmin', these seventy-five-year-old women laugh at me. There's two of them. If there's one thing women are good at, it's swimmin'.'

It's hard to know how to reply to this, except to grin and shake my head knowingly, as if to say: 'I know what you mean. Those women – and their darned swimming!'

Luckily, at this point my dog is ready and I have to pay $1.38 to a younger man who stands by a till. I poke and peer at a handful of coins trying to find the exact money. Meanwhile, the young man rocks sideways from foot to foot. 'Sorry,' I say. 'I'm English.'

'Oh, whereabouts?' the young man says.

'London. Have you been?'

'No, but I know a lot of people over there.'

'Oh, where are they?'

'On the internet.'

'Oh, I see.'

'Thought I recognised a London accent.'

'I know. You people think I talk funny.'

'Yeah. We do.' He laughs.

'Well, we think you talk funny.' And we both laugh.

I take my dog and sit down in a low-backed booth. There are about twenty customers in this small white space, many of them children with their mothers. An old lady flexes her hands as she waits at the counter. The man who acknowledges that women are, if nothing else, good at swimming levers himself off his stool and walks towards a door marked restroom. The dog is good – the sauce is quite something: mincemeat in gravy.

The sky is grey and dank, and so is the road. I head for Clarksburg and stop five miles short, on the western edge of Bridgeport, enticed by the names and logos of several motels looking down on me from a forest of concrete poles that overlooks the junction of Route 50 and Interstate 79, a major north–south route. I check into the Super 8 because, in a spaghetti of freeways and feed roads, it is the easiest to find. But I soon regret that decision.

Room 133 smells musty with damp. Four or five flies are circling. The fridge is in a plastic tray – perhaps it leaks. It's leaning over at an angle, making it hard to open and liable to pitch forward. And it's humming, almost buzzing, loudly – loudly enough to keep me awake. I push it upright and the noise stops, so I grab a telephone directory and shove it underneath. Should a room like this cost $119 a night? A room in the Super 8 in Winchester cost $68, was a lot better and didn't smell. Does the price almost double because we're near an interstate junction? Judging by the number of parked vehicles, the place is full – so, yes, they charge what they can get away with – and spend as little as possible on maintenance. Super 8 is a huge business owned by an even bigger one called Wyndham Hotels and Resorts; the management of such businesses has to please its shareholders.

Nearby, around the back of a sub-postmodern, red-brick-and-gable shopping mall, I discover Mountaineer Grille, where I sit alone on the short side of an L-shaped bar, observing five men who are taking up all the seats on the long side. All five are middle-aged and wearing smart, ironed shorts – it is still warm outside and the temperature inside is comfortably regulated.

I study the menu and ask the bartender about the salmon; she says it is cooked following a recipe by Gordon Ramsay. I order it anyway. And then we discuss beer; she recommends Two for the Show, an IPA which comes from a local brewery called Short Story.

The two men closest to me are talking intently to each other. Or, to be more accurate, the one nearer to me – who is wearing a baseball cap and an expensive-looking blue-and-white patterned shirt – is talking, while the other – bare head, plain blue shirt – for the most part listens. I can't possibly interrupt them, so I settle down to eavesdrop while pretending to look at my phone.

'I'm a little rough around the edges,' says Fancy Shirt.

'I would guess Mark's good at the little things,' Plain Shirt replies.

'I couldn't do it without a personality like him there. They don't like me. They like him.'

Fancy Shirt, I discover, runs a company that makes – I assume among other things – adhesives, plastic film and plastic covers for thermostats. And – horrors! – a company in White Plains, NY, wants to buy them out.

'I have to succeed, or I'm not doing this any more,' Fancy Shirt says. 'I told my salespeople – don't be friendly with them. They're our competitor. We have to beat them.'

'You want to beat them into the ground and put your foot on their neck.'

'Of course!' Fancy Shirt, who speaks loudly anyway, gets louder still.

I carry on listening and begin to wonder why the conversation between these men seems incomplete. I decide that they are not friends, but acquaintances who happen to meet in this bar – perhaps by chance – now and then; drinking acquaintances whose preferred way of passing the time is talking and listening – unlike the three men to their right who eat and drink silently while watching baseball on the screen above the bar. As my salmon arrives, I realise that neither of them shows to the other any glimmer of weakness or vulnerability, as friends would; nor do they project warmth or humour.

I ask for another beer. Fancy Shirt is telling the other shirt about his new house which, he says, cost $6 million to build. 'I've got the best interior decorator I've ever seen in my life. One hundred dollars an hour. She's probably OCD. She worries away at the possibilities, even after I've made a decision. I have to say, "I won't talk about that any more. Let's move on."'

There are other people here, sitting at tables: a family, couples, two women eating together. But these five men, with their smart-casual clothes and, in four cases, designer baseball hats, intrigue me. They have an air of stolid conservatism. You might see a version of them at a golf club in England. Why are they dining out on Gordon Ramsay food without partners in a bar behind a shopping mall in an unexciting town? Might they be what Americans call 'good ol' boys'? I know that good ol' boys are from the south. I believe they tend to be successful materially and dress conservatively.

They are still there when I go back to my smelly, profitable motel room. I click through the TV channels and find a bearded man in a tight white shirt, who speaks a little too fast, talking about Elizabeth Warren's Accountable Capitalism Act. I discover that he is Jim Cramer and that he presents a programme about stocks and shares and Wall Street called *Mad Money*.

I'm already aware of, and sympathetic towards, Elizabeth Warren – so I am suspicious of this Cramer, who I suspect is going to call her a socialist or a liberal – both of which are considered spooky by the Republican right.

Warren is a senator for Massachusetts who is pitching to be

the Democrat candidate to take on Trump in 2020. With her Accountable Capitalism Act, which will go before Congress, she wants to reinstate the benevolent capitalism that operated before the 1980s – before Ronald Reagan and Margaret Thatcher took the advice of their economic guru, Milton Friedman, and made profit the only legally enforceable goal for corporate executives. Before the Reagan-Thatcher era, companies were legally required to consider their workers, their customers and the regions where they operated, and to make sensible long-term investments, as well as profits. Among many other things, Warren wants 40 per cent of the board members of large companies to be elected by their employees.

Cramer surprises me by broadly agreeing with Warren's ideas. He says that companies that treat their employees well – and he cites some, including Costco and Domino's Pizza – increase their profits.

Good old Cramer. And good old Warren.

17

Stonewall Jackson's Arm

Heading along Route 50 to Clarksburg, I see a sign to Nutter's Fort.
I'm not in a hurry; I don't have to be in San Francisco for weeks, and
it will be interesting to see a fort. I turn off, drive through residential streets for about three miles and fetch up in a dead end outside
Nutter's Fort Elementary School. There is no fort at Nutter's Fort;
there *was*, but it's long gone.

In a side street in Clarksburg I come across a pair of turquoise
men's underpants splayed across a puddle under a concrete bench.
The bench is one of four placed a few feet apart in a square formation
in front of a derelict apartment building with gaping windows. I sit
on one of the other benches – I've been walking for a while – and
muse, but not too much, on the turquoise underpants: how did they
get there? Soon the shirts from last night at Mountaineer Grille,
fancy and plain, come to mind, although there is no connection,
certainly not a conscious one, to the turquoise underpants. I wonder,
for a moment, whether those two men are friends after all. Then
I remember the adhesives, the plastic thermostat covers, the price

of the house and the hourly rate of the interior decorator. A friend would know these things.

Behind the tall, pink abandoned building, grey clouds shift and reveal patches of blue. Clarksburg seems run-down, though there are more signs of hope than in Grafton. On Pike Street workmen are restoring the Robinson Grand Performing Arts Center, which first opened in 1913, but has been closed for five years. Now it is gaining an art deco-style marquee covered in flashing and travelling lights, ready for a grand reopening in October.

On Main Street, the imposing art deco Harrison County Courthouse is well maintained, with war memorials, explanatory plaques, potted palm trees and mown grass in front. A couple come out and walk down the steps on either side of the central railing. They are talking loudly and are soon having a row, standing far apart and waving fingers, if not fists, at each other. I can't catch their words, but my guess is that they are shouting about alimony and custody of children. They walk off in different directions. I turn to look at a bronze statue of a handsome, bearded man on a fine horse in mid-gallop; they look as if they are heading into battle. And they probably are, because they turn out to be Thomas J. 'Stonewall' Jackson, who was born in Clarksburg, and his horse, Little Sorrel.

Jackson was, and still is, a much-admired military tactician. However, in the view of most people who think about such things, he was on the wrong side – the side that wanted slavery to continue. In 2017 a petition, signed by more than 1,100 people, was delivered to the Mayor of Clarksburg, Cathy Goings, asking her to 'take a stand against white supremacy' by having the statue removed. At the moment it is still there, as is the statue of Robert E. Lee in Charlottesville which, in that same year, provoked violent demonstrations and counter-demonstrations during which a thirty-two-year-old woman, Heather Heyer, was killed.

Jackson owned six slaves and was good to them. One was an orphaned child in need of a home, and two asked him to buy them because he was so supportive of black people, both slaves and free blacks. A devout Presbyterian, he broke the law of Virginia by setting up a weekly 'colored Sabbath school', first in his home and then in a church, where slaves were taught to read and write and learned about Jesus and the Bible. He didn't oppose slavery because there is slavery in the Bible. In his book *Stonewall Jackson: the Black Man's Friend*, Richard G. Williams Jr wrote that Jackson was 'no defender of slavery. He accepted it as the mysterious providence of God and worked to lift the existence of the slaves within his sphere of influence.'

He fought for the Confederacy because his state, Virginia, was on that side in the Civil War – even though this estranged him from his sister, a wholehearted Unionist, to whom he had always been devoted. An irony is that West Virginia, where Stonewall Jackson was born, split from Virginia at the beginning of the war in 1861 because its people were mostly small farmers, who had no slaves and no desire to fight for slavery; if anything, the West Virginians were abolitionists. Jackson became the Confederacy's most able general, at least the equal of Robert E. Lee, the commander of the Confederate Army. Some think that if Stonewall Jackson had not died – as a result of friendly fire, which all but destroyed his left arm – in May 1863, the Confederates might have won the Civil War and the history of the United States, and indeed the world, might have been different. He died of pneumonia at the age of thirty-nine, eight days after his arm was amputated. After resting in state at the Governor's Mansion in Richmond, Virginia, he was buried in Lexington, Virginia, where he lived. His arm was buried separately, close to the field hospital, known as Wilderness Tavern, where it was amputated.

I'm not keen on religion, and I detest war and slavery, obviously, but I have a fondness for Stonewall. His last words were: 'Let us cross over the river and rest under the shade of the trees.'

I go into the Clarksburg-Harrison Public Library, a low-slung, modern, brown building and walk upstairs following a sign to 'Reference'. As I reach the top, I see a bald man with circular glasses and a greying beard looking at me from behind a desk.

'Can I help you?'

'Er . . . yes. Thank you. Do you have any books that give a brief history of this region? I'd just like to have a quick look. I'm not here for long.'

'Brief history?' he says and stands up. 'Not sure about brief, but let's have a look.' He walks to some shelves by the wall. He is wearing blue jeans with braces. He bends down, runs his finger along a shelf not far from the floor and pulls out a brown-covered hardback. 'This might help you. It's not exactly brief – I don't think there is a *brief* history. But you might get something from it. You can sit anywhere over there.' He points to a line of tables and chairs and hands me the book. 'Where are you from, may I ask?'

'London, England.'

He smiles. 'Thought I recognised the accent. What brings you here?'

I tell him that I'm driving across the country on Route 50 to San Francisco; that I'm in no hurry; I don't have to drive all the time; I can stop off and try to get some idea of the places I travel through.

'I'd like to do that,' he says. Then he points to the book. 'I hope you get something out of that.'

I sit with *The History of Harrison County* by Dorothy Davis – all 986 pages of it; 'not exactly brief,' as the man said. I scan it, using the contents pages. Indians were here for thousands of years, as they were all over North America. European hunters and fur trappers arrived in the 1760s. Pioneers, many with families, came from the east in the 1770s and raised horses, cattle, sheep and pigs, and produced milk and cheese. Sawmills provided work and wood for building homes. By 1777 settlers were having to 'fort up' – to build forts and, in some cases, live inside them for much of the time to protect themselves from the Shawnee, who were keen on kidnapping and scalping. Roads and railways arrived during the nineteenth century, and coal mining and glass manufacture took off. In the twentieth century, established businesses – notably Carnation, which made evaporated milk, and Maidenform, bra manufacturers – set up factories in Clarksburg.

Dorothy Davis's book was published in 1970, almost fifty years ago. I take it back to the friendly librarian and ask him how the town is getting on now.

He shakes his head. 'I don't know how we survive.' He comes out from behind his desk. 'Many people are sick – some of them long-term. I sometimes think we are owned by the hospital board – by doctors from all over the world. It feels like they are the industry here now.' The town has been in decline since the 1950s, he says. 'Before then there was an elite of lawyers, and there was manufacturing from 1900 until 1950 – mostly of glass.'

'What have people been doing since then?'

'Some have jobs, small businesses. Many are on welfare. There's fracking here now, on the north-west edge of the county.' He shakes his head again. 'But not many of those jobs go to locals. There's a trailer town out there full of workers from Texas, Oklahoma – experts in oil and fracking. So, to add to their troubles, many people are now living in earshot of pumping twenty-four hours a day.'

'Are people angry, or do they suffer in silence?'

He locks his fingers together, rubs his thumbs against one another and grins. 'This is Trumpland – though there are plenty of people who are vehemently against him.'

'Are you . . .' I hesitate, though I think I know the answer.

He laughs. 'Yes. I'm definitely one of them. He's not the greatest statesman.' He pauses and strokes his chin, tugging gently at his beard. 'What's going to happen? No one knows.'

'It's like us and Brexit.'

'Yes. But . . . somehow, I think, we have it worse. It's unpredictable. There's fear and ignorance and chaos at the top.' He looks away, then back again and lowers his voice. 'In Cambodia, Pol Pot took over and murdered everyone who wore glasses . . . Anything can happen.'

'Do people here and across the Rust Belt think Trump's "Make America Great Again" is the answer? Do they blame globalisation? Maybe they are right . . .'

A woman has appeared at his side. 'Excuse me,' he says. I back away and, as he walks with her to his desk, I hear her call him David.

88

Soon he returns. 'The decline here wasn't caused by globalisation. It began long before that, partly because oil began to move around in pipelines. Industry used to be located where the energy was. Then pipelines came and things changed. Glass could be made elsewhere.'

Somehow we wander together the few feet to the balustrade beside the stairs where we look down on the lending library. A woman is staring at a computer screen; a man is scanning shelves, pulling out books and, presumably, putting them back where they belong.

'Some of Trump's support locally,' David says, 'comes from Anglo Saxons who are concerned about losing their heritage. There are plenty of people here descended from the original settlers who came in the late eighteenth and early nineteenth centuries, but they are a minority. They fear the work ethic of Catholics, Hispanics. The Irish arrived here in the middle of the nineteenth century. Fifty years later, Italians, Belgians, Slovaks came.'

He tells me about his 'little house', which he bought some years ago. 'I couldn't now afford a two-bed apartment in town. My neighbour is building a new house. All the workers speak Spanish. They're perfectly nice. I wave them a greeting, but we can't actually talk.'

'Are they illegal?'

'I don't know. I expect so, but I can't ask them.' He smiles. He doesn't seem to care whether they are illegal, but he says that many people would and they would probably support Trump.

I ask him about Carnation milk and Maidenform bras. 'Are they still here or did they move?'

'Carnation left. I'm not sure about Maidenform; I haven't heard mention of them for a long time.' He shrugs. 'The only factory I know of here now makes coat hangers.'

It's time for me to leave. I shake his hand and thank him. 'It's been a pleasure,' he says.

West of Clarksburg, 50 is a smooth, divided highway, lined with low, forested hills. I'm heading for Parkersburg, about 75 miles away, on the east bank of the Ohio River and the last town in West

Virginia. I stop at the Crossroads Café in Pennsboro for a late lunch, sit in a booth at a formica-topped table and order a chicken salad with honey and mustard dressing. On a whim, I add a side order of coleslaw and apple sauce. Why apple sauce? I don't know. It comes with the coleslaw. When the chicken arrives, a loaf of French bread comes with it, and I see that I have too much food – and I don't really fancy the apple sauce. But I do my best, encouraged by a waitress who calls me 'honey' and has a wonderful way of saying 'thank you': 'tha-yernk yew-ew'.

18

Baseball Futures

That evening, after tripping between more beautiful wooded hills, I reach Parkersburg, wander about and go into a lively looking bar called TCB. A young waiter with a topknot haircut tells me that TCB stands for The Coffee Bar – because it *is* a coffee bar, as well as a bar and restaurant. I tell him that there's a pub called the Old Coffee House in London's Soho. He seems interested, or he may be a good actor; whatever, he recommends a beer called Voodoo Ranger, which turns out to be 7.5 per cent proof with a strong, hoppy taste.

I sip this fabulous concoction and think about David, the librarian: how he said that Clarksburg was in decline long before globalisation, because oil pipelines proliferated in the 1950s and, after that, 'glass could be made elsewhere'. It seems ironic, then, that Donald Trump has pledged to bring jobs and factories back to places like Clarksburg while at the same time encouraging the building of oil pipelines by relaxing regulations that protected the environment and Indian reservations. The most egregious new pipeline, the Dakota Access pipeline, runs for 1,172 miles from North Dakota, through South Dakota and Iowa, to an oil hub in Illinois. It was completed in April 2017, after years of legal action, with protesting crowds moved away from the pipe's progress by dogs and riot police. In North Dakota a stretch of pipeline that crosses the Sioux's Standing Rock reservation and runs beneath Lake Oahe, an artificial lake created in the 1960s to provide a source of water, was permitted only after intervention by the president in January 2017.

As I mull David's analysis and Trump's crassness, a baseball game is showing on a big screen, high on a wall several feet away. I notice that the players, though dressed in the usual way and playing on the usual grassy space (a diamond), are children. I ask Topknot about this and he says that we're watching Little League baseball; it's very popular, frequently on television, and this is a live World Series game between Georgia and Hawaii. The players, he says, are between the ages of nine and thirteen.

This seems puzzling. 'What happens to players who are over thirteen?'

'There are other Little League age groups, up to age sixteen.'

I order another beer, Big Timber Porter, from the long list of beers, and something from the entrée section of the menu: salmon with Cajun spices and marmalade. A middle-aged couple come in and sit at a table between me and the screen. The man's head is shaved; he wears a black T-shirt with 'All Gave Some – Some Gave All' written in small, neat capitals on the back.

I watch the baseball and decide to back Hawaii, who are in blue. The score is 0–0 and they are in the eighth inning. The Georgia pitcher, who is wearing yellow, keeps pitching; the batters either miss, hit the ball out, or hit it a short distance and get run out. Then Georgia bat, Hawaii pitch and, again, not much happens.

The bar has emptied a little. The waiters and bartenders are beginning to relax. Topknot comes over to my table, and asks about London and England.

Somehow we get on to politics and, inevitably, I ask him how he feels about Donald Trump.

He frowns. 'It's funny. The man who owns this building – he works upstairs; he's in oil – he was a prime Trump supporter. The woman who works with him can't stand Trump. She cried when he won. But they still work together.'

I reply by telling him about Brexit: how it divides some friends and families, but others seem to get on despite disagreeing. 'But what about you? Did you vote for Trump?'

He shakes his head. 'I didn't vote.' He shrugs. 'If I had, I'd have voted for Trump. I just didn't trust Hillary – the emails and all.' He shrugs again.

'You mean, if you'd *had* to vote for one of them, you'd have voted for Trump? But you didn't fancy either of them?'

'Yeah, that's right. Now, there's so many things Trump hasn't done.' He pushes his glasses up his nose. 'The wall – not that that's a good idea.'

'What about the way he treats women?'

'I don't like that. I wouldn't vote for him now.' He looks over his shoulder. 'I better get on.' He begins to walk away, then turns back. 'You know, anyone other than Hillary would have won that election – even *Bill* Clinton.'

I turn back to the baseball. Still no one has hit a run – and they are in the ninth inning

Topknot brings the salmon, and I ask him about the baseball. 'Is it a draw if no one scores in the last inning?'

He smiles. 'There's never a tie in baseball. They go on until someone scores.' He looks up at the screen. 'This is crazy. Very unusual.' He looks down at the table and straightens my cutlery. 'In Little League they play six innings – not nine like in Major League – and whoever scores most in six wins. Those kids must be exhausted; they been playing since about half past six. But they got to keep going till there's a run. Anyone gets a run now wins.'

The salmon is good, the porter is good, and I watch the boys – they all seem to be boys – play baseball.

It's past ten o'clock when I push the last flake of salmon into the marmalade sauce and eat it. Neither Georgia nor Hawaii have scored and they are in the tenth inning. There are about ten other customers left in the bar; most of them are looking up at the screen. Topknot is by the bar watching and talking to another waiter. He comes to pick up my plate. 'You know,' he gestures towards the screen with his thumb, 'this may be a record for a Little League World Series game. They'll stop them soon. Carry on tomorrow.'

A boy in yellow is batting; he looks as if he is ten, perhaps eleven, years old. He hits the ball into the outfield and runs to first base. Another fresh-faced boy comes up to bat for Georgia. He bats left-handed. A caption shows that his name is Tai Peete and his favourite food is sushi and steak. He hits the ball and runs towards first base, but is run out.

A few minutes later Hawaii bat again. One batter hits the ball into the outfield and gets to second base. The next one gets three strikes and is out. A good-looking, confident boy, perhaps thirteen years old, comes in. As the pitcher draws his arm back, the batter raises his left knee, swings the bat back behind his neck, and unleashes an almighty swipe that connects with the ball, hurling it high to the left and over the fence at the back of the field. A home run! And not just a home run, a *walk-off* home run! The game is over. The batter is mobbed by his teammates – and I am reminded of watching David Bote last Sunday in Annapolis. Hawaii have won 2–0; the boy at second base ran home in front of the batter.

Six or seven people, including Topknot, are standing up cheering; I stand and clap as the hit is repeated numerous times and from many angles. The batter is called Aukai Kea, and he is also Hawaii's principal pitcher. As well as winning the game with the bat, he won it with the ball by stopping Georgia scoring.

Topknot comes over and says that at the end of the eleventh innings the game was going to be stopped and would have carried on tomorrow morning. It was the longest game ever played in the Little League World Series. Once again I have witnessed a record!

I pay my bill, say thanks and goodbye to Topknot, and stroll back to my clean and odourless room at the Travelodge.

19

Lost Among Lawnmowers

I drive on a narrow, undulating road through a hilly outer suburb of Parkersburg, where houses are a mix of scruffy and smart: a place where, perhaps, schoolteachers, plumbers and librarians live. I slow for two women riding horses and squeeze past a tangle of pick-ups outside a white clapboard bungalow with peeling paint. The road meanders on for perhaps three miles, past a convenience store, a low-rise school, a garage – otherwise houses and the odd field harbouring a horse or two. It's warm, the sun is shining and people are riding their tractor-style lawnmowers. Every home seems to have one and someone willing to use it; they mow around their own houses and up to the side of the road, cutting every blade of grass that hasn't been cut by someone else. It seems that no one – not even the owner of a beaten-up pick-up – says, 'To hell with it! Let it grow!' It is this enthusiastic mowing and the lack of dividing fences that gives small American towns and suburbs the appearance of a huge lawn with houses sprinkled on it, like a child's drawing of an imaginary town. And it is the townscape seen in old movies, often starring James Stewart, in which paperboys riding bikes casually hurl morning papers across mown grass onto porches and verandas.

In his book *Second Nature*, published in 1991, the American writer Michael Pollan writes that: 'The conventional design of a suburban street is meant to forge the multitude of equal individual parcels of land into a single vista – a democratic landscape. To maintain your portion of this landscape was part of your civic duty. You voted each November, joined the PTA, and mowed the lawn every Saturday.' Pollan gives examples of the outrage caused in suburban communities by anyone who doesn't keep his or her lawn neatly mown. Such people can suffer abuse, and even be taken to court. Pollan mentions a curmudgeon in Buffalo who likes to have 'a wild flower meadow' in front of his house; over many years, this man has paid $25,000 in fines. The American obsession with lawns, Pollan explains, began after the Civil War when the first suburbs were laid out by a small group of influential landscape designers. One of these, Frank J. Scott, wrote: 'The beauty obtained by throwing front grounds open together ... enriches all who take part in the exchange, and makes no man poorer.'

Pollan writes:

> With our open-faced front lawns, we declare our like-mindedness to our neighbour – and our distance from the English, who surround their yards with 'inhospitable brick walls topped with broken bottles' to thwart the envious gaze of the lower orders. The American lawn is an egalitarian conceit, implying that there is no reason to hide behind hedge or fence, since we all occupy the same middle class.

I'm driving – in fact lost – in this grassy extremity of Parkersburg because today, Saturday, is the second day of the city's Homecoming, a celebration involving fireworks, parades and 'a rubber ducky race'. Many streets and at least one bridge across the Ohio River are closed.

Eventually I come down from the hills, find Route 50 and follow it out of town and over the three-quarter-mile-long Blennerhassett Island Bridge, which shoots over two channels of the Ohio River and a tree-covered island, and takes me into the next state, Ohio. There I set off on a detour along State Highway 7, which follows the Ohio River north towards Williamstown. I want to see the great river properly, in the wild – or, at least, away from the concrete walls and buildings that crowd around it in Parkersburg. And I want to visit Henderson Hall, a plantation house, which I learned about from a flyer I picked up at the Travelodge.

Highway 7 passes through a town called Belpre, where I see a signpost to the History Museum and Underground Railroad. I drive through leafy residential streets until I reach the end of a cul-de-sac and a single-storey building, where a sign announces Belpre Historical Society. Another sign says Closed, and a third reads 'Take Your Own Christmas Photo in Our Sleigh: $5'; this is in bright colours on crisp white paper, so can't have been there since last year, which suggests – today being 18 August – that in Belpre they shop early for Christmas. In front of the building, on a low wall, stand small, painted-plaster figurines of children dressed in clothes that I find hard to describe: Alpine Regency is the best I can do.

The air is cool and the sky is dull with smoky grey clouds. Not far from the strangely dressed kids, a Union flag hangs lifeless from a pole. I turn towards the car and notice a plaque mounted on a post on the pavement. Headed Ohio Historical Marker and, beneath that, Underground Railroad Crossings, a paragraph explains that many escaped slaves, helped by 'agents and conductors', crossed the Ohio River near here.

At Constitution, six miles upriver from Belpre, Judge Ephraim Cutler listened for hoot owl calls that signaled when a boatload of runaway slaves was crossing from Virginia to the Ohio shore. 'Aunt Jenny', a slave woman in Virginia, used a horn signal to alert abolitionist John Stone in Belpre when fugitive slaves were crossing. At Little Hocking, eight miles downriver from Belpre, slaves crossing from Virginia looked for a lantern signal to guide them . . .

Others are named, people who helped slaves 'as they traveled northward . . . to Putnam in Muskingum County where the Underground Railroad merged with the Muskingum River Corridor'.

A light rain begins to fall as I read this. I feel an almost physical fear at the thought of the tortures imposed on the many slaves who were recaptured, and on those who were caught helping them. At the same time, I applaud the bravery of the slaves who sought freedom, and of the people who risked appalling and mortal consequences for helping them.

After Belpre, Highway 7 becomes a sleek, flat, divided highway which barrels north over the floodplain of the Ohio towards Williamstown, with two lanes each way and very little traffic. I find I'm thinking about Topknot and how, when he told me last night that he didn't vote in the 2016 presidential election, I thought of him as indecisive, shilly-shallying. He should have voted; people should take advantage of their democratic right to vote; to vote is to support democracy. Without thinking too hard, I've admired those countries – Australia, Belgium, most of South America and several others – where voting is an obligation enforced by law.

This morning, literally in the light of day, I remember what Topknot actually said and change my mind. He didn't like Hillary Clinton or Donald Trump. So why should he vote for either of them? He didn't shilly-shally. He abstained. To abstain is to make a choice – and a statement: that the candidates on offer are not good enough.

Why should Topknot, or anyone in Australia, Belgium or

South America, be forced to vote for someone whose views or character they find unappealing – or worse?

Ah! But voting was enforced in Athens, the original democracy.

OK ... But I don't care about that. I've changed my mind. Thanks, Topknot.

20

Sacagawea and York

The rain has stopped. The Ohio River is nearby to my right, but I can't see it. I turn right into a road and see that it is called Joe Skinner Road, which, oddly, seems encouraging. Almost immediately, Joe Skinner bends sharp right, and there to my left, grey, smooth and wide – wider than the Thames in London – is the Ohio River.

I stand on grass between trees, gaze at the water and across to woods on the other side. I hear birdsong and a whisper of wind among leaves. Behind me, across the road and set back from it, a line of bungalows is set on higher ground. I glimpsed this river in Parkersburg, but this is the first time I've really seen it, contemplated it.

I associate this river with Captain Meriwether Lewis: the Lewis of Lewis and Clark, the men who, between 1803 and 1805, led the first expedition to cross the continent, from the east to the Pacific, by land. At that time, the Mississippi, roughly one third of the way across, was the western frontier of the United States; little was known of the land further west, which had been visited only by a few fur trappers, most of them French Canadian. Thomas Jefferson, president at the time, wanted the expedition, which he named the Corps of Discovery, to find a river route to the west coast so that the United States could begin to establish control of that coast. Lewis and Clark were to research the flora and fauna that they found in the west and send back samples, and they were to set up trading and diplomatic relations with the Indian tribes they would inevitably encounter. Jefferson persuaded Congress to fund the Corps of Discovery and appointed Lewis as its leader. Lewis immediately invited his army friend, William Clark, to join him as co-leader.

In the summer of 1803 Lewis based himself in Pittsburgh and arranged the building of a boat, fifty-five feet long and eight feet wide, with a hold that could carry twelve tons of supplies, a cabin at the stern, a thirty-two-foot mast and a keel. On 31 August, with eleven carefully chosen men, a black Newfoundland dog named Seaman and a smaller boat called a pirogue, Lewis set off on the 980-mile journey down the Ohio River to the junction of the Ohio and the Mississippi. On the way he would pick up Clark and nine more men at Clarksville, Indiana.

It is likely that Lewis sailed past where I am now standing on Joe Skinner Road on 14 September 1803. By then he had travelled 187 miles from Pittsburgh, a tiny proportion of the complete trip. When the party finally strolled on a beach in Oregon on 18 November 1805, William Clark calculated that they had travelled 4,162 miles. I try to imagine Lewis, out there on the water – tall, short-haired, with a long, downward-pointing nose – standing on deck, steering his fifty-five-foot keel boat, chatting to one of his men, pointing to something on the shore, over here, close to where I am standing. What might it be? A goose, an armadillo, a buffalo? They would steer their boat across, shoot it and eat it for dinner.

Thinking about Lewis and Clark brings two people, who aren't on the boat yet, into my mind: York and Sacagawea, my favourite members of the Corps of Discovery. York was William Clark's personal slave. He was the son of Clark's father's personal slave, was the same age as Clark, and had been his slave since they were both

102

children. He was tall and strong, and the only African American in the party.

Sacagawea was the only woman, the only Indian and the only teenage member of the expedition; and she would become the only person to give birth during it. The leaders hired Sacagawea and her husband, Toussaint Charbonneau, a French Canadian fur trapper, as interpreters during the winter of 1804, when they were camped for five months in a fort that they built themselves on the bank of the Missouri close to some Mandan Indian villages and a Hidatsa village in what is now North Dakota. Sacagawea and Charbonneau lived in the Hidatsa village and moved into the fort where, on 11 February 1805, she gave birth to a baby boy, Jean-Baptiste, whom she carried on her back all the way to the Pacific and back again.

Sacagawea, who was perhaps fifteen years old – no one is sure of her age – was not a Hidatsa; she was a princess of the Shoshone tribe whom the Hidatsa had kidnapped some years before. She was tough and able. When a boat overturned and others panicked, she calmly swam about retrieving vital equipment and Lewis's and Clark's diaries. When the Corps of Discovery reached the Rocky Mountains, she recognised landmarks and became its guide. She used sign language to communicate with Indians whose languages she didn't speak, asking directions and arranging for locals to guide the party. And, when the Corps met Shoshone Indians, she recognised her own brother, by then a chief, and burst into tears before playing a role as an interpreter as Lewis and Clark traded with him for horses. It can be argued that without Sacagawea the expedition would have become lost in the Rocky Mountains and would never have reached the Pacific.

Every evening York and Sacagawea worked together to put up a large buffalo-skin tepee, and every morning they took it down. During the night six people slept inside: Lewis, Clark, Sacagawea, Charbonneau, the baby, Jean-Baptiste, and a half-Shawnee, half-French Canadian hunter, tracker and linguist called George Drouillard. York slept outside on the ground beside the twenty-six soldiers who made up the rest of the party.

William Clark became fond of Jean-Baptiste as he grew into a sturdy toddler; he loved to watch him dance and nicknamed him Pomp because of his pompous 'little dancing boy' antics.

A series of deep hooting noises – like a foghorn, though there is no fog – come from the river. A barge, packed high with containers and ungainly, like a double-decker bus, comes into view and slides slowly upstream over the stretch of water where, just now, I saw Meriwether Lewis drifting downstream. I am walking along the bank, not looking at the river, thinking instead. The members of the Corps of Discovery were the first to do what I am doing now: cross the continent on land. They had boats and, at times, horses, and – once they entered the Missouri, just north of St Louis – no maps. They had to hunt and fish for food, trade with and, on occasion, defend themselves from Indians. Not all that many years later – 215 – I have music and air-conditioning in a vehicle that can travel at incredible speed between towns that offer shelter, food, drink and entertainment in motels, restaurants, bars, libraries, theatres, cinemas and museums. They had great difficulty crossing the continent. Well, despite being cosseted with twenty-first-century comforts, I'm not finding it easy either. I get lost. A couple of times, I've been close to panic on a dark, unlit road. I suffer in what feels like aggressive, fast-moving traffic on multi-lane freeways. I get lonely and my time away from home – a piffling seven weeks – seems long. I know that, almost whatever happens, I can't just hop on a plane and go home. I *must* reach San Francisco and get my photo taken on a beach to go alongside the one taken in Ocean City, Maryland; I told everyone in England – friends and relations – that that's what I would do. But I will cope and, compared with Meriwether Lewis, I am lucky.

On the return journey from the Pacific, Lewis left the main party and rode with just three men into Blackfoot Indian territory in what is now Montana; the Blackfoot were known for their aggression; other Indians were frightened of them. Lewis and his men got into a fight with eight Blackfoot, and got away alive only after shooting two of them dead. They then had to ride without stopping for one hundred miles to get away from more furious Blackfoot. Lewis was foolish to enter Blackfoot territory at all. That day he became hot-headed, excitable – a state that came over him from time to time. At other times he was moody – and the calmer Clark had to keep the expedition moving.

Thomas Jefferson thought that Lewis suffered from depression. And, writing in 1996, Stephen E. Ambrose – author of *Undaunted Courage*, a gripping and authoritative account of the expedition – suggested that Lewis was bipolar. Certainly, he had what we now call mental health problems and it is a shame that he didn't seek or receive treatment. As a soldier and man of action, Lewis, like so many young men today, would surely have felt it unmanly to reveal his unhappiness. William Clark was his great friend but, then as now, friends are often unaware of their friends' suffering and are startled when the symptoms erupt. On 10 October 1809, three years after the Corps of Discovery had returned and been acclaimed a great triumph, Lewis shot himself twice, cut himself with a razor, and died in a small log-built inn on a trail called the Natchez Trace in Tennessee.

After the expedition Clark lived in St Louis, married his cousin Julia, and had five children, the eldest of whom was named Meriwether Lewis Clark. Hugely respected and renowned for his role in the Corps of Discovery, Clark became governor of Missouri Territory (later the State of Missouri). From 1809, another child came to live with the Clarks: Jean-Baptiste Charbonneau, the boy whom Clark had nicknamed Pomp. Clark became so fond of Pomp that he offered to have him to live with him and to pay for his education. After some hesitation, Sacagawea and Toussaint Charbonneau agreed, and Jean-Baptiste lived and went to school in St Louis until 1822.

21

Aaron Burr and the Hendersons

There is a bar on Joe Skinner Road, further along. Cars and motor-bikes are parked outside. Two men with lined faces, a day or two's stubble, baseball caps, bellies and jeans are standing outside having a smoke. 'You're a long way from home,' one says, looking at Harpo's New York licence plate.

I explain that I'm from England and that the car is rented.

'Well, you're even further from home.' They both smile – and the one who hasn't spoken yet pulls on his cigarette, holding it between thumb and forefinger.

I say nice things about the river: how it's bigger than any river in England. 'And to think it goes all the way to the Mississippi.' I point back the way I came, to the spot on the bank where I stood and imagined Meriwether Lewis and saw the barge.

'No. No.' They're both saying no, shaking their heads and grin-ning. 'The Mississippi is *that* way.'

'Really?'

'That way,' the talkative one says, pointing the way I had pointed, 'is Marietta ... Pennsylvania, Pittsburgh. West is that way.' He gestures, and his friend turns to look west. 'The Mississippi is west of here.'

'OK,' I say loudly, nodding my head to show respect, and feeling too humiliated to say that I know the Mississippi is to the west.

I follow them into the bar, where a line of men sit drinking. They go to their seats and pick up cans of Coors Lite. I sit in an empty seat next to the quiet one – and we don't talk much. I find out that they are from Parkersburg. 'We come out here weekends to drink beer, watch sports.' He mutters to his friend and glances at the screen in front of us, where two muscle-bound, long-haired men, wearing Speedos and drenched in sweat, pretend to beat each other up.

I drink an orange juice with soda. So my imaginings were all wrong; my Lewis was sailing upstream back to Pittsburgh, where he started. Idiot! Soon I say goodbye, and thank those men for showing me which way is west.

A terrific rainstorm as I drive north towards Marietta and Williamstown. I surf slowly through it for a couple of miles, windscreen wipers on manic, unable to see anything but greyness and water – and the kerb at the side of the road in front of the nearside wheel. As soon as I can, I turn off towards the river on the curiously named Blue Knob Road – a place of warehouses, container storage and mountainous piles of sand. I park across the road from the trees that line the river, sit back and listen to the Barr Brothers album *Sleeping Operator*, spiky and lush, dreamy. A murky grey hints at the river beyond the trees. I turn the volume up to drown out the drumming rain, and close my eyes.

The music is haunting, absorbing, until I sense that the car is gently rocking. I open my eyes. Three feet from my face, something large and black is rotating slowly anti-clockwise: the wheel of a truck. It's followed by a long wall of cream-painted metal and more wheels, three of them. The trees come back into view, but the rocking doesn't stop. More wheels and another wall of cream metal crawl past. Two trucks pull in beside the trees in front of me – and no one gets out. Maybe, like me, the drivers want a break from the relentless rain. Peering through the murk I see the word Halliburton on the side of both trucks. I lean back and close my eyes again. Halliburton means Dick Cheney, vice president under George W. Bush. Halliburton: a company that made excess profits from the Iraq war. I open my eyes, press the switch that locks the doors, and close my eyes again.

Somehow I imagined a plantation house to be a long, low building with a veranda on at least two sides, if not all the way round. Henderson Hall is a three-storey red-brick building in Italianate style: a pillared porch, windows with rounded tops, and a belvedere – a kind of four-way lookout – on top. There is a narrow stone terrace at the front, but nothing that could be called a veranda. The house seems to spring straight from the well-mown lawn that surrounds it; I guess we are too far north and east for verandas.

I am welcomed by a tall, craggy, long-boned man into a long, narrow hall with a grandfather clock, sofas, dark wood chairs, a music stand and floral wallpaper studded with family portraits. A length of red carpet runs from front to back across a dark wood floor. More red carpet, held in place by brass stair rods, covers the middle of a staircase with a banister that curves at the top. The furnishings are familiar: the fusty clutter of the nineteenth century in a Victorian English townhouse, as seen in period dramas on television, in photographs in books and museums and, indeed, in photographs of a house in Dalston, north London, that belonged to my great-grandfather.

I pay $10 and am led to a small room upstairs where I watch a video that recounts the history of the Henderson family from the time when Alexander Henderson – who was matey with the likes of Washington, Jefferson and Madison – acted on a tip from Washington and bought several thousand acres of wilderness here in the Ohio Valley. Two of his sons set up a 2,600-acre plantation, and between 1836 and 1859 his grandson, George Washington Henderson, built this house with a view of the Ohio River; it stayed in the family until 2007 when the last surviving family member bequeathed it to a local historical association. The craggy man wants me to look at the upper floors first. He gives a short talk on each floor when I reach it, and is on hand to answer questions, but I am free to walk around looking at rooms whose uses and contents are described on typed labels.

On the second-floor landing, Craggy Man shows me a wall that is given over to reproductions and transcripts of documents relating to the family's slaves. There were thirty-five slaves at the time of the Civil War, but Craggy Man says that, beyond what is displayed on this wall, not much is known about them. It is only possible to guess at where they lived, he says, while it is thought, but no one is certain, that they are buried under what is now the junction between Old River Road and State Highway 14.

I read a letter from a Henderson to a slave trader, asking if he can supply a fifteen-year-old girl to take on various household chores. The tone is as if the writer is placing an order, and is checking on the price before confirming the deal. Another letter refers to nine runaway slaves and speculates as to where they might be. Then there is an exchange of letters in which a runaway slave apologises for running away, begs to be allowed to return, and is given permission to come back. A handwritten receipt records that a slave catcher was paid $100 for returning a slave. It seems like a lot of money, and my mind flits to the vicious Ridgeway in Colson Whitehead's novel *The Underground Railroad*; I remember the high value of slaves and that they were sometimes sold because their owners needed some cash. I also recall that some slave owners, motivated by fury and injured pride – like Terrance Randall in Whitehead's book – would go to almost any length to recapture a runaway.

The most memorable member of this family was Lorna Henderson. Craggy Man told me all about her, as we stood side by side in her bedroom. When she was sixteen she eloped, got married, bore a son, quickly divorced and went to live in Hollywood, where she tried, without much success, to make a living as an actress. Later she worked as a nanny for Marlene Dietrich and then became a successful private detective, working for Hollywood stars and the US government. All of this – Hollywood, Dietrich, and detectives – seems strange in this place, which I have so far associated with Founding Fathers, plantations and slaves. But then Lorna, who was born in 1895, lived until 1984. Her older sister – older by twelve years – brought up Lorna's son, Paul, here at Henderson Hall, and in later life Lorna came back here to live. She liked to eat chocolates and smoke cigarettes. Her sister and others disapproved of smoking, so she hid her cigarettes in empty chocolate boxes, some of which she pinned on the walls, ostensibly as decorations, but perhaps as hiding places. 'And there they are.' Craggy Man points to a patch of washed-out, striped wallpaper, which forms a backdrop to several faded and mildewed cardboard boxes, on which can be made out, in copperplate lettering, 'Whitman's Chocolates and Confections', and 'R. Wild Confectioner of Parkersburg'; another box carries a picture of red cherries and green leaves, in still-vibrant colours, beside the words 'Chocolate Cherries' in gothic lettering.

Craggy Man ushers me up a narrow staircase to the belvedere, a rectangular room perched on the roof with views in every direction and seats against all four walls. On hot summer evenings, when there was a breeze, the family would come up here to cool down. As well as windows that opened, shutters just above the floor were raised to let the wind waft around people's feet. The slave manager also spent time here, not to cool his feet or even his heels, but to keep watch on the slaves as they worked in the fields.

The flyer I'd picked up at the Travelodge didn't say much about Henderson Hall, but it did mention that two of the early Hendersons, the brothers Alexander and John, played a crucial role in the history of the United States. This was in connection with the politician Aaron Burr, who was an important character in the hit musical *Hamilton*. Burr almost became president in 1800 when, standing against Jefferson, he won the popular vote and tied the vote in the electoral college, but eventually lost after shenanigans orchestrated by Alexander Hamilton in the House of Representatives. Burr had to put up with being vice president during Thomas Jefferson's first term (1801–5). However, in 1804 he shot Alexander Hamilton dead in a duel – in real life, as well as in the musical. He escaped prosecution, although duelling was illegal, and completed his term as vice president – but was unable to continue in politics.

After all that – and, perhaps, in need of something to do – Burr travelled down the Ohio River and recruited support for what would become known as the Burr Conspiracy. He planned to found a new country in the south-west territories of the US and hoped to include the disputed territory of Texas. Some accounts state that he intended to liberate Mexico from the Spanish and install himself as king, *and* take Florida from the Spanish. Burr gained some wealthy supporters, including Harman Blennerhassett, a recent immigrant from Ireland who owned and lived on Blennerhassett Island – the island in the Ohio River that I drove over that morning. Burr began secretly to build an army and an arsenal on the island, while Blennerhassett sought more supporters and approached his neighbours, Alexander and John Henderson, suggesting that they join him in backing Burr. A terrible mistake! The Henderson brothers told their father's friend President Jefferson what was going on, and Burr and Blennerhassett were arrested and tried for treason. After a long and complex trial they were found not guilty but, by then, Burr was deeply in debt and had to escape to Europe to avoid his creditors.

It's as if Burr was trying to thwart Jefferson's aim of spreading the United States and its people across the continent. In 1803 Jefferson, with the backing of Congress, paid Napoleon $15 million for 530 million acres (828,000 square miles) of land west of the Mississippi – land that became known as the Louisiana Purchase. Later the same year, he sent Lewis and Clark to explore and map the newly acquired land and to find a route to the Pacific. Perhaps by sneaking on Burr, the Henderson brothers ensured that Jefferson's vision was fulfilled; without their intervention the history of North America might be very different.

On the ground floor, in the kitchen, a smiling woman takes over from Craggy Man, and shows me nineteenth-century crockery, cooking utensils, shopping lists and receipts for everything from cheese to guns. Craggy Man tells her that I'm from England.

'Oh!' she says, and looks up at me. 'This probably isn't that old for you.' She is holding a white enamel jug with a blue rim.

'Oh, yes it is! We don't have those any more.'

I visit the earth-floored cellar with another friendly woman. We gaze at ancient tools and devices, the purpose of many of which neither she nor I can explain. For the first time, I feel that boredom that often comes over me in local museums where there are too many old nighties, bottles, arrowheads, and fossils.

'They say that the Hendersons never threw anything away,' she says, shrugging – and I believe her.

22

Saloon Cars in Shade

I go for a late lunch at a place called da Vinci's, where my waiter resembles George Costanza from *Seinfeld* – not quite as short, but just as wide-faced and bald. He looks at me with a half-smile, as if I am something he doesn't quite understand, but also as if he isn't going to let that bother him. My order of grilled chicken Caesar salad seems to surprise him. It's 4 p.m. – perhaps a little late, or early, for Caesar salads. And my choice of orange juice with soda water – 'Ice?' 'Yes, please' – makes him cock his head, raise an eyebrow and give the most minimal of shrugs, before he bustles away with a tray balanced on four fingers.

There are other people here, drinking and eating (but perhaps not Caesar salads): two women with swishy hair and two smart-casual men; a Hispanic couple with a lively, white-shirted boy; a middle-aged white couple, he, tall and lean in denim, she, small and round-shouldered – not talking a lot, but apparently quite content. Though da Vinci's is a spacious, upscale Italian restaurant, the décor is plantation-style, and more Malay rubber than American cotton:

113

thick rugs on bare wood floors, trellises stained green, overhanging palms and dim lighting.

George puts my juice on the table with a flourish and a narrow-lipped grin. He brings cutlery and a napkin, arranges it quickly and precisely, and returns with the Caesar salad in a large bowl. 'Anything else you need?' he mutters.

'No. That's it. Thanks.'

Later, he asks if I want coffee.

'Yes, please.'

'With cream?' He puts his head on one side and smiles.

'Milk, please.'

He carries on smiling. 'Haf 'n' haf.'

'Yes, please. Harf 'n' harf.'

He grins. 'OK!' He turns, punches the air and walks off.

When the check comes, it includes a 'tip calculator', suggesting three different percentages of the total. By now I have half a sense that the waiter actually *is* George Costanza. I don't want to offend him. I know that George can get very angry if he feels he has been treated badly, so I add on 20 per cent and wait while he takes my card away. I hold my breath when he returns with my card and a receipt. He puts them on the table, turns to me and grins so that his eyes disappear. 'Thank you, sir. I'm glad you enjoyed the . . . er . . . chicken.'

He gives a little nod and walks away.

I look at the check and see that he is not George. He is Darrin.

As it moves into Ohio, 50 is a divided highway, flanked by grass, woods and low, distant hills, straight and flat with some gentle slopes and curves. It's a dull piece of road. In fact, divided highways *are* dull, I decide, unless they wind up and down mountains.

I bypass Coolville and glide through Guysville, glimpsing a smudge of grey roofs and gas pumps. There is nothing cool, hip, or even hep, about either of them. Long ago both were coal-mining towns. I think of William Least Heat-Moon's fondness for places with strange names; in *Blue Highways* he recalls driving forty-five miles west, when his destination was east, to visit a place that he happened to see on a map: a town called Nameless.

After sixty miles I arrive in Athens, a pretty university town with a long retail strip attached to the studious side of town, like a tangent to a circle. There vast supermarkets, DIY stores, fast-food outlets, bars and motels sit, proud and isolated, behind their own car parks. I cruise the strip slowly – by car, like everyone else – look twice at a bar called Shade, and check into Knights Inn.

Later I drive to Shade. It seems safer to drive than to walk, which would mean crossing four lanes through traffic. As I often do, I park in the wrong car park – Taco Bell's – because I find it hard to differentiate between the entrances to adjacent car parks. It doesn't matter. I'm close to Shade. I just have to step over a low wall.

It's a big place, with screens showing sport, and neon ads for beer – Pabst and Fat Tire. Reggae music coming from somewhere, but not loud. I sit at the bar and follow the bartender's advice: a Mystic Mama IPA from a local brewery called Jackie O. A man called Joe Panik is batting for the San Francisco Giants. Behind the bar, below the screens, above receding tiers of spirit bottles, is a large, framed, black-and-white photograph of Muhammad Ali, teeth bared, glaring down at Sonny Liston who lies on the floor, hands raised as if to say 'Enough'. I take time to study the long menu, and order a fish sandwich: 'An Alaskan Pollock fillet, deep fried golden brown with shredded lettuce, tomato, pickle, American cheese & a side of tartar – $7.69.'

The screen immediately in front of me is showing saloon cars racing round a track in a huge stadium crammed with people. Cars crash into one another – accidentally but inevitably, it seems: they are speeding and the track is crowded. Bits are falling off a car which is a three-dimensional ad for M&Ms with the number 18 on its roof; it is hit again, and spins round on flat tyres, showering sparks. This is like stock-car racing in England, except that the cars look new – until they crump into one another. An older man, along the bar to my left, explains that this is NASCAR saloon-car racing from Bristol, Tennessee; it's called short-track racing because the track is only half a mile around. The stadium, he says, holds 150,000 people – and there they all are, standing up and yelling in the hot sun. 'This is a great sport,' the old man says, unable to look away from the screen.

The bartender is a smiling, open-faced young white woman called Emily who tells me she is a bartender only in the evenings; in the daytime she is a schoolteacher. She teaches young children and it's obvious that she has a big heart and the kids must surely love her. She is busy serving about fifteen people strung out along the bar, so I don't get as far as asking how she feels about Donald Trump. The fish sandwich arrives and a load of French fries comes with it. I get talking to a young man called Aaron, who is sitting to my right: first about the short-track racing, then American football, which leads into rugby, until somehow, eventually, we talk about him. He tells me that although he has two degrees, one of them an MA in accountancy, and works as 'a financial adviser for a very big company', he considers himself lower class. He says that, in America, class is determined by money. 'So Bill Gates, Donald Trump – those guys are upper class here.'

I tell him that this is very different from England, where class travels downwards from the Queen – and has connections with inheritance. As an example of British upper-class snobbery, I mention the late Alan Clark and his quip about Michael Heseltine having 'bought all his own furniture'. And I have to explain who Clark and Heseltine were and are.

Aaron, an interested and intelligent American, is visibly puzzled by the notion that buying or not buying furniture can have a bearing on social class.

I talk about old and new money and how Clark regarded Heseltine as a 'nouve'. This requires a lot more explanation, and I begin to think that I am going into too much detail, and that this good man might prefer to watch cars bumping into each other at speed. But for some reason, the fish sandwich long finished and a second beer mostly drunk, I deliver a dissertation on how the different classes speak in England. I imitate the Queen, tell Aaron that my own way of speaking is middle class and try to convey working-class speech by imitating the way the comedian Arthur Smith speaks – slowly, without aitches.

'You sound like Michael Caine,' Aaron says.

I take this as a compliment and throw in some 'Cor blimey, stone the crows' – something that Smith and Caine surely never say.

'Do people *really* say that?'

'Well, probably not "stone the crows" these days, but "blimey". People say that. I say that.'

Aaron finds this funny, and perhaps enlightening – it's hard to tell. Then he says that the way he speaks, which is peculiar to West Virginia and southern Ohio, is lower class and counted against him in Florida where he worked for a while.

'It sounds to me as if you speak normal, average American,' I say.

'You're English. You can't hear it; you don't know.'

We order more beer and one of us, probably me, brings up Indians and slaves, almost as if they are a single entity: people oppressed by white Europeans. Aaron says he feels some guilt about what happened to both groups; and, in response, I mention the riches acquired by British slave traders, and the British colonising the United States and about half the world, and oppressing any native people who got in their way. And I tell him how I became interested in America as a child because cowboys and Indians played a big part in my life.

'Well, how did that happen?'

'Television, partly. In the nineteen-fifties and sixties, we had series on TV: *Hopalong Cassidy*, *The Cisco Kid*, *The Lone Ranger* were half-hour shows for kids; I watched them while I ate my supper, aged about six, with my toy guns beside my plate ready to shoot at the baddies – who were often Indians.'

'Really!' Aaron seems amazed.

'Absolutely. And not just that. We had cowboy comics: *Kit Carson*, *Buffalo Bill*, *Davy Crockett*. We had cowboy outfits – hats, waistcoats, trousers with fringes. Little plastic model cowboys – and Indians – which we played games with. Then, later, there were TV series from America, shown at about eight o'clock at night. They were longer, about an hour. I watched with my mother's uncle, who we lived with: *Wagon Train, Bonanza, The Virginian, Laramie, Rawhide* with Clint Eastwood. Loads of them. We loved that. You Americans made them. We watched them.'

'I've seen some of that. Old black–and–white stuff.'

'And we got all the movies. John Wayne, Gary Cooper, Henry Fonda. We *loved* all that.' I glance up at the baseball screen. A man called Madison Bumgarner is pitching for the Giants. 'It's strange,' I say. 'In England, in the 1950s, there was less entertainment based on World War Two than there was about cowboys and Indians, a phenomenon on another continent from about a century earlier. I think World War Two was too recent, too much part of the world at the time, to be turned into fiction for entertainment.'

Aaron is still listening. The NASCAR race is still going on; it is 500 half-mile laps, after all. But he isn't watching it. He gets out his phone and shows me the results of his DNA test. 'You send in a swab from your mouth and they tell you your origins.' He says he's disappointed to have no Indian blood. 'I thought there'd be some – a little, at least. I'm about sixty per cent northern European, plus little bits of Spanish, Middle Eastern, Scandinavian.' He thinks he is primarily Irish, but has no idea when his ancestors came to America.

Then, somehow, with another beer, we are talking about politics. Aaron didn't vote in the 2016 presidential election, because he registered too late. If he had, he'd have voted for Trump. 'I didn't rate Hillary and I thought Trump could change things.'

'Has he?'

Aaron sips his beer.

'In the way you wanted?'

He doesn't answer directly. 'People feel run down with little hope of improvement and lowered self-respect. They want Trump to *swagger* for them.' He raises his voice and shakes his head. 'To make America great again.' He waves two fingers on both hands to show he's quoting the president. 'Even some educated people want that. They're fed up with people in Washington having no effect, or a negative effect, on their lives – including Obama.' He stops talking and swigs some beer.

There are fewer people here now. At the bar, just us and a black guy wearing a T-shirt with 'Dilly Dilly' written on it. Aaron says that 'Dilly Dilly' is something people say in advertisements for Bud Light, but he doesn't seem to know why.

We part, firm friends, in the doorway of Shade. I leave Harpo in Taco Bell's car park, and walk

Fortunately he's still there in the morning.

23

Aaron's Conjecture

It's hot. I'm a little tired. I'm sitting on a bench on Ohio University's College Green – in the shade; in the sun it's a frazzle. I'm thinking over last night's chat with Aaron. I like to recall conversations rather than let them float away, because sometimes something drops anchor in my memory; and sometimes I realise belatedly that someone said something significant. Sitting here with my sweaty sun hat in my hand, I remember Aaron saying that people want Trump to swagger for them. He's right, and this explains the hitherto inexplicable – to me – appeal of this lying, bullying man with his disdain for women, immigrants, disabled people – everyone, in fact, except for people who cheer or openly admire him, or belong to his family. Trump is a showman, adept on a stage or podium, where he radiates swagger. In fact, that is *all* he is: swagger. Few people – especially people who are poor and feel uncared for by the privileged political classes – are good at swaggering. A rich man who is a virtuoso swaggerer and who wants to do it on your behalf – while attacking the intellectual snobs and foreigners from shithole countries who have been oppressing you for decades – is a rare treasure; he offers you hope or, at least, revenge, where you had none. All you have to do is vote for him.

Did Aaron come up with this idea? Or did he read it somewhere, or hear it on TV? Someone like Michael Moore, Stephen Colbert or Bill Maher might have explained Trump's appeal in this way.

I watch a group of students – three women and two men, all of them white – walk slowly, collegiately, towards a group of benches under a tall circle of trees. They seem young. Perhaps they are freshmen/women. They all wear Ohio University T-shirts in different designs but the same three colours: white, grey and a kind of washed-out green, or eau de nil. Ohio students are known as bobcats; two of the T-shirts carry that word. Freshmen are encouraged to arrive, take up their rooms, get to know their room-mates, and buy T-shirts in the third week of August, which is about now. On Court Street – the old, pretty, brick-paved main street – shop windows thrust an array of university merchandise at passers-by, including Ohio University Mom and Ohio University Dad T-shirts. Do Mom and Dad buy these so that they can go home to Nameless, Tennessee, sit on their lawnmowers and show off their clever children?

One of the women is taking a photograph of her friends with a swanky black SLR. Two women stand close together, arms round waists, and two men likewise. They all look at the resulting picture, point, giggle and shrug. The photographer steps back to take another picture – and something causes her subjects to rearrange themselves into mixed-gender pairs. One pair have their backs to me, arms round waists: her hand on his hip; his hand on the back pocket of her jeans. The shutter clicks. She lets go of his hip. He lifts his hand and puts it back again, moves it sideways an inch or so, lifts it again, brushes the denim below her belt with two fingers, and takes his hand away: tiny movements, all of them. They drift apart and back into a huddle with their friends.

Is this the first time he's done that? Or are they sophomores, as second-year students are called?

I sip some water from the bottle I refill in motel bathrooms. It occurs to me that group photography provides an excuse for men to put their hands on women's bottoms – and, I hope, vice versa.

After last night with Aaron, I could sit here all day, watching and thinking. Perhaps Aaron's conjecture also explains the appeal of Boris Johnson – another politician who swaggers and whose buffoonery provokes both anger and merriment in his opponents.

I walk up the shady side of Court Street. Among the bars and clothes shops is a New Age gift shop. In the window, between a turquoise hydro flask and a stone Buddha, lie two stickers, both about six inches long. One says: RESIST!. The other: TRUMP LIES MATTER. I smile. I can't help it – because I remember the gloom I felt earlier when, around the corner, where I left the car, I saw a Trump 2020: Keep America Great banner splayed across a second-floor balcony on an apartment block. Except for a scruffy bumper sticker on an old car on the Bay Bridge in Maryland, that was the first ad I had seen for Trump in nine days of travel – and, somehow, though it shouldn't have, it came as a shock.

Soon after it leaves Athens, 50 becomes two lanes with grassy fields, flanked by dense woods, on either side. I pass through Prattsville, a small place, strung along the road, where mown grass is turning golden in the sun. People are indoors keeping cool, except for a man, almost naked in the heat, crouched beside the road trying to unblock a drain.

I click on the radio. A man is talking, sometimes shouting, about Jesus and someone called 'Gard'. After explaining that his ideal woman is 'pure' and 'submissive', this man addresses women directly. 'You ladies! What Gard wants is for you to submit to your husbands in Gard! Back them up! Many men have low self-esteem. Your role is to support them.' I've never understood what 'in Gard' – or even 'in God' – means. Presumably it doesn't mean that women should somehow get inside God and submit to their husbands from that vantage point. The phrase, presumably, is not meant to be taken literally, and is just a mysterious – and therefore godlike – way of aligning God and whatever the speaker wants the listener to do within the same sentence. The tirade builds up, aimed at women who make the speaker angry because they don't submit to their husbands, or, I suspect, to him.

This man is making me nervous, giving me the heebie-jeebies. I switch him off and recover by listening to a sublime piano trio – Keith Jarrett, Gary Peacock and Jack DeJohnette – performing Jarrett's *The Out-of-Towners* live. I also turn off the road, following a rustic sign to Horse Camp, Zaleski Woods. Immediately I am on a narrow lane winding, rising and falling through a dense wood where pines stand straight and tall, and tangle low down with the glittering greens of more buxom trees. Further on, trees bend to reach one another across the road. I stop the car where two lanes meet. There are no signs, no horses or camps or people. I think about Robert Frost and his poem 'The Road Not Taken'. And, engine off, I stay where I am, listening to Jarrett and his friends – as flying insects gather and bounce from Harpo's windows.

24

Mound City

I come to McArthur, a small town gathered round a crossroads where Route 50 meets State Route 93 or, to put it another way, Main Street meets Market Street. It's 2 p.m. The sun burns down. There's no one around, and there's a dusty feel like a Mediterranean town in summer, only without the bougainvillea. Times have been hard here since the 1990s, when several sawmills and a car-parts factory closed. Most of the few shops and cafés are shut – some, it seems, permanently. I hope the locals are enjoying siestas somewhere cool, readying themselves for some fun this evening.

Mullins Pizza, which also carries a sign saying Main Street Diner, is open. It is a diner – it serves burgers and fry-ups and milkshakes and a lot more – but there's nothing cute or self-conscious or retro about it. I discover later that it's been here since 1975. It has black-and-white floor titles, bar stools with chrome legs and two patches of red-painted wall. Two people sit at a table in the window: a severely disabled man in a wheelchair and a woman who is talking to him and feeding him. They are the only customers.

At the bar I pore over a menu and eventually order chef's salad with chicken and, from a choice of dressings, French. As I sit down at a table, a boy aged about sixteen brings iced water in a red plastic beaker. Soon the salad arrives with two sealed plastic pots labelled French dressing. The salad is good; the dressing tastes like the sweet-and-sour sauce served in Chinese restaurants; I've liked that taste ever since I was taken out for a Chinese as a kid in London, so I merrily stir in the contents of both pots.

Later the boy asks about my accent and we get talking. I tell him that I've never been to this part of Ohio before, but I have been to Columbus (the big university city about seventy miles north).

'People from Columbus are mean,' he says. 'They think they're better than the rest of us.'

'Snobbish?'

'Yeah. Snobbish.'

At this moment, the disabled man shouts out something that I can't understand, as he does from time to time.

The boy carries on talking. 'People in Columbus and Cleveland have more money. Costs a lot to live there.' He picks up my empty plate, and tells me that he's originally from northern Ohio. 'Northern Ohio speech is better than here.'

'I can't tell the difference.'

'If you lived in Ohio, you could tell the difference.' He says he came here when he was fourteen. 'It's where my mom is from.'

He asks me where I'm heading and I tell him Chillicothe (sounds like 'chilly coffee' but with a 'th'), a city about thirty miles on west.

He pulls out his phone, calls up a map and, pointing with his finger, shows me exactly how to get there. In particular, he shows me a place where 50 bends to the right but the road appears to go straight on. 'Be sure you go right there,' he says. 'It's easy to shoot straight on if you're not ready for it.'

I thank him, pay and walk out into hairdryer heat.

West of McArthur the road is smooth and curving. I move quickly through a lush valley with woods a little way off to either side.

Gradually the valley widens, the hills recede and huge fields, ripe with maize, appear beneath a big sky: a blue hemisphere that, even as I move through it, holds tight to the horizon – like the skies on the High Plains of Kansas.

Close to Chillicothe, the road is made of concrete slabs and the tyres slap the cracks, making a rhythm like a walking bassline. From Chillicothe I drive a little way north to Mound City. There I stroll around an area of mown grass, said to be the size of ten football pitches, where there are twenty-two rounded, circular mounds, apparently randomly scattered and of diameters ranging from a hundred feet to about half that; one mound, just one, is elliptical rather than circular. I enjoy the stroll and fetch up on the further side of the space where there is a path that leads through trees to the Scioto River. It would be easy to walk around here and think: nicely shaped mounds, probably built by some long-forgotten people to bury their dead, and that's it, and so what?

However, these mounds – and many others in this part of Ohio, close to the Scioto River – provide a route into the history of all North American Indians via the objects that have been found inside.

When the first settlers arrived here in the late 1700s, the local Indians, Shawnee and others, had no idea when the mounds were built or who had built them. Archaeologists who excavated here in 1891 found that they were built over a long period, between 200 BC and 500 AD, and they named the people who built them Hopewell Indians, after a farmer who farmed this land at the time. The mounds were built – slowly, often over generations – from layers of earth alternating with layers of sand, on top of wooden structures that had formerly been used for social gatherings, ceremonies and burials. No one lived here. The Hopewell Indians lived by hunting, gathering and gardening, in small, extended family groups, spaced out along rivers.

Beneath the mounds, along with their dead, they buried a variety of stuff, including exquisitely shaped and decorated clay pots and beautifully sculpted birds, animals, fish and humans. The source material for some of these objects came from faraway places: shark teeth from the Atlantic; conch shells from the Gulf of Mexico; bear teeth from Idaho; obsidian from Wyoming; mica from North Carolina; copper from the Great Lakes region; silver from Canada.

So, 2,000 years ago Indians across a large part of North America were trading with one another – and, to an extent, sharing a culture, now known as the Hopewell tradition. That tradition, which included the building of mounds, stretched from Florida to Canada and from West Virginia to Kansas City.

I leave Mound City the way I entered, through a building that includes a museum, a shop, excellent toilets and two national park officials: a man who is a dead ringer for a friend of mine called Ben Chipps, and a large young woman. Ben Chipps tells me that the mounds are faithful reconstructions of mounds that were bulldozed flat during World War I, when the land was used as part of an army base. I feel a spasm of disappointment – but Ben reassures me. Much time, labour and money were spent on the reconstruction, which followed maps drawn by historians in the nineteenth century; and in 1923 Mound City was declared a National Monument by President Warren G. Harding.

It's five o'clock and the place is closing. As I leave, I hear Ben's large companion ask him, 'What are you doing this evening?' Perhaps she has hopes.

'Oh!, he says. 'Go home. Put my feet up. Watch TV.' He scratches the back of his head. 'Maybe see if I can get around to mowing my lawn.'

25

A Quiet Sundae in Hillsboro

The heat continues into the evening as I drive west towards Hillsboro. The sky is light blue. Wispy clouds lie against the sun in the south. The road is two-lane, traffic-free, a smooth ride across the flood plain of Paint Creek, a tributary of the Scioto, which itself flows south to the Ohio River. To my left, wooded hills rise above fields, and up there, among trees, I glimpse a road, perhaps a lane, winding upwards, like a thread dropped on a carpet. Half a mile on, I turn onto that lane, and find a field of deep green maize as far as the treeline, a white-painted farmhouse and a Dutch barn with a hipped, flyaway roof. I drive on up through woods, bright greens and yellows where the sun falls to my right, bottle greens in the murk to my left. The lane flattens and straightens, maize to both sides, a grand house, smaller houses, all painted white. A stone needle, smaller than trees nearby, points skywards behind a stone wall: a grave or perhaps a war memorial. I turn the car and return to 50.

Now the road is a series of switchbacks and curves. In a hollow beneath trees, black cattle stand sleek and still, waiting perhaps for the cool of night-time. At the crest of a hill sits a low building with a giant ice-cream cone jutting from its gable end. I stop and find an old man behind a sliding window serving an eclectic range of ice creams, sandwiches, burgers and hot dogs. I order a cherry sundae and, after a few grunts and some whistling from inside the window, receive a bowl containing a helter-skelter of soft vanilla ice cream, soused and swimming in cherry sauce. I sit in an out-door shelter eating this delight with a plastic spoon. Across from me, a man with three children, two boys and a girl, allows them to punch one another for a couple of minutes before shouting, 'That's enough!' The children go quiet and scrape up the remains of their ice creams. All four climb into a beaten up, low-slung, matt-black car, which chugs for a minute like a fleet of Harleys before hurtling out of the car park.

As the noise subsides, the only other occupant of the shel-ter, an elderly woman with cheeks like small apples, says, 'You enjoyin' that?'

'Yes. Delicious,' I say. 'Creamy . . . and plenty of it.'

She licks her lips – she is eating an ice cream from a cone – and smiles. 'I live down the road. Most days, I can't resist an ice cream.'

Soon she stands up and says goodbye. And, being English, I expect her to walk to her home down the road. But, instead, she gets into a maroon Datsun and drives east on Route 50.

It turns out that the Buckeye Dairy Bar, where I ate the cherry sundae, is on the eastern edge of Hillsboro, where I hope to spend the night. I follow 50 through the town, up and down several hills – which, surely, give the place its name. There are two motels. I choose one on the side of a hill, where the cheerful Asian proprietor tells me that, because it is Sunday, Hillsboro's bars and restaurants are closed.

I eat almonds and Walmart rosemary crackers in my room. Later I drive around in the dark. A gas station advertises liquor. Inside, the liquor department is closed, locked. A sympathetic cashier shrugs:

she can't sell it on Sundays; the owner forbids it. Downtown, street lights reflect from shop windows – and there is a sprinkling of rain. On a straggling cross street, I come to Burger King where a woman sits at a window, ready to bring me a whopper and fries; I wouldn't even have to get out of the car. I am tempted and may return. I keep on to the edge of town and find a gas station whose owner – bless him or her – treats Sunday like every other day. I come away with a large can of IPA and a pastrami sandwich.

I wake next morning, and soon remember that Cincinnati, the first big city since Washington DC, is just sixty miles away. Before leaving Hillsboro, I drive back to the town centre, the two or three blocks around the junction of Main Street (which is also US 50) and High Street that are Hillsboro's downtown. Last night this area was dead. Now, on Monday morning, it's all heat, noise, movement, people and cars, even at ten o'clock. Policemen are loitering outside Momma's West Main Street Café, and their car is parked in front. I go into the café anyway, because it looks good and it's clearly popular. It's a big space, about half full, plenty of tables; a waitress shows me to one – and I ask about the police, half-hoping a juicy crime has been committed.

'Oh, they come here most days. Have a coffee, maybe a Danish.'

She brings coffee straight away – and I order my favourite American breakfast: eggs, bacon and hash browns.

'How do you like your eggs?' she asks.

'Over easy ... or is it easy over? I can never remember.'

'Over easy.' She smiles and writes on her pad. 'Are you from Australia?'

I smile. I have to. 'No. England.'

'Really! Cool! How do you want the bacon cooked?'

'Oh-oo. Crispy, please.'

'Would you like mushrooms with that?'

'Sure.'

'Tomato?'

'Er ... yeah.'

'And do you want toast with that, and jelly?'

'Er ... yes. That'd be nice.'

She walks off. I take a leaflet about Mound City from my bag and spread it on the table in front of me.

And a voice says, 'Waiters, waitresses always ask how you want it cooked.' A man sitting at a table against the wall, diagonally across the aisle from mine, is looking at me. 'Grilled, I always say.' He laughs.

I laugh.

'I heard you're from England. You just travelling through?'

I explain that I'm driving slowly along Route 50 – I point towards the street – to California.

He nods and asks questions. 'Good road,' he says. 'Beautiful, some of that scenery. I ain't been all the way, but when you get to the Rockies, that'll be somethin'.'

The waitress brings my eggs and bacon. I munch a forkful and glance at the friendly man. He's not young – early seventies perhaps – neat and fit, close-cropped hair, a sharp jawline, and dapper in a black T-shirt and black jeans, all clean and ironed. He looks a bit like President Eisenhower. He's buttering some toast. Will we talk again? I prepare another forkful.

'You know,' he says, 'the only reason Route 66 is popular is because of the song.'

I nod. My mouth is full.

'It isn't that great a road – and a lot of it is gone. Not there.'

I swallow quickly. 'You're right. I've read about that – and I saw it on a TV series.'

'50 is a better road. I like 50.'

He asks about my rental car. I tell him – and he approves of Chevrolet. He himself has an old black Hyundai – he turns and points towards the street – which is very reliable, and a 1992 four-door pick-up with which he's also very happy.

'That's old,' I say.

'Yes, but the new ones aren't so good. Fancy, but not reliable.' He shakes his head almost imperceptibly. 'I've got a forty-two-inch mower attachment, which I can't use because my wife grows flowers and things everywhere.' He says this in a matter-of-fact way, without resentment.

Over an hour or so, I find out a lot about this man. He is eighty-two years old. He comes from Hillsboro, but spent much of his life working as an engineer in Tennessee. 'No degree,' he says with a grin, 'but if you do engineering, you're an engineer.' He has two sons, a granddaughter and a four-year-old grandson. Both sons are mechanics, one of them a genius who works for Texaco on new projects and collects vintage small tractors called Cub Cadets, of which he has fourteen.

When I finish eating, I move to another table – against the wall, facing his – so I can hear him better. Then I learn that Lloyd – I asked his name, Lloyd Satterfield – had poor hearing as a child; he sat next to the teacher in school so as to hear her. 'When I was six, a doctor put stuff over both my ears and told me to swallow. Was like an explosion in my head. It blew my Eustachian tubes open.'

'Wow,' I say. 'That must have been quite a moment.'

He nods, 'Yep.' Then sips some coffee and says, 'I like classical music, orchestral, some country – and big bands: Tommy Dorsey. I don't like Elvis. I went to his house. That man had no taste. Red shag carpet. Yellow walls.'

While we both have our coffee mugs refilled, he tells me about a local sheriff who, a few years ago, was thrilled to be asked to appear as an extra in a movie that was being filmed around Hillsboro. Lloyd smiles just a little as he goes on. 'The man had always wanted to be in a movie. To celebrate, he got very drunk, crashed his car and died.'

'Oh, no!' I say.

'Yep!' He raises his hands. 'So he didn't achieve his lifetime's dream.'

We both swallow some coffee. Then Lloyd goes on, 'Another sheriff went out to a call about a shooting in a remote wood. And he took his wife with him, which he never did usually.' He pauses. 'Well, when they got there, she was shot dead and he was wounded.'

'No! Oh my God!'

'Yep. And local people think that sheriff set it up with hired killers to get rid of his wife – and that his wounding was a mistake, or maybe deliberate to avoid suspicion.' He shakes his head. 'It was strange. He *never* took his wife with him on police work.'

'*You* think he set it up?'

He shrugs and pulls a face – and says nothing.

'Did he get away with it?'

'Yeah! He moved away someplace. He shakes his head again.

And soon he leaves with a firm handshake. 'You have a great trip. I'm sure you will.'

On the edge of Hillsboro a sign points to Hillsboro Ind. Park. I follow it, thinking it will lead to somewhere associated with Indians, only to find Hillsboro Industrial Park.

26

Rock Bottom in Cincinnati

The road runs straight and flat between fields and woods. Every few miles I slow down to dawdle through towns and villages founded in the nineteenth century, where small, older houses with verandas and screen doors sit alongside duller, newer homes, gas stations and Dollar General stores. In Dodsonville, Fayetteville and Marathon respectability presides without swank – and the lawnmowing ethic reaches extremes with acres of close-cut lawn way back from the road. The Stars and Stripes dangle close to the ground from stoops, and the roof of a bungalow is tiled to form the Union flag.

In Owensville, some 150 photographs of local war veterans – from World War II, Korea, Vietnam and Iraq – swing, like pub signs, from telegraph poles. Five feet deep, like outsize cigarette cards, and well designed, they feature sharp portraits – black and white for World War II vets – medals and flags. Some poles carry two banners, and some as many as four.

50 widens to four lanes. I pass a billboard: Frisch's Big Boy: Kids Eat Free All Day Monday. I'm closing in on Cincinnati. 50

widens again: six lanes – a divided highway hanging over the city, built of grey, clean-looking concrete with crash barriers to prevent petrolheads bouncing over rooftops and into the river, hundreds of feet below. I get a stunning view of skyscrapers twinkling in the sun against a backdrop of the wide, curving river, before being swept down into the city, which is not – just here, where I am – a traditional city, more a seething spaghetti of freeways on which cars and trucks move very fast. I lose 50 among the many lanes signed to different destinations, and a light rain begins to fall as I find I am driving south on Interstate 471. The rain intensifies, and I-471 becomes Route 27, a state road heading to a place called Alexandria.

Hungry, and annoyed that I have left the city instead of entering it, I pull into a gas station, buy two bananas, eat one and study the map. The rain is now a storm; I am standing under the overhang in front of the gas station; I will get soaked if I run three yards to the car. Somehow I am able to see the illuminated sign of a Comfort Inn below me in a valley, about half a mile away. Comfort Inns are a little upmarket. It's 3 p.m. and I dither, holding the spare banana. The storm approaches tropical. The Comfort Inn – what a wonderful name for a motel – is calling: 'I am here. I will shelter you, comfort you. You can unpack your stuff, have a shower or a bath, and you can drive into Cincinnati later when the rain stops.' Well, what else can I do? Driving through this storm, back into the city – and finding a motel – without getting lost seems almost impossible.

The Comfort Inn has a covered portico where I park the car. I walk inside without getting wet and am awarded a comfortable room by a charming receptionist; it's a little expensive but a whole lot cosier and cheaper than that damp Super 8 back in West Virginia.

At around five o'clock the rain stops and I head back towards Cincinnati following advice from the charming receptionist, who prints a Google map with instructions and surprises me by telling me that I am no longer in Ohio: when I left the city, I crossed the river and entered Kentucky. Of course, I get lost but, after just a little bewilderment, I drive through the pretty city of Newport, Kentucky, and over the Taylor–Southgate Bridge into downtown

Cincinnati. I spot an outdoor car park, leave the car and walk back towards the river past tall and not-so-tall office buildings.

It's hot and humid, and I wear my floppy hat. On Sycamore Street, beside the pavement, is a curious formal garden where two lush grassy squares are surrounded by twin colonnades of white pillars that support bushy mature wisteria. I walk between the pillars, below the wisteria, and have a sense of being in a cloistered quadrangle. Beds of shrubs and flowers line the grass. This little park is airy and beautiful, even in the heat and humidity. It is overlooked by low grey office buildings linked in a corner by two octagonal towers. All is well designed. What can this be? There is no one around I can ask. I keep walking in the shade of the wisteria and find a plaque that explains. This is the worldwide headquarters of Procter & Gamble (manufacturers of all kinds of stuff, including Ariel, Febreze and Pampers).

After marrying sisters, Olivia and Elizabeth Norris, William Procter, a candle-maker from England, and James Gamble, a soap-maker from Ireland, were encouraged by their mutual father-in-law, Alexander Norris, to start a business together. They founded the company here in Cincinnati in 1837. In 2018 Procter and Gamble employs 95,000 people and is valued at $210 billion.

Across the street from the idyllic Procter & Gamble Gardens, the Taft Theater is to be the venue for *American Idol Live* tomorrow, and on 4 September Alice Cooper will be here. I walk on, keeping a lookout for a street lined with old buildings and bars. But there is none of that. Just wide empty streets, modern office buildings and a few bland shops.

A plaque, screwed to a stained concrete wall, says that the powder magazine of Fort Washington was on this spot between 1789 and 1808. 'Here was stored the ammunition for the expeditions of the Indian Wars (1790–1795) which broke the Indian resistance and opened the Northwest Territory to peaceful American settlement.' Two rivers meet at Cincinnati, the Ohio and the Licking, which flows south for 300 miles through Kentucky. Indians lived along those rivers in the years before the 1790s; Indians from the Hopewell tradition, the mound builders, were around here 2,000 years ago. I imagine Indians under trees beside a river near here living peacefully, doing what people do: finding food, cooking, playing with children, having fun. And then I imagine settlers felling trees, building log cabins, living peacefully, doing what people do: finding food, cooking, playing with children, having fun. Anywhere might be peaceful after you have used guns, powder and ammunition to frighten away the locals, or kill them.

I look up at the wall above the plaque. It's a high wall. The sky is a strip above my head. It's the wall of a multi-storey car park. And I remember the story of Joni Mitchell pulling open the curtains of her room in a hotel in Hawaii, expecting to see paradise, finding a parking lot and then writing a great song. Well, paradise got paved here too.

I walk on humming Mitchell's song 'Big Yellow Taxi', and find Smale Park where, despite the heat, people are jogging in groups and alone beside the river. Waterlogged tree trunks, branches and smaller pieces of driftwood lie on worn grey cobbles at the edge of the water, which ripples and glints in the sunlight. An old-style paddle steamer, painted red and white, is connected to the shore by a gangplank, ready for boarding. Four bridges, including an old suspension bridge and two metal truss bridges, built of girders and struts like giant Meccano, span this part of the river.

I walk away, back towards the city. A man cycles past, and I see the red and concrete stadium of the Cincinnati Reds, a grand structure, spoiled by an architect who seems to have added floodlights as a rushed, unpaid, afterthought; rectangular banks of lights sit tall and narrow, like lollipops on sticks, high and incongruous above the field. It's called the Great American Ball Park and it sits in front of Cincinnati's tallest building, the Great American Tower, which — now that I'm in critical mode — is too big, contains too much glass and is too derivative of the true art deco, which stands, like an admonishment, a few blocks away in the form of the Carew Tower, the city's second-tallest building. The latter was built in 1930 and is beautifully proportioned, brown with hunched shoulders and windows set in vertical stripes of a different brown.

I pass a few tourists, a beggar and a crazy woman shouting quietly – and come to Fountain Square. The charming receptionist circled this on the map, and said that it's the centre of Cincinnati – and has been since the nineteenth century. The fountain is tall – about three storeys of an office block – bronze, glistening, impressive in its intricacies. Children run about in the spray. Adults like me walk around and admire it. A tall female figure, named the Genius of Water, stands at the top with arms outstretched. Water falls from her hands into scalloped dishes, from which it sprays over sculpted scenes with humans and animals, and down to a circular pool.

A few yards away there's a bar. It's a quarter past seven, still hot and humid. I walk through plate-glass doors and am shocked by the sudden chill. I take a seat at a long, dimly lit bar where men, perhaps in their late twenties, sit alone with an empty seat either side of them staring at their phones. Many look as if they have come from an office and taken off their ties. An air of cool is enhanced by dark wood, stainless steel and brass; behind me are low booths with seats for four and dim lights built in. Beers are listed on a menu. I order Crosley Field IPA from a blond thirty-something barman who is curt but friendly. The place isn't dominated by television screens, but I can see one, high to my left. Boston Red Sox are playing Cleveland Indians. Xander Bogaerts, a black batter for the Red Sox, hits the ball into the field between the Indians' basemen and two of his teammates run home: 2–0 to the Red Sox.

Behind the bar and the tiered bottles of spirits, tall stainless-steel tanks can be seen behind a plate-glass window. I ask the barman if they brew beer here at the bar.

'Yes,' he says, 'that's all we sell. Right now, we have eight beers all brewed right here.' He points to the menu. 'That's them. We sometimes have more; it depends.' He says that all the beers are brewed by one brew-master with a part-time assistant. 'And you can't get this beer anywhere else. We don't bottle or can it. You can take some home in a jug, but that's it. Do you want to eat, by the way?' He puts a menu in front of me. 'There are other branches of Rock Bottom,' he says, 'in Denver, San Francisco – but the beers there are different because each bar has its own brew-master.'

I didn't realise that this bar is called Rock Bottom – and then notice that Rock Bottom, Cincinnati is engraved on my glass.

A tall, lean man sits down in the seat to my right; all the seats that have no neighbours are now taken. He mutters something to the barman, who goes away and comes back with a strip of paper, the size of a small cricket bat without the handle, headed My Personal Brewery. Tall Man runs his finger down the beer menu and the bartender leans low over the paper strip clutching a biro. Tall Man calls out, 'Kolsch, White Tiger ... Tall Stacks ... Oatmeal Stout, Crosley Field ... er ... Brown Bear Brown.' And the bartender writes in a jerky scribble. Then he fills six small glasses with different beers and places them in a row on the paper so that each beer is aligned with its name. Kolsch on the left; Brown Bear Brown on the right.

Tall Man gulps down half the Kolsch, sits back and sips a little White Tiger.

'That looks like fun,' I say 'I didn't know you could buy beer like that.'

He turns. 'Yeah! It's called a flight.' He points to the row of glasses. 'A lot of bars – bars where they sell craft beer – do it.'

He has brown skin and short, well-cut dark hair. He asks where I'm from and then why I'm here – and, while I'm explaining that, the man on Tall Man's right – a nice-looking, shorter man – leans across and joins the conversation. Soon Shorter Man and I are learning about Tall Man. He is Indian by race, was born in Kuwait, brought up in Dubai and went to college in Georgia, where he now lives with his wife. He's a software engineer and is in Cincinnati for a few weeks working as a consultant. His name is Raz Ali.

Shorter Man is slim, pale-skinned, with dark hair and a striking profile. He has a great name that mixes jazz and literature: Miles

Pulitzer. Miles grew up in Texas, went to university in Maryland and lives in New York; he too is here for a few weeks, and is working as an accountant on a secret project.

Raz oozes knowledge and self-confidence. He moves around the world a lot. He knows about Michelin-starred restaurants and Premier League football – Manchester United (his team) and Tottenham Hotspur (mine) are analysed. He rates Harry Kane and Hugo Lloris. And he approves of my ordering 'Blackened Creole salmon with mash and green beans'.

Raz pushes his seat back a little. Miles pulls his closer, and says, 'So what are your impressions so far? What do you make of our country?'

'Well ...' I sip my beer. I need to think. They're both waiting for me to speak. It's unlikely that either of them supports Trump. 'I've met a lot of people of different kinds,' I say. 'Many people are dissatisfied, not just financially, and Donald Trump seems to them – *some* of them – to be standing up for them against the conventional East Coast way of doing things which has been making them more and more unhappy.'

Miles is nodding in agreement.

I carry on. 'I picked up an idea a couple of nights ago from a man I was talking to. For those people, Trump is *swaggering* on their behalf – swaggering in the face of the establishment, attacking conventional government, which has not done these people any good for years now.'

Miles says, 'That's right.'

Raz agrees.

'Maybe,' I say, 'Trump is delivering for them in that the economy is booming.'

'It won't last.' Raz shakes his head. 'The trade wars, tariffs, will cause the economy to go the other way before long.'

The salmon arrives. Both of them lean forward and look at it, and want to know if it's good. They both come here once or twice a week but, curiously, have never met before.

The salmon looks good; the flesh is blackened in a pattern like a chain-link fence. I take a small forkful. 'It's great. This is crisp.' I wave my knife towards the ridge of pink fish.

I order another beer, and the talk goes on. We discuss the two-party system: how it doesn't work well any more. The bartender plonks my beer in front of me: New England IPA, paler and a subtler taste than Crosley Field. Miles orders another beer.

The bartender takes my plate away, and we move on to identity politics. Raz's definition is succinct: seeing everything from one viewpoint: as a woman; as a black person; as a gay person; an evangelical Christian; pro-life; pro-women's right to choose.

Raz gulps oatmeal stout, and we switch to the virtues of an amnesty for illegal immigrants to the US. I ask about Dreamers, and Miles explains. 'DREAM stands for Development, Relief, and Education for Alien Minors,' – Raz is looking at the floor and nodding – 'an act that has been before Congress many times since 2001, but never made it into law. It would grant citizenship to the children of illegal immigrants who came here before they were sixteen.'

'The Dreamers aren't that young,' Raz says. 'There are about two million of them. Most are in their twenties and thirties. They work and pay taxes.'

Raz is eating a salad and Miles has some kind of 'healthy' burger.

'There are Dreamers everywhere,' Miles says. 'Some are in the military.'

I make a trip to the restroom, where a man wearing a loud yellow-and-black-striped shirt and shorts stands at a urinal holding his equipment and puffs out his cheeks as if to say: 'Well, this is a necessary inconvenience.' I get back to my seat and notice that the Red Sox are drawing with the Cleveland Indians 3–3.

'When you get to Denver,' Raz says, 'go to Red Rocks. It's a natural amphitheatre, between huge red cliffs. Go to a gig, if you can, any gig, any evening. Or else just walk around the park. It's an incredible place.'

'Also,' Miles leans back, so he can see me behind Raz, who is leaning forward over his salad, 'outside Denver there's a Native

American restaurant with great food. It's called Tocabe' – he spells it, so I can write it down. 'Google it.'

Raz finishes eating. 'I gotta go soon, but tell us about Brexit.' He's smiling and hugging his knee. 'How did that happen?' He sounds incredulous. 'And what in hell is going to happen?'

I shrug. 'I don't know what's going to happen. The problem— '

Miles interrupts. 'You didn't vote for it, did you?'

'No way.'

He smiles. 'I didn't think so.'

'The thing is absurd. It's not just an economic cock-up. It's a cultural one. We have loads of links with the French, the Germans, the Italians, the Spanish – all of them. *And* it threatens the peace that's lasted all this time. It's crazy.'

'About as crazy as electing Trump,' Miles says and wipes his mouth with a napkin. They both smile and climb off their chairs.

Firm handshakes, shoulder claps. 'Great to meet you.' 'Good talking to you.' 'Happy travels.'

Smiles and waves. And they're gone.

I have some beer left. I sip it slowly and watch the Red Sox and the Indians. The Red Sox score in the ninth inning, but it's not enough. The Indians win 5–4.

27

Saved by V. I. Warshawski

I leave Rock Bottom at a quarter past ten. By half past ten I am frantic. I've walked up and down 7th Street twice and can't see Harpo anywhere. I know that I parked him in a car park on 7th Street, so he's been stolen. Thank the Lord, my computer and most of my stuff are at the Comfort Inn in Alexandria, Kentucky – and I have my notebook in the little rucksack on my back.

I decide to scour 7th Street one more time before contacting the hire company and the police. I walk two blocks further west on 7th than I walked before. No Harpo. I turn round before crossing a bridge over a freeway and walk back eight blocks – one long block further than before. I see a car park at the end of the last block. A white car waits, isolated near the middle. Could it be? I'm a hundred yards away. I point the key and click. And there is Harpo – the great Harpo Marx, even – flashing his hazard lights in greeting.

It's raining just a little. I cross the Ohio River on the bridge I took this afternoon, which leads me onto the interstate, I-471. It's

10.45 pm. There's little traffic and the road is well lit. It becomes five or six lanes and climbs a long hill. Earlier there were trucks and cars in every lane; now there is nothing, no tail lights in front of me, and just one car a way behind. Towards the top of the hill, as roads always do when there are more than three lanes, the road divides with signs to many places. I follow the lane signed to Alexandria and am soon driving in darkness, save for the light thrown by my headlights. The Barr Brothers are playing on the stereo. I'm on a straight divided highway with two lanes each way. It's an easy drive, despite the rain. A few pairs of headlights come towards me to my left. Someone driving fast comes up behind, full beam in my mirror for a moment – and an SUV whooshes past. I watch its tail lights until they disappear, perhaps a mile ahead. I come to a built-up area; a glow comes from a couple of houses and then a Sunoco gas station, a splash of white light in the night. Three or four miles on, away from the road, lights shine down on an empty car park with buildings on three sides – perhaps a retail park.

I drive on, looking for Thorntons, the gas station where I bought bananas this afternoon and from where I saw the Comfort Inn at the bottom of the hill. It shouldn't be far. I pass other buildings, lit and unlit. And keep going through the rain. It must be further than I thought.

But I don't see it. I must be twenty miles from the bridge over the Ohio. It wasn't this far. I must have missed it. I drive on – five, ten minutes – to the next turn-off, and head back north. Thorntons gas station must be closed, unlit. So I missed it.

I drive slowly, looking across the lanes to my left, hoping to see a silhouette that might be Thorntons. It was a little way off the road, but well signed and visible, on a side road that led downhill to the Comfort Inn. I don't see it, but it must be there, hard to see in the dark from the farther side of the divided highway. After a long time, perhaps half an hour – I have been driving slowly, peering sideways through the rain – I get back to the junction with I-471 and turn south again. I'm tired, bewildered, a little angry – though angry with whom or what? The Barr Brothers album has ended. Again I drive slowly, watching the side of the road. I don't want music. I have to concentrate. I pass the same lit and unlit buildings, the same gas station, Sunoco – Sunoco is lit, why isn't Thorntons? – the same retail park.

Again, I drive for twenty, twenty-five minutes. And turn north *again*. This time I drive faster. I am cross – cross with myself, cursing that it has taken me all this time to realise that I am on the wrong road. I don't know why it's the wrong road, but it must be. At least I have a plan. I'll turn and come back yet again, go into the Sunoco gas station, which is clearly still open, though it is now more than half-past midnight, and ask for help.

I park beside a gas pump and walk quickly through the rain. There isn't a store here, just a small space where a young man with dark hair is staring at a computer screen.

'Sorry to bother you. I've somehow got lost. I'm looking for a Thorntons gas station which is near a Comfort Inn.'

He looks at me. 'Sorry.'

'I'm looking for a Thorntons gas station, which is near a Comfort Inn. I'm staying at the Comfort Inn, but I can't find it.'

'I don't know . . . Sorry.' He looks back at his screen.

'You don't know where there's a Thorntons . . .?'

'No.' He glances up at me. 'Sorry.' He looks away.

I go back to the car, get into it and drive on. 'How crazy! How ridiculous! How insane ' I'm talking to myself, shouting to myself, thumping the steering wheel. The only thing now is to turn round at the next junction, go back to Cincinnati, somehow borrow a phone or a computer and find out where the bloody Comfort Inn is.

I come to the retail park and turn into it. The car park isn't completely empty. There's a blue pick-up in one corner. Maybe there is someone here. Three or four warehouses sit in darkness, but there's a light coming from the back of what looks like a DIY store. I stand in the rain and ring a bell beside a plate-glass door. And, incredibly, someone is coming. A woman. She looks at me through the glass for a moment. And the door opens. 'Hello,' she says. She has spiky blonde hair with two or three hi-res pink tufts.

'Sorry to bother you. I'm lost. I'm looking for a Comfort Inn near Thorntons gas station.'

'You're on the wrong road,' she smiles, almost laughs.

'No! Really?'

'It's on Route 9. Come in. I'll show you how to get there.'

'Thanks. That's fantastic!'

She turns on a light and we walk through to a room at the back. Music – hip-hop – is playing, and it's warm. She leans over a laptop and calls up Google Maps. 'Where are you from? You sound like English – or Canadian?'

'England. London.'

'Wow! Well, what are you doing here in the middle of the night?' she laughs.

'Travelling through, slowly. East coast to west coast.'

'OK! There it is. Comfort Inn.'

I can see the motel and Thorntons.

She taps the track pad and the map scales down. 'And we're here.' She moves the cursor.

She shows me more than once how to get from here to the Comfort Inn. It's about four miles, but complicated. And she offers me a biscuit from a tin. 'It's free. I'm the janitor here.' She laughs. 'Security, you know.' She's wearing jeans and a striped men's shirt. Something about her – a carefree self-confidence, perhaps – makes me think of V. I. Warshawski, the Chicago-based private detective created by Sara Paretsky. The biscuit looks like a chocolate-chip cookie but, when I bite into it, it's softer and seems to be filled with peanut butter.

I look down at the laptop. 'Where's Alexandria?'

'Alexandria?' She slides the map up on the screen to show me that Alexandria is south of where we are now. I must have almost reached it earlier.

'So which town is the Comfort Inn in?'

'Er ...' She zooms the map out and points with the cursor. 'Wilder. Here.'

'Wilder! Never heard of it. I'm such an idiot. I thought it was in Alexandria.' I'm an idiot, but I'm relieved. Thanks to this smart young woman, I now know where I am – and where the places that matter are.

'You're travelling, you said?'

I explain – and I ask how she became a janitor.

'It's easy. Anyone could do it.' She's a graduate student studying for a master's in architecture; her job as a janitor gives her some extra income.

'But you just let me in. I could have been anyone.'

'I can tell by looking at people. I knew you were a lost English guy.' She chuckles. 'If I didn't like the look of someone, I'd leave it locked. It's never happened, but I can get back-up here in no time.'

A clock on the wall shows 1.25 a.m. She lets me out of the door. I thank her many times for her help and the biscuit.

'You're very welcome. Drive safely. That way.' She laughs and points south. 'Then, don't forget: turn and drive back.'

28

Sadness, Anger and Guilt

A yawning man who is trying to smile lets me into the Comfort Inn. It is three and a half hours since I left Rock Bottom.

I walk through my room and into the bathroom. There I drink some water, flex my shoulders and stare at a framed photograph of a white horse being nuzzled by a slender chestnut foal. Seven or so miles from Rock Bottom to here! If I'd walked, I'd have been in bed an hour ago – if I hadn't died from exposure or drowned. I think about satnav and why I'm making this crazy trip, which feels, once again, like an endurance test.

I unlace my shoes – and remember the driftwood on the shore of the Ohio River and the paddle steamer. Then Raz and Miles, those beers, the blackened salmon – and V. I. Warshawski.

In the morning I set off for Cincinnati and, less than twenty minutes later, park in a lot on 3rd Street. I walk via Rosa Parks Street to the National Underground Railroad Freedom Center, an intriguing boxlike building with glass at ground level, brown bricks above, and slim concrete sides. It looks like a well-filled sandwich standing on end: watery sardines and chocolate between two slices of white bread.

The glass-fronted foyer is airy with a high ceiling, a gift shop and not much else. I take a lift to the third floor and soon experience a rerun of the anxiety induced by the curving walls of the National Museum of the American Indian in Washington. It is hard to know where to go among several exhibitions, which themselves are laid out in circles, curves and tangents. But I soon shake off this mild vertigo in the exhibition called From Slavery to Freedom. I wander slowly among others studying letters, lists, WANTED posters, timelines, pictures, objects, diaries, tools, whips, reconstructed living quarters – on crowded ships and plantations – all representing the years between 1619, when the first slaves were shipped from Africa, and 1888, when Brazil was the last country in the Americas to make slavery illegal.

I repeatedly find myself beside two middle-aged white couples. Amid the misery, we manage to smile at each other. We lean in to study paintings, engravings, drawings and life-size tableaux sculpted in bronze: slaves roped and chained; stacked on racks below the decks of ships crossing the Atlantic; whipped and tortured; bent double picking cotton; exhibited for sale in street markets. I feel sad, angry and guilty. We white people did this; the private and public wealth of the British grew on the scarred, aching backs of these people – grew out of their lives and their premature deaths.

I stand in front of a collage painted in black and white. Among the many images: a map of Africa; a three-masted schooner waiting at anchor off a beach; a man and a woman lying below deck with no room to sit up; women picking cotton; men digging up rocks. At the centre of the collage is a poster headed:

To be sold and let
by public auction
SLAVES

A young black couple and their daughter, aged about eight, stand close to me. They are dressed as if for a wedding: the man in a dark suit, the woman in a floral dress with a straw hat. The girl's hair is braided into beautiful cornrows, her skirt and blouse immaculately ironed.

I exchange glances with the man. His expression is blank and so is mine. We both look back at the painting. I wonder whether to say anything, but I walk on. And I remember spending a few days on a campsite in West Germany in the late 1960s. I was with English friends and we got to know a group of German teenagers. One evening, after some beers, they said 'Sorry' to us. 'What for?' we said. 'For the war,' one of them said. 'We feel bad.' 'Not your fault,' one of us said. 'You weren't born.' They talked about their parents and what they had done back then: some were exonerated; some were felt to be guilty in some way. And so it went. We tried to make them feel better.

It is clear to me why the Freedom Center is here. In the geographical sense, because it is on the northern shore of the Ohio River, which separated the slave states to the south from the free states to the north for hundreds of miles. Thousands of slaves crossed this river to freedom, with difficulty and in great danger, many with the help of the conductors of the Underground Railroad.

In the broader sense, the Freedom Center is here because this pitiless, prolonged humiliation of one race by another must be remembered and contemplated. That long episode, when black Africans were owned and, for the most part, tormented by white Americans, ended. But slavery didn't. Another exhibition, 'Invisible: Slavery Today', on the same floor of this building, makes me angry all over again. High-tech screens and dimly lit, life-size tableaux display images of the degradation of five types of modern slavery: forced labour, bonded labour, child slavery, sex trafficking and domestic enslavement. As I come away from a peek into the sordid room that is the home of an enslaved sixteen-year-old prostitute in South-East Asia, statistics loom up in the murk: 'Globally some 12 million children are trafficked each year – source UNICEF.'

At the front of the building, away from the exhibits, windows look out over the river. In the foreground, on a flat roof, an eternal flame burns in memory of the candles that were lit as signals to escaping slaves in the windows of underground railway workers: white people and free blacks who risked – and sometimes lost – their lives to help.

On the floor below, a sturdy wooden building stands alone in a large space. It has a few small barred windows and two strong doors. A notice tells me that this is a slave pen, built in 1830, and brought here from a farm in Mason County, Kentucky, sixty miles south of here. It is thirty feet by twenty-one feet and has two floors. Male slaves were kept, chained to shackles, on the upper floor, women and children on the lower floor – sometimes for days, sometimes for months – by a slave dealer called John Anderson. There might have been sixty-five slaves in this little building, kept in debilitating heat, amid nauseating smells, with buckets for sanitation, straw on the floor and a hearth for the women to cook what food they were given. When the market was at the right price, Anderson would march his slaves 750 miles to Natchez, Mississippi, a journey that took between thirty-seven and forty days; sometimes he took them further, as far as New Orleans. It has been estimated that, in modern money, Anderson made $800,000 annually from dealing in slaves.

The only upside to this awful part of an awful story is perhaps frivolous when seen alongside the horrors inflicted on so many men, women and children. One day a male slave escaped from this building and ran. Anderson chased him on horseback. The horse tripped. Anderson was thrown, hit his head on a rock and died. Anderson had no sons. His daughters were not keen on dealing in slaves, and closed the place down. Learning this didn't exactly make me shout hurray, but at least, like Hitler and a few others, an evil man got his comeuppance.

29

Hoity-Toity in Burger King

For the first time I manage to leave Cincinnati in the direction I want on the road I want: west on Route 50, which soon narrows to two lanes and runs alongside the Ohio River. I stop at the United Dairy Farmers (UDF) gas station; I don't need gas but I'm hungry – it's almost 4 p.m. – and the convenience store looks promising. I choose something I've never seen before, a UDF Southwest Chicken Salad Shaker: an assembly of vegetables and chopped chicken in a clear plastic beaker with a dome-shaped lid, similar to those used for iced coffee in takeaway coffee shops. Inside the lid is a plastic container of dressing.

As I stand in line to pay, I read the label: 'Fresh Ingredients. Handcrafted.'

I lean sideways to look at the man behind the till; he is short, bearded and about thirty. The man in front of me reaches the front of the line and Bearded Man says, 'How you doin'?' in a quiet, reserved voice.

The customer is tall with bulging biceps. He shouts back, 'Terrific. And you?'

'Not so bad,' Bearded Man says quietly.

When it's my turn, I hand over the salad and say, 'This looks like a good idea. I suppose I just tip that in' — I point to the dressing — 'and shake it.'

'I think so. I think it looks pretty good.' He holds it up, turns it round and peers at it. 'I never tried it, though.'

'Oh! Is it a new thing?'

'Well, I just don't want to spend five dollars finding out if I like it.'

'You're right. It is expensive,' I say, feeling guilty that I can afford something that he can't — and, worse still, I hadn't even looked at the price.

He beeps the barcode with his beeper. 'Actually it's four dollars sixty-nine — but still nearly five dollars.' My guilt intensifies. I've read Barbara Ehrenreich's book *Nickel and Dimed: On (Not) Getting By in America*, in which the author struggles to live on the income from a variety of low-paid jobs, including shop work.

I pay and he hands me the salad. 'Thanks,' I say.

'You're welcome.' He smiles thinly and turns to the woman behind me in line.

White puffy clouds with grey undersides lie beneath a big blue sky. To my left, the grey of the river; to my right, scrubby trees among workshops and warehouses. Where shall I go to shake my salad? I turn off left following a sign to Shawnee Look-Out in the hope of being able to look out, as I presume the Shawnee once did, and shake it there.

I drive along a narrow, winding, up-and-down lane, through sunlit, leafy woods and straggling villages. Five miles on, I arrive at Shawnee Look-Out Golf Club, where I'm told that I can't enter without a permit, although I can buy one for $14. I think of the Shawnee and all they endured so that, 200 years later, a bunch of strangers could aim a little ball at a hole. Already guilty about spending $4.69 on a salad, I certainly can't spend $14 on

153

somewhere to sit and eat it; it isn't as if I am going to spend the day playing golf – or hiking, which the permit would also allow. I park in a small car park facing some trees near the entrance to the golf course, shake my salad and eat it, standing up beside the car, with the plastic fork supplied. It's good and therefore, to me at least, worth $4.69.

A huge bird, which might be an eagle, soars above Route 50 as I drive through the pretty village of North Bend. Close to five o'clock, I enter Indiana where there are T-shaped telegraph poles, with two cross pieces, spaced evenly along the right side of the road. I'm thinking of spending the night in Seymour, which is about seventy miles on. I pass through Lawrenceburg, which blends into the next town, Aurora, where the river bends south while Route 50 continues on west, straight and flat through green fields. The Eagles' *Greatest Hits* roll from the speakers. On the left side of the road, more T-shaped telegraph poles, with just one cross piece, rock by in a rhythm picked up in the corner of my eye. The highway is empty, as it is in my memories of movies like *Two-Lane Blacktop* and *Easy Rider*. I sit back in my seat, relax my shoulders, and tap my thumb on the steering wheel along with the Eagles and the telegraph poles, which somehow are in sync. Despite the heat, I turn off the air conditioning, let the windows down and try to focus on the road and the landscape. But my mind won't empty. Instead, I think about guilt and try not to feel it – neither for being born white, nor for what my ancestors may have done, nor for being able to buy a chicken-salad shaker without thinking about its price. But it's not easy. Is this why I drink beer most nights?

After miles of fields filled with maize and milo (usually called sorghum in the UK), 'Peaceful Easy Feeling' comes on – and again I sit back and lower my shoulders. It works a little. I come to the town of Versailles, whose name promises beauty and formality. Instead there is a rash of billboards, then McDonald's, Kwik Car Wash, Subway.

The land is flat, as perhaps it will be for more than a thousand

miles across Indiana, Illinois, Missouri, Kansas and the beginnings
of Colorado, until the Rockies emerge. Long open fields are lush
with yet more maize and milo. A railroad track, edged with low
telegraph poles, appears to my right. A small, white post-office
van is following me at a distance. It comes closer, and I see that it
is driven by a woman. A freight train sits stationary on the track
to my right; it is long, very long, a mile of boxcars and open
wagons piled with sand. The white van has dropped back, fifty,
a hundred yards.

Abruptly, US 50 is closed and I have to detour onto State
Highway 750, an empty road, patterned with the shadows of trees.
For miles the white van stays with me until eventually we return
to US 50 and enter the outskirts of Seymour. There a Knights Inn
sits beside a junction with a north-south interstate. I cruise through
Seymour on 50 to see what else there is, and glance at the rear-
view mirror. A brief pang of loss; the white van has gone – turned
off without a word – or even a flashing of lights. There is little else,
so I turn back and check into the Knights Inn.

Later, I drive the cross streets of Seymour in the dark, looking
for a bar – and don't find one. All right. No beer tonight. No
problem. Fed up with driving in the dark, I leave the car at the
Knights Inn and set out to walk to a Burger King, a half-mile
towards the centre of this dead town along Route 50. I cross the
forecourt of a Shell garage, and begin a strenuous and wobbly
hike along a springy grass verge – there is no pavement beside
50. There is dampness in the air and on the ground. Cars and
trucks loom up from behind spraying light, gravel and drops of
water. I wonder why I am doing this, and think about going
back to get the car. Instead, I retreat from the road and cross
several forecourts, some of which – Chilis, Starbucks, Bonanza
Steak, Quality Inn and Long John Silver's – are well paved and
lit. Others, abandoned, potholed and muddy, rot in darkness
in front of defunct businesses. I use my phone to light my way,
and spot rats in a huge, overgrown lot between Quality Inn and

155

Long John Silver's. Perhaps to keep the vermin out, Long John has put up a high wall that I can't climb; instead I retreat to what was once an exit to Route 50 and bounce along the verge to Burger King.

Two young men sit at a formica table, munching. They are the only customers. A young white woman, who is perhaps a goth, stares at me from behind the counter; half her head – the right half from my point of view – is shaved; the other half is covered in blue-black hair, elaborately, beautifully, arranged in long, narrow plaits interwoven with blue beads. Above her the menu stretches to the ceiling and the side walls, with outsize pictures of burgers, chips, onion rings, coleslaw and lettuce leaves.

'Hello,' I say.

She nods. 'How can I help ya?'

'I'll just have a look at this.' I pick up the printed menu and stare at it. At the same time I am distracted by her arms, both of which are covered in tattoos, some of which look as if they were drawn by Aubrey Beardsley. 'Er ... I'll have ...' She is staring at me and it is clear that I bore her. 'A bacon cheese chicken royale.'

'D'ya wanna drink with that?' She taps some buttons on the till.

'Actually, sorry, I won't have that.'

'Oh!' She sniffs and sighs – and taps at the till.

'Sorry. I'll have a ... king fish and a Coke.'

She looks at me. 'Sure?'

'Yes. That's what I'll have.'

She turns to the till. Tap, tap, tap.

'Fries?' She's not looking at me now. She's looking sideways at the darkness beyond the window.

'Yes, please.'

Tap, tap, tap. 'Eat in or take out?'

'Take out.'

She looks out at the almost empty car park. 'How did ya get here?'

'I walked ... from the Knights Inn.'

'Walked! From Knights Inn! My God! No one ever did that.

156

I thought ya musta come in a cab.' She's smiling a little – or is she smirking?

'No. I walked. It wasn't great, but it wasn't that bad.'

'Well,' she says, as I pay. And that's all she says.

She turns away to assemble my dinner and put it in a paper bag. She's certainly not impressed by someone who walks to Burger King from the Knights Inn. And nor am I – and now I have to walk back.

30

Back to Begin

In the morning I see a Coin-Op launderette, a little beyond Burger King on the other side of 50. I've been away for twelve days and need to do some washing. I carry my washing in a large JD Sports plastic bag into a big, clean space, lit with strip lights. A sign says: 'Please do not sit on washing machine.' Why do people want to do that? Is it something sexual? Fans hang from the ceiling, rotating slowly. I study washing machines, dryers, a slot machine that sells small boxes of soap powder, and a change machine that provides the necessary quarters.

I can see only one person, a woman of about thirty with a friendly face; she has a phone to her ear. I change $6 into twenty-four quarters – I'm going to need them – and buy a small box of Tide for seventy-five cents. Front loaders cost $4; top loaders $2.75. I look at both for a while, decide on a front loader and open its door.

My being new to this must be obvious. The friendly faced woman has finished her phone call. She comes over, looks at my bag and says a top loader would be best; she even shows me where to put the coins. I'm grateful. Not only has she saved me $1.25 – but I soon realise that, if I had blown $4 on a washing machine, I'd have had to change a $20 bill into eighty quarters to buy enough time in a dryer, and would have been left with about seventy-five quarters.

I sit on a low chair for the twenty-eight minutes that the front loader takes to wash my clothes. There's a cool, cleanish feeling in here. Music comes from a radio somewhere and accompanies the whirring noises of washers and dryers. I write a postcard to my grandson Fred. A middle-aged guy in a red T-shirt, blue shorts and flip-flops wanders happily by. The Eagles come on – a song I know, but can't name, is drowned out by my top loader entering a spin cycle. When the cycle ends, the Who are shouting 'Talking About My Generation' – strange that this song I first heard more than fifty years ago, and didn't like much, is playing in a Coin-Op in a small town in Indiana. I've never been keen on the Who. Give me the Stones, the Animals, the Kinks or the Beatles.

I use a trolley to move my clean clothes to the dryer. There I am helped by the supervisor – a white woman with straggly blonde hair – who has appeared from somewhere. Drying will take half an hour, she says. Five minutes of drying costs twenty-five cents. She says I should put in six quarters all at once. If you put them in one at a time and check your clothes for dryness between coins, you have to endure a two-minute cool-down period each time. I compromise and put in five quarters.

I sit in the low chair again and find I'm thinking about the Shawnee and the golf course. I can't blame the golf-course entrepreneurs for the demise of the Shawnee. That would be unfair, just as those kids on the campsite in Germany can't be blamed for starting World War II.

Tom Petty died recently. Now, in this Coin-Op, he is snarling 'I won't back down'.

A no-nonsense kind of woman, pursed lips, red face, comes in with many bags of washing. She drops four coins on the floor, two dimes and two cents. She picks up the dimes and leaves the cents. She goes out to her car. Shall I pick up the cents? Would that be low-grade, greedy behaviour? I pick them up. She comes in with more bags of washing, but I get away with it. She is wearing jeans and a tie-dye T-shirt, and her short hair is tied back with an elastic ring. I guess she has several children and a job, and no time to pick up small coins.

I leave with all my clothes, except those I am wearing, clean and folded, and drive on into Seymour along 50. I call into the visitor centre to check if there is anything nearby that I shouldn't miss, and learn about Medora Bridge, which I will visit this afternoon. I sit at a low bar in Townhouse Café, a warm and busy place with several women waiters. I order chef's salad and have a brief chat with the owner, a blonde woman called Val, who tells me that Townhouse was founded in 1962 and has had only three owners since then. 'We get top, middle and lower types here. Everyone,' she says. I'd like to ask her to define these three types, but she has to rush off. Instead, I look around. There are workmen with grimy hands and saggy shorts at the bar to my left, and beyond them an old man with a grey ponytail; to my right, a neatly dressed old man with hearing aids. Sitting at tables behind me are a group of young women with several children; a young couple with two children; three long-haired, unshaven men; two smartly dressed, subtly lipsticked, middle-aged women with an apparently prosperous silver-haired man. All these people are white, which perhaps reflects the make-up of the region, and that I am now well inside Middle America – and that Seymour, though it calls itself a city, is a medium-sized market town.

An earnest man with large nostrils has sat down next to me; he is wearing a black singlet which reveals muscly arms and shoulders. He tells the bartender that he doesn't want coffee because it is bad for the health. This remark serves as a cue for the chef, who is standing behind the bar, to tell Black Singlet all about his own health. The nub of it is that Chef had his blood pressure tested a few weeks ago. 'It was 297 over 178,' he says, almost with pride. Can that be right, I wonder? He went to hospital, 'Where they told me I was lucky to be alive. I'm fifty-two years old. They treated me for five days and, when I left, they said I should lose weight, which I have been doing. I weighed 397 pounds [about twenty-eight stone] and now I'm down to 287 pounds. I don't eat or drink certain things and now my blood pressure is right down.' He speaks in a matter-of-fact way, without a smile or a shrug, and moves on to tell Black Singlet the details of his father's health and other people's – down to their exact blood pressure at different times. Throughout most of this, Black Singlet has been enjoying a plate of beans and a glass of water. Early on, it was clear that he would have liked Chef to stop talking and go back to the kitchen. Now he finishes his meal, stands up, walks to the till, pays while Chef is still talking, says, 'Bye Greg', and walks out.

On the road to Medora, State Road 235, I go through a town called Begin and marvel again at the strange names that people give to their towns. As I drive through Begin, I see its name several times above road signs announcing speed limits. I leave Begin, head on towards Medora and drive for many miles – far further than I expected. The road gradually narrows so that it seems less and less like the wide, sweeping highway that I turned onto from Route 50. Eventually I decide that I have taken a wrong turning. I turn round and drive back to Begin, where I pass Medora High School . . . and begin to wonder. An old man with a white goatee beard is walking along the road slowly and stiffly with his arms out from his side. He is slim and wiry, wearing black jeans and a checked shirt. I stop the car and let down the window. 'Excuse me. Is this Begin or Medora?'

'Begin? No. Nowhere called Begin round here. This is Medora.'

Those road signs . . . the start of each new speed limit! BEGIN 50. BEGIN 40. BEGIN 30. What a complete and utter idiot! Again!

'Can you tell me how to get to Medora Bridge?'

'You can get there, but you'll have to come back the same way because the road's closed. Drive down here and over the railroad, turn left at the stop sign, drive to the end and through the "Road Closed" barrier. You can get through there and you'll get to the old wooden bridge – not far.'

I thank him warmly and start to drive off.

161

The old man calls to me. I stop the car and he walks back to me a few yards. 'Don't worry about the "Road Closed" sign. It's open to local traffic, and that's what you are.'

I thank him even more warmly than before. He has been helpful and friendly – like most Americans.

His directions are accurate. I reach the bridge in about five minutes and find a structure like a long wooden barn with a pitched roof, white-painted entrances at both ends, and brown-painted walls. There is no one here – and the place is quiet. To my left, which I sense is to the east, a shallow river lined with trees ripples and sparkles in the sun and, where it is still, reflects the sky; near its banks, where trees overhang, the water is murky green.

I walk up the paved slope to the bridge's entrance and look through a dark tunnel towards a square of dazzling light. This is the longest covered bridge in the US: 431 feet, built in 1875 to carry local people and their carts and wagons across the East Fork of the White River. I walk in, treading on thick oak planks that carried horses and, later, cars. As my eyes adjust to the darkness, I see the intricate balance of planks and joists, and the curving beams that form the trusses. Everything is made of wood, held together with wrought-iron bolts. When this bridge was built, many bridges in the US were covered. Left uncovered, a wooden bridge would last for about twenty years; covered bridges might last a hundred years. When the nationwide network of US routes was built in the 1920s and 1930s, US 50 crossed this bridge, which then was wide enough for cars to pass each other. When cars became wider, the bridge had to become one-way. In 1935, US 50 was rerouted four miles to the north – where it is now – but the bridge was used until 1972, when a concrete bridge was built close by.

I come out at the further end where a narrow road winds through fields. Viewed from this side, the river water is brown and reflects the trunks of trees and the light that passes between them. I remember Stonewall Jackson and his last words: 'Let us cross over the river and rest under the shade of the trees.'

31

French Lick

I pass a sign on 50 to Monroe Res – which I hope is an Indian Reservation. I turn the car and drive back. The reverse of the same sign says Monroe Reservoir. I try to shrug rather than curse, turn the car again and drive on for miles through verdant countryside with, here and there, a herd of mooching Friesians.

After an hour of slow driving I reach Bedford, a small city with a courthouse, which suggests it is the capital of a county. 50 goes straight through the middle and doubles as 16th Street, which, in turn, becomes the south side of the courthouse square. I park and wander about. In front of the courthouse the largest US flag I have ever seen swirls in the breeze above a huge sculpture of a woman in flowing robes standing on a tall plinth holding what looks like a giant twig from a Christmas tree. Seen against the deep blue sky and its drift of cotton-wool cloud, the monument and the flag reach out like the Statue of Liberty or a call to the barricades. This is the Soldiers, Sailors and Pioneers monument and celebrates everyone who fought or suffered on behalf of the US up to and including

World War I. The plinth has gorgeous pre-Raphaelite-style reliefs on each of its four sides. Arranged around it are smaller memorials to the dead and the veterans of wars since 1918: World War II, Korea, Vietnam, Iraq and Afghanistan – and a memorial to seven policemen who died in the course of duty between 1875 and 1998.

Bedford was a well-known stop on the Underground Railroad – and, I imagine, escaped slaves would have felt some relief on arrival, although they would still have been vulnerable to slave catchers. Slavery was banned in the first constitution of Indiana, which was written when the territory became a state in 1816; in 1820 all remaining slaves in the state were freed.

I walk around the square, admiring its old red-brick terraced buildings, some of which have high, square false fronts of the type seen on wooden buildings in westerns – a sign that, although I'm not quite yet in the west, I am getting there. It's little more than 200 miles now to the Mississippi and St Louis.

I turn off 50 and head south to French Lick for two reasons: its name and because Al Capone went there for his holidays. The drive through the Hoosier National Forest (Hoosier is the official name for a resident of Indiana; no one seems to be sure why) is beautiful, hilly and wooded. And it turns out that the road to French Lick is more fun than its destination, and offers literal proof of Robert Louis Stevenson's assertion that 'to travel hopefully is a better thing than to arrive'.

French Lick got its name in the early nineteenth century. It was the site of a trading post run by French settlers who chose the location because it was close to springs and a salt lick, a place where animals will go to lick naturally occurring salts and minerals.

In the 1920s French Lick was a hellraiser of a resort – a hopping and a jumping place with thousands of visitors, speakeasies and jazz, and – what's more – the place where tomato juice was invented. Now it's a dreary place, clean and pleased with itself; a place of luxury spa hotels, manicured golf courses, a giant 'Las Vegas-style casino' and shopping, which means Gucci, Louis Vuitton and similar overpriced tat with a logo. It's as if, at some time in the twentieth century – perhaps during the Reagan-Thatcher era – wealthy people forgot how to have fun and consoled themselves by buying stuff, *any* stuff, that poorer people couldn't afford. Such stuff is well known to economists, who call it 'Veblen goods', after economist Thorstein Veblen, who noticed in the nineteenth century that some products defy the normal laws of supply and demand. With Veblen goods – a common example is diamonds; another might be Gucci scarves – the higher the price, the more can be sold, and vice versa. To put it another way: would anyone buy a Louis Vuitton bag if its regular retail price was $10?

The place is redeemed a little by the view from street level of the wooded hills that surround it, and by a trompe-l'oeil mural of a terrace of old shops painted in a distressed style on the side of an old building, which harks back perhaps to the time of Al Capone. However, the best feature of French Lick is the public restrooms, which occupy an insignificant brick building between two almost empty car parks. Here women go to the left, men to the right, and in the space between is a plastic rack stuffed with copies of the *Official Visitors' Guide* to French Lick. From this I find out about the hotels, golf courses and shops – which, like the people, are so high-end that most of them are hidden behind gates and protected by bouncers.

In this part of town, the old town, I see: two men, who are fixing a street light; two women, one bronzed, the other pale; and no children. But, on the edge of town, I drive along a strip where life as most of us know it continues, with people, gas stations and fast-food joints.

In the shade of early evening I drive back to 50 on the same road. Beside me, face down on the passenger seat, is the *Official Visitors' Guide*. Pictured on the back cover, a couple aged about forty walk in casual clothes past a box hedge, behind which, in soft focus, are trees and a large building with two red towers – presumably a hotel. This attractive couple hold hands and smile at each other with plenty of teeth. The photo is captioned 'Visit French Lick'. This artless ad reminds me of a series of clever, artful ads for vodka, which appeared beside the escalators in London Tube stations in the 1970s. In one of them a photo of a couple smiling, but looking away from each other and not touching, was captioned: 'They think we're just good friends, but we've discovered Smirnoff.'

I fetch up after 9 p.m. at Theroff's Motel, an independent motel in Washington, Indiana. The receptionist tells me that if I want to eat something tonight, I'd better get down to Pizza Hut pronto. It's just along the road, but I will have to drive.

Phew! I arrive in Pizza Hut in time – and they even have beer. 'Budweiser or San Miguel?'

'San Miguel, please.' Anything but Budweiser.

I order some pasta, fetch some salad from the help-yourself salad island – and become aware of loud chat and laughter from a group of people who are sitting, partly hidden, behind a frosted-glass screen. There seem to be about twenty adults and almost as many children celebrating something.

As I eat my salad, a woman wearing a long, plain, maroon dress to her ankles emerges from behind the screen and walks past my table. She has a white cotton bonnet, called a kapp, on the back of her head, with tie-strings hanging down over her ears. I guess that she and her friends are Amish, or perhaps Mennonite. More women in white kapps come past, and a girl wearing trainers; all of them wear floor-length dresses in blue, green or maroon. Men and boys, wearing plain shirts and long trousers, walk by. Some of them smile at me. A man with a little boy says, 'Hi.' The chat and laughter from the long table behind the screen continue.

My chicken alfredo tagliatelle arrives, and I ask the waitress who these people are. 'Amish,' she whispers. 'There are a lot of them around here.'

When it seems that they have all returned from where they went – the restroom, I presume – they suddenly go quiet. Has someone given a signal? Are they praying? After less than a minute, they get back to talking. And then laughing.

An older man with a grey beard comes by. He smiles. His trousers have perfect creases. Later the same man stands near my table, studying the bill.

The Amish leave noisily before I do. When I get up to pay, I find two women sitting in a booth are encouraging the waitress to lose weight; she is, perhaps, a little podgy. In another booth is a young woman who looks too thin. A man sitting with her says to the waitress, 'She lives on pop.' None of the Amish – more than thirty of them – children or adults, looked either thin or fat.

32

Four Boys and a War Hero

Robert Mueller's inquiry into Russian interference in the US election of 2016 features on television news every morning, and along with it comes Michael Cohen, the president's former lawyer. Today we viewers are treated to a new name. David Pecker has been helping Cohen to pay off women, including Stormy Daniels, who claim to have had affairs with Donald Trump. Did Trump take this man on because his giggle-inducing name seemed appropriate to the job in hand? I do wish he had, but he's actually an old friend of the president, and the owner of the *National Enquirer, Men's Fitness, Fit Pregnancy* and many other magazines.

West from Washington, 50 is a divided highway. There's little traffic, but a lot of noise. The road surface is sending up a high-pitched whine; sometimes the tyres almost squeal. Suddenly, a curt message appears on the dashboard telling me to change the engine oil. Bloody cheek! Why should I? I haven't driven Harpo that far; he can't need fresh oil already. I drive a little faster between fields of maize and somehow bypass the city of Vincennes, where I was intending to stop and look around. I realise the mistake when I arrive in a city called Lawrenceville and discover that I have left Indiana and entered Illinois.

I decide to drive back the eleven miles to Vincennes, but first take a quick walk around Lawrenceville in burning sunshine, which sharpens the edges of all solid objects, particularly buildings and cars, and blackens all shadows. Outside the imposing courthouse, built in 1889, a printed board gives some history illustrated with photographs and engravings. In 1842, in the previous courthouse, a woman named Elizabeth Reed was tried and found guilty of murdering her husband. She was hanged on the edge of town; she is the only woman ever hanged in Illinois. The square around this courthouse is similar to the square in Bedford: old buildings – a hundred years old or more – each the width of a single shop front, each of its own design, showing bare bricks or pastel paint, some with elaborate cornices at roof level, some with western-style box-shaped false fronts, are jammed against each other, forming thriving, colourful terraces. As in Italy or Spain, there is no one around now in the heat of the day, but these shops and smart-looking offices are clearly in business.

I return to Vincennes, park outside Old Chicago Pizza and Taproom, which was clearly a cinema not long ago, and stroll up Main Street. Each block is a terrace of late-Victorian buildings, all of them different, well maintained and decorated; I'm reminded of Bedford and Lawrenceville, but there is more life here and effort has been made to market the street as a whole. Flowers bloom in hanging baskets and concrete tubs, but this is not overdone, and American flags, but not too many, droop here and there. Floral banners hang from retro-style black lamp posts celebrating Indiana's First Main Street and give the date 1732, which seems early for a main street. A watermelon plant, complete with a nascent watermelon, sprawls low on the pavement outside a restaurant called Pea Fections and, further along, a banner hanging from a lamp post announces the annual Watermelon Festival, which includes a seed–spitting contest.

This is a street of restaurants, bars, cafés and shops, many of which have punning names: Olde Thyme Diner, Pretty Posies Floral and Gift Shop, Main Street Paw Spa Dog Grooming. As I walk, I hear Bob Dylan singing 'Like a Rolling Stone'. Across the road, outside the Record Cellar, a grey–haired man sits on a bench, stares down at the pavement and nods along with Dylan. A shop window is given over to a biography and photographs of Red Skelton, the comedian, who was born in Vincennes in 1913; the Red Skelton Museum of Comedy is on Red Skelton Boulevard in the university part of the city.

Main Street ends in a park, the George Rogers Clark National Historical Park. At its edge, a plaque honours François–Marie Bissot, Sieur de Vincennes (1700–36), a French–Canadian explorer and soldier who built a fort here in 1732 'to protect the claims of France in the New World'. At that time France's territories in North America, known as the Province of Louisiana, stretched north from New Orleans into Illinois and Indiana. The last of the three sentences on this plaque begins, 'In 1736, Vincennes was burned at the stake by Chickasaw Indians . . .' This happened during the Chickasaw Wars, when the French, allied with the Choctaw, fought the British, allied with the Chickasaw, for the right to trade along the Mississippi. During a battle at a village called Ogoula Tchetoka, now in the state of Mississippi, the Chickasaw captured nineteen French soldiers, including Vincennes, and burned them to death. The eventual victory of the Chickasaw and the British in this little–known war had a big influence on the development of North America and the United States.

I walk into the park. The sun bears down on my sun hat. Clouds shaped like boats and cigars float in a deep blue sky. Somewhere cicadas are scratching. And I am the only human here. I come to another plaque and learn that the park is named after Lieutenant Colonel George Rogers Clark, who was a hero of the War of Independence. In February 1779 he arrived here with 160 men after an eighteen–day march and captured Fort Sackville from the British.

During that war, he fought and won many battles against the British in what was then known as the Northwest Territory (now Indiana, Ohio, Illinois, Michigan, Wisconsin and Minnesota). When the British surrendered that territory in 1783, the size of the newly independent United States doubled and Clark gained the soubriquet 'Conqueror of the Old Northwest'.

There were two conquerors of the Northwest in the Clark family. George Rogers Clark was the elder brother of William Clark, who travelled even further north-west as co-leader, with Meriwether Lewis, of the Corps of Discovery sent by Thomas Jefferson in 1803 to find a route across the continent to the Pacific. I find that I am wondering whether, like his brother, George Rogers Clark had a personal slave to help him conquer the north-west. And, if so, was he as resourceful as the mighty York?

I walk on over mown grass and reach an embankment overlooking the wide, brown and beautiful Wabash River. There is nothing on the other side except a riverbank shrouded in trees and, somewhere out of sight, a memorial to Abraham Lincoln. Vincennes is on the east bank and in Indiana. Over there is Illinois. A fine five-arch road bridge, the Lincoln Memorial Bridge gleams white in the sun; it was built here because this is where twenty-one-year-old Abraham Lincoln crossed the Wabash with his pioneer family on their way to a new home in Illinois in 1830.

Close to the bridge, at the bottom of a flight of steps, are three upright, rectangular stone panels, each about ten feet wide. The history of the river crossing, the town and the region is inscribed on them, in beautifully engraved capital letters. I read that there was a ford here and that the Wabash 'was crossed by a buffalo trace, an ancient path worn by countless animals and aborigines in their migrations between east and west ... Vestiges of a remote past and forgotten races' have been found. Indians, French explorers and missionaries lived here. And then: 'From France, England won this region.' Only to lose it to George Rogers Clark in the War of Independence. After that war, pioneers, 'seeking new homes in Illinois and beyond the Mississippi', crossed the river here. A wooden bridge was built after the Civil War, and was replaced in 1931 by 'this bridge of concrete ... It commemorates the opening of the west and the expansion of our country from ocean to ocean.'

I walk towards the park's centrepiece, the George Rogers Clark Memorial, which is grand and circular, built of white stone, ringed by massive Doric columns, with a dome on the top. It was built in the 1930s, dedicated by President Franklin Roosevelt in 1936, and is in the neoclassical style with a hint of wedding cake.

Four studious boys have arrived from somewhere, clutching notebooks and pens. They are climbing the steps to the memorial. I follow them up, and in through tall doors. Inside, on a marble plinth, in the centre of the circular space, stands a larger-than-life bronze statue of the great man, portrayed as he was when, on his own initiative, he led his men here to take the fort from the British. Back then, in 1779, George Rogers Clark was twenty-five years old. Now the young, handsome hero gazes for ever into the distance: defiant, hair swept back, cape flowing from his shoulders, hands resting on his sword, which pricks the ground between his feet. He is lit from above – the dome is shallow and made of glass – and a huge window above the door throws light on his face.

He is surrounded by seven murals, each of them twenty-eight feet tall and sixteen feet wide. Five show scenes from Clark's life as a soldier. Two record the results of his success. In one of these, an official reads a proclamation granting the right of US citizenship to the people of the Northwest Territory. In the other, a crowd including Meriwether Lewis, co-leader of the Corps of Discovery, watches as the American flag is hoisted and the French flag lowered in St Louis in March 1804. The message of this last mural is that the spread of the United States across the continent would not have happened had George Rogers Clark not taken Fort Sackville from the British in Vincennes in 1779. If the British had kept the fort, they could have claimed the Northwest Territory and the United States might have comprised just the original thirteen states.

I spend some time admiring these murals. The more I look, the more I like them, though – and perhaps because – they seem behind their time. They were painted by Ezra Winter, a celebrated muralist, aided by six assistants, in 1933 and 1934. For the sake of accuracy, Winter and his team hired models and posed them in costume. In each picture, people do things – ride horses, fight, wade through a river, talk, fire rifles, shake hands, make proclamations – in the foreground, while as a backdrop, usually at the top of these tall paintings, dreamlike trees, hills and sky look down. To my uncertain eye, these paintings are, like the building itself, in a neoclassical style and hark back to Ingres, David and Poussin.

One of the studious boys is sketching in his notebook. The other three are looking around and chatting quietly. They are wearing long trousers and blue, short-sleeved shirts. I guess they are about fifteen years old. One of them – the smallest one, who has the longest hair, and is perhaps their leader – glances at me.

'Pretty impressive,' I say, waving my arm towards the murals. 'I love these paintings.'

'Yeah,' the boy says. He points to the statue. 'And he's so cool.'

'Yes. I guess he was,' I say. 'He changed the course of American history.' They're all looking at me now. 'Are you from Canada?' one of them says.

'No. London, England.'

All four say 'cool', and one says that his parents have visited London. They want to know what I'm doing in Vincennes.

I explain about Route 50 and driving to San Francisco.

There is some amazement, more 'cool's and some 'wow's. They would all like to go to California. They've all been to St Louis, which is less than 200 miles; one of them flew to Florida for a wedding.

I tell them how much I like their town, and we talk about their school; everyone there does projects on George Rogers Clark. It's something they have to do, but they like doing it and try to find out new things. The smallest one says, 'Yeah! Did you know that he fell in love with a Spanish woman called Teresa, but she didn't love him, so he never got married and died poor and alone after having his leg amputated?'

'No. No. I didn't know that. Why did he have his leg amputated?'

'Because it got burned . . . in a fire.'

'Really! Is that right?'

'Yes,' he says. 'I read about that.' His friends mutter their agreement.

I look up at the vigorous young man cast in bronze. 'Blimey . . . that's sad.' I can't think what else to say. I leave the boys and the memorial, and walk back towards the river.

A man in a uniform and a straw cowboy hat is coming towards me along the paved embankment: a National Park ranger. He says 'hi' and asks if I need any help.

'Actually, I'm looking for somewhere where I can sit in the shade and eat my lunch.' I pat my bag where I've got almonds, cheese and rosemary crackers from Walmart.

The ranger leads me to some steps that go down to the river. At the bottom, up against the embankment and in its shade, is a low wall.

I eat cheese, stare at the water and think about what the boy told me, about the dashing hero who changed the world but died poor and alone. Something, or perhaps two things – George Rogers Clark's amputated leg and the tranquil view across the River Wabash – remind me again of Stonewall Jackson.

33

Tecumseh and Other Indians

After lunch I bump into the ranger again. He asks if I've seen 'the pylons', and points to them. They are along the riverbank, about fifty yards away, a pair of rectangular stone columns standing at the entrance to the Lincoln Memorial bridge. 'Those both have neat sculptures of Indian chiefs,' he says. 'Take a look. Some people say those are Tecumseh and his brother. You know Tecumseh? Big-deal Indian chief.'

'I do know him. He *was* a big deal,' I say.

'Well, if you're interested in Tecumseh,' – he pushes his hat back and wipes his forehead with the back of his hand – 'there's a carving, a wooden sculpture that's definitely him. Just carry on along the river path after the bridge – about two hundred yards.'

'OK. Why are there statues of him here, in Vincennes?'

'Well,' he looks at the ground. 'He was from round here. He was a famous Indian, a chief, a warrior. I don't know too much about him, but he tried to organise the Indians, the different tribes, you know.'

*

The pylons stand facing each other on either side of the road. Both have a relief carving of an Indian chief in full headdress cut into the corner facing the road and the park. These carvings are about ten feet tall, and exquisite. They have an angular, art deco look – which isn't surprising, since they were made in 1933 by a French sculptor called Raoul Josset.

I walk on along the riverbank, and remember that the ranger pronounced 'Tecumseh' as 'Ticumsa', and that he and I were both calling Indians Indians. Indians call themselves Indians. I've discussed this with Indians I've met. They don't mind being called Indians; they are proud to be Indians. Native American or Amerindian is acceptable, but only politicians and ignorant foreigners avoid calling them Indians.

The Tecumseh sculpture stands on a patch of grass a little way back from the river. My first impression is of a totem pole about twenty-five feet high. It shows just Tecumseh's head and neck, carved out of an oak tree and greatly elongated. Two huge feathers rise from his hair, which is long and falling around his neck. He has a hook nose, a firm, dimpled chin and lines in his cheeks. I've seen paintings of this man, which make him look a lot more handsome and distinguished.

A plaque explains that in '1810 and 1811 Tecumseh defended the rights of his people in meetings in Vincennes with William Henry Harrison, Governor of the Indiana Territory'. As well as being a great leader – his people and his warriors were devoted to him – Tecumseh was a deep thinker and a forceful orator. Though he died so long ago, in 1813, many of his speeches were written down and have survived. Protesting about a treaty that Harrison had signed so as to obtain land from a local chief, Tecumseh said:

> The way, the only way to stop this evil is for the red men to unite in claiming a common and equal right in the land, as it was at first, and should be now – for it was never divided, but belongs to all. No tribe has the right to sell, even to each other, much less to strangers ... Sell a country! Why not sell the air, the clouds and

176

the great sea, as well as the earth? Did not the Great Spirit make them all for the use of his children?

Tecumseh travelled north to the Great Lakes and south through Tennessee to the Gulf of Mexico, visiting tribes of Indians and making speeches. His dream was to unite as many tribes as possible and establish an Indian nation in the Old North West, the region that George Rogers Clark had won from the British in 1783. Some tribes followed him; many didn't. With his brother, Tenskwatawa, who was a holy man known as 'the Prophet', he founded a Shawnee village in present-day Indiana, which became known as Prophetstown. Indians from other tribes were attracted to Prophetstown: some by Tenskwatawa's spiritual teachings, others by Tecumseh's call for an alliance to protect their land from the Americans. This led to Tecumseh's Federation with, at one time, 5,000 loyal warriors spread across the north-west.

When Tecumseh went travelling in 1811, he told Tenskwatawa to evacuate the village if an American army approached. With Tecumseh away, William Henry Harrison, the Indiana governor who lived in Vincennes, moved on Prophetstown with 1,200 soldiers. Instead of leaving, as instructed by his brother, Tenskwatawa attacked the Americans and lost the ensuing battle at Tippecanoe. The Americans then burned the village to the ground.

When the British attacked the Americans from Canada, as part of the war of 1812, Tecumseh and his men joined them. Together they took Detroit from the Americans, and Tecumseh was designated a brigadier general in the British army.

After a battle to take Fort Meigs in Ohio in May 1813, Tecumseh intervened to stop a band of Indians, led by another chief, massacring American prisoners. News of this made Tecumseh a hero among his enemies, the Americans. Later that year, on 5 October, the Americans won the Battle of the Thames. Tecumseh was killed in the fighting – though no one is sure how he died.

After Tecumseh's death, his arch enemy, William Henry Harrison, who would later become President of the United States, wrote: 'He was one of those uncommon geniuses which spring up occasionally to produce revolutions and overturn the established order of things ... If it were not for the vicinity of the United States, he would perhaps be the founder of an empire that would rival in glory that of Mexico or Peru.'

In *The Penguin History of the USA*, Hugh Brogan wrote: 'Towards the end of [the Indians'] days of freedom and power, one man of genius among them, the Shawnee Tecumseh, saw the truth and realised that only by uniting in one nation might the Indians save themselves. Tecumseh was a great general, a compelling orator, a generous and humane man. But his vision came too late ...'

So was Tecumseh the greatest Indian of them all? What about Crazy Horse and Sitting Bull, the Sioux chiefs who defeated Custer at the Battle of the Little Bighorn, and fought tirelessly, with words as well as warriors, for the land and freedom of their people.

Or Geronimo, the Apache leader who held out longer than any other Indian chief against the white men, despite their guns, railroads and irrational conviction that it was their 'manifest destiny' to own and rule north America.

Or Chief Joseph of the Nez Perce, another great orator, who fought and negotiated endlessly in an ultimately hopeless attempt to save his people and their land.

Or Osceola, leader of the Florida Seminole, a tribe who disappeared into the Everglades in the 1830s when the other tribes of the south-east were being sent by force, and by the notorious Indian Removal Act, to Indian Territory in what is now Oklahoma. The Florida Seminole never signed a treaty, still call themselves 'the Unconquered People' and, nowadays, are business hotshots who own and run the worldwide chain of 124 Hard Rock Cafés.

Or the three founders, back in the fifteenth century, of the Iroquois League of Six Nations: Dekanawida (the Great Peacemaker), who had the ideas but couldn't convey them because he had a stammer; Hiawatha, who did the talking; and Jigonhsasee (the Mother of Nations), whose home became a meeting place for warring chiefs. (The Iroquois Hiawatha has no connection to the poet Longfellow's fictional character who fell in love with Minnehaha.)

Perhaps it's foolish to try to single out one Indian as the greatest of them all. Yet, in *The Shawnees and the War for America*, Professor Colin Callaway writes: 'To some Tecumseh is simply the greatest Indian who ever lived. He failed to achieve his goals, but his dream of a pan-Indian coalition has inspired generations of Native Americans.'

I drive back across the Wabash into Illinois. Each time I cross this river, the time changes, because this is where Eastern Time becomes Central Time, if you are going west. I've adjusted my watch twice today already and I will again when I next stop driving, and so lose the hour I retrieved about three hours ago.

I shoot past Lawrenceville and continue on a flat, straight road through fields of maize and soya. I pass a sign saying DO NOT PICK UP HITCHHIKERS and instantly recall an apparently true story called 'White Sands' by Geoff Dyer, one of my favourite writers. (I say 'apparently' because Dyer likes to blur truth and fiction. He doesn't seem to think that the distinction matters, or perhaps even exists; I agree with him, up to a point – with regard to his writing, rather than mine.) In 'White Sands' Dyer is sitting in the passenger seat of a car that is being driven along a remote highway in western Texas, towards El Paso; the driver is his wife – who in this story is called Jessica, though Dyer has told us in a foreword to the collection that her name is Rebecca. They see a man hitchhiking and pick him up. A few miles later they see a sign that says DO NOT PICK UP HITCHHIKERS: DETENTION FACILITIES IN THIS AREA. The rest of the story relates how the three people in the car deal with this information.

For me, in this empty part of southern Illinois, there is no hitchhiker. But, half a mile after the sign telling me not to pick them up, a sign points to CORRECTIONAL FACILITY. Having read Dyer, I am half-expecting this – and a small shudder erupts inside my head.

In Olney I make a detour following a sign to East Fork Lake.

179

There, I stand in the shade of trees, gaze at ripples on water and listen to two gatherings of cicadas; one bunch is sawing away at a high pitch without stopping; the other makes sounds an octave lower and only intermittently. A way off two or three men fish from a boat. I munch a couple of biscuits and wonder about the cicadas. Am I listening to a hen night interrupted by catcalls from boorish men?

I get back on 50. The land is flat, the sky huge and beautiful – clouds float high up and there is silver in the west. The road is straight and raised above the land on either side; it was built by Indians thousands of years ago, a causeway across marshes. An old, narrow road appears to my right and crosses three rusty truss bridges. Notices say it is closed. I guess that this is the original Route 50, built in the 1920s.

I pass an isolated shop called 00 Western Wear. I'm getting into cowboy country – not far now to the Mississippi, where the west begins.

34

Love Stories

I drive into Salem and pass the Continental Motel; it looks a little wacky and independent. A few yards on, I see a sign on a pole in front of a US flag: 'American Legion Post 128'. Next to it, a notice says 'Open to the Public'. I check in to the Continental Motel, and find two *china mugs* – not the usual throwaway beakers sealed in plastic – in my room for tea and coffee. I turn on the TV and think about the American Legion. What would that be like? Would it be full of old soldiers? What would they make of me – if anything?

I have to find out. After all, I can always leave; there are other bars in Salem.

I open a green door in a low, newish, red-brick building, and walk in. Two men, both of them white, are sitting at the bar with a big space between them. They turn round. 'Howdy,' the man on the left says, and smiles. The other man has a good look and turns away.

'Hi,' I say.

'What can I get ya?' A slight, blonde-haired woman speaks from behind the bar.

'Oh! A beer please.'

'Bud. Bud Light?'

'Do you have any IPA?

'We got Porch Rocker. Samuel Adams.'

'Sure. That sounds good.'

Both the men – I'm now standing in the space between them – have bottles of Bud Light, and glasses. The bartender puts a glass and a brown bottle with a green label in front of me. The bottle is cold. I pour slowly to avoid froth. And take a sip. It's fine, with a lemony taste.

'That good?' The bartender is holding a wine glass; she reaches up to hang it from the canopy above the bar.

'Yeah. Great, thanks.' And it is great: cold and refreshing, as beer should be at the end of a hot day.

'Where are you from, may I ask? You don't sound ...' The bartender tilts her head and scrunches her face. She reminds me of Reese Witherspoon.

'London, England. I'm just travelling through.' I explain my east-west journey as best I can. 'I flew to Washington DC and rented a car.'

'I never been that far east, not as far as Washington or New York. I been to San Antonio to see my son – in the air force.' She looks too young to have a son in the air force. 'I went to Chicago for three months. Didn't like it. I'm a small-town girl.'

The man who said 'howdy' turns towards me, a tall man – leaning back against a bar stool with his feet on the floor. 'I wouldn't want to go anywhere else. I do well for around here. I went to South Carolina for a while. Wanted to come back. Small town – I like it.' He holds out his hand. 'I'm George.'

'David,' I say and take it. He looks me in the eye. I guess he is in his thirties. He has a fit, outdoor look about him, a moustache and stubble, big hands and deeply tanned forearms.

'I'm Arra,' the bartender says.

'Arra,' I repeat her name as we shake hands.

She says that she is named after her great-grandmother who was German, and that her mother's side of the family is Irish.

I say something about history seeming to unfold as I drive west. I mention the waves of settlers, the War of Independence, wars against Indians, the Civil War and slavery.

George says, 'You know there were black slave owners – and there were Indians who owned blacks?'

'Really? I didn't know that. Seems strange.'

'It's true.' Arra is leaning on the bar nodding.

George says, 'I'll show you. Gimme a moment.' He picks up his phone and taps on it.

I glance around the room, at bare brick walls with posters, notices and small framed pictures. Five or six people are sitting at tables. It's cosy; the lighting is muted.

'This is it.' George looks up at me and reads from his phone. 'William Ellison – former black slave – became the wealthiest black property owner in South Carolina. In 1860 he owned fifty-three black slaves, making him the largest of the one hundred and seventy-one black slaveholders in South Carolina.' George hands me his phone. 'Here. Take a look.' Arra is still leaning on the bar. They both seem keen for me to know that there were black slave owners.

I scan a Wikipedia page about William Ellison.

'Interesting, isn't it?' George says. 'Slaves could buy their freedom, and then like anyone else get rich, buy land and slaves to work it.'

'I didn't know that.'

'Same with the Indians. You can look that up too.'

Arra wants to know more about London and me: what do I do there?

I tell her that I edit books and do some teaching.

'Well, I'm a bartender.' Arra laughs. 'And George digs holes – big holes.'

'Yeah!' George smiles. For a second I imagine him bent over a shovel all day. 'With a back hoe. And I inspect water towers as well – for Marion County. I got two jobs.'

'Does that mean you have to climb up the towers?'

'Yep. It's wonderful up there. Views all across Illinois – and further. So flat here, you can see for ever.'

'So you climb, like up a ladder?'

'Yep.'

'God! I couldn't do that.'

He smiles. 'Afraid of heights? Noodle legs, I call that.'

'How high are they?'

'Ninety to a hundred and eighty feet.'

'My God! Is there someone with you?'

'Not always, but usually. He stays on the ground.' He sits back on his stool and puts his heels on the rung above the floor. 'I just love working outdoors. You know, I was a high-school dropout. Now I earn more than my friends who went to grad school, and they have thousands of dollars of debt. I worked in a factory before.' He grimaces. 'God, I hated that. It was so repetitive.'

'I worked there too,' Arra says. 'The car-headlight factory. It was a horrible place to work: no windows, artificially lit, no air con, very hot. Then I worked in the tail-light factory.' She looks at George. 'You didn't do that one. That was bad.' She looks back at me. 'They do headlights in Salem, and tail-lights in Flora, a few miles down the road.'

'Yep. I walked out in the end.' George sounds angry, and tells me how the manager said he was not making enough headlights. 'But I was working on a faulty machine. They took the machine away for one day to repair it. On that day I worked on a functioning machine and made way over the quota of headlights.' Then they gave him back his old machine. It hadn't been fixed properly, but the supervisor still got at him for making too few. 'So that's when I walked out.'

I order another Porch Rocker and George lets me buy him a Bud Light. Arra brings them, and I ask George if he has ever been in the military; we are in the American Legion, so I guess that he has.

'No,' he says with what seems like some regret, as if perhaps he hadn't done his duty. 'My father persuaded me. He'd been in Korea

184

and he didn't want me to go through the things he'd been through: the things he'd seen and done. He never told me what those things were – I don't think he ever told anyone. But they hurt him – I know that – always. He pretty much begged me not to join. So I didn't. And then he passed away a year later.'

Before George has finished telling me this, his phone rings. Now he looks at it – and frowns. 'Excuse me,' he says and walks out to the car park.

I order another beer and a pizza topped with pulled pork. Arra brings the beer and moves along the bar to talk to someone.

George returns after a few minutes. He doesn't look happy.

Arra comes back and looks at him; she looks worried too. 'Crystal?' she says.

'Yeah.'

'Again?'

'Yep.' George takes a breath.

'You gotta go.'

'No. We're gonna wait and see.'

'OK. Want a beer?'

'Please.' George turns to me, smiles and raises his eyebrows. 'A while ago I got married to Crystal – eleven years older than me. She already had four kids with her first, abusive husband, who left her and went off with someone else.'

'A schoolfriend of mine,' Arra says and pulls a face. 'That was awkward.'

'I was seventeen when I met Crystal. She was twenty-eight. We got together and I asked her to marry me, but she wouldn't. She'd just come out of an abusive relationship and she wasn't ready for another commitment.' He pours beer into his glass, and takes a gulp. 'Then I had a car crash and almost died. Ran off the road into a ditch, spun over three times and turned twice and landed upside down. I was thrown out about fifty feet and lay unconscious for an hour in a field till someone found me.'

'Was it dark?'

'No. It was daylight. This guy saw the overturned car and looked around; he figured there must be someone somewhere. Lucky for me.' He swallows more beer and wipes his mouth with the back of his hand. 'I had a broken face. I've got metal plates in here.' He points to his left cheek, which looks normal, if a little bony. 'I broke all my ribs, punctured lung. They didn't think I'd survive. And when I came to, I was angry and wanted to get out of that hospital. I was pullin' out the IVs. My dad and Crystal persuaded me I must stay there.

'After a while they did tests of my body and my mental capacity, and let me out for Crystal to care for me – she has CPR and first-aid qualifications. And,' he sighs and takes another swallow, 'I took eighteen months to get back to normal. I was in bed much of that time. And during that she said she'd marry me, because, she said, she realised how much I meant to her, how she'd miss me if I died.' He smiles then, and picks up his beer.

'Wow! You're a lucky man.'

'Yes.' He smiles again, but the smile turns to a frown. 'Now we have a problem – a boy who's getting into trouble, doesn't come home when we tell him to, and ... worse, bad stuff.'

Arra is talking to some people sitting at a table. George goes out for a cigarette and I eat the pizza that has been sitting on the bar for a while. I think about these two people: how they are in a network of friends and relations who have known each other for years, maybe all their lives – Arra is thirty-nine, George thirty-six. They want to be here – nowhere else.

Both of them reappear. Arra leans on the bar and tells me that she is married to a man who is twenty-six years older than she is. 'Clifford. He's a tattoo artist. He's well known around here.'

George says, 'Clifford is legendary. A real cool guy.'

Arra was married and had her son – the one who is in the air force – when she was nineteen. Her husband died when their boy was five. 'I still miss him,' she says, 'but I love Clifford. I brought up my boy by myself, did all kinds of jobs, supported us. And this' – she looks around and waves an arm – 'this is the best job I ever had. Bartender manager. I love it.'

George puts his glass down on the bar and says he's going to go home, but he'll come back.

Arra tells me about her sister, who is married to a fundamentalist preacher. 'He says I'm a sinner, working in a bar, being married more than once – other stuff!' She grins and then says, 'It's awkward.'

I mention Jeanette Winterson and her book *Oranges Are Not the Only Fruit*. Before I can say that it's about being brought up by fundamentalist Christians, Arra tells me she's read it, and loved it.

I'm not sure why, perhaps I'd had too many beers, but I mention that Jeanette Winterson is a lesbian.

'Well,' Arra says. 'I'm bisexual. I've been with one or two women. I was always a tomboy and played with the boys. Most of my friends are men now.'

George returns. All is well. His boy came home. Arra brings more beer and this time I have Bud Light – I don't like it, but I fancy a change. I ask them both the question that's been in my mind all evening: 'How do you feel about Donald Trump?'

'I *love* Trump,' Arra almost shouts.

George says, 'He just says what's in his mind. He's not a politician. He doesn't bullshit.'

'There's a civil war in the United States,' Arra says – and a steeliness comes into her face. 'It's already started. Between those who believe people should be given what they require and those who believe they should work for it.'

'What about the stuff he's said about women? Is that OK?' I ask.

'It's just locker room,' George says. 'Garage talk.'

Arra shrugs. 'The Democrats and the Republicans don't like Trump because he's not one of them. He doesn't bullshit.' She gives me a stare and shrugs again. 'We get many people who come into this bar who are against him. We have arguments.'

George says, 'What I like about him is that he does what he said he'd do.'

'What about the wall with Mexico?' I say.

'Well, at least he's trying,' George says.

187

Arra says, 'He's not a politician. They talk, say they'll do something and then never do it.'

'He doesn't need to be president.' George raises his hands, palms upwards, and looks at me. 'Doesn't need the money, the four-hundred-thousand-dollar salary. He gives it away.'

'They make him keep one dollar,' Arra says.

'He gave his first salary to the National Parks.' George fills his glass with pale yellow beer, Bud Light. 'He was asked in the nineteen-nineties – you can see the clip online – if he would ever stand for president. He said, "No, but I'd be a good one."'

'Has he made you better off?' I ask.

'Yes. A bit.' Arra nods. Her elbows are on the bar, her face cupped in her hands. 'He says things I wish he wouldn't. People in this bar say things I wish they wouldn't.'

'Yeah,' George laughs – and names someone.

'Right! But what can you do? You live with it.' Arra's phone goes ting! She looks down at it. 'It's him. Donald!'

George grins. 'Her phone bings when Trump tweets!'

'No!' I say.

'Really. It's true.'

Arra looks up and shrugs. 'He's just letting me know what he thinks about South Africa.'

George stands up. 'Real good to meet you.' He leaves with a firm handshake and a 'Hope we meet again'.

Soon I leave too. Arra comes to the door and out into the car park. She takes a deep breath and gazes up at the stars. 'I had eleven miscarriages and an ectopic, but at least I got one – my boy.' She looks at me and back up at the sky. 'Maybe I'll be famous after I die, like Emily Dickinson and Edgar Allan Poe.' She smiles and hugs me. 'Have a wonderful trip and keep safe.' I leave her, standing in the dark, gazing upwards.

35

Dr Jazz in Lebanon

On morning television more and more people are 'flipping' to tes-
tify to Robert Mueller against Donald Trump; 'flipping' seems to
mean giving evidence in return for leniency towards past criminal
activity. I don't expect Arra cares about this. And there is sad news
about John McCain, the popular Republican senator who stood for
the presidency against Barack Obama; he has decided to receive no
further treatment for his cancer.

Later I eat a croissant and a banana in the café of a giant supermarket called IGA. The television is tuned to Fox News, which is
reporting a brouhaha in Texas about 'taking a knee', the kneeling
by black players in the NFL during the national anthem in protest
against police brutality and racism. The Republican Senator Ted
Cruz is angry with the Democratic Congressman Beto O'Rourke
for supporting the protesters.

I move on and sit in Walmart's car park, waiting for torrential
rain to stop so that I can run in and stock up on almonds and apricots. Meanwhile, I'm transfixed by some guitar music on the radio:

acoustic, beautiful, intricate, rhythmic – sort of Spanish. Who is playing this? Pat Metheny? Martin Taylor? Santana? Yes, quite possibly Santana. The rain eases, but I go on sitting there as the music winds up and down and around and along and up again. And then the DJ says, 'Slash, "Obsession Confession".' Slash! I thought he was just a hellraiser.

I find what I want in the cathedral quiet of Walmart and then see, on a sign hanging over a long, broad aisle, the words Tire and Lube. Does this mean that Walmart can change Harpo's oil? It does. I run through the rain, jump into Harpo and drive into Walmart's garage. A small, friendly woman gets to work under the bonnet, and a man in the lube admin department wipes the rain off my glasses. The job takes thirty minutes, during which I buy a pair of Wrangler shorts, and costs $53; as well as fresh oil, Harpo has a new filter and his dash is reset to remove the officious message.

It rains as I head off towards St Louis. The road is two-lane, bumpy and flat – like the landscape, which is covered in maize. The sky is closed in, lined with moisture, dark grey – the air is warm. I pass through several small towns and, as the rain lifts, stop in Lebanon. In West St Louis Street, the road is red brick and late Victorian buildings sit close together, all different in colour, shape, roofs, cornices, balconies, doors, windows – all of them pleasing, looked after, appearing to be proud of themselves.

From across the street I see Dr Jazz Soda Fountain and Grille, a red-painted building with a first-floor balcony, white-painted, over-hanging the pavement, supported by four slim columns. A strange collection of stuff with a retro feel is displayed inside the bay windows either side of the door. To the left, among much more: a Colt revolver; a Scrabble board; a boiled egg in a stainless-steel egg cup; a mechanical cocktail shaker; an old television showing what looks like an episode of *The Phil Silvers Show* (aka *Sergeant Bilko*). To the right: a saxophone; an old milk bottle; an old, full Coke bottle with its lid on; an elegant red pushbike with a gearstick on the crossbar; a sign announcing 'God Bless America'.

I have to go into this place. Inside a waiter called Maia shows me to a booth. It's five o'clock; there are about eight other customers. Nat King Cole is singing 'Ramblin' Rose' and Maia brings me iced water and a menu. I ask about the name, Dr Jazz.

'Well, this building is a hundred and sixty years old and was originally a drugstore. So it's called "doctor" because of that. And' – she looks up at the ceiling – 'it's called "jazz" because the owner likes the music of the period between 1920 and 1970.' She smiles and retreats while I look at the menu. The booths and tables are dark wood, and there is plenty of mahogany behind the bar, but the bar itself and the stools in front of it are chrome and red formica and leatherette: classic diner.

I wouldn't have eaten anything at all right now if I hadn't walked in here but, when Maia returns, I find myself ordering chicken Caesar salad. I ask her about the diner counter and stools.

'Those date from 1932,' she says. 'And we have the oldest soda fountain in the US, from 1886. There,' – she points, I think, to a cleanly designed gunmetal tap – 'and those milkshake makers,' – she points to an enamelled green tower, about two feet high, from which hang glass and metal spouts – 'are from the nineteen-thirties and we still use them.'

'Wow!' I say, as Maia looks around.

'And that icemaker,' she says, 'with Coca-Cola on the side?'

I see it, and nod. 'Yep.' I'm fifteen feet away; it looks like a red plastic box.

'That's from 1952.'

'Wow! You know such a lot.'

'I should do. I've worked here for six years.'

She wanders away. There is a lot of stuff in a long cabinet behind glass at the back of the bar: old photos, old telephones, signage, packaging, ads, toys, a shiny saxophone – mostly from the first half of the twentieth century. There is an old telephone box – an indoor, American one – on the way to the toilets. The menu is packed with images, and includes an invitation to Dr Jazz's 'It's a Wonderful Life' show during November and December: 'Come home to George Bailey's' where 'the table is set with all the Baileys' favorite traditional

191

foods while the heart-warming show reminds us all that "No man is a failure who has friends".'

This place is a museum as well as a bar and restaurant. In a way, I love it. There's stuff here that is good to look at and that should be preserved somewhere. There is an air of reverence as well – as if the place is hallowed – a restaurant where the waiters and wait-resses, as well as being charming and nice-looking, are curators. I can't imagine relaxing here. I suddenly think of Mullins Pizza in McArthur, Ohio, where there was no stuff and a disabled man might shout.

36

Contentment in St Louis

Low in the sky, light pokes through the murk – and the moon is there, high up, behind thin cloud. Closer to St Louis, the cloud thickens and the sky lowers overhead, like thick smoke, while an intense light floods the horizon. Soon the cloud lifts. 50 speeds across East St Louis in sunlight – and I think of Miles Davis, who grew up here in a comfortable way; his father was a dentist. His former home has recently become a museum – but it's 6.30 p.m., too late for that.

Suddenly I see the famous arcing arch. A giant gleaming hairpin, more striking than its photographs, the Gateway Arch must be two or three miles away on the farther bank of the Mississippi. Soon I cross a bridge – nondescript but for some metal superstructure – glimpse an America's Best Value Inn, low to my right, and pull up at traffic lights in St Louis, Missouri.

My room at America's Best Value Inn is on the second floor and opens off a concrete walkway. From there I can see the Mississippi

300 yards away, beyond three car parks, through a thin forest of railings, lamp posts and telegraph poles. It is disappointing, the short stretch that I can see: straight, and narrow when compared with its ever-rolling grandeur down south at New Orleans; and the further bank is featureless, with East St Louis hidden behind trees. The scene improves when a long, dark barge floats into view – bringing with it a tiny hint of Huckleberry Finn.

The chatty young man on reception tells me that to find bars and restaurants I should go to an area called the Landing. 'That's short for Laclede's Landing. Some guy who landed there a while ago; I'm not sure about the history exactly.' He laughs, gets out a grey, photocopied map, turns it to face me and draws a rectangle on it. 'That's the Landing. Those blocks that go down to the river, there.' It isn't far. My snap decision to stop at this motel is looking like a good one. 'Just walk straight through Lumiere Place, which is right here.' He points to the map and then waves his arm behind him. 'It's just along, outside here, left and then right.' He draws on the map, so I can't go wrong.

Outside it's growing dark, but the air is still warm. I walk through the Lumiere District, which seems to comprise several car parks and three swanky new hotels – one with matching casino. Large, shiny cars wait by the curb and chauffeurs hobnob with doormen wearing bulky suits. I cross a road and the atmosphere changes to narrow streets, old buildings, bars and restaurants with tables outdoors, and real people – young and old, black and white. I hear loud music, cheering and clapping and walk under a railway bridge towards it. I come out in a park, at the base of a grassy slope where several hundred people sit watching a band on a stage set up against an old stone wall beneath the arches of Laclede's Landing Metro station. The audience are in near darkness; the stage, the wall and the arches are lit. People sit in groups, many on their own folding chairs, children race around, and food and drink is sold under canvas gazebos. A large black man is singing the blues and playing guitar, backed by bass and drums.

I get talking to a man who has a small child asleep on his

shoulder. He tells me, in a loud whisper, that the singer is called Kingfish. 'He's only nineteen, but he's been performing for a while, comes from Clarksdale, Mississippi.'

'Reminds me of B. B. King,' I say.

'Well . . . you're smart!' He raises his eyebrows. 'He was taken up by B. B. King's drummer. He's played with him, Tony Coleman.'

'Oh! Well, there you go.' I smile, and stand in the dark basking in the satisfaction of being called smart by a man who clearly knows about the blues, which I don't.

I watch and listen for about twenty minutes. Kingfish, whose real name, I learn, is Christone Ingram, is a brilliant guitarist and a good singer – but it's 8.30 p.m. and I'm hungry.

I walk back the way I came, along 2nd Street, and go into a bar called the Lou. It's a busy sports bar with lots of neon and music that is loud, bland and heavy on bass. I think about leaving to get away from the noise, but end up sitting at the bar with a beer. The man next to me drinks and looks at his phone. On a screen above the bar, the Boston Red Sox are losing to the Tampa Bay Rays 10–3. I eat a salami and cheese salad and watch the baseball – and wonder why I didn't buy a burger in the park and keep listening to the great Kingfish.

Then I hear a woman's voice, pure and hurting, singing a blues number. The thumping racket has stopped. The voice is accompanied by a guitar – and a pedal steel or a slide guitar. This is fabulous music; someone in the bar has changed playlists and turned the volume down. The same voice begins a new song – more upbeat. Maybe they have put on a CD – a jazz trio: vocals, guitar and pedal steel. I can speak to the bartender now without shouting, so I tell her I love this music and does she know what it is.

'It's that duo who are playing outside. We're piping them in.'

'It's live?'

'Yeah.'

'Just outside here?' I point over my shoulder with my thumb. 'Can I take my beer out and listen?'

'Sure.'

'Are they busking?'

'Not really. We pay them to be there, Fridays.'

I pick up my beer and go out. There are tables and chairs on the pavement. Two musicians, a black woman and a white man, are sitting with their backs to the window of the bar. She is singing and playing an electric guitar; he is sitting to her right and playing slide guitar, with a dobro on his lap and a steel slide on his finger.

I sit a little way away. The woman's eyes are closed. She sings in a strong, bluesy voice with her mouth against the microphone. As the song ends, the man looks up and smiles; he has brown hair streaked with grey, tied back in a ponytail. The woman glances at me, expressionless; her hair is pushed back behind her ears and falls in corkscrew curls. He adjusts the tuning of his guitar; she counts, 'One, two, three, four.' And they start a new song. Her voice moves from plaintive to pained to angry; he plays a complex lead, and she plays a percussive rhythm, hitting the strings from the bottom upwards.

Two women sit at a table close to mine. They talk quietly and seem to be listening as well. Otherwise, it's just me with these musicians; I feel privileged. A balmy evening with a little breeze, but still warm. I sip my beer and look around and up at the sky, and feel unusually content. This is a lot better than watching the Red Sox.

The woman is singing, eyes closed, hands caressing the guitar; and the man leans over his dobro, picking with the fingers of his right hand, shifting the steel slide with his left. People stroll by and stop. Some put dollar bills or coins in a bucket that's sitting on a table; some go on into the bar. Most of the time the audience is us three – and all the people in the bar. Sometimes, when a song ends, they go straight into the next one; sometimes the man announces the next one and I feel as if he is talking just to me. He doesn't sing. On the guitars they share the lead and the rhythm, swapping, it seems, when they feel like it. She has a lovely oval face, which is usually still with concentration; occasionally she smiles at him and us, the audience, or shrugs.

He plays a Hawaiian tune, twangy and intricate, on the slide guitar; and she strums an emphatic rhythm. After a while, he puts down the dobro and picks up a conventional guitar, a Les Paul, and she announces a Jimmy Reed tune, 'Honest I Do'. She sings it with great passion, and hearts break when she pleads with her man to tell her he loves her.

When that ends, he says that they are taking a break. But they just sit on their chairs and pick up bottles of water.

We start talking and – after we get me and what I'm doing here out of the way – they, mainly he, tell me a lot. They're married; he's fifty-five, she's fifty-eight, and they've been playing together since he was fourteen. She's called Sharon and he's called Doug. They're grandparents and both of them say, with big smiles, how great that is. She's a full-time musician and plays bass in other bands and on recordings but, when they play together, which they do often, she plays guitar. He wishes he was a full-time musician, but has to earn extra cash working as a furniture restorer and French polisher.

I ask if I can buy them a drink, and fetch them both a beer and one for myself. As Sharon starts a new song, Doug drops a finger pick in his beer, which splashes into Sharon's face. They both laugh and she starts again; then she stops and says to me and the two women, 'By the way, this song is my own composition.'

When they pause again, I go in and through the bar to the restroom. In the bar there is thumping music – apparently live – with a woman shrieking like a screech owl into a microphone in a way that seems unrelated to the backing music.

Outside, I tell Sharon and Doug about this awful music and that there's a woman who can't sing. 'If they want live music, they should have you in there,' I say.

'No, no.' Doug smiles 'That's karaoke.' They both laugh.

They play till about ten-thirty. Sharon goes into the bar and Doug solos for a while on his Les Paul. Then he starts to pack up guitars, speakers, microphones. Almost on a whim, I say, 'How do you feel about Donald Trump?'

'I *hate* him,' he bellows. 'He's an embarrassment. I wish he'd never been elected.'

197

'I thought you might say something like that,' I say.

He laughs. 'Too right!'

I put $10 in the bucket.

'Hey! That's kind. Thanks.'

Sharon comes back and I say again that I love their music.

'We're on tomorrow at the Blues Museum if you want to come by: eleven a.m., 6th and Washington.' She's putting her guitar in its case. 'But I know you've gotta get on to San Francisco.' She gives a thin smile and shrugs.

'No. I'll come. I'm going to stay here another night.'

I leave them and walk back into the park, past litter-pickers clearing up after the Kingfish gig. From the top of the slope I can see the Gateway Arch above a stand of young trees, shining beneath a silvery moon. I walk towards it and watch as the light moves along the arc of steel as I get closer. Then I see that, by looking at the thin band of the arch in a different way, I can make it seem as if the light is on the underside of the band and not on its top, and at the same time, shift my perception as to which end of the arc is nearest to me and which is furthest away. The longer I stare at the arch, the harder I find it to decide which end is nearer to me, and which side is the top and which side is underneath. I walk a little closer, but the confusion remains. I am confronted by a visual riddle, similar to those found in the 'impossible art' of M. C. Escher. I think about walking closer until I get close enough to see the legs of the arch on the ground; then I would know which end is nearer to me. But, although it is still warm at 11.30 pm, it is late and dark among the trees. And what will I learn? Only something I know already: that one or other of the arch's feet is nearer to me. Does it matter?

I turn away, walk down the hill, under the railway bridge and back into 2nd Street. I remember last night: Arra shouting, 'I *love* Trump.' And a few minutes ago: Doug bellowing, 'I *hate* him.'

Back in my room, I scroll through the TV channels and am surprised and thrilled to see the English singer-songwriter Nick Lowe sitting in a chair in front of an audience talking to an American, who turns out to be Jim Nelson, editor of GQ magazine. Soon Nelson asks about Lowe's song '(What's So Funny 'Bout) Peace, Love and Understanding?', and Lowe tells him how the idea came to him in the early 1970s, after the hippie dream had come to an end.

A guitar sits on a stand between Lowe and Nelson. Lowe picks it up, strums a catchy rhythm, and sings the song with great feeling. The audience clap loudly. It seems as relevant now as it ever was.

37

Gateway to the West

I walk in the thick shade of a concrete underpass, and out into hot sun. It's Saturday morning, and there aren't many people around. Nowadays the old downtowns of big cities are empty, especially at weekends when office workers stay in their homes in suburbs and satellite towns.

But it feels good to be in St Louis, the famous outpost on the Mississippi, close to its meeting with the Missouri. In my mind, I am halfway across America. Though I am a little less in terms of miles, this is where the west begins – and the east, with its industry, government and high-flying academia, ends. Here was the frontier until long after Lewis and Clark floated back here after crossing the continent in 1806. In many ways, it's still the frontier. From here, on the west bank of the Mississippi, the big country stretches out. A glance at the map in my road atlas shows, in the east, a dense tangle of roads connecting thousands of cities and towns, while to the west just a few roads run, for the most part, horizontally across the map, east to west. Between here and the Rockies in Colorado are the flat lands of Missouri and Kansas, 900 miles of crops and cattle. I've driven the dense and urban east. Now I look forward to the emptiness of the west where, perhaps, I will move more quickly.

At the National Blues Museum, Sharon and Doug are setting up on a stage in a large room. They won't be performing till noon – nor will anyone else; it's just them today. Doug suggests I look at the museum itself. 'It's pretty interesting.'

It is – and it's big enough but not too big. It gives the story of the blues in words, photographs and artefacts – mainly sheet music, records and musical instruments – beginning with the 'work songs and field hollers' in the cotton fields of the nineteenth century and carrying on through to the strange phenomenon of white musicians in the UK – the Rolling Stones, the Yardbirds, the Animals – playing blues in the 1960s and bringing it back to America with the 'British invasion'. In between came gospel; ragtime from the state of Missouri – and St Louis in particular; the first professional blues artists like W. C. Handy, Bessie Smith and 'Blind Lemon' Jefferson; and jazz, which grew out of the blues in New Orleans and migrated during World War I, when the Storyville district of that city was closed, up the Mississippi via St Louis, to Chicago, where jazzmen such as King Oliver, Louis Armstrong, Sidney Bechet and Jelly Roll Morton took hold.

'Without a major recording industry,' a caption tells me, 'St Louis became a live music town.' Since the early days, 'its central location, next to the Mississippi River and alongside the north-south railroad lines, made it a landing place for musicians coming up from the south and those headed east or west'.

I can't resist the opportunity to stand on a stage, behind an old-fashioned steel microphone, in front of a life-size black-and-white photograph, taken in 1920, of Mamie Smith and her Jazz Hounds; the latter comprise a lively quintet of trumpet, trombone, clarinet, fiddle and piano. Another visitor kindly takes my photograph.

The Sharon and Doug gig is an exclusive event for members of the museum only. Doug makes sure I am an honorary member for

201

the day, which means I get a badge to pin on my shirt and a free lunch – barbecued chicken, rice, broccoli, carrots, crisps, a tangerine and a bottle of water – to eat while watching and listening. We, the audience, sit at round tables. Some black children dance, and their mother joins them. Sharon and Doug, who are known as the Fab Foehners – Foehner being their surname – sit side by side, as last night, shrouded in blue light. Doug does the talking – and even mentions 'David Reynolds, a fan from London, England'; everyone turns round and stares, and a small girl comes right up to me for a closer look. I'm sitting at the back so I can see everything, even a man at a mixing desk at the very back who works hard throughout. They play wonderful music, blues with real feeling, for a long time. Perhaps because the audience is larger and more attentive than last night, Sharon talks and smiles more. They end with last night's showstopper, 'Honest I Do'.

But that's not the end. We in the audience demand an encore and we get 'Death Letter Blues'. And then we get another: Lightnin' Hopkins's 'She's Mine'.

And that's it. We hug in the foyer, and I plead with them to come to London sometime.

It's 2 p.m. and burning hot. I walk towards the Gateway Arch. I want to see it in daylight. Last night it was lit up – and I couldn't decide which side was up and which was down. Now, I decide that the lit side must have been facing down, since lights can shine on it only from below. Why didn't I think of that yesterday?

But ... there was a bright moon last night. It would have been shining from above – obviously. Maybe there weren't any lights on the ground. If there had been, both sides would have been lit. Wouldn't they?

I walk through the Gateway National Park towards the arch and come to an illustrated information board that tells the story of Elijah Lovejoy whose 'print shop once stood here in Locust Street'. In the early 1830s Lovejoy printed and edited the *St Louis Observer*, an anti-slavery newspaper, and therefore irritated many people in what was then a slave state. In 1835, he wrote a fierce editorial attacking a mob that had carried out a lynching. The mob broke into his shop and destroyed his printing press. For safety, he moved with his wife, Celia Ann, and son, Edward, across the Mississippi to Alton in Illinois, a free state, where he set up another press and another abolitionist newspaper – and where Celia Ann bore their second child. Alton was a haven for escaped slaves, yet many of the inhabitants were pro-slavery and resented abolitionists who protected escaped slaves. In 1837 a mob attacked the warehouse where Lovejoy kept his printing press. Lovejoy was shot five times and died trying to defend himself and his press.

John Quincy Adams, the sixth president of the United States, said that Lovejoy's murder produced 'a shock as of an earthquake throughout this country'. When John Brown – he of the song 'John Brown's body', which Union soldiers would sing twenty-five years later as they marched into battle during the Civil War – heard of Lovejoy's martyrdom, he said: 'Here, before God, in the presence of these witnesses, from this time, I consecrate my life to the abolition of slavery.'

And what about the two children and the young wife? Well – a descendant of Elijah, Martha Lovejoy, works at the US State Department's Office to Monitor and Combat Trafficking in Persons. It's salutary, in the middle of a bland park, to find a reminder of how things were less than 200 years ago – and to think of how they are even now.

In a corner of the board that tells Elijah Lovejoy's story is a map of the park with a 'You Are Here' arrow; it shows paths and lakes, the arch itself, the Mississippi, and the interstate highway which, until it was covered over with grass and a curving path in 2014, separated the park from downtown St Louis. It also shows the grid of old streets and buildings that were razed in the early 1940s to make way for the park and a monument, which turned out to be the arch, though its design was delayed until after World War II.

From the top of a grassy bank, I look down at the Mississippi. Grey water, an old truss bridge away to the south, a helipad on a tethered barge connected to the shore by gangplanks, a few cars parked nearby. Further on, in the lee of the arch, broad steps lead down to the embankment, where a line of horses and carts wait to take tourists for a trot, and an old-style riverboat, with funnels and balconies, is moored to a pontoon on which sits a smart white-painted pavilion offering riverboat cruises.

Another information board is headed Miles of Steamboats and shows a sepia-tinted photograph of this same riverbank with perhaps thirty riverboats – like the one that now hosts cruises – crammed together at a quayside packed with barrows, horse-drawn carts and men unloading them. A caption says: 'Steamboats waiting to load and unload their cargo lined up for miles along the Mississippi River. Field calls of dockworkers filled the air. You might have heard whisperings about the Underground Railroad.'

I watch as a white-painted boat – a kind of modern-day tugboat – pushes ten long barges, arranged in pairs, slowly upstream. The tug is leaving a churning, frothy wake.

I think about the old streets that were knocked down in the 1940s; they were said to have been a slum by then. Had they been preserved, they would now, perhaps, form a cool neighbourhood of bars and apartments – like the streets of Laclede's Landing: a place for students, artists, and perhaps some affluent techie folk, attracted by a mix of heritage and a view of the Mississippi. Instead of that there is now this monument to which I am now getting close: the world's tallest arch, the tallest manmade monument in the western hemisphere, and Missouri's tallest accessible building. Yes, you can go up to the top. Will I do that? I'll wait and see – but I'm not keen on heights.

Why was it built? Because the locals and the nation, represented by the US government, wanted a monument to the westward expansion of the United States and to all those who made that happen: from Thomas Jefferson, who in 1803 made the deal with Napoleon known as the Louisiana Purchase, whereby the US gained a vast tract of land west of the Mississippi and doubled its size, to the unsung pioneers who set off on the Oregon Trail. And why was it built here? Because the founders of St Louis, French fur trapper Pierre Laclede and his stepson Auguste Chouteau, landed here, on this riverbank, in 1764.

I'm underneath it now, and can see that, as well as its astonishing height – which I could see when I was way off, over there, across the river – its legs, or feet, are much further apart than I expected. And I can see it's triangular in section, with one side facing up towards the sky, and two sides facing at an angle towards the ground – though they face the ground far away, perhaps as far away as the invisible horizons on either side of the arch. The sides of the triangle gleam where the light of the sun falls on them, and are a flat grey where they are in shade. Its triangular shape explains the arch's ambiguous appearance – the optical confusion it creates – from a distance, in daylight and at night.

It is a tremendous spectacle, many times more tremendous than the restored streets that might otherwise be standing here. The world has plenty of heritage buildings and old downtowns – but there is nothing else like this.

38

Poet With the Kirbys

Underneath the arch, right underneath, under the ground, is a visitor centre. Broad steps lead down from the west side of the arch. Inside, I gawp at the queues for the trams that travel up inside the arch to take punters to the top. I walk away and square up to the Museum of Westward Expansion. Can I cope with another museum – the second of the day? And it's a big one. I can see that it's packed with stuffed animals, carts and wagons, life-size cowboys and Indians, teepees, bronze statues, paintings, photographs, charts, tabletop models, information panels – and hundreds of people, children and babies milling around. And it's strong on design and lighting, much of it dim.

I tiptoe in, as into a cold ocean, and soon wonder whether to jump in or back out. There must be some logic, but I can't uncover it. It's like shopping for clothes in a department store: trousers are mixed in with shirts, sweaters and coats; jeans are piled on shelves at one end of the store, and other, subtly different jeans are piled up at the other end, thirty yards away. It would be good if these modern museums were to put arrows somewhere, suggesting a route. Of course, I and many people, including children, would then ignore them, but at least we'd have a direction from which to deviate.

But I grouse too much. I am learning a lot. The local Indians were the Osage; they lived in villages, in oval-frame houses covered with hide, went in for farming as well as hunting, and were very tall – most Osage men were between six and seven feet. Before them, 800 years ago, mound-building Indians established this area – where the two mighty rivers meet – as a major trading centre. In the nineteenth century the city became sophisticated and cosmopolitan, attracting immigrants from Europe as well as from all over the American continent, and even voluntarily from Africa.

There is much here about Thomas Jefferson – in particular that he got the bug for westward expansion from his father, Peter Jefferson, who was a co-founder of the Loyal Land Company, one of whose aims was to find a way overland to the Pacific.

I learn from a photo caption that the revered – by military tacticians – General William Sherman, a Civil War general on the Union side, who later became commanding general of the army, based himself in St Louis during the 1870s so as to direct US military strategy against western Indian tribes. On occasion Sherman was merciless, allowing his men to slaughter women and children alongside adult warriors – and he was feared and respected by the Indians, who called him 'Great Warrior Sherman'. It is ironic, then, that Sherman's full name, revealed here in small print crediting the photographer who took his portrait, was William Tecumseh Sherman. According to Sherman himself, his father, who was a lawyer from a prominent family, 'caught a fancy for the great chief of the Shawnees'.

There are salutary statistics on display. Estimates suggest that before the arrival of Europeans in 1492 there were between 9 and 12 million Indians; in 1890 there were 248,000 – the numbers decimated by European diseases, whisky, starvation after being removed from their homelands, and war. Between Independence in 1776 and 1847, 559,219,894 acres of land were 'seized' from the Indians by white men. Indians did attack wagon trains, but not as often as old Hollywood movies suggest; pioneers, or 'overlanders', often fired the first shot – perhaps out of nervousness. In the years between 1840 and 1860, 426 Indians were killed by overlanders, while 362 overlanders died at the hands of Indians.

Eventually I have had enough. On the way out, I negotiate tables piled with knick-knacks and buy some postcards of the arch. On the back of one of them, I read that the arch's height is the same is as its width, 630 feet, and that its triangular section, which narrows considerably from the ground upwards, has equal sides; in other words, the arch is a monumental equilateral triangle.

I peer out into the heat and daylight, and wander west towards the Old Courthouse. This is similar to, and smaller than, the Capitol in Washington DC: a central dome above columns and pediments. Once the tallest building in St Louis, it is now like a jewel in a bucket of concrete turds. I know that it is beautiful inside, with murals and columned galleries lining the dome, but it is a museum and I have had enough museums.

To my left, two blocks away, I can see Busch Stadium – a lump on the cityscape made of red brick. Commonly known as Busch III, it is home to the St Louis Cardinals National League Baseball Team. Like its two predecessors, Busch III is named to promote Budweiser beer, which was first brewed in St Louis in 1876 by Adolphus Busch – and is still brewed by Anheuser-Busch Brewing Association. The stadium is called Busch, rather than Budweiser or Bud, because stadiums cannot be named after alcoholic drinks. In his book *American Heartbeat*, the English writer Mick Brown describes the decision to build a sports stadium so close to the Old Courthouse as 'an act of planning similar to relocating Wembley Stadium beside Westminster Abbey'.

It's dark outside but still very warm. I go into an Irish pub called Tigin, and am greeted by an American bartender, Kirby, who is a fan of West Ham United and Bayern Munich – the latter because his German teacher at school showed videos of Bayern games with a German commentary to help the class learn. Kirby passed his German exams and became a fan. There is another bartender, a young woman who also seems to be called Kirby. Can that be right? Both Kirbys ask for my first name and call me by it. They do the same with a man named Darrell who has sat down further along the bar.

A screen is showing the St Louis Cardinals playing the Colorado Rockies. The score is 0–0. I order a beer called Poet, and shepherd's pie topped with colcannon. The Cardinals have a fielder called Tots.

The beer is dark, a little sweet and delightfully cold. But soon I feel cold. The air conditioning is turned up high, and I'm wearing only shorts and a T-shirt – as I have for days now. Darrell is wearing a sweatshirt, and a man sitting to my left is wearing a thick tweed jacket. I can see why, but he can't have walked through the streets wearing that, surely; it's at least ninety degrees outside. He must have come in a taxi and run across the pavement.

Female Kirby brings the shepherd's pie. The colcannon is delicious – there's spring onion in there – and I feel warmer. Male Kirby says that his favourite footballer of all time is Philipp Lahm, the full back who played for Bayern for fifteen years, and captained them and Germany. He fetches a drink for Darrell, comes back, leans on the bar and says he rates Antonio and Arnautović at West Ham, but doesn't think much of Felipe Anderson, who wasn't worth the £36 million that the Hammers paid for him. Then we talk about my team, Spurs – which seems weird in an Irish bar in St Louis where there's a choice of baseball or boxing on the screens. Kirby rates Harry Kane – who doesn't? – and the great defender Alderweireld.

Tweed Jacket and Kirby get into a sophisticated conversation about the Cardinals; neither is happy with the way they have been playing and they mention names that mean nothing to me. Lots of ads for cars come on during the baseball tonight; they run along the bottom of the screen during the dull bits, but never when a pitch is about to happen: Hyundai, Chevrolet Cruze, and 'Kia – driving to success'.

Kirby takes my empty plate and asks if I want dessert. 'We got Guinness ice cream.'

'Guinness ice cream!'

'Yep. It's real cool. Comes with a brownie.'

'OK. I'll try anything.' And I order a pint of Guinness to go with it.

Two women are boxing on one of the screens. Mikaela Mayer, who has boxed for the US in the Olympics, is fighting someone called Edina Kiss. Mayer hits Kiss hard on the chin and then on the cheek. Kiss falls on the floor near the ropes – and gets up. Mayer keeps punching Kiss in the face – and Kiss keeps moving backwards. It seems unfair; Mayer is much taller than Kiss and has a longer reach. The round ends. Kiss is from Hungary and has come all this way to fight Mayer in Arizona. The next round is the same: Mayer punching and Kiss backing off. I'm longing for Kiss to land a mighty uppercut on Mayer's chin. Why am I so aggressive? At least my aggression is in sympathy with the underdog. But Kiss lands very few punches; instead she takes them in the face and on her body.

The Guinness ice cream arrives with a cherry on top. It tastes like Irish coffee.

At the end of the third round – there might have been six – the referee stops the fight, and awards it to Mayer. Well, I'm relieved – and I suspect that Kiss is too. The baseball continues; the Rockies are leading 1–0. The Cardinals make it 1–1 in the eighth inning. I sip Guinness and decide to watch till the end. And the Rockies' batters go crazy; there are no home runs, but almost all of them are hitting and running and reaching base. By the end of their eighth inning, they are winning 9–1. Male Kirby and Tweed Jacket shake their heads, as the Cardinals achieve nothing in their last inning and the game ends.

I say goodbye to the Kirbys, go outside – and suddenly get warm. Bliss! It's too hot in the day. Now, a few minutes after 11 p.m., it's a little humid but the temperature is perfect.

I stroll over to Gateway Park. The moon is bright behind wisps of cloud; the air is damp and carries the scent of long grass and of a wild herb that I can't name. The arch rises above the trees, lit – I am sure now – from below, and not by the hazy moon.

39

Another Gift

CNN has the news that John McCain has died. Tributes are being paid. Among them, his friend former Senator Kelly Ayotte says she hopes 'his passing and the attention given to him will bring about an improvement in the way we do politics', a clear reference to the shortcomings of Donald Trump. McCain was the American equivalent of a British one-nation conservative, a reasonable man who was willing to work with political opponents to make his country and the world a better place – a type of politician that is becoming rare. I have one beef with him: his choosing the far less reasonable Sarah Palin as his running mate when he stood for the presidency against Barack Obama in 2008.

McCain planned his own funeral. He wants George W. Bush and Obama to speak, and decreed that Trump is not to be invited.

I walk to the Laclede's Landing Metro station to take a ride pretty much for fun. A train comes in and, as I am about to get on it, a worried-looking black man approaches holding what I take to be coins. Can I give him two dollar bills so he can buy a ticket? I hand him two dollars. He puts something in my hand, says 'Sorry,' and hurries away. I jump onto the train just before the doors close, and look at what is in my hand: the frame – or it might be called the chassis – of a large watch. No hands, no watch face, no clock-work – just a fake gold ring studded with fake diamonds. I'm a fool, of course – but I feel sorry for the panhandler; he was anxious, bedraggled and, almost certainly, poor.

The train goes underground. I'm sitting close behind the driver, who is calling out each stop as we get to it, and telling people which side to get out. This carriage seems almost new: steel poles; grey plastic seats, with bright red rails and soft pads for bottoms and backs. A notice reads 'Concealed weapons prohibited on these premises'. At the 8th and Pine stop, two middle-aged women wearing Cardinals shirts – white with two red cardinals sitting on a yellow twig across the front – get on; one has MOLINA 4 on the back, the other MARTINEZ 18. We come out into daylight, and the driver sounds a raucous hooter as we approach a level crossing. A couple get on. She feels a pair of seats with the back of her hand before gesturing to the man that he can sit down.

I look again at the wreck of a watch: a worthless ring with a pair of sprockets on each side, across each of which a spring-loaded lug was once fitted, enabling straps to be attached so that someone – the panhandler? – might wear it on their wrist. How did it become this dull remnant of a once shining and useful accessory? Perhaps it stopped ticking. Someone took it apart and meant to mend it – but never got as far as putting it together again. It's the second object that I've been given. The penny with a cross cut into it that a kind man gave me high up in the Alleghenies – to 'keep you safe' – is in my pocket, as it has been every day since then. Keeping it with me is becoming an obsession. But what shall I do with this 'gift' – for which I paid two dollars?

I look out of the window at low buildings and a swathe of blue sky. I've left the skyscrapers behind and am heading for Forest Park, a district in the west of the city where the 1904 World's Fair was held. I am hoping to dip quickly in and out of the Missouri History Museum, where the Jefferson Gallery is dedicated to the St Louis World's Fair, and to emerge with a postcard to send to a friend in London called Mike. Mike knows more than anyone about the first World's Fair, also known as the Great Exhibition, which was held in London's Hyde Park in 1851; he takes great interest in later World's Fairs but has never been here.

I get off the train into stifling heat – so hot it catches in my throat. I've only once felt hotter; that was twenty-five years ago in Delhi. I clamp my sun hat on, am glad of its wide, floppy brim, and plod a couple of hundred yards to the museum, an elegant, two-storey building with columns, a balustrade on its roof and a hint of art deco. It was built in 1913 with money earned from the huge success of the 1904 exhibition, which took four years to build and landscape, was open for seven months, spread over 1,200 acres, visited by almost 20 million people, cost \$15 million, and made \$600,000 in profit.

Once inside I scamper round the Jefferson Gallery, and stop in front of a series of contemporary paintings of the fair by John Ross Key – detailed outdoor vistas painted in oils. Key depicts a fantasy fairyland, a Shangri-La of palaces, castles, lakes, fountains, waterfalls, gardens, monuments and statues, peopled by women in long dresses, carrying parasols, and men in straw boaters. Inside these dreamlike buildings was the produce of fifty-three countries, and of forty-three of the then forty-five US states – as well as live exhibits that included pygmies from Africa; the Igorot tribe from the Philippines, complete with elephants; Tlingit people from Alaska; twenty American Indian tribes; and the formidable Apache chief Geronimo, then aged eighty, who was permitted to sell his autograph and handmade bows and arrows. Twice a day the second Boer War was re-enacted by 600 soldiers: British, Boer and native South African tribesmen. Visitors included President Theodore Roosevelt, Thomas Edison, Helen Keller, Scott Joplin, the fifteen-year-old T. S. Eliot, who was born and raised in St Louis, and Jack Daniel, who submitted his Tennessee whiskey to the World's Fair whiskey competition and won the gold medal for the finest whiskey in the

214

world. Some visitors from around the world and from elsewhere in the US stayed for a month, while many locals came every day.

At the rear entrance to the building a museum guide tells me that only two of the 1,500 exhibition buildings remain. 'They were designed to be removed. Most were taken somewhere else or scrapped straight away.' One of the surviving buildings is now the St Louis Art Museum. 'It's over there, past the golf course,' he points. 'I wouldn't walk there. Not today. The effective heat – how hot it feels because of the humidity – is a hundred and seven degrees.'

In the museum shop, the man behind the till is friendly – he wants to know where I'm from, where I'm going, and why – and helpful. 'You know the first forty miles west from St Louis on Route 50 is a freeway – or expressway ... parkway, beltway.' He raises his hands in the air and laughs. 'They call it all kinds of things, and I don't know which is right.'

'I'm glad you don't know,' I say. 'I don't have a clue.'

'It's got lanes, you know what I mean? They drive fast – so you might not see much. You have to look straight ahead and watch for trucks.'

'Even on a Sunday?'

'Yep. I reckon. They'll be there.'

I thank him, and leave the museum with a paper bag full of postcards. I was there for less than an hour.

40

Small Matters

The man at the till was right. There are plenty of trucks belting along. I sit behind one for a while and grow bored with seeing nothing but a pair of dirty white doors. I pull out to overtake and soon find I am driving at 80 mph, passing long lines of trucks and cars. My speed must be illegal, so I slow to 70, and then 65 – but soon a truck looms up in the rear-view mirror like an ocean liner, so I step on the gas again.

The man at the till was wrong about one thing: 50 hasn't become an expressway or a beltway or anything like that. It's now much more exalted: it's Interstate 44 and I'm stuck on it for about forty minutes.

I come off onto a blissful two-lane road and look up at blue sky with clouds like floating tigers. I dawdle along an undulating, softly curving road lined with trees through which I can see fields. It is seventy-six miles to Jefferson City, the capital of Missouri, where I hope to spend the night. There is no hurry: it's only 4 p.m. I pass signs to wineries – sweet grapes and sweet wine, perhaps, under this huge, sunny sky.

In a small town called Beaufort, an armadillo lies with its feet in the air beside the road – dead, not sunbathing, I fear. And so 50 winds on through pleasant countryside, past small matters – 'Puppies. Maltese Morkies. For Sale' – until it becomes four lanes and slides into Jefferson City.

I turn into downtown, park and walk. It's almost 6 p.m. The place is quiet, sedate, leafy with a nineteenth-century feel. There are few people or cars or bars – and no hotels that I can see. I look through railings at the governor's mansion, and uphill through his beautiful, sunlit garden, past his twee fountain, to the domed Capitol, another small replica of the Capitol in Washington. At the bottom of the hill, to the north, are railroad tracks, and a line of trees through which I glimpse grey-blue water: the Missouri.

I return to the bustle of 50 and check into the Baymont Inn. From there I drive half a mile west, and find what I have now come to expect on the edge of a city: a strip lined with gas stations, fast-food joints, supermarkets and DIY stores. I go into Applebee's Neighbourhood Grill and Bar; it feels like one of a chain (later I learn that there are 1,830 Applebee'ses). Something that might be 1990s soul music plays as I enjoy cedar salmon with maple mustard glaze, while chatting intermittently and amiably to a waiter called Marc. Two screens face me. One is showing an episode of *Family Guy* with subtitles, which means that I can follow the dialogue despite the loud music. It's very funny – but I'm distracted by the other screen, on which a violent psychopath is punching the life out of another man while pretending that they are wrestling. Across the bar, a man who looks like Bruce Springsteen, who must be watching the same antics on a screen above my head, thinks it's funny and ascribes the aggression to the attacker's red hair, of which there is hardly any: a couple of toothbrushes at most.

A woman comes up to the bar. She is looking at her phone. A waitress calls from across the bar, a distance of eight feet, 'How ya doin'?'

She gets absolutely no response.

The waitress looks at Marc and shrugs. Then at me, shrugs again and purses her lips.

For dessert, Marc persuades me to order a brownie bite: '350 calories' the menu says. Am I crazy?

It's tasty and as I eat it, everyone gawps at a screen at the end of the bar. A man has won $900,000 playing poker. And it seems that he is being given it in cash.

The showers in motels are usually over a small, low bath. The knobs, buttons and taps that operate them are different in every motel. I have to study them and try them out while wearing my glasses. This morning my glasses get splashed with cold shower water. I take them off. Where to put them? I usually put them on the lavatory cistern, which is often, as in this instance, next to the bath. I get into the shower, start it up and remember that I have forgotten to bring the shampoo, which is on the other side of the room, beside the basin. I climb out of the shower, cross the room and find three little bottles. To distinguish one from another, I have to put my glasses on. Conditioner? No. Body lotion? No. Shampoo? Hurray! I get back under the shower, turn it on and remember that I have forgotten to take my glasses off. They get a thorough splashing. I take them off. Where to put them . . .?

I pick up a copy of the *Jefferson City News Tribune* and a map in the motel foyer, head back into downtown and find Lewis and Clark Trailhead Plaza, a small park that slopes down towards the railroad and the Missouri. On 4 June 1804, three boats containing Lewis and Clark's Corps of Discovery passed this place on their way upstream. Clark's diary and writing by other members of the Corps suggest that they stayed in this region for at least two days. I try to imagine them in their three boats on this wild stretch of river, looking out for Osage Indians and stopping to hunt for deer, before this city was even a hamlet.

At the top of the slope bronze sculptures of five members of the expedition stand on a semblance of a rocky bluff overlooking

218

a small pond containing a row of spurting fountains. The bronzes show: Lewis; Clark; Clark's slave, York; George Drouillard, the expedition's chief hunter and tracker; and Seaman, Lewis's Newfoundland dog. I don't like to carp – especially when a lot of effort has gone into something – but this commemorative assembly is somehow unsatisfactory; it lacks the vigour or oomph that these men, who achieved so much, deserve. Or, to put it another way: the men and the dog are too small, and the fountains are too big.

I walk downhill to the railroad and peer at stationary goods trucks from behind a wooden fence. I hear the clatter of a train and hold my phone still to film a red and yellow engine and a long line of well-used trucks – none of which matches another – roll slowly past.

Back from the railroad, behind a – mercifully – closed museum, I sit on a bench in the shade of an old oak, eat a breakfast of blueberries and read the *Jefferson City News Tribune*.

An article on page three is headed 'How to Survive a School Shooting 101'. The piece is syndicated from Omaha, Nebraska, and reports that in that city, children aged from ten upwards are being offered lessons in responding to an armed attack at their school. The writer attended the introductory course (in the US, '101' means 'introduction') where children and teachers learned 'how to block a classroom door with desks and chairs, how to wrestle a gun out of the hands of an intruder and how to tie a tourniquet tight enough to stop the flow of blood'.

The piece goes on to say that the 'core message ... is ... you don't have to cower in a corner as bullets ricochet around you. You can run, you can hide or you can fight back is a message that's appealing to a segment of parents, teachers and kids who feel some school responses are too passive.' The writer takes a balanced view. There were eight kids and six adults at the course she attended, so the idea is perhaps not popular, although the cost of the course, $65, might be a deterrent. And she quotes a director of student services who wrote in a letter to parents,

'While practice is important, we also recognize that there is a fine line between preparing children and raising their anxiety to levels that interfere with learning.'

I swallow a spoonful of blueberries and think of my grandchildren.

41

Chief High Bow Thunderburk

There's a view on the long hill down from Jefferson City. I stop the car and stare: hills, woods, golden fields, green pasture and black cattle that look like slow-moving ants. My road is out there – bits of it, like ribbons scattered in the distance. Without the road, this might be paradise, and I wonder whether Indians delighted in it, or whether for them this was just the way things were.

I drive on. Little cliffs appear either side of the road, blasted to make it level.

Black calves browse in a field dotted with trees and, after a town called California, the road narrows to two lanes. Space seems to grow beneath the wide-open sky, and the landscape begins to feel western with fields of maize, mooching cattle and clumps of rusting pick-ups in grassy front yards. A junk shop is surrounded by acres of rubbish. West of a small town called Syracuse, on the wall of a low, white-painted warehouse, I glimpse a sign that says 'The Indian Store'. I drive on, find somewhere to turn, and go back.

As I get out of the car, a small woman comes out of the store and suggests I park further from the road. 'They come round that kerb pretty fast.' She points to a bend.

The store is long and narrow and, at a quick glance, packed with stuff: feathers, bones, knives, clothes, rugs, toys, beads, jewellery, arrowheads. These are everywhere, on tables, shelves, hanging on the walls.

The small woman is wearing a green cardigan and is perhaps in her sixties. 'You have a look round,' she says. 'Take your time. You live round here – close?'

'No, no. I'm from England.'

'From England. I've got a daughter–in–law from England.'

Her son, she tells me, lives in Seattle. He met an English woman, who works in an English airport, online. She was able to get cheap flights and visited him for two years. Then they got married and she came to live in Seattle. Both had been married before, and both had children.

I feel tentative about asking, 'Are you Indian at all?' though it seems a reasonable question in an Indian store.

'No, but my husband was. He was Choctaw Indian. He passed away last year.'

I say I'm sorry. And I discover that her name is Arlene, and that, astonishingly, she is eighty-five years old. 'We started the store here sixteen years ago, and around that time he discovered that his great-great-grandfather was a full-blood Choctaw chief. He met his wife on a wagon train, and they wanted to get married, but they wouldn't let him because he didn't have a last name. He was just Chief High Bow. The Indians didn't have last names. But anyhow, he took her last name in order to get married. So he's listed as Chief High Bow Thunderburk.'

'Thunderburk?'

'Thunderburk.'

'Was that her name?'

'Yes. That was her maiden name.'

'Interesting name,' I say.

'Sounds kinda English doesn't it? Does it?'

'Could be. Well . . . I don't know.'

'German?'

'German. More likely.'

We discuss where the Choctaw are from. Arlene says Oklahoma, after they were sent on the Trail of Tears from Georgia by President Andrew Jackson. 'I read about that,' she says. 'The soldiers went in there with wagons in the dead of night in wintertime, and got those Indians, and put them on those wagons, and made a lot of them walk. And some of them didn't even have shoes or a coat or nothin'. And a lot of them froze to death on that trail.' She is looking at me and shaking her head.

'Including children and pregnant women.' I say. And we both curse Andrew Jackson once more.

Arlene shows me a knife made from the jawbone of a black bear – a fearsome-looking thing, not something I want to take on a plane back to England. 'And this knife,' she picks up another large implement, 'is made from the leg bone of a white-tail deer.' And then another. 'This is from an elk. They are made by a Chippewa Indian called Turtle Man. He lives in Minnesota.'

'I've got a bronze thing up there,' she says, 'from the Trail of Tears.' She points high up on the wall. 'See it? The horse, and the Indian with his spear and his head drooped over.'

'Yes. So sad.' The image, stamped into bronze, is familiar – it looks similar to the sculpture *End of the Trail* by James Earle Fraser, which has been much copied.

We talk about Andrew Jackson and his Indian Removal Bill. Arlene agrees that it is a travesty that the plan to have him replaced on the $20 bill by Harriet Tubman has been shelved by Donald Trump.

I wander around the shop, up and down, picking things up, putting them down, gawping. I see things my grandchildren might like, and earrings perhaps for my wife. Do I want to carry stuff all the way to San Francisco?

I guess it can just sit in the boot of the car for three weeks.

I speak to Arlene again and she says she is part Indian, after all.

'But I don't know what part. I'm originally a Scot, but my daddy was part Indian, but I didn't know what part. He didn't have the facial hair and the high cheekbones. He told us we were part Irish, part Dutch, and part Indian.'

Then she tells me that, when Indians were going to be sent to reservations, many dressed to look like white people. 'A woman came in here. She must have been about forty years old. And she said, "I just found out that I'm Indian. My grandmama told me we was Indians." And she asked her, "Grandma, why didn't you tell us we's Indians?" And Grandma said, "Honey, if I'd a told you, we'd a starved to death."'

'On a reservation,' Arlene explains. 'And they changed their name. They took a last name, like Smith, Jones, Grant. They took a name and just passed it off. You know, and just acted like whites do. A woman at the Mormon church here, where they do genealogy, told me a lot of Indians did that in order to keep their land.'

A young couple come into the shop. The man has been here before, and knows Arlene; it seems as if he has brought a new girl-friend here on a date. I disappear, and gaze at a shelf of handmade wooden toys. I've been round the shop twice already and am still finding new things. I choose a clever arrangement where four chickens are attached to a wooden disc with a handle like a ping-pong bat. When I shake this thing the hens bend over and peck at the ground. I tell Arlene that I want to buy it for my grandson. She is keeping a small pile of stuff for me by the till: earrings, a bamboo pipe, a small mechanical chicken and the chickens on a ping-pong bat.

She says, 'You have grandkids, and then you have great-grandkids.'

'I hope I live that long.'

'I got great-great-granddaughters,' she says.

'Great-*great*-granddaughters,' I say.

'Yeah. My great-granddaughter has had twin girls.'

We talk about Indian names, a woman called Wendy whose Indian name is Windy because she was born on a windy day. 'Because the first thing they see is what they name their baby.' She knows a boy called Running Fox and a woman who works in a café in Syracuse who is called Blue Skies.

I pay with a $20 bill, which brings about another mention of Andrew Jackson. 'Terrible man he was,' I say, looking down at his overcoiffed, shaggy-eyebrowed face. 'What do you think about Trump?'

'He's a accident waiting for a place to happen. I don't know about the guy. Everybody's been saying we need a businessman in there instead of a politician. Well, he's neither. I don't know how many times he went bankrupt.' She rolls her eyes and hands me four dollar bills.

I shrug as I take them.

And Arlene goes on: 'He's got property all over everywhere. He's doing things no president ever did. You didn't ever see presidents texting at night.'

'That's really odd,' I say.

'And he's so critical about everybody. Anybody that don't like him. Then, boy he just—'

'Like John McCain. He was very rude about him, wasn't he.'

'Yes. Like, when he was dying, he didn't say nothing.'

'Do you think the people who voted for Trump – some of them – have changed their minds?'

'A lot of them are.' She nods with eyes wide open. 'There's a lot of them going to the Democrats.'

'Can I ask?' I think I know the answer. 'Did you vote for Trump?'

'No. No, no, no, no. Uh uh.' She waves a finger sideways, backwards and forwards.

'Did you vote for Clinton?'

'I did. I felt I needed to vote for somebody. And I didn't really want Clinton in there, but I didn't really want Trump in there—'

Arlene talks about Medicare and Medicaid, and how Trump has made a mess of it. 'It started out that everybody could afford the insurance. But it ended up that the premiums went up. And they were paying thirty-five dollars for a doctor; now it costs them a hundred and ten dollars to go to a doctor.'

225

'He's messed it up in just two years?' I'm leaning against a table covered in drums and tambourines.

Arlene has sat down on a stool. 'And Lord help us if he's in for another two years.'

'Well, he might not be.'

'All of these foreign countries hate us now. We are not even working with the NATO nations, the ones who are supposed to be helping us with our wars.'

'He seems more friendly with Putin than anyone else.'

'Oh yeah. And we never had anything to do with Putin. We never had anything to do with Russia.' She looks down and scratches her nose. 'And now he's started that tariff with Mexico and China. And it's hurting the farmers.'

We talk about the minimum wage, which, Arlene says, is $7.25 an hour in Missouri. 'You can get that in McDonald's and places like that. Suppose you've got three kids to support. You've got to pay social security on that and you've got to pay taxes. You'll be lucky to come home with five dollars an hour.' She looks at me and shakes her head. 'You know. You can't do it. If you go and apply for food stamps or something like that, you can't work anywhere, because, if you're working at one of those seven-dollar-twenty-five-cent jobs, they cut you out. Your benefits and everything, they cut you out.' Arlene stops talking and looks at me.

She smiles and goes on. 'This boy I know. He works. His girl-friend had a baby. He gets behind on his child support. They take his driving licence away. So how can you get a job, support a baby, without that?'

'Is that as a punishment?' I say.

'Yes. And if that doesn't work, they put him in prison.'

'For not paying?'

'For not paying – and when they go into prison their child sup-port keeps going on. If he's paying four hundred dollars a month, when he gets out he's got to pay maybe seven thousand dollars of back child support before he can get on to paying what's due now.'

'So he's got no hope.' I shrug.

226

'And he goes back to prison.' Arlene shrugs. 'It's screwed up. The whole government system is getting bad.'

'Maybe it'll get better soon. It must. Maybe they will impeach him.'

'I'm hoping.' She smiles again.

We talk about primaries, and midterms and the chances of the Democrats, and are interrupted when the door opens and a man and a woman come in.

He has grey hair, swept back. 'What kind of Indian stuff you got here? What tribe are ya?'

'Oh, I'm a Heinz Fifty-Seven.'

Three of us laugh.

'I don't really know,' Arlene continues, 'and when I asked my dad what I was, he said, "Part Dutch, part Irish, part Indian, now go play."'

The woman is slim; she has dark eyeshadow and dark hair pulled back tight to her head. Arlene encourages them both to look around. The woman wanders off.

The man tells us how, for three years in the 1970s, he lived on an Indian reservation near Santa Fe with a tribe called the San Ildefonso. He was introduced by a white friend who was close to one of the elders. 'You have to be welcomed in. They size you up for about a year. They find out if you're a genuine person. And all that kind of stuff. And once you're accepted, you're accepted for life.'

'That happened with Windy's boyfriend. You know Windy, the Lakota Sioux that I told you about. Her boyfriend went up there to work on the reservation in South Dakota. And they started dating and everything. And after a time the tribe adopted him.'

She goes on to tell us more about Windy. 'So she came back here and was living with Kent. She had three Indian kids and her sister had a baby and she adopted it. She has got some land up there on the reservation, and she's a sun dancer and she had to go back to South Dakota every year and dance – to keep her land, you know?'

'Yeah,' I say. And Grey-Haired Man says it too.

'She had to do that for five years, and they have to dance without

227

eatin'. And after the five years – after she got here and got back to eatin' and everything, she said, "Boy! It was a job." Doing that dance, because I think they have to dance for three days.'

Grey-Haired Man tells us about the San Ildefonso tribe dancing. 'Out there in the mountains at seven thousand feet, it's bitterly cold. A full-blown blizzard can be blowing and they're out there.'

'They have to dance, yeah,' Arlene says. 'And she has to. It's non-stop.'

'And you're not wearing much clothes either so,' Grey-Haired Man chuckles. 'It's freezing cold and they're just dancing.'

I tell everyone that it's time for me to leave.

Grey Hair asks my name, and I tell him, of course.

'I'm Tom Brooks. Good to meet ya.'

'I've been here about an hour, haven't I?' I ask Arlene.

'Well, that – hey, that's fine. You're welcome any time, OK? Bye. Bye, bye.'

42

Among Mennonites

The road is just beautiful: a huge sky with puffy white clouds – a Magritte sky; trees all along the side of the road, all kinds of trees, deciduous, conifers, and I can see right over them; rocks and low cliffs. Gliding gently downhill now with 'First Song' playing – a track on *Beyond the Missouri Sky*, the sublime album made by Charlie Haden and Pat Metheny. According to Harpo's temperature gauge, it is ninety-five degrees outside.

In the clean central square of the fragrant-sounding Sedalia, in the lee of a long, low courthouse, I stand in front of a memorial to the dead of all wars from World War I to Vietnam. High on a plinth a soldier is striding between shreds of barbed wire draped from broken posts; in one hand his rifle with fixed bayonet; in the other a grenade, which he waves in the air as if it were a cricket ball and he has taken a difficult catch. I stare at the soldier and peel a banana. It's old, this banana; it was old and ripe when I bought it in a garage yesterday. A chunk of it falls to the ground. I pick it up; it doesn't look too clean, so I carry it towards a bin. Distracted by the ornate Victorian buildings in the courthouse square, I forget about the bin. Instead I bite into the banana chunk, and my teeth hit something hard. I manage to find it, pull it from my mouth. It's black, a fragment of tar.

I walk the empty, low-rise streets. The sun beats down and no one is outdoors. I come to the Ozark Coffee House: small and old-world from the outside; brushed-steel coffee canisters, pine furniture, armchairs and cushions on the inside. I am greeted by two young women in long dresses. One is blonde and smiling, the other dark, quiet and industrious. I sit at one end of a long table and the smiling one brings cappuccino and a menu. She wears a small white bonnet on the back of her head. I look at the other woman, who is at the bar; as she turns away I see she is also wearing a bonnet. I guess they are Mennonites. There are just two other customers: a young woman in a yellow armchair; and another on a high stool at a shelf against the wall, peering at a laptop. I order a wrap with corn and black beans.

The smiling one gives me a code and I take my phone online. In England Spurs are drawing 0–0 away at Manchester United after eight minutes. A loud family come in, speaking Spanish. They sit along the table from me: several children, their mother and their grandmother, who wears plenty of make-up: heavy black eyeliner and red lipstick.

Twenty-four minutes and still 0–0. I've been chatting to the blonde woman, who can hardly stop smiling. She knows now that I'm from England and travelling slowly towards San Francisco, and she has confirmed that she is a Mennonite and the coffee shop is owned by Mennonites. She asks where I'll stay tonight. I don't know, but suspect I'll stay in Kansas City, which is about ninety miles down the road, or in Independence, which is close to, almost a suburb of, Kansas City and is the famous jumping-off point for the wagon trains that took settlers west in the nineteenth century.

Smiling One has another idea. She thinks I should stay at a place called Lee's Summit, which is on Route 50, just a few miles before Kansas City. 'It's three o'clock. You could get there around five,

five-thirty. There are motels and restaurants. Go and look at Kansas City and Independence tomorrow.' She picks up my phone and using her thumb calls up a map, shows me where to go.

I haven't looked at a map on my phone once in all these days. I'm hugely impressed. 'You're really good at this. I thought you people were in the nineteenth century. You seem to be in the twenty-second.'

She laughs. 'I'm not that good. I just try to keep up with my husband.' She looks at the photo on my phone's home page. 'Is this your granddaughter?'

'Yes. She's called Flo. And I've three ... no, four grandsons.'

'She's sweet.'

She recommends two restaurants in Lee's Summit, shows me their web pages on my phone, takes my biro out of my hand and writes their names in my notebook: Kansas City Joe's and Jack Stack. And she recommends places for me to visit in Kansas City.

We are joined by a big man, whose beard is shaped so that it follows the outline of his chin. He might be Smiling One's husband. He introduces himself as Justin, and talks about Kansas City, which he says is 'really neat'. And he tells me about Mennonites. They are Christians who are committed to peace, and the first Mennonites came to America with William Penn, who founded Pennsylvania, in 1682. Since then they have come in waves at different times, from Russia, Holland, Poland, Germany and Switzerland, to escape persecution by Catholics and Protestants.

Somehow our conversation moves on to politics. And when I mention Trump, he looks glum and shakes his head.

'Do you think some people who voted for Trump have changed their minds?'

'Likely,' he says.

'Did you vote for Trump or Hillary?'

'Well, we don't' – he shakes his head – 'vote.'

'Oh! Is that part of the religion?'

'Yeah.' He points up at the ceiling. 'We believe in ...' He's still pointing.

231

'That you'll be OK.'

'Yeah . . . I think so.' He smiles.

Before I go, I tell the two women what a great place their coffee shop is.

'Why thanks,' says Smiling One. 'We like it. We like how it's small and we meet people. And Justin is a big part of it. He roasts the green beans for us, so our coffee is always very fresh.'

'Yeah, upstairs,' Justin says, and points to the ceiling with a little less reverence than when he was pointing at God.

I walk away thinking what great people those Mennonites are. Then I remember reading books by the Canadian Miriam Toews, who was born a Mennonite. Some of her Mennonites were strict, authoritarian old men who interfered in other people's lives and didn't like people to have fun. Well, obviously there are Mennonites and Mennonites.

I check in to a Super 8 motel close to a roundabout in Lee's Summit, where the receptionist gives me directions, which I write down, to Jack Stack Barbecue. If I don't get lost, I'll be there in nine minutes. As I drive I remember that Pat Metheny's father had a car dealership in this city, and that the great guitarist grew up here – and indeed returns from time to time. I miss a turning and take twelve minutes to reach Jack Stack.

The place is busy with many people sitting at tables. The bar is different; a young couple are sitting at one end beside a row of empty chairs. I sit a few seats away from them and order a local beer, Stockyards Black, recommended by the bartender, who is called Shannon. She is about thirty-five, friendly, talkative, and busy washing glasses, polishing the woodwork and pouring drinks for waiters to take to tables. Before settling here, she lived in Florida, South Carolina and Hoboken, New Jersey. She came west to be with a boyfriend, broke up with him but stayed. 'I couldn't afford to go back, but I liked it anyway. It's cheaper, less pretentious; the people are slower and have more time to talk. And you get much more apartment for your buck.'

I eat grilled salmon while Shannon arranges glasses in a dishwasher and recommends places I should look out for in Kansas City. She tells me about Mennonites and the Amish. 'Mennonites integrate with modern technology, see doctors, use computers, wear sunglasses, drive cars,' she says. 'The Amish don't do any of that. They use horses and carts, are great builders and build houses and sheds for other people.' She slams the dishwasher shut, pushes a white knob and says, 'Mennonites are very good farmers.'

I think back a few days to that jolly group of men, women and children in Pizza Hut, in Washington, Indiana. They were probably Mennonites, not Amish. There were no horses or carts in the car park.

43

Wagon Train

As a kid I loved the TV series *Wagon Train* and watched it regularly in the early 1960s. Wagon trains featured in the cowboy comics I read, and in westerns that I saw at the cinema. And for my ninth birthday my mother gave me a book called *Great Stories of the Wild West*; in it I read the tragic but exciting true story of the Donner party.

So perhaps in pursuit of a childhood dream, I leave 50 at Lee's Summit and make a detour along a concrete freeway to Independence, the city where, beginning in the 1830s, wagon trains assembled before travelling west to Oregon and California. By 1869, when the First Transcontinental Railroad reached Oakland on San Francisco Bay, bringing the notion of travelling west by covered wagon to an end, more than 400,000 settlers, gold miners and businesspeople had taken the Oregon Trail from Independence. Still more had travelled on the California Trail and the Bozeman Trail, both of which followed the Oregon Trail before branching off.

The pioneers arrived in Independence after a few days' travelling up the Missouri by steamboat from St Louis. It was the last place where they could stock up with provisions for the long trip west, which would take about five months, and it was where pioneer families would join others to form wagon trains, which were often led by professional guides. After leaving Independence they would cross hundreds of miles of grassland before having to climb, with their horse- or ox-drawn wagons, over two huge mountain ranges, the Rockies and the Sierra Nevada. I'm not sure what I'll find at Independence, but there will surely be some acknowledgement of the city's role in westward expansion.

In the centre of the city, I park near the Jackson County Courthouse, an elegant and imposing redbrick building; Independence is the capital of Jackson County. At the east entrance a statue of Harry S. Truman, President of the United States from 1945 to 1953, stands on a tall plinth – this is Truman's hometown. He holds a walking stick, planted firmly on the ground, and looks squarely ahead. He wears a double-breasted suit with a three-pointed handkerchief in the breast pocket, while creases radiate from the button that takes the strain of holding his jacket closed. This is not to say that Truman looks fat – far from it – just that his jacket looks a little tight.

I wipe sweat from my forehead, slap my sun hat back on and walk slowly around the block that is filled by this symmetrical building. The west side is identical to the east. An identical plinth stands outside the entrance. The only difference is that the ghastly Andrew Jackson is sitting on a horse on top of it. He is billed as 'General Andrew Jackson', rather than president, although this ruthless man, who brought in the cruel and deadly Indian Removal Act, was both at different times.

I am disconcerted to read on the plinth that this statue was presented to the people of Jackson County by Harry S. Truman. I have always thought of Truman, who became president at the end of World War II when Franklin Delano Roosevelt died in office, as a good man, whereas Jackson was an out-and-out villain.

Nearby, on a patch of grass, stands a rough, reddish slab on which

235

an engraving of an ox-drawn covered wagon sits above the words HERE THE OREGON TRAIL BEGAN.

Around another corner I find the tourist information centre and am greeted by a charming National Park ranger called Wade – who confirms that this is Harry Truman's hometown, and he and his house and his wife, Bess, to whom he was married for sixty-two years, are its main attractions. When I ask about the wagon trains and the Oregon Trail, Wade whips out a map. 'We have the National Frontier Trails Museum. It's just a few blocks.' He draws on the map to show me where to go. He looks at a clock. 'In five minutes we'll be showing a short film about Truman. You're very welcome. It's free.'

For five minutes I study Harry Truman books, postcards, key rings and fridge magnets. From the magnets, I find that Truman came up with numerous aphorisms, including 'The buck stops here'. Among the others are: 'If you want a friend in Washington, get a dog'; 'Not all readers are leaders, but all leaders are readers'; 'It's amazing what you can accomplish if you do not care who gets the credit'; 'I never did give them hell. I just told the truth and they thought it was hell.'

The film has plenty of nostalgic, black-and-white footage, both of domestic life at home with Bess and his family in Independence, and of formal presidential occasions. It seems that Truman was bright, likeable, hard-working and modest. He failed as a farmer, and a clothing business he founded went bankrupt. In 1922, at the age of thirty-eight, he decided to try politics and was elected as a judge. In 1934 he became one of the two US Senators for Missouri and in 1944 was elected Vice President of the US.

When he was president the buck stopped with him in a big way on two occasions. In August 1945, in order to end World War II in Japan, he authorised atom bombs to be dropped on Hiroshima and Nagasaki, the first, and only, use of nuclear bombs. And in 1950 he took the US into the Korean War; three years later, after 3 million people, many of them civilians, and including 30,000 Americans, had been killed, the war ended in a ceasefire. Meanwhile, in 1948,

Truman was one of the founders of NATO. The Korean War makes me think of the American Legion in Salem, Illinois, and George, the inspector of water towers, whose father saw such suffering during that war that he persuaded his son not to join the military.

Through all this, Truman came home to Independence whenever he could. And he declined to stand for a third term in 1952, although he could have. Instead he wrote, 'I have had all of Washington I want. I prefer my life in Missouri.'

'Truman seems like a really nice guy,' I say to Wade when the film finishes.

'Yes. He was pretty unusual. Just a regular guy. He never expected to become president, but he did OK. He turned into a statesman – and a lot of people liked him, especially here.'

'Very different to Trump,' I say quietly.

'You know, Trump is the first president – even counting those who were generals – who has no connection to politics.' Wade's tone sounds critical, but when I ask if he voted for Trump, he says, 'Because of my job, I can't reveal my preferences.'

Wade said that there are real covered wagons at the Frontier Trails Museum, so once again I head for a museum. I walk ten blocks in sweltering noontime humidity, and reach what appear to be the suburbs of Independence: neat clapboard bungalows where the rocking chairs on the stoop look down on close-shaven lawns.

As I walk through the museum, I follow the progress of pioneers on the Oregon Trail, and get further and further from Independence until I reach Oregon. By then I've read stories, and extracts from diaries and letters, and am brimming with admiration for these people who suffered months of sweat, discomfort and privation to get to where they wanted to be. I've seen them in photographs and paintings, and looked at the stuff they took with them: tools, blankets, furniture, toys, boxes of everything from champagne to sardines – and I'm grateful that the amount of stuff is limited, so that visitors like me don't glaze over and wander off in search of coffee, as we often do in museums.

I study the California and Santa Fe trails. And then I read extracts from the writings of members of the Donner party. After delays early in their trek, the group got stuck in snow and took refuge in huts in the Sierra Nevada mountains, where they were snowed in for four months. Virginia Reed Murphy, who was thirteen years old at the time, wrote this some years later:

> On the evening of February 19th, 1847, the first relief party reached our cabins, where all were starving ... But with the joy, sorrow was strangely blended. There were tears in other eyes than those of children; strong men sat down and wept. For the dead were lying about on the snow, some even unburied, since the living had not the strength to bury their dead ...
>
> Out of the 83 persons who were snowed in at Donner Lake, 42 perished, and of the 31 emigrants who left Springfield, Illinois, that spring morning, only 18 lived to reach California.

I come to a Conestoga, a long, strong, elegant wagon, which could carry six tons and was named after a river in Pennsylvania. This one is empty but for three boxes and a bag of grain, probably to show – as I learn from a caption – the clever way that the base boards curve down into the middle, lengthways, to prevent the load moving. Conestoga wagons carried freight all over the USA, in particular on the Santa Fe Trail, which was a trading, rather than a migration route.

However, Conestogas were too heavy to be hauled across the prairie, the desert and up into the Rockies. Further on, standing in a convincing patch of scrubby desert, I find the more humble yet iconic covered wagon – an ordinary farm wagon roofed with canvas stretched across hoops. These were nicknamed 'prairie schooners', as fleets of them sailed west stuffed with the children, parents, sustenance and stuff of settlers. This one is filled with barrels, sacks, trunks, billycans, a hunting rifle and a china doll in a long grey dress.

I read more extracts from accounts written by travellers. Indians were a worry for many emigrants: some tried to steal horses and guns; but many were friendly. This was written after the event by Jesse A. Applegate, who was seven years old in 1843:

> We camped below and near an Indian town of the Kansa tribe . . .
> It was said those Indians grew corn, beans, and pumpkins.
>
> I admired several of the Indian men I saw there. They were more than six feet tall, straight, and moved with a proud step; wore blankets drawn around their shoulders, and leggins. Their hair was shorn to the scalp, except something like a rooster's comb on top of the head, colored red . . .
>
> In crossing the river the Indians assisted our people in swimming our cattle and horses . . . Those Indians were friendly and accommodating.

Illness was another problem – and often fatal. James Wilkins wrote this on 15 June 1849:

> Passed a great many newly made graves today, and find a great deal of sickness amongst the emigrants, almost in every company we pass. Diarrhea running into cholera are the prevailing complaints. One poor woman is badly situated, having lost her husband and two children, several men sick and not able to do anything, she is forced to drive herself and one little girl drives the cows.

After the exhibits I come to a box of period clothes provided for visitors – probably children – to try on. I put on a coonskin, Davy Crockett-style hat and take a selfie. I look like a drunken uncle playing charades at Christmas.

44

Kansas City Jazz

I drive west out of Independence along Truman Road and slow down to look at the Truman Home, a large, white-painted Victorian house with gables and verandas. Guided tours are available, but I'm passing on that.

Half an hour later, I park beside a large office building on 12th Street, Kansas City, get out of the car, sit in the sun on a low wall and try to work out where I am by studying the Kansas City map in my road atlas. A classic art deco skyscraper – the type that has shoulders – is fifty yards further up the road. The Mennonites and Shannon at Jack Stack Barbecue told me to go to the Power and Light district. Perhaps this is it.

A woman comes up to me and asks if I know where the entrance is to the building behind me.

'Sorry, I don't know. I'm not from here. Do you know where the Power and Light District is?'

'Oh sure.' She points. 'It's just there: two blocks west. This, here, is the business district.' She points at the art deco skyscraper. 'That's

City Hall. This is the Courthouse.' She nods towards the building beside us – the one that she can't find the way into.

I walk up Main Street, then across and down Baltimore Avenue. The city is hot and empty. A bar has four customers; a coffee shop just two. Three men in blue overalls squat on the pavement, eyes half-closed, backs to the wall in a patch of shade – as if they were in Mexico, but without the hats.

By chance, I pass the tourist board, where a woman sits behind a big desk. I ask her where the Missouri is and if she knows anywhere that I can hear some jazz. She's chatty and knowledgeable. We talk about the Kansas City sound, and how this is the place where jazz moved on from big band to smaller groups and improvisation. I know this much and that Count Basie was here with his big band and encouraged his musicians to improvise, and that Charlie Parker, the high priest of bebop, was born here. 'Why did that happen here?' I ask Chatty, Knowledgeable Woman.

'Two reasons,' she smiles. 'The location: in the middle of the States. Everyone came through here if they were travelling between the coasts – by plane or train. I mean in the nineteen-thirties, forties, that kind of time. And they stopped off because of T. J. Pendergast.' She pauses, as if wondering what to say next.

'Who was he?'

'He ruled the city in the twenties – late twenties – and thirties. He was a politician and kind of a gangster.' She pauses again. 'So the city was very liberal. Pendergast liked drinking, gambling ... having fun, I guess. He ran the police and everything. Prohibition hardly happened here. Bars and clubs were open all night, and there were a lot of them. The musicians played their regular gigs – probably in big bands – and then met up later in bars and jammed. All night sometimes, they say.'

'So that's when people like Charlie Parker started improvising?'

'Right. Apparently.' She pulls out a map of the city. 'And they came from all over, the musicians. There was lots of work, lots of fun, and the out-of-hours stuff when they jammed with each other and worked out new ways to play.' She unfolds and smooths the map on her desk. 'And they competed, you know. Who can play the longest solo – or can come up with something new?'

She turns the map round to face me, and draws a circle in biro. 'This is where it mainly happened: 18th and Vine. And the Jazz Museum is there too.'

She draws more circles on the map: two places where I might see jazz this evening. And then suggests I take the free streetcar north up Main Street to reach the Missouri.

Getting on the streetcar is like walking into a fridge: pleasant for a short while but then too cold. The car isn't crowded, stops frequently and takes about fifteen minutes to reach its northern terminus. From there I walk, as instructed, down an alleyway which becomes a boardwalk, elevated above railroad tracks and a riverside path; it ends in a broad platform high above the Missouri, which is grey-brown, wide and roiling. On the further bank, dense, green woods. More eye-catching are the rows of small padlocks – all of them, I hope, symbols of undying love – attached to the fence that prevents people falling into the river; I have seen this kitsch, yet touching, phenomenon on bridges in Paris and Dublin.

A creaking, airless lift takes me to river level. I walk east along a path flanked by trees and shrubs until I come to narrow concrete steps leading down to the river itself. I wanted to see it again before it bends north, away from my route west, and up through Nebraska and the Dakotas to its source in Montana. Once again, I think of Lewis and Clark and their men (Sacagawea didn't join the party until it was way north of here) seeing this place – until then the forested home of Indians – for the first time. Thirty years or so after they slid by in 1804, a man named McCoy set up a trading post just south of here. His supplies came by riverboat and were unloaded onto a flat expanse of rock, which is here now on the riverbank. At first, he named this place Westport Landing, but as a town grew up, it was named Kansas after the local Kansa tribe of Indians.

*

The sky has darkened to a deep purple-grey, and the air has cooled. I'm walking towards the Phoenix, a jazz venue ringed on the map by Chatty, Knowledgeable Woman. A few drops of rain splat on the pavement. Within a minute a jagged line of lightning cracks the sky, followed by a deluge. I sprint to the steps of an office doorway and join a man who is smoking a cigarette. He takes a pull, taps off some ash and says, 'It'll blow by.'

'How long, do you think?'

He stares up at the sky, which is almost black and split by lightning. After a loud crack of thunder, he shrugs. 'Five minutes.' He pulls on his cigarette. 'Maybe ten.' He flicks the butt across the pavement and into the stream that is running down the gutter. 'Gotta get to work.' He smiles and pulls the door open.

I wait till the rain seems to have eased, then run and stop in another doorway thirty yards on, where I wait and run again. Repeating this process four or five times, I reach the Phoenix, a corner bar with clear plate-glass windows. I stand on a large doormat and shake off water. Rain is piling down onto the pavement outside. My hair and shoulders are soaked and cold. My shorts somehow are dry. I take a seat at the near end of the bar. Two female bartenders are chatting to customers further up. Between me and them a young man is poring over a fat hardback book. One of the bartenders, dark-haired, dark-skinned, comes over and greets me. I order orange juice with soda and ask if there will be live music.

'Seven p.m.,' she says. 'Open mike.'

'Will it be good? Or ...'

'Well, it's not exactly open mike. There's a great pianist and anyone can jam with him.' She makes a face. 'So some of it'll be good. Some of it's kind of' – she rocks her hands with open fingers in a gesture of uncertainty – 'OK.'

She asks where I'm from, and the other bartender joins her. We talk about London, England, Kansas City and St Louis, and decide all of them are cool. They urge me to stay in their city a few days. I can see great jazz if I do that – and I can go to the Jazz Museum, which is also great.

243

They both go off to pour drinks. It's 5.15. Do I want to stay here till 7 p.m. to hear some jazz that has been damned with faint hand gestures? I paid to park the car till 6.30. I drink orange juice and watch water streaming across the pavement.

I leave at 6 p.m. – the rain has almost stopped – take the streetcar back down Main Street and collect Harpo. I head south down Main Street. At some point I am sure to come to a ring road or even to my road, 50, going west. I'll find a motel, come back into the city tomorrow and go to the Jazz Museum; in my mind the excitement of 'jazz' more than cancels out the ennui of 'museum'.

I stop at traffic lights and become aware that someone in the back of an SUV has his window wound down and is trying to attract my attention. 'One of your brake lights ain't working,' he says.

'Oh no! Thanks,' I say.

'You're welcome.' He's young and rather overweight. A layer of flab encircles his jaw like an uncooked pork sausage. He raises his window. He seems to be smiling.

I drive on ... and on ... and on ... for thirty minutes without seeing any sign to a main road out of the city. Soon surely I will reach Route 50 or Interstate 35, with which 50 shares the road for a few miles. Eventually I find I am indeed on I-35 south, which is also 50 west. It is dark and rain is falling again. Soon I turn off, following signs to motels. By 7.45, I am at the Holiday Inn – pricey, but cheaper, I guess, than the Hilton next door. And the receptionist tells me that I'm in a town called Olathe; he stresses the word as he would Oliver.

In my room, I find Olathe on the map. It's twenty-two miles south-west of Kansas City and well placed for driving on west. Olathe is an American Indian word for beautiful – and a name often given to newborn girls.

I go into the bathroom and am surprised to see two loo rolls sitting on adjacent rollers, *both* of them folded to a point! I think this over as I take the lift down to reception. I shouldn't have been surprised. After all, you get what you pay for.

45

Tittering Rednecks

Over breakfast I watch a hoo-ha provoked by a man called Ron DeSantis, who has lost a Republican primary in Florida. DeSantis has accused the man who defeated him of 'monkeying' up the state. The winner, Andrew Gillum, is black. Outrage, quite rightly, has broken out. While keeping an eye on this, I decide not to go back into Kansas City. I would love to tour the Jazz Museum, but I'll leave it for another time. It'll be good to move on west. There's a way to go and I have a deadline enforced by my plane ticket out of San Francisco.

I put my case in Harpo's boot – and remember the brake light. Can I buy a bulb and fit it myself, or do I need to find a garage?

On the empty feed road that connects the Holiday Inn to the Hilton and a couple of restaurants, two men are laying new kerb-stones. It occurs to me that it'd be worth checking the lights before going to a lot of trouble to fix them – after all, this is an almost new car and no warning light has appeared on the dash to announce a faulty bulb. I stop, let down the window and ask one of the men if he would mind looking at my tail lights while I push the brake pedal – and I explain why I am asking. Luckily he is the kind of person who likes to help others. He stands behind the car. I put my foot on the brake. And, in the mirror, I see him smiling and shaking his head.

He comes round to my window. 'They're fine. Both shining brightly. Someone was trying to be funny.' He shrugs and raises his arms.

A cloud lifts; my day is free of trouble. I thank the man several times and drive out onto the interstate, which is doubling as Route 50. I know from the map that this cheeky takeover goes on for almost a hundred miles, so I plan to leave the interstate about four miles on and make a long detour on Route 56, which loosely follows the Santa Fe Trail.

I think about the young man who seemed to smile after telling me my brake light didn't work. It was a prank, wasn't it? There were four men in that SUV; perhaps they were all in on it. Maybe they were riled by Harpo's New York plates, which meant they were riled by the man they took me to be: a man from the east coast, from that elite which, until Trump got in its way, had always governed them high-handedly, had sent them to fight wars and failed to provide them with a decent living when they returned, shocked and miserable. Maybe that was it. The fat-rimmed face comes into my mind: a redneck smirking; a car full of rednecks tittering.

I drive on – and remember the film *Deliverance*. But . . . come on! It was a prank; it might even have been a mistake.

Shreds of cloud float in a clear blue sky above Route 56, the driving is easy and I'm struck by long, green vistas and glimpses of cattle. When I was about eight I read a monthly cowboy comic called *The Kansas Kid*. This is Kansas; empty but for telegraph poles and weathered fence posts supporting rusty barbed wire.

The slopes become steeper and the land wilder, though still green and lush. I'm in the Flint Hills, so named because erosion has left flint near the surface and just a thin layer of earth above rock, making this cattle, rather than grain, country.

I drive into a town called Burlingame and am struck by a sign on a street corner: Redneck Days – Downhill Derby – September 1st. That word again – used with pride. I stop because I like the look and feel of the wide main street as it bakes in the midday sun. I walk between old two-storey buildings with false fronts, and imagine horses hitched up outside saloons, and Gary Cooper peering from a doorway holding a cocked Colt 45. Images from classic westerns – *High Noon, Once Upon a Time in the West* – play in my mind as I walk back to the car and drive on.

The distances between towns and villages are getting longer. The road is stretching out; the countryside is suffering fewer intrusions from gas stations, fast-food outlets, industrial parks – or from cities and towns with their courthouses and war memorials.

Fifty miles on, I turn off at a sign to 'Old Stone Barn', and find a carefully restored grey building standing on a gentle slope in a green meadow; a plaque tells me that it was built in 1871 to house livestock. Nearby is a flat space, the size of a small football pitch, surrounded by a sturdy metal fence. A sign says Rodeo Arena. To one side is a tiny portable grandstand with short rows of bleachers that look as if they are made of aluminium. A dozen or so small calves stand in a pen and stare at me. I've watched a few rodeos and know that they will be lassoed, trussed up with rope and held down with a knee on their necks. This happens when a competitor shows great horsemanship and manages to lasso one of them. Sometimes the calves survive untied – the limited time given to the rider is up. Then, quietly, I cheer. I can't help being on the side of these little creatures – they are tiny calves faced with aggressive people on horses.

As I walk by, a small black calf comes to the fence and stares up at me with big, brown eyes shielded with sloping lashes. I sense that he might be saying, 'Hey! Can you get me out of here, please?'

Closer to the road, white windowless buildings cluster behind a sign announcing Morris County Noxious Weed Dept Warehouse – Control Your Noxious Weeds! Downhill from there, in the shade of a clump of cottonwoods, an old concrete table is flanked by concrete benches and a post with an ashtray screwed to it. I sit down, turn my back on the noxious weed warehouse, picnic on dried apricots and rosemary crackers, watch the calves – and contemplate setting them free.

Two miles on I stop in the small town of Council Grove and walk up and down Main Street, which *was* the Santa Fe Trail. I see post-cards through a shop window and go in. Two women are sitting behind computers, and this shop is the Chamber of Commerce. The postcards are free, as is a wall full of information leaflets, and the two women are happy to stop their work and chat. They wish me luck with driving to San Francisco; it'll be a lot cooler there, one of them says. They are enthusiastic about their town. I must walk up the road to the Neosho River, one says, because the crossing there, where the river is shallow and lies on rock, is why the Santa Fe Trail came through here and why the town grew up. They tell me to visit other sights, all of which are a short walk away.

I take a handful of free postcards and set off for the river. I look down on it from a bridge; it's shallow, narrow, and snakes through a pretty park. I walk on and reach Council Oak, another sight the women wanted me to see. The stump of a tree sits below a protective roof. On 10 August 1825 this was a flourishing oak beneath which US officials and Osage Indian chiefs sat to sign a treaty allowing European Americans to travel through Osage territory to Santa Fe for the rest of time; the Indians were paid $800. After that, the Santa Fe Trail – 900 miles long, two-thirds of it west from here – was open. At that time Council Oak stood in a shady grove of trees where wagons gathered into trains before moving on west; the grove gave the town its name.

I walk back across the river, on down Main Street and come to the Last Chance Store, a grey stone building built in 1857. The name was used to advertise the place with slogans like 'the Last Chance for Bacon, Beans and Whiskey'. And it really was the last chance; from here traders travelled 600 miles through land that belonged to Kansa, Cheyenne, Arapaho, Comanche, Kiowa and

Plains Apache Indians. There might be opportunities to trade, but there were no shops.

Council Grove is now a quiet town. But until 1880, when the railroad to Santa Fe was completed, a huge amount of trade between the US and Mexico travelled this way (Santa Fe and what is now the US state of New Mexico were then in Mexico). Stuff made in factories in the eastern US and Europe moved west, while furs, rugs, silver and mules came east. In 1860, a local businessman recorded that '5,405 Mexican and Euro-American traders, 1,532 wagons and 17,282 mules, oxen and horses passed through Council Grove', and, in 1863, it was reckoned that $40 million worth of goods were hauled through the town. I remember the Conestoga that I saw in the Frontier Trails Museum in Independence. Those wagons would have been like that – long with a downward curve inside and able to carry 12,000 pounds, six tons, of stuff.

I drive south on state highway 177, a narrow road across the Flint Hills, which will take me back to Route 50, twenty miles south. The sky, clear blue overhead and paler towards the horizon, lies beneath low cumulus clouds which advance across the sky in formation, like Lancaster bombers crossing the North Sea in World War II. The land is flat, treeless moorland, spacious and undemanding – no buildings, no cattle – with low hills way off to east and west. I stop in the turn-off to a ranch, and take a stroll; rough grass, a deep brown green, stretches all around and the warm air smells clean.

I drive on and come to a decorative sign, 'Tallgrass Prairie National Preserve', set in front of a car park and an information centre, which turns out to be shut – it's almost 5 p.m. – though there are leaflets, and benches on which to sit and read them. Before the arrival of Europeans in the US, there were 170 million acres of tallgrass prairie. It was all over the country, but mostly in the eastern prairies, in a strip stretching from Manitoba to Texas. Less than 4 per cent is left, much of it here in the Flint Hills; this preserve has 11,000 acres. The tallgrass grew as tall as a cowboy's hat, and bison, on which the Plains Indians depended for food, clothing and shelter, ate it and lived in it.

I walk uphill along a path to a wall. There a notice explains that if I walk another four miles, I will see bison. I'm tempted, but it's getting late.

Back in the car park, a couple with three children get out of a car and set off walking along the road. The smallest child, a two-year-old boy, was crying before they started, so Mum is carrying him. The middle child, a four-year-old girl, is hanging on to Mum's jeans. Meanwhile, Dad is striding out and not looking back; the oldest child, a girl aged six or seven, is trying to keep up with him, but it's not easy, and she is soon halfway between her parents.

I hope Mum is going to get Dad to pay more attention to his children. But what do I know? Maybe they aren't his children. As some clever dick once said: 'Never judge a man by his umbrella; it may not be his.' Anyway, I stop gawping and drive off.

I think about the great William Least Heat-Moon, author of *Blue Highways*. I knew that he wrote a book called *PrairyErth*, a highly regarded study of a small region of the US – but I didn't know where it was. Just now I learned from a leaflet that it is right here. *PrairyErth* is about Chase County, Kansas, which contains the Tallgrass Prairie Preserve and the road I'm now driving on.

At Strong City I join 50, now disconnected from Interstate 35. I head on to Hutchinson, where I arrive in the car park of a motel called Motel 6 in time to watch the sun set, in pink, purple and gold behind a gas station called Love's – whose apostrophe is heart-shaped.

46

At the Polo Sports Lounge

Inside Motel 6, the receptionist seems gloomy. And when she sees my driving licence, showing the Union Jack and my address in London, she becomes grumpy as well, shrugging her shoulders and declaring, 'An Englishman ripped me off six hundred dollars.' She stares at me as if I might be him.

'That's *terrible*,' I say. 'But I would never do that. Not all Englishmen would do that. That's really bad.' She is still staring at me – and holding my driving licence in the air as if it were damning evidence. 'I'm really sorry that an Englishman did that.' Still she's staring. 'If I knew who it was, I'd try to get your money back.'

'Well,' she lowers her hand and shakes her head. 'It was very upsetting.'

'I'm really sorry.'

I think she has accepted that it wasn't me. Perhaps she has asked herself why, if it were me, I have turned up looking for a room. She is looking down at the motel's register.

'What happened?' I say.

She writes in the register and deals with my credit card. 'Room 251, upstairs.' She hands me a key, scratches her neck and looks me in the eye. 'Well ... I got to know him online. We became very friendly and, after two years, he said he wanted to send me some gifts: some items of jewellery, a purse, other things.' She glances out of the window towards the remains of the sunset. Remembering is clearly painful. 'Nothing came. Then I was contacted by US mail and asked to pay a hundred dollars to get the gifts; I thought it was a revenue charge – customs duty, you know? This happened again, and then again, until I had paid six hundred dollars, but I never received the gifts.' She looks back at me, shakes her head and looks down. 'So I gave up. I'd been fooled.'

'Well, the worst thing is that you were misled ... deceived, I mean.' She must have become fond of this English blackguard.

'Yep,' she says. She looks up at me for a second, and then down again. For her it was a romance; maybe she had hopes of a new life away from Motel 6. 'There's no elevator. The stairs are over there.'

'I'm sorry you went through that.' I turn away and wheel my suitcase towards the stairs.

Later, when I ask if she can recommend a restaurant or bar where I might get something to eat, she is still a little edgy. But she fills me in on the Hutchinsons: we are in South Hutchinson, which, her expression betrays, isn't as classy as plain Hutchinson, which is up the road and across the river.

'Which river is that?'

'Arkansas.'

'Oh, right. That's a big river.'

'Yep. Goes to Wichita that way' – she points behind to her right – 'and Dodge that way' – she points towards the car park. And she mentions two or three restaurants in Hutchinson.

I like the sound of the Polo Sports Lounge – partly because it stays open late; it's already half-past eight.

She tells me how to get there. 'Once you're across the river, Hutchinson is on a grid. You need 30th Avenue and Main.'

There's a space at the small, square bar. I ask the man sitting next to it if it's taken.

'It is – by you,' he says loudly. I thank him and sit down. His name is John, and on my other side, my right, is a man called Dave, who introduces himself.

They are both middle-aged and white. John has short-cropped hair. Dave has well-cut grey hair and a strong, handsome face.

They ask what an Englishman is doing in Hutchinson and I give the usual answer: driving across the country, Route 50 to San Francisco.

I look at the menu and ask about the fish: 'Mahi mahi. What is that?'

'It's good,' says Dave. 'It was probably caught in the ocean around Hawaii. But what's really good tonight is the pasta special with seafood. I've got that on order.'

A dark-haired man, who has evidently been standing behind us, leans in and says to me, 'Tonight my pasta special is especially special.' He smiles – and I assume he is the chef.

I order a small IPA and the pasta special. The dark-haired man introduces himself as Jason, and then speaks to Dave. From this I learn that Dave's brother has died, just this week, and that he is the second of his brothers to have died. 'Just me and my sister left,' he tells Jason.

When Jason leaves, I tell Dave that I'm sorry about his brother. 'It must be hard,' I say.

'It's hard.' He raises his hands and shrugs. 'He was sick. We knew that. The funeral wasn't good. And I didn't much like the obit. I didn't get a chance to give my opinion. My brother's children organised it. Here people are buried three days after they die, almost as a rule. So there isn't much time to get things right.'

Dave was in the military for twenty-four years, and is now fifty-four. 'I specialised in dealing with prisoners of war pretty much my whole career.' He worked in France, Germany and Italy, but not the UK, and for much of his career he trained military prison warders.

I ask if he was in Iraq.

'Yep. I arrived soon after Abu Ghraib. Was horrible.' He isn't looking at me, but I can see his eyes have narrowed into a squint, and his left fist – the one I can see – is almost imperceptibly clenching and unclenching. 'Should *never* have happened.' He sips from a glass of red wine. 'There were a lot of things we learned from that. One was' – he jabs his finger down towards the bar – 'realise how easily what you do can turn up on the internet.' He turns towards to me. 'Of course, people should *never* treat prisoners like that. But if they're tempted to do something . . .' – he pauses – 'inappropriate, they should remember it'll show up sometime.'

Somehow we get to talking about politics. 'I voted for Obama, against McCain, because I didn't like Sarah Palin. I liked McCain, but he made a mistake in choosing Sarah Palin as his running mate.'

'So are you a progressive Republican? Is that right?'

'Yes.' He smiles. 'Now. Whaddya think of this? I came up with this pun about McCain versus Trump: "The lion of the Senate will be remembered long after the lyin' of the White House is long gone."' He laughs. 'Whaddya think?'

I smile. 'It's good. Yeah.'

'It's *not* good. You're too polite.' He laughs again. 'It's just funny, if it's anything. Things like that come into my head. I don't know why.'

'So you're not keen on Trump?'

'No. I'm not.' He speaks quietly and moves his eyes from side to side – which seems to mean you have to be careful what you say. 'It's the first time in history we've had a president like this, who isn't a politician, who makes so many crazy decisions.'

'Do you think Trump will be impeached?'

'Quite possibly, if the Democrats get enough seats in Congress.'

'So then you would have Pence. How would that be?'

A plate of pasta, thick with squid, shrimp and clams, is put down in front of Dave, along with cutlery wrapped in a napkin. He pulls out a fork and prongs a pair of shrimps. 'Pence is an ass-licker; he's right there behind Trump. He would be more conventional as a president, but he has very right-wing religious views. It'd be different – perhaps better.'

My food arrives. Dave says, 'Isn't there a guy called Johnson who's causing trouble in your country?'

'You mean a fattish guy with ridiculous blond hair?'

'Yeah! That's him.'

We order more drinks and keep talking. Dave recommends that I go to Greensburg, a town further west and about twenty miles south of 50. 'It was flattened by a Tornado F5 in 2007. It's now been rebuilt on ecological lines. It's incredible what they've done there – well worth going to see.'

'OK. Sounds interesting. What does F5 mean?'

'It's the highest rating – the most destructive tornadoes. With winds over 200 miles an hour. Almost every building in Greensburg was blown down, or away. People were killed – ten or eleven, I think.' He sips his wine. 'Go have a look. That town is now something new, something hopeful – if you know what I mean.'

The John who was there when I arrived has gone. Another John, a skinny, bearded man, has turned up and is talking to Dave from across the bar about a local matter, of which I know nothing. I stop listening and stare blankly at a screen showing American football – until I hear bearded John's voice raised and a little angry. He is saying that statues of Confederate heroes, like General Robert E. Lee, should be left where they are because they are part of history; moves to have them taken down are liberal. PC nonsense.

Dave points out that most of these monuments were put up in the 1920s – decades after the Civil War whose military heroes they are supposed to celebrate; Dave says that they were put there to reinforce white supremacy and the laws that enforced segregation.

I can see that John isn't really listening. However, he calms down and they talk about segregation here, in Hutchinson, and whether there were Ku Klux Klan marches in the city in the 1950s and early 1960s – when segregation was being threatened by the civil rights movement.

I'm startled at this mention of the Ku Klux Klan, and then amazed to hear them speculate about whether the KKK were in full costume, *if* they marched here. 'I thought that KKK stuff only happened in the Deep South,' I say, 'in places like Alabama and Mississippi.'

'The KKK were in lots of places, usually in secret,' says John. Both of them say there was a lot of racism in Kansas in those years – and likely a chapter of the KKK, but they don't know for sure. 'The Stars and Bars might have been waved around a bit,' Dave says, and explains that the Stars and Bars is the Confederate flag.

Bearded John leaves. Dave and I have another drink, and somehow begin to talk about writers and books. Dave likes Steinbeck, especially *The Grapes of Wrath*. 'You know,' he says, 'that book was disapproved of when it first came out because it was so raw, and the language was raw too. At school – would you believe? – we read Dickens, Chaucer and Shakespeare.'

'Chaucer! Wasn't that a bit heavy – all that Old English?'

'Yes. It was.' He grins. 'But we had to do it.' He swallows some wine. 'I like Tom Clancy. He wrote great Cold War stuff. And' – now he looks a little sheepish – 'I'm a big fan of Hunter S. Thompson, especially his book about the Nixon campaign – you know? *Fear and Loathing on the Campaign Trail '72*.'

'I've not read that. But I like his writing. He was a great original.' Dave is nodding. 'He invented a new way of writing.' I swallow some beer. 'I always felt sympathy for him as a man, a human; I think he was tortured, disappointed, by the world – and he got it all out in the writing.'

Dave is still nodding, and then says I should see *Where the Buffalo Roam*, the movie that stars Bill Murray as Hunter S. Thompson.

It's past midnight, but there are still plenty of people here. Someone – Jason perhaps – produces a bottle of red wine called 19 Crimes. Amid much hilarity, it's explained to me that this is an Australian Cabernet Sauvignon and is named after the number of crimes for which convicts were transported down under. A little is poured into a glass for me to taste – and it tastes good.

I say that it is time for me to leave, but I'm presented with another glass of IPA by dark-haired Jason, who I now realise is the proprietor of this excellent bar. He has been smiling at me in an approving way from his seat on the opposite side of the bar for some time now.

When I finally manage to leave, Dave says goodbye several times and repeats, once again, that I must visit Greensburg. Jason shakes my hand, pulls a glass from a shelf and hands it to me. 'For you. A souvenir.'

I thank him and look at it and turn it round. 'Oh!' I say. 'This glass has the name of the bar on it!'

'Well, I wasn't gonna give you just a glass!'

Jason comes out into the car park and points in the direction I should go. 'Stay on Main. Across the bridge. And straight on. You'll be fine.'

47

Back to the Santa Fe Trail

In the morning I run into my receptionist friend and she is very matey; there's none of yesterday's brooding gloom. She wants to know what I did last night and is pleased that I liked the Polo Sports Lounge; she goes there occasionally – but she wouldn't sit at the bar. 'We sit at a table, have a drink and something to eat.'

50 is flat, straight and empty. So empty that I try out Harpo's cruise control for the first time. I set it to 65 mph and it works fine. I touch the brake and am back in control. I've driven all this way with my foot on the gas – what an idiot! I set cruise control again and wiggle my toes.

I stop in Stafford, a small town with a wide main street where a few cars are parked at an angle, nose to pavement. I walk up and down, and something – perhaps the red-brick surface of the street; perhaps the contrasting levels of affluence – reminds me of Middleburg, the opulent small town in Virginia with its old and pretty buildings and shops selling French clothes. Here many shops are closed, some permanently. Grey blotches deface the cream paint of the shapely sign proclaiming 'The Curtis Café Air Conditioned' and the neon tubes that once traced its letters are in fragments; the Curtis Café has clearly been closed for some time. However, the small cinema shows movies on Friday and Saturday evenings and Sunday afternoons, and across the road, a sign with the single word Pizza in faded red letters sticks out above a restaurant that is open from 4 p.m. to 9 p.m.

As I get back to the car, a woman's voice says, 'You come all the way from New York?' She's middle-aged with blonde hair cut in a bob and a deep, outdoor tan.

'Further than that. From London, England.' I explain how and why I got here.

'Welcome to our dying town,' she says.

'Your cinema's open.'

'Well, we're lucky to have that. I even go occasionally. No, the town is just about alive and ticking. We're lucky to have two state businesses here – both water-related. They give work to people.'

She and her husband – who, it turns out, is sitting in the driver's seat of a grey pick-up right next to us – are farmers. 'We grow milo, soybeans, corn, some cotton. Plus wheat, which is harvested in June.'

'You grow cotton this far north?'

'Yes. Because of the hotter weather we get now.'

'Has it got a lot hotter?'

'Yes. We farm close to town, just east of the airstrip, with irrigation from an aquifer that replenishes itself. It's kinda bowl-shaped. When I was a kid, we didn't use irrigation. Didn't need it. Now it's much drier.' Pale lines show around her eyes and on her cheeks, and I guess they come from years of squinting in the sun.

I ask if her husband minds waiting while we chat.

'Oh, he's OK. He's used to me talking to people.' I look across at him and he smiles. 'But I'd better go. Now, you have a great trip and drive carefully.'

'Oh. I take care. I drive slowly.'

'Well, don't drive too slowly. That can be dangerous too.'

*

Straight, and raised a little above flat cultivated fields, 50 stretches ahead apparently for ever: two lanes of gravel-beige tarmac divided by a faded, broken, yellow line – with my beloved telegraph poles, evenly spaced, to the left. And no trees, so the sky falls to the horizon all around. I play John Fogerty's album *Wrote a Song for Everyone* – reworkings of his Creedence Clearwater Revival hits – set cruise control and tap my feet.

Seventy miles on, I will detour south to Greensburg. But before that I take a right and drive north on an empty country road about twenty miles to Fort Larned, which was built by the US Army in 1859 to protect travellers from hostile Indians on the Santa Fe Trail.

In front of a row of cars, in the bleak, sun-baked space outside the post office in the town of Larned, the Stars and Stripes dangles at half-mast in honour of John McCain.

Another flag is flying at half-mast at the fort, a few miles west. Long, low, nineteenth-century, brick barracks are arranged around a grassy parade ground, about the size of two football pitches. I look into dusty rooms furnished, as they would have been, for officers: a grand piano, a low comfortable bed with mosquito net, a vase filled with dried grasses, a draughts board, a writing desk with pen and ink, a trunk, a washbowl and jug, books, clothes. I follow two elderly, patrician white Americans, a man and woman, who peer through windows and doorways at this stuff. We carry on round until we reach a shop where a woman asks if we want to see a film about this fort.

I don't. They do. I make an excuse and walk out into the sun and the warm breeze, which is still ruffling the flag. I'm bored with this fort. I've been to forts like this before in South Dakota and Texas. It's similar: dusty and lifeless. In the 1860s and 1870s this place was a village, almost a town, teeming not just with soldiers, but with civilian men and women: soldiers' wives, friendly Indians, Mexicans, European Americans, army laundresses, travellers, traders, teamsters, hunters. In 1867, a company of black cavalrymen, from the US Army's all-black 10th Cavalry Regiment, was stationed here. As well as barracks and military stores, the fort had shops, a hospital, a cemetery, a laundry, a bowling alley and, in a special hut, a billiard room. Now most of this is gone and tourists like me rattle around.

I cross the Santa Fe Trail, now grassed over, as I walk to the car – and drive away with John Fogerty, south to 50, then further south towards Greensburg.

48

Greensburg 1: The Tornado

As I drive into Greensburg, I see only new buildings: a hospital, shops and attractive, low-level detached homes built from wood, sitting on their own grassy plots. This is the town that Dave in the Polo Sports Lounge said had been rebuilt after being destroyed by a tornado. It looks good, as well as new.

I follow a sign to the Big Well Museum and Visitor Information Center and park outside a striking piece of modern architecture featuring a circle and two – or perhaps three, depending on how you look at it – semicircles. A notice says that it closes at 6 p.m.; it's 5.45. I go in and am greeted by a friendly woman called Terri who explains that, like most of Greensburg, this museum was built after the tornado flattened almost every building in the town on the night of 4 May 2007. Before that disaster, Greensburg was known for its big well. 'The world's largest hand-dug well,' Terri says. 'It was dug in the 1880s.

'People used to come to our town just to see our incredible well. Now they come to see our incredible new green town as well. It's all here in our exhibition.' She leads me round the end of a white-painted wall into a huge circular space. 'This is the well.' She walks to some railings and leans over.

'Wow!' I'm standing beside her, looking down into a deep hole, wide enough to accommodate a spiral staircase twisting down to the bottom. 'That was dug by hand?'

'Yes. You can read all about it in our exhibition' – she waves at the long circle of wall, which is covered in text, diagrams and photographs – 'and you can find out about the tornado and the rebuilding of the town. You can see that now if you want to – I'll stay till you're done – or you can come back tomorrow.'

There is no one else here, so I check that she doesn't mind working late just for my benefit.

'That's OK. I got stuff to do.'

I buy a ticket for $5 and spend about forty minutes looking, reading and walking through 360° in a clockwise direction. I learn about the well in ten minutes: 109 feet deep, thirty-two feet across, it was dug in 1887 and 1888 by gangs of twelve to fifteen men using shovels, picks, half-barrels, pulleys and ropes. It supplied the new town of Greensburg and the approaching railroad with water until 1932; it was then covered and turned into an attraction.

I move on to the tornado, the force and size of which is hard to imagine. Often called a twister, a tornado is a rotating column of air, caused by a coming together of warm moist air and cooler dry air that drops from a storm cloud and spins as it travels. From a distance it looks like a spinning funnel of cloud. The Greensburg tornado was on the ground for sixty-five minutes, during which it travelled 28.6 miles. It moved through Greensburg at around 18 mph, like a car cruising slowly through a built-up area. But, unlike a car, it was 1.7 miles wide, and the wind it brought with it moved at up to 210 mph, which 'with rotational wind shear' increased to more than 260 mph. In ten minutes the one and a half square miles of Greensburg was flattened.

A warning was issued by the National Weather Service at 9.37 p.m. The tornado siren, right here next to the Big Well, then wailed until 10 p.m. Nonetheless, eleven people died that night, at least sixty people were injured and 95 per cent of Greensburg's homes and businesses were destroyed.

What happened after that is moving and inspirational – and displayed on these walls. Some people left the town, feeling they had lost everything, but more stayed. Just a week after the tornado, at a town meeting in a huge tent, one resident suggested rebuilding as 'a model green community'. It took a while, but gradually this idea caught on. After a year of discussions and meetings – during which many residents lived in trailers on a park built specially, to the south of the town – on 19 May 2008, the city council ratifed its 'sustainable Comprehensive Master Plan'. This required all municipal buildings to be built to certified environmental standards. Kiowa County, of which Greensburg is the county seat, or administrative centre, made the same undertaking: county buildings were to meet the same standards.

Federal and state money was available for communal resources, such as utilities, roads, schools, the hospital. Homes and businesses relied mainly on insurance or investment. Rebuilding happened quickly. By the spring of 2010, the ten turbines of the Greensburg Wind Farm were supplying all the town's energy needs – and a whole lot more, which was 'placed back on the grid and offered as renewable energy credits for other Kansas Pool customers'.

Near the end of the display I come to a panel headed 'Living in a Sustainable Town'. It says, 'Greensburg has embraced the concept of sustainability in all its rebuilding efforts.' And then that, because 'building green' is more expensive than conventional building, 'everything from recycling building materials to aiming towards net-zero homes, offices, and farming was thoroughly debated'. The text continues, 'The outcome? Not only increased community spirit, but also pride in doing something absolutely unique.'

A final panel tells how the achievements of the people of Greensburg have spread. City planners have come from all over the

US and beyond to see how the town works and how they might make their own communities more green. People from other towns that have been hit by tornadoes have come to learn how to cope. A common question: 'How do you include all your citizens in the process?'

The answer given is 'a collaboration of the private and public sectors, faith-based organisations, and other resources ...' I would say, from what I've learned in the last half hour, that you have frequent discussions and consultations and, though people often disagree, you make great efforts as a group to remain friendly and to concentrate on the common goal. The people of Greensburg share certain sources of inspiration; near the beginning of this story of rebirth, the most fundamental were stated: 'Love of Greensburg and its community; the joy of overcoming challenge; and finally one very simple fact: Greensburg is home.'

I find Terri and she asks if I want to walk down the stairs to the bottom of the well. I tell her I'm not crazy about that idea: I don't like looking down from a height, and won't walking back up be exhausting?

'Come with me,' she says. 'I walk down and up every day. It's good for me.'

Terri, incidentally, is a comfortably covered woman of about forty, wearing tight blue jeans.

So I walk down, round and round on the metal stairs. And the 109-foot depth isn't as far as it looks. The wall is made of flat grey stones held together with cement. The stairs stop at a viewing point, and I look down twenty feet at a circle of green–blue water.

'It all seems very neat and tidy,' I say.

'Well, it was all rebuilt, except for this wall, after the tornado.' She waves up towards the roof, which, like the rest of the building, is circular. 'None of this was here. This place is much neater than it was – and safer. There's a lot of that in Greensburg. Places that are better than they were before.'

We start walking back up, and Terri stops at the first of the many landings. 'I stop for a rest at every landing,' she smiles as she draws breath. 'Twenty-one steps between landings.'

When we reach ground level, she suggests we walk up one more flight to the rotunda beneath the roof. Here there's a circular gallery with windows all round, giving a 360° view of the town. As we walk around, Terri points to the three buildings that weren't completely demolished by the tornado. One is the grain store, a group of concrete tubes more than twice as high as the telegraph poles.

'Why didn't that blow down?' I ask.

'Good question. People think it's because it was full of grain.'

Everywhere there are new homes, built of wood, most of them sizeable, all of them different, with walls, roofs, gables, verandas painted in muted greens, blues, greys, browns, maroons. And there are gaps, grassy spaces.

'Some people moved away,' Terri says, 'took insurance money and sold the land their homes had been on. Some have rebuilt on the same land. Some, from outside, have bought land and built. But there are gaps.' She points at one and then another. 'We hope they'll be filled. The population is down from about twelve hundred to around eight hundred and fifty.'

'New people are coming?'

'Yep. This is an attractive place – and work is going on to encourage people to come here to live.' She points to a large building with a red-tiled roof. 'That's the Best Western Motel. Just built. Just opened. You should stay there tonight. And, if you want to get a beer at the bar and drink something, go to the Cannonball. It's cool: busy and friendly.' Again she points. 'You can't quite see it from here, but it's there, on Kansas Avenue, a couple blocks east from Best Western.'

We walk downstairs and towards the door. I thank her for staying open late and being so helpful.

'It's been fun,' she says.

49

Greensburg 2: The Mayor and the Judge

I check into the Best Western and find the slickest, tidiest motel on Route 50 so far and two loo rolls folded to points. I drive to the Cannonball and around the back to its crowded parking lot. As I walk towards the back door to the bar, a small man in a red T-shirt is coming the other way. He tells me I'm a long way from home – he's seen Harpo's New York plate. I tell him that he's right and explain myself. Then I say that I'm pleased to be in his town and that I'm intrigued by the story of the tornado and its aftermath.

'Well,' he says, 'I was the emergency management co-ordinator that night in 2007. I'd love to talk to you more, but I've got to leave.' He begins to move away. 'The mayor and his wife – she's a judge – are in the bar. You should meet them.'

'Oh! I wouldn't want to disturb them.'

'They're great people. They'd want to meet you.'

A large, grey-carpeted room is filled with white-topped tables and plenty of people, none of whom is conspicuously the mayor or a judge. The bar is at the end close to the door. I take the nearest empty seat, which turns out to be a little low – my chin isn't far above the counter. The bartenders are both busy, and no one seems to notice my arrival. I pick up a menu. One of the bartenders comes over and I order a small glass of IPA and a nacho salad.

Both arrive quickly. I load up a nacho with lettuce, tomato and mayonnaise – and an extremely tall man leans over my shoulder and says, 'You sound like you're from Texas.'

Dumbly, I start to explain that I'm from—

He tells me he's joking and holds out his hand: 'Bob Dixson, I'm the mayor. I heard that you're from England.'

I put down the nacho, stand up and do my best to be matey. Bob is a lean, grey-haired man, wearing an open-necked shirt and blue jeans. He asks if I will join him and his wife.

'That's very kind. Are you sure I won't be interrupting?'

'Of course. If someone from England visits our town, we want to meet him.'

I walk with him to a table against the wall. One bartender follows, carrying my nacho salad, and the other brings my beer. Bob introduces me to Ann, an elegant, dark-haired woman with sparkly eyes. The Dixsons are eating tacos; Bob is drinking beer and Ann is drinking wine.

They want to know about London and my drive from Maryland.

I try to scoot through half of America with quick recollections of Annapolis, DC, Patsy Cline, Cincinnati, St Louis, Kansas City and of frequently getting lost.

They listen and make sympathetic comments.

I mention my quick visit to Fort Larned. 'Actually, I found it a bit dull. Nothing much happening. I've been to other forts like that.' Should I have said that? Was it disrespectful? Forts are part of their history.

'If you've seen one fort, you've seen them all.' Bob laughs and raises his hands.

Someone comes up and speaks to Bob, and I find myself talking to Ann. I ask how she became a judge.

'Well, I'm retired now. I just fell into it. I'd been a magistrate.

'To our grandchildren, the town as it is now is all they have known,' Bob says. 'The new house, which we've built with our old age in mind, is different – largely one floor. But, to our grandchildren, it's their grandparents' home.' He lifts up his hands, grins and shrugs one shoulder. 'It's better to live in the present than to dwell on the past. We have shown the grandchildren photographs of the old town, which was like all the other old towns, with a main street paved with red bricks and full of old buildings. And they've seen photos of our old house. But it's not important.'

I ask about the talks Bob does: how he goes about it.

'I do them with PowerPoint – you know: show pictures of the stuff we've done. And I always begin by saying that the green stuff has nothing to do with politics. I tell them that our ancestors, when they first came here to the High Plains, took care of the land, the earth. They knew that their lives and the future of their children and grandchildren depended on it. That's all being green is, I tell them. It has nothing to do with politics.'

It's time for us all to leave the Cannonball. Bob insists on paying for my beers and my food. And he says that, if I'd like to, it would be a pleasure for him to drive me around the town tomorrow and show me a few things.

And, of course, I say, 'Yes. Thank you.'

50

Greensburg 3: The Democrat

In the morning I meet Esther, an elderly woman, who is cleaning up in the breakfast room. When she hears that I will be meeting Mayor Bob, she says, 'He's great – and his wife and daughter.'

She has a damp cloth in her hand as she tells me how the tornado changed her life. 'We had a family car dealership – me and my late husband. It was destroyed by the tornado and, because the population shrank, there was no point getting it going again. I do this' – she waves the cloth – 'to keep busy, and it gives me a little extra cash. I've always liked to be busy. We – my husband and me – used to travel all over the States buying parts for small aircraft; that was our business. We went to Maryland, Buffalo in New York State, all over, driving in tandem. I often drove a U-Haul for us to put the parts in when we collected them.'

I drive to the Arts Center, where I had arranged to meet Bob. Ann is already there and Bob turns up as I arrive. No longer a judge, Ann runs this centre, which is named 5.4.7 in memory of the night of the tornado and those who died. It includes a gallery, white-painted and full of light, where there is a display of metallic art, much of it exquisite and finely detailed.

Bob explains that he has to go to his office to take a conference call about a meeting of a committee that he chairs in Washington. He apologises; he won't be able to drive me around, but he's arranged that their daughter Stacy will do that instead, and he will meet up with us later.

Stacy arrives, Ann makes coffee and we sit down and chat. Stacy is tall, with dark hair and an open, pretty face. She has two children and a husband, and is Greensburg's head of tourism – a role for which she is fully qualified, she explains. 'It's nothing to do with Dad.' She laughs.

We get into her SUV and drive two blocks to her parents' house; it's large and low with shrubs and climbers out front. Then on to her house, a little smaller and equally attractive. 'We bought a standard design offered by a builder and modified it to suit us,' she says. 'A lot of people did that.'

'How long did it take for people to get their new houses?'

'Most of the rebuilding was done in three years. The town was full of builders: from places like Kansas City for the municipal buildings, and more locally – Dodge and around – for the homes. Some builders had queues of people waiting for them to build their houses.'

We drive on. 'I find it hard to imagine how it used to be,' I say.

'Well, they were old buildings, wood, with two storeys – and my parents had an attic on top. That was a beautiful old house.'

'And verandas?'

'Yeah. Or porches. They all had them. Places for people to sit out – often on rockers. Some of them wrapped around two sides of the house. Those houses were a hundred years old, like you see in most old towns – in streets where people live, away from Main Street. The new houses mostly have porches too.'

'Do you find you can imagine, think back, to how it was?'

'Yes. But I like it the way it is too. You know, it's on the same

273

grid. The streets are where they always were – so there are people living right where they did before.'

We drive into another residential street. 'You know what I miss,' Stacy says, 'almost more than anything: the trees. We had tall trees which met across the streets during the summer. There was this great canopy of green, so in places you couldn't see the sky.'

Now the sky is everywhere – and the sun. There's no shade. There are little, new trees – perhaps ten feet tall – and a few survivors of the tornado, but they are small and stricken, with missing limbs and their tops blown off.

We drive on and stop outside the new hospital on Kansas Avenue, the east–west through route. It gleams with steel and glass. 'This is much better and bigger than the old hospital,' Stacy says. 'It's what was needed anyway, and it's in a better, more convenient place.'

We go south – past more new homes and some empty lots – to an area of grass divided by a grid of dirt roads, which are sprouting weeds. Stacy stops somewhere in the middle of this. 'This is where FEMA, the Federal Emergency Management Agency, funded roads and temporary homes in trailers for three hundred families.' She points to a patch of grass. 'My parents lived there. It was weird. The trailers all looked the same – and people used to walk into the wrong one! After a while my dad put a plant outside so they knew which trailer was theirs.'

Stacy takes me to the school, a low, two-storey, extremely modern mix of wood, concrete and glass. We go inside and walk along a long, wide, curved passage. Children with their teacher are coming the other way, paired up in an orderly line. A boy breaks away from the rest, comes up to Stacy, kisses her and returns to the line.

'My son,' Stacy says – and the teacher smiles. 'All ages are in one building, but they have separate bits of it.' We see children eating their lunch and look into a classroom. Everywhere there is plenty of space and huge windows giving natural light. 'The school has a platinum rating, the highest,' Stacy says, 'for greenness.'

Driving again, we pass a flag at half mast. 'John McCain seems to have been a good guy,' I say.

Stacy agrees – and then when I mention Trump she twists her face. 'I'm probably the most left-wing of my family; my brother calls me a . . . Democrat!' She laughs.

'There are progressive Republicans, aren't there?'

'Oh sure. McCain was one.'

I tell her that I've met perfectly nice people who say they love Trump.

'Oh yeah, in that bar you were in last night, there were people who would shout that they love Trump. A problem is that things in this country have become very polarised now.'

'It's the same for us. We're divided by this crazy Brexit.'

'I know,' she shrugs.

We come to another new, well-designed building called Kiowa County Commons, where there is a museum, library and media centre. Bob is waiting for us in the museum. Here I don't take much in, except for a life-size cardboard cut-out of a small grey-haired man in a checked shirt, blue chinos and deck shoes, who worked for more than fifty years at Hunter Drug Store on Main Street, serving sodas and floats. His name was Dick Huckriede and he was popular with adults and children; his job title was general clerk, but he didn't mind being called a soda jerk. He stands against the wall in the museum, smiling respectfully and looking utterly content.

Stacy drives me back to the Arts Center and Bob follows. A customer is pondering the metal sculptures and Ann is sitting at the table.

'I've seen and learned such a lot,' I tell her. 'It's amazing, wonderful, what's happened here.'

'I want to tell you something,' Bob says as we sit down. 'Two things saved this community: FEMA – that's the Federal Emergency Management Agency – their creation in six weeks of the temporary community, that trailer park you saw; and the school board's insistence that the next semester of schooling, beginning in August, should happen, which meant trucking in temporary classrooms. If the kids had gone off to schools in neighbouring towns, they and their parents might never have come back. Those were the two key factors.'

'Otherwise the community would have fragmented?'

'Very likely,' Bob says.

'Probably,' Ann says.

Stacy nods. 'Yep.'

Bob goes on, 'The public buildings were rebuilt at public expense via FEMA. But homes weren't. Insurance covered a rebuild, but that doesn't put your life back together. Nothing does. You've lost your stuff, your community, all you were accustomed to. You have to start again – and many people suffered PTSD. Some moved away and didn't come back. Many stayed. New people came and bought empty lots and then built homes to their own design. Some stayed, rebuilt and never talk about it. Some do talk. It's better to talk, we think.'

Ann and Stacy agree. And Stacy says, 'It was an old town with services that needed to be renewed. So the thing created opportunities – as long as people stayed together.'

'OK,' I say, 'there's one thing I want to ask you. It's trivial, but how did you know I was in the Cannonball last night? Did the guy in the red T-shirt come in and tell you?'

'Yes, he did.' Ann smiles. 'Ray. Ray Stegman.'

'He told me he was in a hurry to get away.'

'He was, but he came back in,' Ann says. 'He wanted us to meet.'

'Ray is a great guy,' Bob says. 'He was the sheriff here at one time. He was the emergency management coordinator that night in 2007 – he still is. He was a few miles out of town and he saw the tornado coming; he rang the guy who operated the siren and told him, "Leave it on until I ring you back and tell you to turn it off." It went off after about twenty minutes when the electricity went down. I think he maybe saved some two hundred lives.'

'He was one of many who didn't got the credit due to him,' Ann says.

Bob shakes his head, gives a weary sigh and says, 'There are a lot of them.'

Ann goes to check on her customer, who is still gazing at sculptures. Stacy, Bob and I sit in silence. Ann comes back and sits down.

'You know what's amazing,' I say. 'How I got here. I met a man in a bar in Hutchinson who said, "You should go to Greensburg. It's really interesting."'

'A man in a bar in Hutchinson, huh?' Bob laughs and slaps his knees.

'Then, when I got here, I saw a sign to the Big Well, went there and met Terri, who showed me round there – and said I should go to the Cannonball.'

'Terri,' Ann says. 'We know her.' She smiles.

'Then, in the parking lot at the Cannonball, Ray Stegman comes up because my rental car has New York plates, and says, "You're a long way from home," and it goes on from there. And he even goes back into the bar. I mean, what a great guy!'

They are all looking at me.

'I'm sorry. I must stop wittering.'

'Wittering? What's that?' Ann asks.

None of them knows what wittering means – so it can't be part of American English. I explain. 'Talking too much in an incoherent fashion.'

They laugh.

Eventually I leave, with repeated goodbyes.

Ann: 'It's been so great. Come and stay. You and your wife have a permanent invitation. Please come. We have plenty of room.'

Me: 'It'd be hard for us to reciprocate; our house is quite small; we have a spare room, about half that size' – I gesture to the small room at the back of the gallery – 'and only one bathroom, but ...'

'That doesn't matter.' Ann smiles.

And I think, no, it doesn't.

51

An Old Acquaintance

The road to Dodge City stretches into the haze, a shard of tarmac piercing the horizon. On either side ancient telegraph poles, like flimsy crucifixes, march in line.

Dodge is even hotter than the other hot places I've been lately: 104°F according to Harpo's onboard thermometer. I park on Gunsmoke Street, clamp on my sun hat and walk about twenty yards to the Red Beard Coffee Shop, recommended by Stacy for its air-conditioning as well as its coffee and its atmosphere. It's cool in both senses, with plenty of bare red brick, distressed wood, meditative music and a gleaming motorbike on a shelf above the restrooms. The three other customers sit alone with their laptops. So no talking, except with the barista, who is curious about my accent and wants to go to London. I order an iced latte, and she talks me into a slice of coffee cake to go with it. It's soft, sticky and delicious. And it's 3 p.m. Save for a handful of almonds, I haven't eaten since breakfast.

I sit in front of my notebook for half an hour, enjoying the peace and the chill. My mind meanders to last night at the Cannonball. Someone – perhaps me – used the word 'sustainable'.

'Sustainable?' Bob said. '*I'm* sustainable.' And then: 'In other words, *cheap*. Thrifty, frugal, *cheap*.'

I walk out into the heat. I visited Dodge eight years ago, during a north-to-south road trip, enticed by its history. I was disappointed. I love westerns and the happy-go-lucky, footloose image of cowboys, and I find gunslingers racy and attractive – perhaps because, in my mind, they look like Robert Redford and Clint Eastwood. Dodge is the world capital of gunslinging, so it should be my kind of place. But, sadly, it isn't.

In the 1870s and early 1880s cattle were driven here from Texas to be moved on east by rail. Cowboys would arrive after months on the trail, desperate to tumble into the saloons, gambling joints and whorehouses. Drunken fights with fists, set off by petty insults, cardsharps and disputes about, or with, women, were frequent. Some of these, but not many, turned into gunfights. As well as businessmen and cowboys, the town gained a population of gamblers, conmen and bums – and a reputation for lawlessness.

The part of Dodge on offer to tourists seeking the truth about Wyatt Earp, Bat Masterson and Doc Holliday is, for the most part, a gimcrack place peddling myths, cowboy hats and key rings. It's called the Boot Hill Museum and the entrance fee gets you a walk past and through an anodyne reproduction of the old Front Street, 'a show with Miss Kitty and her cancan girls', a mock gunfight and dinner. You can also glance at the Boot Hill cemetery, a scrap of grass on a slope, adorned by a few phoney wooden crosses beneath which there are no corpses.

It's not all bad. You can see photographs of Earp, Masterson, Holliday and lesser-known gunmen looking mean behind the droopy moustaches that, like shaved heads and bull necks now, were all the rage with men of violence in the 1880s. And an exhibition called The People of the Plains gives insight into what life was like on the vast flat plains around here, for Indians, cowboys, soldiers, buffalo hunters and pioneer families through displays of photographs, tools, weapons, clothes and reconstructions of daily life.

I skip these attractions this time, and drive out through dusty industrial outskirts where two large and amusingly-named meat-packing companies, Cargill Meat Solutions and National Beef, help Dodge's economy to thrive.

After a few U-turns, I get on to Route 50 heading west, a fast road across a flat, treeless landscape. Grey clouds swirl overhead, while towards the horizon a greenish-blue sky is studded with small, bright clouds, like puffs of white smoke.

I soon reach Garden City, and find that I'm crossing Route 83, the road I grew fond of when I drove its length from Canada to the Mexican border eight years ago.

I get lost in downtown, park, walk around and, by chance, find myself outside Traditions, a soda fountain and sandwich bar that has been here, just off Main Street, since 1943. I went into this place twice on the same day, 2 July 2010, in the morning for a coffee, and in the afternoon for a sandwich, which, after persuasion from the owner, a man called Mike Wade, was followed by a cherry-flavoured ice-cream soda. I got talking to Mike and found that he had bought this wonderful and well-preserved café six months before. He had been in 'auto-body work' for some years and wanted a change of lifestyle. I remember hoping that he would make a success of Traditions; he had hinted that he had bought it when sales were falling as shoppers migrated from Main Street to the edge of town, where the likes of Walmart and Sears had set up their megastores.

It looked the same from the outside. Would it be the same inside, with the chrome-and-leatherette revolving stools, and the 1950s painted menu with root beer at five cents and banana splits, two dips for twenty-nine cents? And would Mike still be there? I pulled on the door and went in. Yes and yes! The only difference seemed to be that Mike was wearing a lurid, tie-dyed T-shirt.

Of course, he didn't remember me. But, after the initial surprise, he made out that he did.

'I'm from London. I'd driven here slowly from Canada. We took each other's photos, and you said you'd put mine on the wall next to Elvis.' I look around. Elvis is no longer there. And nor am I.

'Oh yeah! Yeah. I think I remember.' He is frowning with concentration and his index finger is raised.

'I wrote a book about that trip. You're in it. Mike Wade.'

'Really?'

'Yeah. You could find it on the internet.'

'I don't have internet. I don't believe in it.'

We talk for fifteen minutes. Traditions is thriving. 'I expanded the menu a bit. More sandwiches. More pies. Good lunchtime trade. Office workers. Some shoppers still. And kids love it: the sodas and floats and sundaes.'

'You got this right,' I say. 'You've got what people go to Starbucks for — coffee and sandwiches — but better than Starbucks' mass-produced stuff. And you've got the retro sodas and ice creams.'

Mike has to go. He still has the car he bought in 1975 and he's taking it to a high-school reunion. 'I'm going to lead a drag on Main Street, which means driving up and down looking at girls. We used to do that every night.'

'Isn't that illegal these days?'

He laughs. 'Maybe.'

I try to pay for the coffee I've been drinking, but he won't let me. 'See you in eight years.' He waves an arm as he walks off.

I check in to America's Best Value Inn and head out to the Clarion Hotel bar, a place where, eight years ago, I had an enlightening conversation with a farmer and an agronomist who was employed to advise the farmer — he was a big-time farmer with two big farms — how to look after his land. Tonight I sit in the same seat I sat in back then. The place seems louder with music and chat — it's Friday — though there are fewer people at the bar. I order an IPA, and tilapia with sweet potatoes.

Next to me two young men are having an intense conversation and drinking Bud Light. Suddenly they order drinks from a bottle kept on a plinth in a glass case next to a bottle of ten-year-old Bushmills. It turns out to be Chivas Regal, which, somehow, I know was Hunter S. Thompson's favourite whisky. While I ponder whether to tell the young men this, the bartender pours the Chivas into shot glasses and the young men tip the nectar down their throats. Then they take sips of Bud Light. To me this seems the wrong way round: I would drink the insipid beer as quickly as possible and savour the whisky.

And why is the Chivas Regal kept in a glass case when there are two rows of single malts on shelves?

The tilapia arrives with a sachet of brown sugar. I ask the bartender what the sugar is for.

He isn't certain but he thinks it's to go with the sweet potatoes and the butter.

I eat and watch American football on a screen across the bar. The Wisconsin Badgers coach is called Paul Chryst.

Without warning the music is turned up and a light is shone on a spinning mirrored ball hanging from the ceiling. I'm sitting in strobe lighting and my tilapia is winking at me. Then five middle-aged women begin to leap about, screeching, behind me. More people, including the Bud Light and Chivas men, start to leap about shouting. In the more ordered world, a caption runs along the bottom of the screen telling me that Tiger Woods has three birdies and two bogeys.

I eat quickly, and wonder why American football players have a neatly folded little white towel hanging from the back of their extremely tight trousers.

And soon I escape.

52

McCain, Bascue and Ferlinghetti

The television in the breakfast room of America's Best Value Inn is showing John McCain's funeral. A middle-aged couple are watching as they eat. I pour bran flakes and milk into a polystyrene bowl and sit down. The funeral hasn't yet begun. The guests are milling about in the aisles of the Washington National Cathedral, chatting as if at a cocktail party. Small groups of grey-haired men are shaking hands and gently patting each other's backs. Not sure who any of them are – but that's Hillary Clinton. And there is Obama, and that must be Michelle Obama with her back to the camera. And there's Bill Clinton. And George W. Bush. A big man who looks familiar is milling around smiling – it's Al Gore. And that's Ivanka Trump and her husband, Jared Kushner. McCain, who planned this himself, pointedly and famously didn't invite Donald Trump – which is hardly surprising, since Trump denigrated McCain's service as a pilot during the Vietnam War. McCain was shot down on his twenty-third bombing mission, badly injured and imprisoned for five and a half years in Hanoi, where he was tortured and beaten. He received several medals, including the Distinguished Flying Cross. 'He's not a war hero,' said Trump. 'He's a war hero because he was captured? I like people who weren't captured.'

As I toast two slices of bread, the guests take up their places in the pews. A dignified elderly woman sits in a wheelchair, and the commentator says that she is McCain's 106-year-old mother. A camera zooms out, and the cathedral is revealed to be a gothic gem with soaring columns and a vaulted roof.

The Obamas, Bushes and Clintons are in the front row. Meghan McCain, John's daughter, speaks from the pulpit, movingly and through tears, about her father for several minutes. Then a song is sung to the tune of 'God Save the Queen'. I don't catch the words because a man with short hair, wearing a crisp yellow T-shirt with Harley-Davidson printed on the back, arrives and says, 'Do you mind if I change the channel?' He is speaking to me and the middle-aged couple.

'Er . . . no,' the middle-aged man says.

'OK,' his partner says.

'Sure,' I feel compelled to say.

Harley-Davidson man seems agitated, tight-lipped, close to becoming aggressive – which perhaps he would have, if the three of us hadn't been so docile. He picks up a remote, stares at it and pushes buttons. I wonder what's going to happen. Does he want to watch a game show? Or a soap?

The screen goes blank. And then the very same scene comes back on. The difference is that FOX NEWS is displayed in the corner of the screen instead of CBS. The singing finishes, and Senator Joe Lieberman speaks. He is dry and amusing, a Democrat senator and a great friend of the Republican McCain. Then, to save him the climb to the pulpit, Henry Kissinger is helped to a lectern close to McCain's flag-covered coffin. I didn't realise he was still alive. A voiceover says he is ninety-five. His voice is even deeper than it used to be, and he pays a solemn tribute.

I go to the breakfast counter and run into Harley-Davidson Man.

I try to be light-hearted. 'I thought maybe you wanted to watch a movie,' I say.

'I prefer Fox News,' he says, without smiling.

I leave the breakfast room, go to my room and turn the television to CBS. I want to pack my bag and get moving, but find I'm lounging on the bed watching George W. Bush, a man who used to seem terrified when he had to speak in public. Today he is articulate and well prepared. He is followed by Obama, who is moving, statesmanlike, and timing his words and phrases perfectly, as usual. He quotes Ernest Hemingway, whom McCain admired: 'Today is only one day in all the days that will ever be. But what will happen in all the other days that ever come can depend on what you do today.' Obama goes on, 'What other way to honour John McCain's life of service, than to, as best we can, follow his example?'

There's a theme to these speeches, especially those by Lieberman, Obama and Meghan McCain. They are certainly a hymn to America – the Declaration of Independence and Abraham Lincoln have been invoked – but there is a more specific message: the speakers have hailed McCain's humanity and wisdom, his willingness to make compromises to improve people's lives, to work across the Republican–Democrat divide. As well as a tribute to McCain, this is a rebuke to the absent Donald Trump. Meghan McCain made this clear when she said: 'We gather here to mourn the passing of American greatness – the real thing, not cheap rhetoric from men who will never come near the sacrifice he gave so willingly. America does not boast, because she has no need to. The America of John McCain has no need to be made great again, because America was already great.'

After Obama, a choir sings 'The Battle Hymn of the Republic'. The line, 'Glory, glory, hallelujah! His soul goes marching on' is repeated with sublime descants – and a soft man weeps.

I drive towards the library, and Garden City seems a better place than its neighbour Dodge. There is less dust and no gaudy pretension. Perhaps there is truth in their names. Here, trees, grass and flowers grow where they were placed: beside sidewalks. And old buildings, public and private, seem to be cared for.

A bronze, life-sized Mark Twain sits on a bronze bench outside the library, legs crossed, arms folded and not at all gaudy. He dangles an open book over his knee and stares with curiosity at library-goers, who look back in awe at his moustache, eyebrows and quiff, and wonder whether to sit down next to him. Eight years ago I sat down and cosied up, but to do it again seems unnecessary.

Inside I wander about looking at books and am smiled at by a young librarian with painted nails and a thin blue jumper.

I sit down at a computer and google 'Garden City immigrants'. I know that Garden City is famous for successfully integrating thousands of immigrants to work in its meatpacking plants. City planners, social scientists, journalists and film-makers come here from all over to see how it works. But I'd like to see if anything has changed in the Trump era.

Meatpacking began here in the 1970s when the city's leaders decided to admit a meat-processing factory to keep their town alive and prevent it becoming a ghost town like so many remote towns on the prairies. They knew such a factory would need immigrant workers and took steps to recruit them. The meat industry grew, with more factories, more cattle and more corn grown to feed them. More immigrant labour was needed – and the city contin-ues to recruit and welcome immigrants from Mexico, the central American countries, Somalia, Ethiopia, India, Vietnam, Laos and Myanmar.

Sometime in the 1990s Garden City became a 'major minority community', meaning there are more children of immigrants than of US-born parents in the city's schools. Even though Kansas is a conservative Republican state, most locals are happy with this. Many factors have combined to make it work: the city govern-ment, Chamber of Commerce, churches and charities have always worked hard to help newcomers to fit in; immigrants are nothing new – there have been many Mexicans here since the 1900s when they came to process sugar beet ; many nationalities and races live here – twenty-seven languages are spoken – so locals aren't swamped by any single group, and enjoy a range of cuisines, shops and cultures; for years it has been seen that immigrants work hard and pay taxes; and finally, there is near full employment and the city thrives.

I find a story on the National Public Radio website with the headline 'A Thriving Rural Town's Winning Formula Faces New Threats Under Trump Administration'. The author, Frank Morris, quotes the local sheriff who says that 'another Trump administration executive order could force local law enforcement to check the immigration status of otherwise law-abiding citizens'. The sheriff, Kevin Bascue, goes on to say that such action might cause the end of what the city has 'worked so hard over many, many years to make happen here. I think our community would be a dying community without the immigrants that have come to fill in the gaps, and to grow business.'

Bascue says his force will cooperate fully with federal immigration agents, 'but with an eye toward preserving Garden City's winning formula – which starts with immigrants'.

Hurray for Kevin Bascue!

I drive to the coin-op laundry on West Fulton Street, which is also Route 50, and get talking to the manager about McCain's funeral. She says she'll watch it later, and I tell her that Obama made a great speech.

'Oh yeah! He's a great speaker,' she says.

'Three presidents were there, but not Trump,' I say.

'Well, he didn't want him there. They didn't get along.'

She doesn't expand on this, but I sense that she sympathises with McCain rather than Trump.

While my washing rotates, I read a book of poems by Lawrence Ferlinghetti, *A Coney Island of the Mind*. I feel a bit of a ponce – but so what? Why am I worrying? There are just three people here. Maybe they are all poets and fans of Ferlinghetti. Who knows?

I move my clothes over to a drier and carry on reading. I come to these lines in the poem titled 'I Am Waiting':

and I am waiting
for a way to be devised
to destroy all nationalisms
without killing anybody

I close my eyes – and remember Nick Lowe singing 'What's So Funny 'Bout Peace and Love and Understanding?' and the studio audience clapping.

I take my stuff from the drier and put it on a steel table. Then I fold shirts, T-shirts, socks and smalls under the indifferent gaze of an old man with a stick, a white moustache, and a lifetime in his eyes.

53

The Clutter Murders and Truman Capote

Holcomb is a small town on Route 50 seven miles west of Garden City. It would be an unremarkable place if it weren't the site of the brutal murder of Herb Clutter, a popular local farmer, his wife, Bonnie, and two of his children, Nancy and Kenyon, in their own home during the night of 15 November 1959. The murders, the police investigation, the conviction and the execution of the two perpetrators are conveyed in gory and gripping detail in Truman Capote's book *In Cold Blood*.

Capote, already famous as the author of *Breakfast at Tiffany's*, and his childhood friend Harper Lee, soon to be the author of *To Kill a Mockingbird*, spent a large part of four years here talking to everyone involved: the Clutters' family and friends, police, lawyers, jailers and the two murderers as they awaited trial – and then their execution in 1965. Capote celebrated publication of *In Cold Blood* in 1966 by holding a black-and-white ball at New York's Plaza Hotel to which

540 guests, including John Steinbeck, Frank Sinatra, Greta Garbo, Marlene Dietrich, Andy Warhol and Jacqueline Kennedy, were invited and asked to wear masks. Capote called the ball 'my great big, all-time spectacular present to myself'. No one from Holcomb or Garden City, where the men were held in jail and put on trial, was invited. The book became a bestseller around the world, earning $6 million. A film followed a year later and was nominated for four Academy Awards.

Some locals were offended by Capote's appropriation of their tragedy and grief for his own ends. Perhaps they felt that this strange man from an exclusive literary clique in New York, a world of which people from the High Plains of Kansas had no knowledge, had grabbed a piece of their history and culture and run away with it – like Elgin with the Marbles. Some were offended because Capote introduced inaccuracies and, in particular, put words in people's mouths; Capote never took notes and claimed that he could remember long conversations. Furthermore, some felt that he had sympathy for the murderers – a pair of misfits from deprived backgrounds. Capote defended his book by asserting that it was a new form, what he called 'the non-fiction novel'.

The park in the centre of Holcomb is announced with a large sign: Holcomb Community Park, Dedicated to the Herb and Bonnie Clutter family. I park and walk across mown grass, passing swings, a children's playground, a picnic table with a roof, and plenty of trees. I come to a wide gravel path leading to a large brass plaque headed 'Clutter Memorial', mounted on stone and supported by a low brick wall. Behind are a box hedge, low fruit trees, small pines, a pair of cypresses, rose bushes, lavender. Two stone benches face the plaque at an angle. Everything is neat and respectful. I stand up to read the plaque which, in five paragraphs, tells a lot about the lives of the four Clutters who died that night in 1959 – and mentions the two elder daughters, Eveanna and Beverly, who had by then moved away from home. A single sentence states that the four were 'killed ... by intruders who entered their home with the intent of robbery'.

I sit on one of the stone benches and think about the contrast between these five paragraphs and Capote's book. The plaque was put here in 2009 to mark the fiftieth anniversary of the Clutters' deaths. The idea came from Bob Rupp, a local man who in 1959 was seventeen and a high-school basketball star; he had been dating sixteen-year-old Nancy Clutter and was the last person to see the Clutters alive. Obviously Capote hadn't met the Clutters – though he tried to find out about them. The five paragraphs celebrate four lives. The book turns four deaths and two killers into something more than simple facts; perhaps, given the book's success, Capote created a legend. If I were a local, or a friend of the family, I know which I would value. But if I were a New York sophisticate who had never been to Kansas – as Capote hadn't – where would I stand? But perhaps that is a silly question.

For miles 50 stays close to the Arkansas River, and is flat, straight and empty. I coast towards Colorado under a dome of blue.

I have postcards to post. In the small town of Syracuse, I find the post office and park fifty yards up the road where parking is permitted. I walk back along the sidewalk and watch a dirty white pickup stop in the middle of the road outside the post office; an elderly man gets out, leaves the door open and the engine running, and hurries into the building. By the time I get there, he is coming out clutching a handful of mail.

'Howdy,' he shouts.

'Hi,' I say, as he slams his pickup into gear and drives off.

Straightaway a car comes round the corner, parks in the same place, a door is left open with the engine running and the procedure is repeated. This time I say, 'Howdy.'

'Howdy,' comes the reply.

Beyond Syracuse, the road begins to rise and fall. Soon it becomes a switchback, like the A30 between Salisbury and Stockbridge, and in the rear-view mirror I see miles of tarmac bunched like a concertina.

I cross into Colorado and stop at a picnic area on the edge of a town called Holly. Amid the din of grasshoppers scraping their legs together, I sit at a concrete table eating almonds and apricots. A grasshopper lands on the table, and then another. I watch them spring up and away and see that the grass is alive with their constant hopping. Some seem to skim or fly long distances, ten feet or so, keeping close to the ground; perhaps they are locusts.

At another table, some way off, a couple are eating a formal lunch with knives and forks, off plates, on a tablecloth. They have glasses, bottles and lots of plastic boxes. They are chatting away, undisturbed by locusts.

I sit at a formica table eating a sandwich in a branch of Subway inside the gas station in Holly. Three old-timers in baseball caps, ventilated with mesh, sit at a table by the window. One of them is looking out at the sky, which is blue but for a few small puffy clouds low down. 'Think there'll be a storm?' he says.

'You bet,' says one of his friends without looking up.

The gaps between towns and villages are getting longer. Fifty-five miles on from Holly, I look for a motel in Las Animas and fail to find one. I press on twenty miles to La Junta and stop at the Travel Inn, which – for tonight at least – is run singlehandedly by an elderly (Asian) Indian man who smiles a lot. I take twenty minutes to check in because he is constantly interrupted by phone calls and queries from other guests. Intermittently while I wait, a loud unexplained bing-bong noise echoes around the tiny reception area. After several minutes the much-harassed, but still smiling receptionist disappears into a back room and returns with a flannel, which he wraps around a small box attached to the wall near the door.

After that there is no more binging or bonging – and gradually it occurs to me that I, more than anyone, had been causing it. The flannel is blocking a censor that was setting off the bing-bong whenever anyone came through, or walked close to the door.

54

Bent's Old Fort

In the morning I drive around in search of breakfast. La Junta is a reasonable-sized place, but short on bars and restaurants. Last night, the only restaurant I could find was full, so I ate in Pizza Hut. This morning I don't see anywhere – and am about to give up when I notice a crowd of cars parked close together on Colorado Avenue. It's Sunday, so perhaps their owners are inside an inconspicuous church. I drive closer and see CAFÉ on a sign above a blue awning. Some people are on the pavement outside, chatting. I park, cross the pavement, pull back the door and walk into a large room crammed with people, chat and laughter: families, groups, couples, loners sitting at a low bar; waitresses rushing all over, one young waiter, and a grey-haired man with a moustache at the till by the door.

I sit down at the bar. A dark-haired waitress pours me a mug of coffee and gives me a menu and I find that this place is called the Copper Kitchen. For the second time on this trip, I order my favourite breakfast: one egg over easy, bacon, hash browns and toast.

The waitresses know everyone, and they have the time to

chat – perhaps because there are so many of them. Two seats along from me a heavyset man has been reading a Spanish-language newspaper. Now he is confiding something to the dark-haired waitress; it seems to be a health issue and she shows her concern.

A few minutes later, he is talking quietly to another waitress. This time I pick up that he has a hospital appointment tomorrow and is worried. She talks to him for some time, frowning in sympathy, looking for an upside, saying it may not be as bad as he fears.

I think back to the Townhouse Café in Seymour, Indiana. This place is similar. Both are what Americans call 'mom-and-pop cafés' and are increasingly rare.

Later still, I get chatting to the dark-haired waitress, who turns out to be the daughter of the owner.

'This café seems to be the centre of town, the hub of the community,' I say.

'Yeah. It pretty much is,' she says. 'It's been ours since 1988, but there's been a café right here since way back. An old-timer told me there was a place here in the nineteen-fifties.'

'There was no one in the streets,' I say. 'Then I opened the door and they're all in here.'

'That's right. People come in because they see all the cars – and they're amazed. We only do half-day today, and some weeks it's our busiest day of all seven.' She looks along the bar to see if anyone needs anything. 'We just do breakfast and lunch. Some of the delivery men say that the places that try to do all three don't work. Besides, when would you get time to clean? I'm here sometimes – there's a lot of cleaning – till five p. m. And I want to see my family.'

'Yeah. People work too much these days – those who have jobs, that is.'

She smiles and pulls a zip over her lips. 'Yeah! Those who have jobs!'

Was that a reference to layabouts who stay at home watching television? Or to government policies not providing enough jobs? I suspect the former.

I pay her dad at the till.

He smiles and says, 'Thank you for coming in. You come again, please, whenever you can.'

Bent's Old Fort is not far from La Junta. I've seen enough US Army forts but, from looking at pictures and reading about Bent's, I know this one is different. It's older, built in 1833, with their own money, by brothers William and Charles Bent, and their business partner, a French aristocrat called Ceran St Vrain, whose family had been dispossessed during the French Revolution. Pictures of Bent's Old Fort show an adobe building topped by crude battlements – the kind of hot, dusty hideout that might feature in westerns set around the Mexican border, such as *The Magnificent Seven* and *Pat Garrett and Billy the Kid*. A woman called Susan Magoffin stayed there for twelve days while on honeymoon in 1846, and wrote that it 'fills my idea of an ancient castle'.

I drive uphill out of La Junta on to a treeless plateau of brown scrubby grass that reaches every horizon. I pass two horses, a chestnut and a dark bay, and see no other living creatures. This is the kind of landscape that would appeal to Cormac McCarthy and J. G. Ballard. After four miles I pass a sign announcing Comanche National Grassland and realise that I'm on the wrong road. I've been driving south-west when I should have been driving north-east.

Eventually I reach the car park at Bent's Old Fort, which I can see – long, low and earth-coloured – in a hollow about a quarter of a mile away. I take a leaflet from a perspex box which explains that I can walk directly to the fort along a paved path and, if I want, I can come back on the hiking trail which loops round by the Arkansas River for one and a half miles.

As I am looking at this, a man and a woman – youngish, both wearing shorts – come towards me. After some howdying, they tell me they have just walked the hiking trail. 'It's a nice hike, along the river, not too long,' the woman says.

'You could do it backwards,' says the man. 'Like, start from here. That way, if you buy stuff, you don't have to carry it all along the trail.'

I'm looking at the bag he is carrying and wonder what's in it. Key rings, dishcloths, packs of cards? 'Maybe I'll do that,' I say, and look up at the sky. 'It's a nice day for a walk.' It is: sun and streaks of white cloud.

The man looks at his watch. 'Well, you could go that way and you'd be there by one o'clock, in time for the tour – which takes one and a half hours.'

'One and a half hours! Do you *have* to go on the tour?' I'm thinking of getting straight back in the car.

They both laugh, and he says, 'No. But it's really interesting.'

And she says, 'There's a movie, and they dress up and act things from back then.'

I thank them and begin to walk the trail. It's a pleasant stroll among shrubs and small trees beside the Arkansas River, which is surprisingly insignificant: narrow, shallow, brown and broken up by sandbanks.

The Bent brothers and St Vrain built their fort here, on the Santa Fe trail beside the Arkansas River, which was then the border with Mexico, so that they could trade with that country, and with fur trappers, who by then were catching beaver in the Rockies, and with the local Indians, the Cheyenne and Arapahoe, with whom they were very friendly. Indeed, William Bent married a Cheyenne called Owl Woman and spent time living with her in her village, where he was known as Little White Man.

After thirty minutes I reach the fort, which has a chunky adobe look, pinkish brown like unpainted plaster. The Stars and Stripes flies over the entrance at half-mast. I walk in and find a large, gravelled space with a well in the middle and rooms built against the outer walls, below the battlements. Crenellated turrets stand at the north-east and south-west corners, and the place smells of leather and horses. Twenty or so people and their kids are wandering about, and five or six staff, dressed in period clothes with floppy hats and bandanas are sitting around. Steps lead to the upper level, where lookouts would have stood scanning the horizon, muskets ready. There are rooms up here too, including one for Sarah Magoffin, one for the French aristocrat, and a billiard room.

As well as the adobe walls, which are four feet thick, the fort is held together by huge logs, some of which look like whole trees. The place is sturdy and earthy, a setting where anything could happen, violent or peaceful. To me, it reeks of the romance of the Wild West. I just love it and it should be available as Lego. And yet it is real. Or almost real. Well, let's face it, it is an accurate reconstruction built in 1976 – something I wouldn't have guessed if I hadn't read it in the brochure. Reconstruction took 1,000 craftsmen fourteen months.

And it's all free. When I leave, I'm given a lift to the car park in an electric buggy by one of the guides, who is dressed as a ruffian in a green shirt and floppy cowboy hat. I offer him a dollar at the end of the ride, but he says, 'No, no. We get paid.'

55

Bikers

A group of tables sits in the shade of some tall trees close to the way out from Bent's Old Fort. Two shining motorbikes are parked and two men are sitting at a table; otherwise no one is there. It's almost half-past two. I decide to stop and eat some nuts and apricots, and try to park Harpo without blocking the bikers' view across to the fort and beyond.

I go to a table a little away from theirs. They're bikers; they won't want to talk to me, I think. As I sit down, one of them calls out, 'You passing through?'

I expect they've seen Harpo's New York plate and, as usual, I explain what I'm doing.

'This is a great time to be driving through the Rockies,' says one of them, a large man with grey hair tucked into a blue bandana. 'The schools are back and the aspens are turning. Great scenery around Cañon. Look out for that.'

'You get lonely, driving all this way on your own?' the other one, a lean, dark-haired man, asks.

'Yes. Sometimes. I listen to music.'

'Oh, what do you like to drive to? I play the Eagles a lot.'

'That's amazing!' I almost shout. '*I was just about to say the Eagles.* I love "Take It Easy".'

'Me too,' he says. 'Standing on a corner in Winslow, Arizona.' He speaks the line rather than singing it. 'We been there.'

'Yep. We have.' The grey-haired one grins.

We introduce ourselves. Grey hair – he looks like Father Christmas – is Geoff; he tells me he was born in 1947. Lean, dark hair is Paul. He is four years younger than Geoff. Thin-faced with high cheekbones, he could be a native American.

'We've been riding together for thirty years,' Geoff says.

'Long time' – Paul nods and smiles – 'and we're still friends.'

Their bikes are beautifully polished with gleaming chrome.

'So you go long distances, to places like Winslow, Arizona?' I ask.

'Sometimes.' Geoff blinks and pushes back his bandana. 'We've been over the Rockies, Utah, Wyoming. Today's just a Sunday afternoon out.'

We talk about their bikes. Paul's is an Indian 800 Scout, a beautiful machine with shining black paintwork and lots of gleaming chrome. 'Made in USA,' he says.

Geoff's is a Kawasaki 800. 'I got a fifteen hundred at home, but the eight hundred is faster. I use the fifteen hundred to carry my wife.' He chuckles, and Paul grins and looks skyward.

And then the conversation takes a surprising leap. 'You're English,' Geoff says. 'Do you know the TV show *Are You Being Served?*?'

I almost laugh out loud. 'Yes, of course. It's quite old now.'

'I love it,' he says. 'It's my favourite show.'

Paul is smiling and shaking his head. 'It is funny.'

Geoff especially likes Mr Humphries, the camp shop assistant, and we talk about how, when the show was first shown in the 1970s, no one talked about him being gay, but everyone knew. 'I don't think they could make a show like that now,' Geoff says.

'Probably not – but then comedy has moved on,' I say.

Paul agrees. 'But a lot of the old stuff is still funny.'

'Oh yeah!' I say. 'What about *Sergeant Bilko?*'

'He was something, Phil Silvers,' Paul again.

We talk about other American shows, going way back to *Burns and Allen*, *I Love Lucy* and *The Mary Tyler Moore Show* and forward to *Friends* and *Seinfeld*.

'You know the other English one I really love?' Geoff adjusts his bandana, smoothing it back.

'Er ... *Monty Python?*'

'No. That one – what's it called? – with Hyacinth Bouquet.'

'I know,' I say. 'She was so funny. What's it called?'

'*Keeping Up Appearances*, isn't it?' Geoff says.

'Right,' I say.

Paul is smiling, nodding and then shaking his head. He looks at his watch, and then at Geoff. 'We ought to go, man.'

'Yeah. I'd like to talk with you longer, but we do have to go.' He sighs. 'We're meeting some people – at a cemetery.' He stands up and zips his jacket.

'Great to talk with you, David.' Paul holds out his hand. 'You have a great trip. I'm sure you will.'

'Well, David, I'm real glad we met. It's been fun. Take care.' Geoff shakes my hand, and points upwards towards the west. 'Don't drive too fast round those bends up there.'

'Great to meet you too,' I say. And then something I say only in America, 'So long.'

They put on their helmets, climb on their bikes, drive away with Geoff in front and hold up their hands in a synchronised wave.

Only now do I eat my almonds and apricots – and then I drive away, back towards Route 50 at La Junta.

Beyond La Junta, I pass some ugly feedlots. There is no grass. The cattle stand in mud, their heads nodding in and out of troughs. Do cattle display body language? These seem to, and they're saying: *I hate this place – and the food; I'd rather eat grass.*

After a small town called Swink, I see a dim, dark blue shape above the horizon, way ahead, below the bright blue of the sky. Is that the Rockies? Surely not yet. I'm forty miles from Pueblo, and the Rockies are a way further.

I drive on under a beautiful cloudscape and listen to the Eagles. A sign – Pueblo 18 miles – slips past. A purple silhouette rises above the horizon ahead. That *must* be the Rockies!

Pueblo is big and built up and suffers from Interstate 25 running low above it, north–south, on a flyover. I cruise around and check into the Baymont Inn.

Later I sit in a booth in a lively Mexican restaurant called 3 Margaritas; I drink a tasty beer called Modelo Especial and eat a vast plate of chicken fajitas with tortillas. As the evening wears on, a table full of happy folk sing 'Happy Birthday' in Spanish. When they start again in English, I join in and clap. This Modelo is good stuff.

The breakfast room at the Baymont is crowded with adults and children. A huge screen is showing a band called Why Don't We; two of its members have Meet-Me-in-McDonald's haircuts. No one except me is looking at Why Don't We, whose name, I presume, was hit on by a think tank of marketing wizards. And I don't look for long.

I walk south on South Union Avenue in Pueblo's old downtown. Boxy two-storey buildings, dating from around 1900, all different, with decorative cornices at roof level, butt up against each other to form terraces. A few are bars and restaurants; more are antique shops or junk shops. There aren't many people around this Monday morning. The meat-and-potatoes, shoes-and-sweaters shopping is happening somewhere else. I look down from a bridge at the Arkansas River Walk, a tourist trail – with boat rides available – which winds past bars, restaurants, shops, art, sculpture, bridges and waterfalls; this was created not long ago by a restoration of the original route of the Arkansas River, which was diverted after a flood in 1921. Now the trail is almost deserted; no doubt it's packed at weekends and in the evenings.

A few blocks further south I cross the post-1921 Arkansas River. Also artificial, it is unnaturally straight, has sloping concrete banks and several low stone spits running right across, presumably to slow the current. A man stands in the middle of this ugly, neglected mess, fishing; the water comes up to his ankles.

I walk north again and turn off to the Pueblo Union Depot, a handsome disused railway station. Opposite is a café where I sit on the street, drinking coffee and listening to jazz, among others who seem to have time to sit and listen and stare.

I return to the car and drive out of Pueblo. I'm taking a break from Route 50 now. I will spend a week south of here, in New Mexico, resting with someone very special. So, like the interval in a theatre, this is a perhaps an opportunity to fetch a drink or visit the restroom or both. I will come back to Pueblo in seven days and carry on driving west.

56

Close to the Edge

The Quality Inn is just off Route 50 on the west side of Pueblo. Robert, the receptionist, is tall, brown-skinned and keen to talk. He was born in North Carolina and came here not long ago from New York. 'I wanted to look at the opportunities here, now that they have legalised marijuana. I bought five acres of land.'

'To grow marijuana?'

He laughs. 'No ... Well, perhaps.' He shrugs. 'It's more an investment. Prices will rise here. And having land with something happening on it will set me up legally in Colorado. I'm gonna begin with a pig on it.'

'Really?'

'Yeah.' He grins. 'Just so something's going on there.'

'And can you make money out of marijuana?'

He learned to cook when he was a child, he says. 'So I cook gourmet dishes containing marijuana. I might sell them, like in a farm shop. My star dish is a cheesecake with wonderful ingredients: vanilla, cinnamon, a dash of Jack Daniel's and, subtly, marijuana.'

Robert has other ideas as well. 'California makes a lot of solar energy. In summer it doesn't need it all. What to do with the rest? I like thinking about, researching these things.' He breaks off to suggest places that a young couple might go for dinner. Then he looks back at me. 'And, you know, you can make water in a world that needs it by using old, defunct air-conditioning units. They make water out of the air by cooling it; it comes out of them and falls on the sidewalk. Harness that. Someone – let's call him Bob – can make the water. Someone else – call her Susan – can work out ways to purify it and all that.

'I got no kids. I can try these things out. I can move around. I almost went to California, which I love, but this is the place now – in five years it'll be booming.'

'Because of the legalisation of marijuana?'

'Not just that. That is already bringing in more people. But the attitude. The tax breaks they are offering for ideas, for investment.'

'You know,' he says, 'travel helps people to learn, and you learn most if you have no plan, no itinerary.'

I eat at a local place recommended by Robert. It's called the Red Lobster. I order salmon.

The waiter is small with short, shiny dark hair. 'Do you want the dinner portion or the lunch portion?'

'I don't know. What's the difference?'

'Dinner is two pieces of salmon. Lunch is one.'

I'm glad he asked. 'The dinner portion, please.' It's 9.30 p.m., after all, and I'm hungry. The salmon is good. Almost as good as the Shock Top Belgian White beer.

50 is straight but for two bends, and runs through scrubby desert all the way – thirty-three miles – to Cañon City. Beige mountains with dark green summits lie on the horizons ahead and to the sides. I park diagonally to the pavement in a space on Main Street and walk about. This is the town that Geoff and Paul like. I can see why: the mountains are here, almost in the town, between buildings, at the

ends of streets; and the place is clean – as if recently swept and rained on and dried in the heat. Hard edges separate sunlight and shade. Pink and red Victorian brickwork shines out against the deep blue sky, and arched windows and fancy cornices rise above storefronts with blue, red, grey and green awnings. The town seems comfortable, a little elegant, but without pretention; plenty of working pickups are parked among the cars.

I have some cards I want to post and I pass a man sitting on a bench. 'Excuse me. Do you know where there's a mailbox?'

'No. I work for the refuse department.'

It's too hot to look for a mailbox. Instead, I find cool and shade in a café called the Bean Pedaller (which is also a bike-repair shop). I order coffee and a choc-chip muffin from the nice-looking waitress and mention the extreme heat that is grilling the sidewalk.

She smiles. 'It's supposed to stay hot for a week after Labor Day, and then start to cool.'

'Oh! Well, when's Labor Day? I hope it's soon.'

She smiles more broadly. 'It was last Monday, a week ago today – so that doesn't exactly add up.' She wrinkles her nose. 'But it could be cooler tomorrow. Who knows?' She hands me a plate with the muffin on it. 'I'll bring your coffee over.'

I sit at a table by the window, which is filled with large cactuses and an antique pedal bike.

About three miles west of Cañon, I turn off 50 onto a road that promises a view from high up a hill – or is it a mountain? – to my right. A sign says Skyline Drive. A notice says that the road is one-way, which is unusual outside of cities, but there must be a way back nearby. I drive through a stone arch and follow the lane – it's narrow, definitely a lane.

Yes. It really *is* narrow. The tarmac – old and cracked – is just wide enough for Harpo. The lane becomes steep. I climb rapidly and see that there is a steep precipice to my right. A strip of dirt about a foot wide is all that's between me and the precipice. No barrier, post, fence, anything to prevent a car – Harpo, for example – going

305

over the edge. I *hate* heights. They make me feel funny. But I have to keep going. I can't turn round. Even it were allowed, it would require a twenty-four-point turn, during which Harpo and I would slip over the edge.

I take the only action possible. I grip the steering wheel, stare straight ahead at the road – not sideways at the ever-increasing drop – and drive slowly forward. Thank the Lord there are no cars behind me, hooting and flashing their lights.

I climb even higher, and – horrors – there are now precipices on both sides of me. I glance at the valley floor – it's like looking out of the window of a jumbo jet – and quickly look away. I'm trapped. And now the lane plunges down – I have to apply the brake – and up again. I feel as if I'm riding a rollercoaster, but it isn't on rails; I have to steer along this narrow track.

A rock wall appears to my left – a temporary respite, but only to one side. And after that a lay-by. I pull in and park, take some breaths and get out of the car. I look around; it's OK as long as I keep away from the edge. A wrought-iron bench rests on concrete slabs close to a flat stone that would make a good picnic table. I stare down – way, way down at houses and streets, trees and grass. Beyond is a low grey ridge and further still a green valley and mountains, rocky mountains. And bright sky with clouds, flat-bottomed and puffy, rolling this way. Across the lane another valley, smoke rising, hills, mountains and more clouds, sunlit from above – yes, I'm looking down on them.

A small, silver car arrives and parks behind mine. A young couple get out, stand and gaze. And take selfies.

'Would you like me to take your picture?'

'Yes, please,' she smiles.

I tell them how terrified I am. 'Standing here is fine. But driving on that narrow strip with those drops both sides . . .'

'Oh. It's quite safe,' he says. 'You just gotta drive slowly. We done it often.'

'We did it in the dark, in the rain, the other night.' She smiles again and shrugs.

They must be crazy! Though they seem quite normal: both tall with plenty of hair; friendly and full of humour. Yet we're standing between two precipices.

He says it's safe. And I know it is. I can drive a car along a narrow road. That's all I have to do. Except it's up in the sky. The Skyline Drive. I look along the lane, up to where the road bends and then seems to end in the sky. That might be the highest point. After that, there could be a long plunge down to earth. Like a ski jump. 'How much further is it?'

'About another half a mile,' he says, 'and you come out somewhere down there.' He points down and to the left.

I get in the car. 'Drive safe,' he says.

'OK. I'll try. If I don't, you can phone . . .'

I drive on, up around the bend and over the summit. And then – the worst bit yet – absolutely nothing either side of the lane, which is just wide enough for the car, and a sheer drop both sides. I drive past another parking place – I want to get this over with – and from there, to my relief, the way is down. But still heart-pounding. A hairpin bend on the edge of a precipice. And another hairpin. A car catching up behind, a silver car, the nice couple.

On, on down – and somehow I'm in a residential street in a town. A sign tells me I'm in Cañon, the town I left about forty-five minutes ago.

I park outside someone's house and just sit. I promised myself a whisky when I reached the bottom – I have a miniature bottle of Jura, given me by my daughter before I left London. 'In case of a medical emergency,' she said with a grin. That *was* an emergency. But now? Better not. Instead I gulp water from the bottle.

57

Cannabis in Colorado

Before leaving Cañon for the second time, I have a good look at the map and see that 50 follows the valley of the Arkansas River, curling through the Rockies for some sixty-five miles to Salida. This time I drive quickly past the turning to Skyline Drive and emerge in spectacular country, wild and rocky with the shallow, fast-flowing river always close to the road. Cliffs of jagged, pink-tinged rock sit on both sides; shrubs and low trees grow on earthy hills, and through gaps I see mountain ranges, blue and bottle green in the distance. I stop often to stroll and breathe the clean air, untroubled by people or cars.

At Salida, 50 becomes Rainbow Boulevard, a broad strip flanked by fast-food outlets and gas stations, appended to a dozy old town shaded by verandas and pines. Quiet shops and bars fill three blocks of F Street, Salida's main street, which ends at a bridge across the ever-present Arkansas River.

I return to Rainbow Boulevard and cruise up and down, eyeing motels. I settle on the Circle R because it's not part of a chain; it has a dated, art-deco feel without seeming old or run down, as some of the chain motels do. The proprietor is friendly – it's clear that he owns the place – and my room, though not large, has the feel of a small house.

Further along Rainbow Boulevard is a marijuana store. I don't want to buy any but I'd like to have a look.

Like most edge-of-town stores, the 3D Cannabis Center is a detached building with its own car park. However, unlike other stores, it has no window displays, no brash posters proclaiming this week's special deals; it doesn't even have swing doors. Rather, it's a pink, single-storey blockhouse with one small window, one small door and a two large signs announcing Retail Cannabis.

As I park, an elderly woman with a stick is being helped through the door by a young man wearing a baseball cap and one of those beards that just outlines his jaw. As I walk towards the door, it closes. I push on it and find it's locked, so I ring the bell. No one comes. A sign says All Welcome, and a smaller one says that customers must be over twenty-one. I ring the bell again. Nothing happens. As I walk away, Baseball Cap and Beard appears with the elderly woman and helps her to her car.

'Are you open?'

'Of course. Welcome. Come in.' He apologises. 'I had to help that customer.'

I follow him into a waiting room, and explain that I don't want to buy anything; I'm from England and am just interested.

'Fine. No problem. We want to spread the word.' He waves his arms. 'As long as you have photo ID.'

I show him my passport. Then he ushers a man who is already waiting through a door into a room where the cannabis must surely be. It seems that only one customer can go in at a time.

Decorative pipes, bongs, books and free leaflets are set out on glass shelves. I sit down and read a leaflet called *Marijuana in Colorado: What you should know before consuming cannabis in the nation's first state to legalize*. It's useful information, under headings: 'Edible Products', 'Concentrates', 'Vaporizer Pens', 'Where

309

to Consume', 'Driving', 'Be Safe and Sensible' and 'The Facts' (which briefly explains the law). People buying alcohol in shops and pubs might learn from a similar leaflet.

As I read, a woman comes in from outside – the door is no longer locked – sits down and waits. A minute later another woman arrives. None of us makes eye contact or speaks. It's like being in a dentist's waiting room in a culture where dentistry is, for some reason, embarrassing.

After a while, the man is shown out and Baseball Cap and Beard leads me into a small square room. 'Have a look around. Feel free,' he says, 'and ask me any questions you want.'

Glass cabinets stand against three of the walls and display numerous products: cake, biscuits, sweets, gum, chocolate, tincture, resin, vape oil, inhalers, pain-healing salve and more. Much of this is branded and sold in boxes, packets and jars. Large glass jars, like those used for sweets in old-fashioned sweet shops, contain different types of grass, which are sold by weight.

'It's such a good thing,' I say, 'that this is legal.' (I've long thought that cannabis should be legal; I went to the Legalise Cannabis concert in Hyde Park in 1967.) 'When did the law change?'

'It was legalised for medical use in 2009 and then for sale to over-twenty-ones in 2014.' He waves his hands. 'But it took a while to sort it out locally and there was a lot of detailed stuff, sorting out secure supplies, manufacture, all that.'

'And other states are making it legal?'

'Washington State already. And there are about five who have gone some distance.'

'It'll be everywhere before long ... even England.'

'Yeah! That'd be good.'

'It's interesting this is happening in the era of Trump.'

He laughs. 'Well, he's all about money. So he likes it. I even got some tax back – two hundred dollars.'

'Oh, because you started a new business?'

'Well, no. We pay a lot of tax. They're very pleased with us.

So pleased, they gave us some tax back to encourage us.' He pulls a face, as if to say, *How about that!*

I've taken up three minutes of his time – and kept people waiting. I thank him.

'You're welcome. I hope you come back, man.'

58

A Fish in the Arkansas

In the evening, while it's still light, I lean on the bridge at the end
of F Street and look east along a shallow stream, perhaps one hundred feet across, flowing over and between flat stones. To my right,
seat-sized rocks are arranged in a small amphitheatre around a tiny
beach. A group of men in shorts sit and chat, and a man in a black
T-shirt stands ankle-deep in the water. This is the Arkansas River,
again, and that water, carrying bacteria from that man's toes, will
flow – through Cañon, Pueblo, La Junta, past Bent's Last Fort,
Garden City, Dodge City, Hutchinson, Tulsa, Muskogee and Little
Rock – some 1,400 miles to the Arkansas's confluence with the
Mississippi, and from there south 400 miles to the Gulf of Mexico.
This is my final encounter with the Arkansas. Its source is less than
fifty miles north of here, close to Mount Elbert, at 14,440 feet the
tallest mountain in all the Rockies, from Canada to New Mexico.

Beside me a young guy stares down into the water. 'See the trout,'
he says and points.

I follow the direction of his finger. 'Behind that stone you mean? . . . Yes, I see it.' A dark shape, perhaps eighteen inches long, pointing towards us. 'It's facing upstream. That's what they're supposed to do.'

'I guess. I'm just learnin' to fly-fish. There's another one.' He points again.

I peer into the water.

'You from round here' he asks.

'No. I'm from England. I just drove in here.'

'I thought I caught an accent.' He smiles. 'First time I've been here. Neat place.'

We talk about England and Denver, where he comes from, and fishing.

When he has to go, I cross the bridge and look west. The river is darker, made opaque by reflected light from the sky. Half a mile away, above the trees where the river bends, is the blue silhouette of a mountain.

Bridges and riverbanks are good places to meet people; flowing water is calming and there's something to look at and talk about. I remember meeting an artist on a bridge in Maryland, weeks ago now.

I wander around looking for somewhere to eat and am taken by a place called the Fritz which, from outside, looks like a busy bistro in Paris: small tables, wine bottles, chatter and a high bar where a row of people are sitting.

Inside it looks exactly the same.

I sit at the corner of the bar on the only empty chair. To my right a couple sit at right angles to me and to my left a man is fiddling with his phone. He's smart-casual, fit-looking, with a neat haircut and a pressed gingham-check shirt; I guess he's in his fifties.

We get talking when I ask him what his newly arrived meal is; it looks really good.

'Steak Fritz with fries,' he says and I order it too.

We get round to what I'm doing here and I mention my terror at driving the Skyline Drive.

313

I'm relieved when he nods. 'I know. I've been on that road. My brother lives near there. I had to sit in the back seat of a 4x4. I couldn't see anything, not even the edge of the road – just the drop.'

His name is Duane. He grew up in Nebraska near the Niobrara River, which I walked across on a footbridge a few years ago. He tells me why the Nebraska Sand Hills are as they are: glacial movement about 12,000 years ago combined with winds from the Rockies. I ask how he knows this.

'I'm a geologist. I work in oil and gas exploration.' He turns and looks me in the eye. 'I'm fifty-seven years old. I know a lot of stuff.' He chuckles. 'But I'm still a little boy really.'

'Yes. So am I.' I nod my head and look towards him – perhaps I'm hoping that he can see the little boy as well as the man. My Steak Fritz arrives. Delicious and uncomplicated: steak – the first steak I've had on this trip – chips, and hollandaise sauce.

I ask how he feels about fracking.

He sighs. 'It's been going on for fifty years. The opposition to it is whipped up by people with a green agenda.' He winces. 'What is new, but not very new, is the ability to drill sideways into rocks and push sand into cracks which are mostly already there. This facilitates extracting oil or gas from those rocks.' His hands are resting on the bar. He raises them a couple of inches. 'I don't think fracking is dangerous. In the UK it's easier to whip up opposition because the land beneath people's houses is owned by the Queen or the Crown, so, theoretically, fracking can happen below people's homes without their permission. Whereas in the USA people own the land under their homes' – he laughs – 'right down to the centre of the Earth. Anyway,' – he lifts his hands again – 'oil and gas won't be used in a generation or two, either because they will run out or because political pressure will bring about use of renewables instead.

'Meanwhile,' he says, 'we all owe our lives and our ways of life to nitrogen. That you can be here, having travelled so far, talking to me, is down to nitrogen. We depend on it, and we get it, thanks to the power derived from oil and gas.'

I don't know much about nitrogen, and think of saying, *What*

314

about oxygen and hyrdrogen? Instead, I ask what he thinks about Trump withdrawing the US from the Paris climate-change agreement.

'I think Trump is *despicable.*' He almost spits the word – and then he grins and shakes his head. 'Despicable. I've disliked him ever since he was on *The Apprentice*. But him withdrawing from the Paris Agreement isn't very significant, because it was never ratified by Congress in Obama's time. I *do* think the idea of politicians setting a target for the earth's climate is absurd. You know, politicians saying it mustn't get more than two degrees hotter. Obama and the Democrats say that kind of thing because they depend on the green lobby for funding and votes.'

'So is it OK if the Earth gets more than two degrees hotter?'

'No. It would likely be a disaster. But scientists, not politicians, know what to do. They can deal with this, can set their own targets – sensible ones. Give them money, give them encouragement. But don't make them follow instructions from politicians – you know, no more than x degrees by y date – that can screw us all up.'

I find I'm agreeing with him; he talks a lot of sense. We both order another drink – red wine for Duane, IPA for me.

'Did you like McCain?'

'Yes I did. But he made mistakes. With Russ Feingold – the Democrat senator – he pulled off a bi-partisan initiative to limit the money political campaigns can use or accept in donations. Well, it backfired. It limited donations, but it's brought about a new form of funding by specific-interest groups, who are dictating the political agenda.

'Everything now – the debates on CNN, NBC, ABC and CBS and Fox – is directed by PR people who are in it for the money; they will support whichever cause pays them and frequently switch allegiance because someone else pays them more. Every question you hear asked is put down by a pollster.'

'How about the Founding Fathers,' I say. 'Did they get it right?'

'The Founding Fathers!' He grins. 'Did *they* get it right? That's a huge question.' He's still grinning. Now he lifts his hands and almost punches me on the shoulder. 'The Founding Fathers. Well, they were incredibly shrewd to build in the checks and balances that they did build in – and especially keeping religion out of government.'

'Well, I rate Jefferson, partly because he was such a good writer.'

Duane nods. 'And he bought the West from Napoleon.'

'And they were right, definitely, to separate Church and state. You know that the Queen is head of the Church of England?'

He looks surprised. 'No. I didn't know that.'

'And we have bishops in the House of Lords – Anglican bishops. And religion, emphasising Christianity, has to be taught in our schools – though parents can withdraw their kids.'

'Some states make rules like that,' he says, 'despite the Founding Fathers.'

He swallows the last of his wine, pays his bill, and shakes my hand warmly. 'It's been good to meet you and talk. But I talk too much.'

There's a hold-up on F Street. I sit in a line of cars. And pull out a little to see what's happening. A large deer, or perhaps it's an elk, is standing in the middle of the street. Minutes pass before it wanders off into a side street.

59

Golden Eagles

The woman who cleans the motel rooms at the Circle R is outside my little house with her cart loaded with sheets, towels, soap and shampoo. She has long dark hair and is about forty. A young black guy stands beside her holding a broom; he seems to be her helper. She points up into the pure blue of the sky. 'See them?' Five or six large birds are circling quite low above us. 'They're golden eagles.'

'Really?'

'Yes. When I pray, I always see them the next morning. If I forget to pray, they aren't there.'

'Wow!' I look up again. I'm sure she's right. They are golden eagles. They look golden and have huge wingspans.

'I'm Native American. I have a feel for these things. They come from the other side. They go real high, higher than any other bird, above the wind. Or they'll come in low, like here now.'

I look up again, shading my eyes from the sun. 'They're wonderful. I'm from England. We don't get these there. There are some in Scotland, I think.'

'You from England?' The young black guy is speaking. 'Liverpool? I love the Beatles.'

'Oh. OK. I like them. I'm from London.'

'Oh.' He looks disappointed.

'You know *Abbey Road*?'

'Yeah, I love that record.'

'Abbey Road is in London. They recorded the album in a studio there.'

'Oh, I didn't know that.'

The Indian woman is pointing to the eagles again. 'They're around town in summer. You'll see them down at Safeway and Walmart. They come down and pick up stuff. Sometimes they'll pick up a little dog and carry it way up high, and drop it to break the bones so they can eat the bone marrow. That's what they really love.'

'Oh God! That seems cruel.'

'Yep. It is.' She pulls a face – or is that a ghoulish grin? 'Nature's like that.'

50 is smooth, two-lane and free of traffic as it climbs between tree-covered mountains. Above me, forests of green conifers are patched with the yellows of autumnal aspens and eastern larch. After forty minutes of gliding uphill through gorgeous, ever-changing, sun-filled mountains, I reach the top of Monarch Pass, where the frontage of a souvenir shop and café – the only building in a large car park – announces Monarch Crest, Continental Divide, Elevation 11,312 Feet. To the left, or east, of these words is the word Atlantic; to the right, or west, Pacific. Hitherto, the rivers and streams I have crossed on this trip have flowed into the Atlantic; from here on they will lead to the Pacific.

Driving down is more difficult, with much slowing down for bends, cars on my tail and a sign that says, 'Truck ramp for run-aways 3½ miles'. Are you supposed to drive that far around these tight bends without brakes? When I reach the ramp, which is an uphill stretch of stones, there are tyre tracks in it. After nine miles of braking and spinning the steering wheel, I come down onto a flat

318

road across a broad valley, past meadows, streams, pools and grazing cattle, with bosomy hills a way off on either side.

I come into Gunnison, where the wide Main Street has a western feel; false-fronted buildings sit among the familiar, staid mix of Victorian buildings. The place is alive with young people and bicycles; there's a university here somewhere. I have a soft drink and a hummus sandwich in a bar called the Alpine Brewing Company, and get talking to a man with white hair and a trim moustache. He's on a trip from his home in the mountains outside Los Angeles to visit his daughter in Denver.

I tell him that I find the traffic on freeways in big cities hard to handle.

'I've been commuting into LA every day for thirty years. Sometimes I still take the wrong lane off the freeway, and drive around and back to avoid the risk of a crash if I change lane.'

I'm glad to hear this. 'So it's not just me who finds it difficult.'

'It's hard,' he says. 'You have to drive at the same speed as everyone else, for safety. If the limit is sixty-five and they're doing seventy-five, it's safer to go seventy-five.'

After Gunnison, 50 follows the Gunnison River and the landscape changes again into a world of dreamy lakes, wild marshes and low hills. As I drive on, the lakes become more wild and their water a greener blue, and the low hills grow into bare mountains and mesas, the flat-topped, steep-sided hills that rise above plains, . Further still, trees reappear and again I'm among mountains coated in conifer and aspen.

I reach Montrose, cruise past a line of fast-food joints, park in downtown and walk about. I remember the woman in the tourist information office in Gunnison saying, 'The town itself doesn't have so much to offer as the surroundings have.' This seems to describe Montrose also.

A few miles out of Montrose I'm confronted by a sign: When You Die You *Will* Meet God.

Soon I'm in Delta. It's 7 p.m., and I check into the Riverwood

Inn. Outside my room a strip of lawn leads down to the Gunnison River. I walk out and gaze across the water as the sun sets, golden behind the trees on the other bank.

I eat at Daveto's, a busy mom-and-pop Italian restaurant, patronised by men in shorts and recommended by the owner of the Riverwood Inn. I'm shown to a booth. There's no bar to sit at and no television showing sport or anything else; nor, from my booth, can I hear anyone else's conversation. I look out of the window at Main Street. Dusk has fallen and no one walks past. The back of the illuminated sign that says that Daveto's is open flashes red and blue; across the street, the words Wells Fargo are lit up in yellow; cars are parked and occasionally one drives past.

A friendly, concerned, middle-aged waitress brings me a beer, Blue Moon Belgian White, and a salad which includes two tiny crackers wrapped in cellophane. And I go on looking out of the window. I sit, stare and think. It feels good.

In the distance, behind the Wells Fargo sign, illuminated white letters are coming out of the dark and moving from right to left. Holy Co—. I am hoping for Cow, but it's Communion Sunday 10.15 a.m.

My baked ravioli with sausage arrives. It is 'smothered' – a word much used on the menu – with 'marinara', a thick tomato sauce in which I sense chillies and capers; and smothered again in melted cheese. This is quite a nosh-up, but I'm hungry.

My first pedestrian – a man in a pink shirt, blue jeans and a baseball cap – walks past the window. Suddenly I remember Duane last night – not that he was wearing a pink shirt – saying that nature doesn't give a damn about humans (or small dogs, if the cleaner at the Circle R Motel is to be believed). The world will go on when all this consumption of cheese, pasta and tomato sauce, and oil and gas, has ended. The golden eagles know what they want and how to get it.

60

Call a Marine

Donald Trump is on the morning television news talking about 9/11 – yesterday was the seventeenth anniversary. He makes that annoying circle with his thumb and forefinger and is clearly trying to win votes. He is followed by a succession of fit-looking middle-aged folk telling us how they once suffered from a variety of medical conditions – constipation, inadequate catheters and Crohn's disease – but that they are now all better thanks to the products they are holding in front of the cameras. Film of people fleeing the coasts of Virginia and the Carolinas ahead of Hurricane Florence comes on as I switch off and head for the breakfast room.

There I drink coffee and spread Smucker's Grape Jelly on toast, while a middle-aged couple sit on the other side of the room: she bottle blonde and on the large side; he tall and lanky with long, straggly hair. 'Look at this,' she says. She spreads a newspaper on the table and points. 'This gun. It's big and new. Do you think we should get one?'

He looks and doesn't seem keen. He stands up, crosses to the breakfast bar, puts bread in the toaster, comes back and sits down.

'Do you think I should apply for a job as a bus driver?' she says.

'You could. If you want.'

'If I went to Denver, would you come with me?'

He grunts.

I leave Delta and drive into another startling landscape: scrubby, treeless, desert-like country – marked with long, low, flat mesas – where almost nothing green is growing and all is earthy brown. This is the western slope of the Rockies, lower than Monarch Pass but still 5,000 feet above the sea. Here, beneath an intense blue sky, 50 is a four-lane divided highway skimming the top of the world.

The country becomes greener as I approach Grand Junction: cypresses and cottonwoods beside the road; horses in a white-painted post-and-rail paddock; a sign to a vineyard. 50 bends, climbs and falls on its way through the city, a large and hilly place with long outskirts at both ends. Grand Junction has an orchestra, a theatre, upscale shopping, kayaking, fishing and golf, but all I want is to get my hair cut. At the western end I turn and drive back east. Somewhere back there I saw a small building signed Hill Top Barber Shop.

I'm lucky. A man is just leaving. A woman with wavy dark hair and brown eyes greets me and waves me into a red-leather barber's chair. She wraps a stripy cloth around me and smiles. 'So-oo, what can I do for you?'

She's looking at me in the mirror. 'Oh ... I'd just like it tidied up and shorter please.'

'OK. That shouldn't be too difficult.' She sprays my head with water as if I were a houseplant, and starts combing. 'So where are you from? I guess not from here.'

I explain. She stops cutting for a while, stares at me in the mirror and listens. There's no one waiting, and no one else in this little wooden building, which is like a large beach hut. She asks questions, and I find I'm talking more about myself than I have to anyone during this trip. To explain my interest in North America, I tell her about my grandfather, an alcoholic accountant who in the early years of the twentieth century became unemployable after being sacked for stealing from his employers in London.

She's snipping at my hair again, and glancing at me in the mirror.

'He was forced to leave his home and his wife and son, and ended up living on the streets for four years, sleeping on benches, eating in soup kitchens. Then he was helped to emigrate to Canada, and fetched up working on the railroad in a small town in Manitoba.'

'OK!' she says.

'Twenty years ago I went to the town in Canada where he'd lived to see if there were any traces of him. It was the first time I'd been anywhere in North America beyond the East Coast.'

'And were there . . . traces of him?'

'Yes. I met an old man in his nineties who – when he was a baby – lived next door to him. He didn't directly remember him, but he remembered his parents talking about him. The old man's father had a pair of boots made by my grandfather. They were the best boots this man ever had, his son said. After spending a year building a fence along miles of railroad, my grandfather became the town's cobbler. In the end I wrote a book about all that.'

Then I ask her about herself. 'I was born in LA. And then we moved to near Gunnison – that's when I got to like this part of Colorado – but then my dad died, and we moved back to LA. I got married there, got divorced and came back to live near here, in a little town called Pitkin – you'd have passed the turn to it, off Route 50 before you got to Gunnison. I bought the gas station and the general store and brought my kids up there.' She stops talking, bends her knees and peers at the back of my neck.

'So do you commute to here from there?'

'No, no. My daughter went to college here. And I moved here. I like it. I got married again. My husband is a builder.' There's a buzzing noise as she cuts my hair at the back with an electric clipper. She switches it off. 'Did you say you wrote a book?'

'Yes.'

'What's it called? Can I buy it?'

'Well ... you could, but—'

'So what's it called?'

'*Swan River*. That's the name of the town in Manitoba where my grandfather went.'

She's picked up her phone. I can see her in the mirror, tapping on it. She holds it up and peers at it. 'Is your name David Reynolds?'

'Yes.'

'There's a copy for thirty-five dollars.'

'No. That's ridiculous. There should be some used paperbacks. They'll be much cheaper.'

She keeps tapping her phone, using both thumbs, and eventually buys a copy for $1.50, plus postage. And she carries on cutting my hair.

'Eyebrows?'

'Yes, please.'

She does a quick blow-dry and comb, and holds up a mirror so that I can admire the back of my head.

'Great,' I say. She whips the cloth from my shoulders and I stand up. 'That's great. Thanks. And it's been fun.'

'Fun for me too,' she smiles as she folds the cloth. 'And I'm getting a book to read. I love reading.'

I'm about to ask her how she feels about Donald Trump, when the door opens and an elderly man comes in, followed by a woman.

'Hello, Marianne,' he says and grabs both her hands.

'Jeff. Jeff, this is David – from London, England. David, this is Jeff and this is Anna.'

'Oh!' says Jeff. 'We were in London recently. Had a great time ... but Big Ben wasn't striking.'

'Oh, I know. They're trying to mend it,' I say.

'We met on a cruise ship.' He points to Anna who is small, dark-haired and perhaps Chinese-American. 'She was security on the cruise ship, and she got me to leave the dance floor one night at three a.m. That's how we got together.' He laughs. Anna doesn't seem quite so amused.

Jeff is thin and wiry, wearing a baseball cap and a navy-blue

T-shirt with the words Royal Marine Commando stitched in gold thread beneath an embroidered crest. He sees me looking at it. 'If you need any help, call the marines.' He chuckles. 'You know, our marines were modelled on yours. Ours were founded in a bar in Philadelphia.'

'After Independence?' I ask, desperately trying to think of something to say.

'Actually, a little before.'

'Well, you needed marines to win your independence.'

'That's right!' He chuckles again. 'And you know what, you were lucky to get shot of us unruly people.'

'Yeah, we're fine without you.' Jeff and I laugh. Anna smiles thinly.

I pay Marianne, and say goodbye to everyone. As I open the door, Jeff calls out, 'Don't forget. Any trouble, call a marine.'

61

Global Warming at the Strayhorn

As I leave Grand Junction I begin to arrive in the wonderfully named Fruita; the latter is almost a suburb of the former. Over the short piece of land in between, the dull brown flatness continues, although to my left, not far away, are hills – perhaps mountains – where pinky-orange rock is studded with greenery: shrubs, small trees, perhaps conifers.

In Fruita I turn left at a sign to the Colorado National Monument. It looks interesting; the road is leading to the mountains – and what is this monument? After a couple of miles I am driving alongside dramatic towering cliffs, like the ones that Indians look down from in all those westerns.

I take a turning to the right, again signed to the monument, and stop the car to study a map on a plinth. Four miles down this road is a visitor centre and a twenty-three mile loop of road, called the Rim Rock Drive, is marked. I look up and see tiny cars, way above me on stripy yellow cliffs. I can see that they are driving along the edges of sheer precipices with no guard rails or any protection from a sudden slip of the steering wheel. I drive on and come to a kiosk where a woman wearing a cowboy hat and the National Park uniform is selling tickets. She says that some people feel a little dizzy on the Rim Rock Drive and that even the four miles to the visitor centre is along unguarded roads at some height.

After my heart-pounding, nightmare panic on the Skyline Drive, I have ruled out driving along narrow roads on the edges of precipices. The nice woman lets me come in, turn round and go out again without paying.

I drive on along the side road from Fruita. There is no traffic, so I stop frequently to gaze up at majestic cliffs, striated in reds, pinks and yellows, and canyons filled with green shade. I come to a parking place for hikers, stop and study some information on another plinth. Independence Monument is a two-and-a-half-mile hike from here. Further on, at three and three-quarter miles, is a rock formation called the Kissing Couple. Hikers are told to follow the track and stay on it, because leaving the track disturbs wildlife, and to take away *all* their litter because 'the tiniest crumbs can cause upset tummies for lizards and ants'.

I decide to try hiking – walking, in fact – a few yards, maybe a hundred yards; I spend a lot of time driving, so that will be good. I take a bottle of water, my hat, and my phone to use as a camera. I walk on rocks up a gentle slope and quickly feel puffed, but something makes me go on. I follow a sandy trail beside a fence, behind which are some swanky houses with swimming pools. The trail turns away from the fence and heads up towards a ring of cliffs striped in every shade of pastel red from plum to the palest pink. Then it narrows between dry shrubs and a stony slope that falls away, worryingly, to my left. I clamber up flat grey rocks amid a strong smell of pines, and say to myself, 'That's enough. Go back.'

But I go on. And on and on. There's a kind of bliss here in the hot, scented air – alone under a vivid blue sky with these beautiful rock formations.

On a sandy stretch of path, among sagebrush and prickly pear, I see footprints. A man-size, zigzag pattern appears again and again, clearer than the other prints. I reckon this Man Friday has been here today – and there is no sign of him walking the other way, back towards the car park where two cars were parked.

The track is heading towards a vertical grey rock. It looks as if the path ends here. But it doesn't. I climb over shiny flat rocks, and on the other side is soft, sandy soil – and the footprint. That guy has been here; the path *must* go on.

A forked rock, tall and narrow, rises high behind a ridge in front of me. Could that be the National Monument or the Independence Monument? I keep going and keep thinking, *Is this foolish? If I slip on one of these loose stones and fall, no one will know – there is no one anywhere near.* But always I want to see what's round the next corner, over the next rise. I come to a cliff wall, which seems to soar for miles into the blue, cloudless sky. Surely a dead end. But there's the track going on to the left.

I go a little further, thinking this really is enough. I can't see where the track might end or whether it will get round the next sheer cliff wall. I must have walked two and a half miles by now; the forked rock is probably Independence Monument. I stand still, grasping at this magical place, holding on to it: the sun, now low and whitish; the warm air; the hot rocks and boulders; the stones, sand, scrubby plants, cactuses; the scents of pine and sagebrush; and the reds, browns, yellows.

My mind turns practical. It's after six o'clock. Allowing for dawdling, stopping and staring, it's an hour's walk to the car. I won't get to Utah tonight. I should find a motel in Fruita.

I hear voices – some way off. I can't see anyone, but they seem to come from further up the trail. I keep looking and spot two tiny figures far above me, on the opposite curve of this cliff – a woman wearing a pink T-shirt and a man in a black one. I can see a line from them to me, around and down this vast wall of rock; I can guess where I would have to go to complete this journey, to see Independence Monument from bottom to top. And – to hell with it. It's too late in the day. I've done this and loved it.

Pink T-shirt and Black T-shirt gradually come closer behind me; they're laughing and talking – the woman with that shrill, surprised tone that young American women often have. Eventually they catch up with me. I'm standing still drinking water; they smile and say hello – and keep walking and chattering.

I follow more slowly. The cliffs are a mass of light and shade, and even the low sagebrush throws long, wispy shadows. And now those trainer prints are going the other way.

Back in the car park, Pink and Black are standing, chatting, drinking water. I sling my hat into the car, and realise that they're saying a long goodbye. Two cars: one is hers; one is his. They are still talking when I drive off.

I check into Fruita's Super 8 motel and, taking advice from the man on reception, walk a block in the twilight around a dried–up field to the Strayhorn Grill.

At the bar I get talking to a handsome, weather-beaten man with thick hair and an enormous moustache. He's wearing a subtly patterned shirt and a baseball cap. After explaining how I come to be in Fruita, I tell him about my walk.

He nods. He's been on the same walk.

'I saw the Independence Monument, but I didn't see the Colorado National Monument,' I say. 'Where is that? I couldn't see it on the map out there.'

He leans back on his bar stool and laughs. 'No. You wouldn't. It's not a monument, as such. It's the whole place – all those cliffs and canyons – about twenty thousand acres.' He twiddles an almost empty glass of red wine. 'A national monument is like a national park, only not quite as restricted. National parks are set up by Congress. National monuments are designated by the president. This was Taft – around 1910. He knew this area. He wanted to protect it.'

We get on to what he does. 'I buy and sell cattle at auctions for clients all over: Utah, Wyoming, New Mexico and around here.'

329

I know there is a water shortage right now and ask if it affects his business.

'Yes. It's a big problem, especially this year. People are selling proportions of their herds, fifty, sixty per cent. Many, particularly breeding females, are being sold to ranchers in the north where there's more water.' He stands up, walks around the bar, picks up a bottle and pours himself some more wine.

'You must be a regular customer,' I say.

'Oh! No. I own this place. Well . . . with Sheryl, my wife.' He smiles and points along behind the bar to where two women are standing: one has neat blonde hair and is wearing a blouse; the other has short dark hair and bare, tattooed arms. He comes back and sits down. 'About the drought: whatever is causing global warming, whether humans are causing it or not, it *is* happening and it's happening all over the world – look at the Arctic, the Antarctic – *and* we must do something about it.'

He's a friendly man. He tells me his name is Bill, and he seems in no hurry to do anything except drink slowly and chat, while I sip IPA and eat chicken salad.

When I mention Trump, he frowns – as many people do. 'I think the man is despicable.'

'Someone else used that word to describe Trump – a geologist I met in Salida.'

'Well, it's accurate.' He twiddles his glass. 'We hoped that having a businessman in the White House might produce some policies that would help us, and' – he almost sighs – 'some of them are helping, perhaps. But he's the kind of businessman who will do anything for money, without regard to other issues.' He swallows some wine. 'There are certain standards that, I expect in Europe too, we expect our leaders to stick to – and he doesn't.'

I mutter my agreement and say something about Obama.

Bill looks wistful, puffs out his cheeks. 'Obama is a good man, but very liberal. He wants to help everyone, and, of course, we want people with disabilities to be supported; we all go along with that. But it went too far.' He pauses. 'I'd rather there were free contraception, paid for by us, than us paying for women to have babies, fifteen thousand dollars a year.' He speaks quietly, without rancour. 'There are people who are better off not working than working.'

'Most people want to work,' I say.

'But they get out of the habit, and working doesn't make them any better off.'

I finish my salad. The tattooed bartender takes my plate away.

'Would you like a piece of one of Sheryl's fruit pies? She's famous for her pies. Have a piece on the house.' He calls Sheryl over and the tattooed bartender comes too. 'Sheryl. Meet David. And this is Jamie.'

Big smiles and howdies.

'David's driven from Maryland to get here – and he's moving on to San Francisco.'

'Wow!' says Sheryl. 'Can I come with you?'

'And me,' says Jamie.

Sheryl says her peach pie is good today, and goes off to heat up a slice. Bill asks Jamie to fill up my beer. And we talk about the Indians. 'I'm sorry for them,' he says. 'They live on all the worst land. I work for some tribes, selling their cattle. But going into their reservations can be difficult. If you go on their land, find someone and ask permission. Be very respectful.'

The peach pie arrives; a scoop of ice cream is melting on top.

I ask Bill if he's read Dee Brown's *Bury My Heart at Wounded Knee*.

'I did, when I was young. I was very moved by it. My grandfather was a doctor, lived in Oklahoma. He treated Quanah Parker, the Comanche chief. Parker was a civilised man who lived in a big house and all that. At the same time, he ruthlessly killed many white men. But in defence of his people's way of life.' Bill sounds admiring rather than critical.

'A lot of those great chiefs – Sitting Bull, Crazy Horse, Geronimo – killed a lot of white men. but I can't help feeling sympathetic.'

Bill nods. 'Yep. We have to live with that. It's part of our history.'

The peach pie is delicious. I'm the only customer left in the bar. I eat up, drink up and pay my bill – a chicken salad and one beer. Big thanks. Handshakes. 'Good luck. Come by again.'

62

Grey-Green River

At Fruita, Route 50 joins Interstate 70 and the two continue together almost 300 miles to Salina, Utah. To avoid driving on an interstate, I take Route 6 west out of Fruita. After about ten miles I reach a small, dusty town called Mack and a sign that says 'Through traffic left to I-70'. I ignore this and drive straight on – if I have to, I can always turn back. The tarmac road continues, although the yellow line in the middle is very faded, as if a decision has been taken not to bother with it since the traffic is all on the interstate.

I pass the back of a large wooden sign supported on two posts. I stop the car to see what it says on the front. Beneath a cut-out painting of mountains and fir trees are the words 'Entering the Centennial State of Colorado'. So I must now be in Utah. Across the road is a beaten-up trailer home, some farm implements and two horses eating grass in a fenced-in field. I drive on. A cloud of dust comes towards me and resolves itself into a dirty white Toyota, which shoots past.

The landscape becomes semi-desert, flat, brown and featureless.

And, twenty minutes – perhaps fifteen miles – after the Colorado sign, in a stony lay-by, four letters are hand-painted in red, one above the other –

U
T
A
H

– on a small piece of board nailed with a single rusty nail, at a crazy angle, to a post.

So, it's a fact. If I wasn't there already, I'm in Utah now.

I drive over a cattle grid. The tarmac is cracked. The desert is more sand than shrub, and stretches for miles towards distant hills. No sign of humanity. How often does anyone drive along here? If ever. Ten miles on, a yellow road sign carries an image of a cow and the message Open Range. And, curiously, a line of telegraph poles appears, crossing the desert heading north-east, at an angle to the road. I stop, stand in the hot sun, and count them: sixteen, growing ever smaller and more like matchsticks until they vanish, carrying three wires, into a hazy distance.

A breeze cools the heat of the sun, and I drive on with the windows down, air-conditioning off. Where is this road going? Somewhere. It can't just peter out. I suspect this was once Route 50, the original, laid down in the 1920s.

I catch a sound, a faint hum – which grows louder and familiar: trucks on an interstate. Soon I see it to my left. It has to be I-70/Route 50. I come to a T-junction, a narrow, well-maintained road – left towards the interstate, right to somewhere unknown. I choose left and, as I come close to the approach road, two deer, mother and child, wander across. I slow. They stare, and skitter away.

I'm on I-70/Route 50, travelling at 60 mph with cruise control and my toes waggling. I want to reach Salina, where 50 will be liberated from 70, with as little interstate driving as possible. I turn off at the first opportunity, onto a road numbered 128 and head towards Moab, forty-five miles to the south-west; from there I'll return to 'my' road further along.

Here there is more scrubby desert, with the line of the horizon broken by low mounds and ridges. And soon there are trees to my left, through which I can see the grey of a river – and then an old suspension bridge beside a smooth concrete arc, which carries this two-lane road. I pull into a rest area and read an information board. The old bridge is Dewey Bridge, built in 1916 and intact until 2008, when a seven-year-old boy playing with matches caused a fire that destroyed its wooden, single-track carriageway. And the river is the Colorado River, which I crossed back in Grand Junction close to Marianne's barber shop, where its meeting with the Gunnison River gave the city its name.

Here the river is opaque, grey-green and about fifty yards across, with low rocky banks and no sign of a boat. I think about John Wesley Powell, a great American. Despite losing his right arm fighting on the Union side in the civil war, Powell was a man of action as well as a college professor. In 1869 he led the first expedition to travel the complete length of the Grand Canyon by boat – an adventure described in his bestselling book *The Exploration of the Colorado River and Its Canyons*. In 1883, as director of the United States Geological Survey, he became unpopular for advising correctly that land west of the 100th meridian (which runs through Dodge City) was too dry for farming and homesteading.

I cross the bridge and drive with the river close to my right, and soon I'm among stunning red rock formations, which rise up on both sides. Like the Colorado National Monument, the landscape is studded with imagery from westerns – and, indeed, many films, not just westerns, have been shot around here, notably *Thelma & Louise*. It takes me an hour and a half to drive the thirty-five miles to Moab because I keep stopping to gaze up at extraordinary shapes: pencil-thin buttes standing on conical peaks, brick-like mesas sitting on and squashing sharp ridges, a sphinx with the slopes of a mountain for a skirt. Closer to Moab, the landscape expands; cliffs and peaks,

335

and their attendant mesas and buttes, stand apart from one another, further from the road, becoming ever more majestic. Here there is space, in the lee of a pair of monumental mesas, for cattle to roam like beetles on a cathedral floor.

Moab is a pretty town, its hot pavements clogged with dawdling people in hats, shorts and shades. I go into Back of Beyond Books, cool and well stocked, and sneak a look at a local guidebook. I learn that I have just driven along the south-eastern edge of the Arches National Park, famed for its 2,000 natural sandstone arches, and perhaps one reason for the tourists and souvenir shops. I try two of Moab's motels, but am told they are full because the town is packed for its annual music festival.

I take US Highway 191 north-west out of town and skirt the western edge of the Arches National Park, crossing a broad desert of brown sand sprinkled with parched shrubs. Muddy hills, sprouting rocks striped with an eerie chemical green loom on my right, and craggy cliffs and long, low mesas stand a way off to my left. I come to the entrance to the Arches Park. It's 6.30 p.m.; dusk is coming on. Too late for sightseeing.

I get back to 50/I70 thirty miles west of where I left it, and follow it for twenty miles to Green River.

There is one room left at the Super 8. 'It's a disabled room. That OK?'

'Yes. That's fine.'

And it is – a perfectly good room with plenty of railings.

63

Mormons in Walmart

Next day I drive up and down Green River's straggling Main Street, past fast-food outlets, RV parks, a coin-op laundry, a carwash – and Ray's Bar, where last night I ate mahi-mahi with chips among boisterous locals who weren't unfriendly but were, understandably, preoccupied with talking to one another. On the bank of the Green River itself, where Main Street crosses it, stands the John Wesley Powell River History Museum – a low, modern building with plate-glass windows. Shall I go in? I'm off museums, but I have a soft spot for the adventurous Powell. I admire his speaking truth to power: telling businessmen and railroad magnates, who had much to lose, that homesteading wouldn't work in the west.

I go in and find that, though Powell features – there is a recon-struction of the boat he took through the Grand Canyon, with a waxwork of the great man sitting in an armchair amidships – the museum also covers the entire history, prehistory, geology and explo-ration of the region. I spend a not unpleasant hour absorbing what I can about colonists (including the Spanish), Indians (principally the

337

Ute, after whom this state is named), and outlaws (principally Butch Cassidy and Sundance), and then head out of town.

Turning north, I drive for mile after mile on a two-lane road through sandy, scrubby desert, its dry waste softened by strange hills and mounds like the feet of giant elephants – and, further away, long ridges, both low and mountain-high, flat-topped or rising in steps. An occasional gentle bend or stretch of bridge with, regularly, every three miles, a half-mile of passing lane. Emmylou Harris's *Red Dirt Girl* plays, and for a while I let the windows down and hang my arm out in the sun. In fifty-five miles two cars pass, and the lights of a truck, a mile behind, shine like diamonds in the mirror. Otherwise there is no sign of man but for a defunct gas station displaying a worn advertisement for jerky. This kind of distance driving is relentless; somehow it's so simple that I'm having to concentrate harder than I might driving down Piccadilly.

At last I come to a gas station and pull in. It's 4.30 p.m. I'm hungry. I sit at a Subway table eating a six-inch ham sandwich and watch flies fooling around in the window.

Five miles on I hit the city of Price – and the shock of humanity: parked cars, a child in a buggy, Walmart, the King Koal Movie Theater and Utah State University Eastern.

At the information centre the door is locked. A young woman appears and opens it; she looks as if she's on her way out. 'Have you come for the meeting? It's upstairs.'

If only I'd said 'yes', what might have transpired? Would I have got away with it, like the man who went for a job interview at the BBC and ended up on the news answering questions about the internet?

'I was hoping to get some information about motels.'

'The information centre is closed. But what did you want to know?'

'I was thinking of driving on to Helper. Do you know if there are any motels there?'

We're standing on a grey carpet in the reception area; this kind woman is holding two bags and a ring binder. 'There's one, but I wouldn't stay there.' She makes a face and shudders. Then she looks out through the glass door – 'I'd recommend the Greenwell Inn, which is right there.' She points across the road. 'That's the back of it. Just drive around the block. My boss used to stay there – and it's not expensive.'

I thank her. 'It's really kind of you to help – after you've closed for the day.'

'That's OK.' She looks at me and smiles. 'But I don't work at the tourist centre.' She nods towards the reception desk. 'I'm an attorney. This is the county courthouse. The information people have a room upstairs.'

At the Greenwell Inn the receptionist is a very chatty, youngish woman – so chatty that I think she won't mind my asking if she's a Mormon. She isn't, but she doesn't mind being asked.

She gives me a door key and a voucher offering a discount at the Tangerine Eatery on the other side of the car park. When I ask if they sell beer, she says I should go to the bar downstairs, which is called Wooly's Lounge.

'Wooly's Lounge?' I'm not sure that I've heard correctly.

'Yes. Wooly's Lounge.' She smiles and shrugs. 'I've no idea why it's called that.'

'I'd quite like to meet some Mormons,' I say. 'Maybe there'll be some at Wooly's Lounge.'

'They won't be in there because they don't drink,' she says.

'Well, maybe I'll go to a coffee bar.'

'There won't be any there either, because they don't drink coffee!' She's laughing.

'Do they drink tea?'

'Maybe' – she doesn't seem sure – 'occasionally.'

'Well, where do you think I might meet Mormons?'

'Walmart.'

'Walmart?'

'Yes. Really. That's where you see them.'

'I don't think I can go up to someone in Walmart, and say,

"Excuse me. Are you a Mormon?"' Now, like her, I'm giggling.

She calms down. 'I can recognise them. They have a glow.'

'No!'

'Yes, really. It's hard to explain.'

'So I should go to Walmart and look for someone with a glow. How many Mormons are there in this town?'

'I would say about fifty per cent are Mormons.'

'So there's an even chance in Walmart. And there must be a pretty good chance outside in the street.'

'Yes. But probably better not to go up to people in the street.' She's holding a hand in front of her mouth, and trying not to laugh. 'It might be a little easier in Walmart.'

'You mean sidle up to someone who's looking at the bananas, and say something casual about bananas – kind of as a way in?'

She's staring down at her keyboard, hand still over her mouth. Her shoulders are shaking. She doesn't seem able to speak.

'You could' – she breaks into a giggle – 'try that.'

'Is it true that the men have five wives?'

She looks up and shakes her head. 'No. These days they only have one. The multiple-wives thing is seen as a joke.'

A couple have arrived wheeling suitcases. 'Good luck,' she says – and turns to them.

64

Love and Indecorum

I go into the Tangerine Eatery and take the stairs down to Wooly's
Lounge, a dark basement with a pool table and a bar at the far end.
The bartender is talking to the only other customer. He breaks off
and brings me a bottle of Hop Rising Double IPA; he's young with
short, spiky hair, a bent silver ring through his lip and a goatee beard
which lacks the usual moustache component. He goes back to the
other customer, and it becomes apparent that he is interviewing him
for the job of bartender. The man doesn't strike me as much of a catch
as a bartender: when asked to name a drink – so that he can be shown
how to enter it into the computerised till – he can't think of one.

He leaves. I order a BLT from the menu – and the bartender,
whose name is Kyle, and I get talking.

'I got a wife and a five-year-old boy and a little one. As well as
this job, I work as a waiter in a restaurant called Wingers.' In both
places he's paid a little more than the minimum wage, which is $7.25
an hour. 'Plus tips,' he stresses. 'Tips are important for bartenders and
waiters.' He gestures with his thumb to a glass that sprouts dollar bills.

I ask if he is a Mormon, though I suspect that he isn't, since he is the manager of a bar.

'I was raised a Mormon but I left when I was about seventeen. I was drinking and smoking – I'd been smoking since I was fourteen.' He starts pulling glasses from a dishwasher. 'It just didn't fit with my life. My parents didn't seem to mind. My grandmother did. "Won't you come back to the church?"'

'So were your parents born Mormons?'

'My dad was. My mother wasn't, but she went to church as required.'

'Is that like every Sunday?'

Kyle explains that Mormons have to go to church at a certain time on Sundays, depending on where they live – in which of the city's wards. 'I got fed up with that. Also, the church takes ten per cent of everyone's income. They even come knocking on your door saying, "You owe a hundred and thirty-two dollars."'

While Kyle is telling me this, another young guy arrives and sits on a bar stool close to me. He's lean with glasses and is wearing a yellow baseball cap backwards. Kyle opens a bottle of Bud Light and puts it in front of him. His name is Timmy.

'What do they do with the money?' I ask. 'Ten per cent of people's incomes is going to stack up.'

'They build more temples, and they pay tax,' Kyle says. Timmy is rolling a cigarette. He looks up. 'They don't pay taxes.'

'No?' says Kyle. 'Well, what do they do with the money?'

'Oh. They help people out,' says Timmy.

My BLT arrives and, while I munch it, Timmy tells me that he is a musician. He writes his own songs: rap and hip-hop. Sitting on his bar stool, he sings one of them, a slow ballad, unaccompanied. His voice is low, rasping.

'That was good,' I say – and I mean it.

'I got thirty-six albums available for download. All you have to do is go to my website.' He writes the address in my notebook. 'I'm MC Timmy.'

He tells me that he finds collaborators on the internet whom he

342

doesn't actually meet. 'They hear my songs and ask if they can put music to them, or they add to them, flesh them out.' He shows me a video on his phone: Timmy is singing and I can see a man playing guitar; it sounds good. 'I never met that guy. He just wanted to do my songs.'

Timmy orders himself a beer and gets one for me. 'You know, one of my ambitions in life – it's on my bucket list – is to see Chelsea play live.'

We talk about football and travel, and I find out that Timmy works as a chef in the restaurant upstairs. He hasn't yet been outside the United States, but he's hitched around a lot.

An older man – not that old, about thirty-five – comes in with a dog, a beautiful black German shepherd called Ava. 'Her parents,' he says, 'came here from Czechoslovakia, so she's first-generation American.' He strokes her head and she looks up at him. 'She would protect me even from myself,' he says. 'One time, I had a gun that was malfunctioning; she put her paw up to stop me trying to fire it.'

Two women come in, collect beers from Kyle and go to the pool table. Then a small, young, disabled man arrives. He's a friend of Kyle and Timmy. He asks if he can feed Ava a potato croquette, which Kyle has heated up specially.

'Of course,' says Older Man. And Ava takes it from his hand.

Someone says they wish there was a strip club in Price. Older Man is enthusiastic. Timmy is amused at the idea rather than keen.

'I'd get my wife to work there.' Kyle says. 'She'd earn a lot. She's got a great booty.'

'My wife could work there too,' Older Man says with a smile.

Kyle says, 'My wife really does have a great booty.' He fiddles with his phone and shows a photo to Older Man and Timmy.

'All right,' says Older Man.

Timmy says nothing, but waves a hand in a hasty salute.

Then he holds it up to me: a picture, taken from the back, of a woman wearing suspenders and no knickers. He quickly whips it away. Luckily I don't seem to be required to comment.

I buy beers for Timmy and me. Kyle prises the tops off and says, 'It's great being a barman because of all the different people I meet. Some white Africans came in.' He speaks as if they were really weird.

'They might have been from South Africa,' I say.

He looks blank, so I tell him about apartheid and Nelson Mandela, whom he has heard of but isn't sure why. We talk about segregation in the US, which he knows all about. 'That was bad,' he says.

'It was crazy,' I say. 'Down in the south the white people would dance the night away to a famous big band, all black musicians and led by a black man, and then the band couldn't stay in the hotel where the ballroom was, because it was only for whites.'

'Real bad.' Kyle shakes his head.

'That used to happen to Duke Ellington, you know.'

'No. I don't know him.'

Two youngish guys arrive and Kyle makes them cocktails in what look like old jam jars.

The small man – I've picked up that his name is Zach – has sat down next to me. He is urging Kyle to make something, a drink I presume, for his mother, because he has to get home. Zach is about four foot six tall; one of his hands is bent backwards; his head is rather lopsided; the tops of his ears curve over.

'I gotta go,' he says to me. 'I have to have dialysis tomorrow.'

'Oh, I'm sorry.' I say. 'Can you get a transplant? Any chance of that?'

'Yes. I'm being tested for that. And my brother is too. And if my brother isn't a match, Kyle has said he'll be tested.'

'Oh! That's good of him. Are you good friends?'

'Yeah. Kyle is my best friend. We were neighbours from years back. Kyle taught me to walk. I didn't walk till I was ten. They told me I wouldn't be able to.' He looks away and then back. 'They said I wouldn't live after birth, but I did. Then they said I wouldn't live beyond five, but I did. They kept telling me I wouldn't live, but I did.'

'That's great!'

344

From his slightly wonky face, his big eyes look into mine. 'Don't underestimate a handicapped person. They'll prove you wrong.'

'And Kyle taught you to walk. That's great.'

'Yeah. He's like a brother to me.'

'How old are you now?'

'I'm twenty-four.'

'Is Kyle the same age as you?'

'He's a bit older. Twenty-seven, I would think. Hey, Kyle. How old are you?'

'Almost twenty-eight,' Kyle calls over his shoulder. 'Here you go.' He turns and hands Zach a container with a drink for his mother. Zach gets off the bar stool and says goodbye to Kyle, Timmy and me.

I chat to Timmy and drink up my beer. I shake hands with him, and then with Kyle, a good man who will give up a kidney for his friend – and show his wife's bare bottom to a stranger.

65

More Giggling in Utah

I drive north out of Price, reflecting that I am near the beginning of the monumental detour provoked by my determination to drive as little as possible on the interstate, which has temporarily taken over my beloved 50. My route to Salina using regular highways takes me on a 199-mile loop to the north. Anyone else would drive 107 miles on the interstate – and get there in less than two hours. But then, I'm in no hurry.

The landscape north of Price is as parched as it was to the south, but here there are long, slow bends in the road, trees, ridges, even cliffs and mountains. The colours are greys and earthy yellows. Mounds that might be slag heaps – this is coal-mining country – sit in front of spectacular cliffs with horizontal stripes in dirty white, cream and beige.

I turn into the town of Helper – mainly because I've read that the museum – *another* museum! – has some relics of Butch Cassidy. It's a pretty town in a rugged sort of way with old, boxy red-brick buildings on a main street that slopes gently uphill until it collides with an imposing stripy cliff. Helper's name comes from railroad engines that were based here in the 1880s to help push trains on their way to Salt Lake City up the steep hills to the north.

An old man is selling antiques and general junk from a shop that's as much on the pavement as it is indoors. 'I came here from New Jersey fifteen years ago and stayed. I like the remoteness, the quiet, the weather,' he says. 'And the people.' He reaches across to an old typewriter and straightens it. 'The local people are easy to be around. And the new people are arty – I like them too.'

I wander into the Western Mining and Railroad Museum and find memorabilia of those industries on which Helper thrived for most of the twentieth century. Some great and colourful paintings, many of them landscapes, hang in rooms on the ground floor: some from the early days of the Wild West; others by painters who live up the street. I suspect artists like Helper's cosy size, its setting in a semi-desert close to mountains and, perhaps, the light that comes from the big sky.

The Butch Cassidy and the Sundance Kid display in the basement is disappointing: a couple of photographs, a WANTED poster, and a flight of four wooden steps from the entrance to the Pleasant Valley Coal Company, which Butch actually walked up before robbing it in 1897. I stand where Butch stood – and have a flashback to playing a note on Patsy Cline's piano.

As I leave, I get chatting to the man who runs the museum. He wants to know where I'm going next. I tell him I'm going up Highway 6 to Soldier Summit, and then to Thistle before turning south to Salina.

He shakes his head. 'There's a serious fire blocking 6 north of Soldier Summit.' He frowns. 'Better not to go that way. We just been hearing about it on the radio. Sounds bad.'

'Oh! OK. I'll work out—'

'Where are you trying to get to? Salina?' He's pulling a map out of a drawer.

'Yes.'

He unfolds the map, holds it up and looks at it. Then he puts it on the counter and swivels it towards me. 'Best way to Salina is to go back to Price and take Route 10 all down here' – he runs his finger along Route 10 – 'till it hits the interstate. Then you got' – he leans low over the map, takes off his glasses and squints at it – 'forty-eight miles to Salina.'

I stare at the map. It makes sense. 'Well, thanks. That's really helpful. I'd better do that. I was just trying to drive on the highways and avoid the interstate.'

He puts his glasses back on, looks at me and smiles. 'I hate interstates, but it isn't bad down there – mountains, you'll see. And 10 is a neat road. Here, you have this.' He folds the map and hands it to me: the *Official Highway Map of Utah*.

I thank him, walk out into the street and put my sun hat back on.

I stop at a gas station on the edge of Price, where an electronic sign tells me it's 2.15 p.m. and 87°F.

That excellent man is right about Route 10. In places it crosses desert, which is broken up by every form of human-shaped protuberance from pimples to buttocks, via thighs, knees, bosoms, hands and fingers – even thumbs. Elsewhere, and closer to the few towns, 10 slides through green, irrigated pasture where cattle – and, just once, sheep – safely graze. Whatever the foreground, flat-topped, striped and skirted mountains rise up behind.

I buy a salad in a gas station, turn off in a town called Ferron, drive three miles and find a blue-green lake at the base of pink mountains, their crests and crevices finely drawn in sun and shade.

I sit among trees at a stone picnic table. Kids walk by with their mother, and say hello.

'Hi.' I grin – and stare at the lake with a plastic fork in my hand.

I sweep onto Interstate 70, which is climbing gently into tree-covered mountains. With my speed at 65 mph I set cruise control – easy, so easy. A small white car swoops past followed by a black four-door pickup. As they pull away, the road gets steeper; the white car pulls over and the pickup surges on. We keep climbing. I

348

pass a huge FedEx truck towing an equally huge trailer. Grey rock walls crowd in on both sides. The road reaches 7,000 feet and slaloms slowly downhill. Mountains, sparsely coated in small conifers, rise on both sides, and a long mesa fills the V-shaped gap between them, like the sea at the bottom of a valley. I try to slow for the constant bends without braking, as cars, and even a few trucks, sprint past in the fast lane, their brake lights flashing at every bend. There is nothing built by humans here except the road itself, the dull metal central barrier, and the yellow signs announcing bends and leaping stags.

170 straightens and flattens. FOOD, a sign shrieks, above advertisements for Denny's, Mom's Café, Burger King and Subway. Mom's Café! Remember that.

A little later, I hit downtown Salina. Few lights are on and there's no sign of a bar. It's 8.30 p.m., and I remember that I'm in Utah, the land of the Mormons. However, painted in large capital letters on the wall of a two-storey building are the words Mom's Café: Famous Home Style Cooking since 1929 – Homemade Pies, Soups and Scones – Great Steaks, Salad Bar – Lunch & Dinner Specials. Around the corner, above the entrance, Mom's is announced in neon. The café is lit up inside – but there are no customers.

I go in and ask if the place is open.

'Yes. We're open. Come in. Welcome!' A woman with a blonde bob which swings around her chin is smiling at me. 'Sit anywhere you want.'

I sit down in a booth. Another woman, dark-haired with a ponytail, is standing behind the bar. She smiles and says, 'Howdy.'

'Hi.' I look at the bar: Coke, OJ, Sprite, nuts, ice cream – no bottles or beer pumps.

Blonde Bob hands me a menu.

'You don't have beer, I suppose.'

'No. I'm sorry. We don't sell alcohol.' She smiles. 'We just do great food.'

'Food is what matters.' I ask for orange juice with soda and ice, look at the menu, and see 'Trout: eight ounces, pink and boneless'.

Blonde Bob brings the orange juice. 'Are you ready to order?'

'I'll have the trout, please.'

'Baked, fried or mashed?'

This alarms me a little. I'd assumed it would be fried in a pan. But American waiters often come up with choices that the customer is forced to make. I think quickly. 'What do you mash it with?'

'Oh! Er . . . A little butter, a little sour cream . . . and chives.' She's standing with pencil poised.

'Sounds great. I'll try that. I've never had that before.'

'Really!' She seems startled. 'You don't have that in England? I'm guessing you're from England, with the accent 'n' all?'

'Yeah. I'm from England. We don't have mashed trout, as far as I know.'

She makes a spluttering noise, bends double and pumps her arms towards the floor. 'No, no . . . *no!*' She's almost shouting. 'We don't mash the *trout*. We mash *potatoes!*' She gasps and looks up at me, and drops her pencil on the floor.

I begin to giggle – which makes two of us. 'Oh-ooh! Right. I thought that was odd, mashing a trout.'

She's the first to calm down. She picks up her pencil and smiles broadly. 'So, start again. With your pan-fried trout would you like baked, fried or mashed potatoes?'

'Mashed, please.'

It's good food. No more customers show up. 'They mostly eat early,' Blonde Bob says. I chat with her about England, the United States, Utah and Salina, and Mom's Café. Descendants of the original mom are still involved, and some of her recipes are still served. Pies were her speciality. For dessert I have her blueberry pie – and go back to my motel happy. Who needs alcohol?

66

'The Loneliest Road in America'

I leave Salina on the familiar Route 50: smooth, ageing blacktop, one lane each way, light traffic. It takes me across a broad plain covered in golden grass, where cattle stand on the remaining green and chew gratefully. Purple mountains sweep down on both sides, and clouds float in the blue like tropical fish. This is perhaps the most tranquil, pastoral scene I've encountered – and it eases the transition between the rivers and red mountains of Utah and the dry desert of Nevada.

I come to the small town of Scipio, which lies on this plain. I park at the edge of a car park close to a church. There are no people here, but plenty of cars. It's Sunday. I can guess where the people are. I stroll on grass under trees and come to a large bell mounted on a plinth built of reddish stone arranged like crazy paving. A brass plaque says that in 1860 thirteen Latter-Day Saint families formed a community in this valley close to the mountains. Three years later Brigham Young, the man who had led the Latter-Day Saints, or Mormons, to Utah, advised them that being close to the mountains put them in danger of attack from Indians. 'He accompanied the men to the center of the valley, laid out the townsite, designated the location for a public square and center of town, and named it Scipio.' In 1869 Scipio's first bishop showed up and used this enormous bell to summon the saints on Sundays.

I drive on through the town, which comprises old houses, their bricks paled by the sun, spaced along a road, and stop to look at a pair of petrol pumps rusting outside an abandoned garage. Edward Hopper is in my mind when, suddenly, there is traffic in this hot, sleepy town. The Mormons are coming out of church.

Soon after Scipio, the road again becomes straight, flat and empty, with just an occasional car or pickup. Again, I am crossing golden grass amid maroon mountains – but on a grander scale; it's as if a football pitch has replaced a tennis court. Pastoral has given way to magisterial; I have a sense of being exposed amid the landscape, rather than enclosed by it; of being alien within it, rather than a part of it.

Delta is the last town on 50 in Utah – although the Nevada border is still eighty-nine miles away. Beyond the town, the flat landscape takes hold again, now with little vegetation, distant mountains and blue sky – beautiful and somehow numbing; I'm growing used to these huge, almost blank vistas.

Without trying to, I'm keeping pace with a tiny black rectangle, probably a mile in front: a car, pickup or truck moving at the same speed as I am. I expect that, like me, the driver has set his speed at 65 mph, the limit here. Sometimes the rectangle disappears in a mirage – and, if a car comes the other way, it appears to merge into it. Nothing moves except this black rectangle. And when it disappears, over a ridge or round a slow bend, there's nothing. And nothing in the mirror. Nothing moving except me.

A lake, or perhaps a salt flat, has appeared on the left; a blue haze hovers over it and softens the outline of the mountains behind. Heat haze, perhaps; according to Harpo, it's 94°F outside. The road veers to the north, away from the lake, and the lake turns silver, glowing, beautiful, becoming more silvery as it recedes – and the mountains lurk behind a purple haze. A battered sign marks a dirt road to Sevier Lake Reservoir. I listen to Dvořák's *New World Symphony* – and feel uplifted, as was the Czech composer – wasn't he? – by sights like this.

Suddenly a deer is standing beside the road, a hundred yards ahead. I slow, stop and watch as it crosses the road and stands in the scrub on the other side. It has curved antlers, large ears and a white behind – probably a mule deer. Where did it come from? There's no cover here.

Now the road is climbing and rounding a ridge. A car is coming towards me and, unusually, there's another behind it. Down on the plain, beyond the ridge, the mournful bit of the *New World Symphony* that was used to promote Hovis bread is playing. In my mind, I see an old man walking up a steep hill in Wiltshire, while in the real world a sign points down a track: You Dig Fossils: 20 miles.

And the road goes on – straight, up, around a curve, down and straight again. A pair of motorbikes pass. And then a US road sign in faded green: Eskdale to the right – perhaps a village. I can't see anything much over there. I've been driving for almost an hour and a half. The *New World Symphony* ended with a thump or two a while ago. Now there's something ahead. Low buildings. A big sign. Nevada!

There's a gas station here at the border, and the Border Inn, which advertises a motel, café, food store and, in larger letters, slots. I'm surprised to see so many cars outside – about ten. I park in semi-shade under pine trees beside an outsize pickup with 'Jim Umhoefer' painted on its side. I go inside and find myself in a café that is also a souvenir shop.

The young Hispanic woman who makes me a coffee gives me a copy of *The Official Highway 50 Survival Guide: The Loneliest Road in America: Nevada* – and stamps it to show that I stopped here.

Life magazine, in a 1986 feature listing 'America's superlatives', described the 287 miles of Highway 50 in Nevada between Ely and Fallon as 'The Loneliest Road in the USA'. (Ely is sixty-three miles west of here.) The magazine quoted a spokesperson for the American

Automobile Association: 'It's totally empty. There are no points of interest. We don't recommend it. We warn all motorists not to drive there unless they're confident in their survival skills.' The idea that this is the loneliest road has been used ever since to promote tourism in Nevada. The handsome booklet I've just been given is part of that – it looks like a passport and has maps, information, photographs and a space for travellers to have it stamped. If you get it stamped in eight specified towns, you can post it to the Nevada tourism people and they will send you a certificate. And the 'loneliest road' has got longer; the tag covers all 409 miles of 50 within the state.

The stamp in my *Survival Guide* says 'Baker', a town on a side road about twelve miles south-west, at the entrance to Great Basin National Park, which has caves, peaks and 'several groves of Bristlecone pine trees, the world's oldest living things'. I'm planning to stop in Ely tonight, but wonder about Baker.

The Hispanic woman tells me there are two small, independent hotels there.

'No big chains?'

She laughs at the idea. 'It's just a little place on a tiny road. You'll see if you go there. You should go to the cave. It's amazing: stalagmites and stalactites.'

I leave the Border Inn, unsure whether to head for Baker or Ely. It's 4.45 p.m.

67

Two Bikers, A Veteran and His Wife

It's 8 p.m. and I'm back at the Border Inn – in room 1, which is a kind of end-of-terrace prefabricated hut, new and comfortable with unpredictable electrics. Next door, in room 2, are my new friends Tony and Mike.

I went to Baker. The Whispering Elms Motel had no rooms. At the Stargazer Inn there was a handwritten message – 'Back in twenty minutes' – pinned to the door. In Kerouac's Restaurant, next door to the Stargazer and part of the same business, the bartender didn't know if they had any rooms. I would have to wait till the man came back. I sat on a wall in the shade for almost an hour.

Meanwhile Kerouac's was filling up. Excited, suntanned young Americans were sitting on the veranda drinking cocktails, chosen from a menu carrying this epigraph: 'Kerouac's is an homage to life on the American road and to feeling at home in unexpected places.'

Eventually, Stargazer Man returned. 'We're fully booked. Sorry.'
By then it was 6.30. I would have to drive to Ely, sixty miles.

I went to Kerouac's and ordered orange juice and soda from the bartender I'd spoken to earlier. I told her the bad news, and that I would move on to Ely.

'Oh, shame! Then you won't see the park or the cave or Wheeler Peak.'

'I might drive back in the morning.'

She pulled a face, and shook her thick, crinkly hair. 'They'll probably have a room at the Border Inn ... You know? That way.' She pointed.

'I know. I've been there – before I came here.'

'I can phone and ask if they have a room.'

And she did. And they did.

Tony and Mike are already at the bar. Tony greets me loudly, while Mike smiles and nods. I order a bottle of stout and sit down next to Mike, a good-looking man in his late forties with greyish hair and a bit of a belly. I already know that they are architects from Columbus, Ohio, and have been biking together for twenty-five years.

'We ride dirt roads and trails one year, proper roads the next year.' Tony is standing up, talking to me over Mike's head. He's tall, red-faced with a stubbly beard. 'Different bikes, obviously. This year we're off-road. Next year we're going to drive the Alaskan Highway on road bikes.'

Tony sits down, leans back and looks at me from behind Mike's neck. He explains that they drove their off-road bikes from Columbus to Moab in a van, left the van at Moab airport, and have been biking on off-the-road trails for two days already. Mike is sipping bourbon and nodding.

'You mean, like across this desert out here.' I jerk my thumb over my shoulder.

'Yeah. That's right. It's great out there. No people, nothing, totally wild. We just—'

A shout comes from the door. 'Am I in Nevada?'

Someone says 'yes'.

'Thank God! So I can get a beer.' A tall man wearing sawn-off jeans walks to the bar. 'Howdy,' he says to the bartender. 'Two Coors Lights please. I got a buddy. He'll be here in a minute.'

I turn back to Tony. 'How do you know where to go, on the trails out there?"

'Well, an amazing guy called Sam Correro has a website called TransAmerica Trail. He's been mapping the trails for years, from Tennessee to Oregon.' He takes a swig from a beer bottle. 'We had an adventure today.' He nudges Mike. 'You tell him.'

'You mean the stand?'

'Yeah. Good story.'

Mike turns to me. 'The kick-down stand for my bike broke, which is a big problem. The only thing then is to lean it against a tree or a telegraph pole. A young guy, about twenty, in the service station where this happened, said, "I've got a bike stand at home that I'm not using. I'll go home and get it. Just wait." So we waited and the boy came back with this stand, which solved my problem.'

Mike pauses, and Tony takes over. 'When Mike offered to pay for it, the boy said, "No, you have it." So Mike gives him a hundred dollars – for something that is worth about ten, maybe twenty.'

'Well, it was worth two hundred dollars to me right then.' Mike smiles and swallows a mouthful of bourbon.

Several slot machines have been booping and bonging behind us. Suddenly a voice shouts 'Hallelujah!' and a sound as if someone is vomiting gravel begins, and continues. 'God damn!' the voice says.

Tony ignores this hubbub. 'We just get away one week a year,' he says. 'We got commitments. I got a wife and a boy. He's twelve. I got married late – I was thirty-five.'

'I been married twice, divorced twice, ten years apart.' Mike speaks quietly. 'I got a boy who's thirteen.'

'Do you see him much?'

'Oh yeah. We're close. He's a little bit attention-deficit disorder, but he's OK.'

Tony goes off somewhere. Mike orders another stout for me, beer for Tony, bourbon for himself.

357

Mike and I talk about his son, who is having treatment. 'But it's expensive,' he says.

I tell him about the National Health Service, that I had some eye treatment recently that cost nothing.

'Cost you your house here,' Mike says.

Tony is back. 'Health and going to college should be state funded,' he says. 'I got a friend who was laid off his job. It wasn't his fault. He got welfare benefits.'

The bartender brings me a chef's salad. Tony asks if I mind him smoking while I eat.

'Of course not,' I say. 'I used to smoke. I still like the smell.' He lights up – and from further down the bar one of the waitresses runs over and gets a light.

Mike mutters quietly to her. He's asking for a bill. 'We got to go soon. We want to be up at five.'

I find that Mike is paying my bill as well as his own. I try to stop him, but he insists. 'Someone did me a favour today, so ... I said, I'd try to do someone a favour tomorrow.' He taps his hands on his thighs. 'So I'm early.'

They leave with a blizzard of great-to-meet-yous and good-nights, and I get on with my enormous salad. Two older, fit-looking people are sitting to my left: a man with short grey hair and a woman with well-tended blonde hair. They pick up on my accent and I have to explain why I'm here, in this remote bar. 'I'm driving to San Francisco.'

'San Francisco's a wonderful place,' the woman says. 'I was at Berkeley, class of sixty-two.' She's bending forward, looking past the man. 'You know, there are only three places in the USA now that preserve a sense of history: Boston, New Orleans and San Francisco.'

I mutter something appreciative about Boston and ask if they've been to England.

'I went there once,' he says. 'I had to fly a plane back to the USA.'

'He was a pilot in the US Air Force. He flew jets for reconnaissance in Vietnam.' She reaches across and holds out her hand. 'My name's Henrietta.'

I shake her hand. 'I'm David.'

'He's John.'

'Howdy,' says John.

'That must have been dangerous, flying reconnaissance.'

'Yeah. It was dangerous. We had to fly high or else very low.' He clears his throat and drinks a little red wine. 'When I got back from Vietnam and hadn't been shot down or injured, when many of my friends had, my mother said she wasn't surprised. She said, "I've always known you were lucky." And I am.' He grins and points to Henrietta.

They are both seventy-eight, though they look ten years younger. He's from Maine and she's from Illinois. They live in Tucson, Arizona, and have another home on the coast in Oregon, where they go in the summer when Tucson gets too hot. They're on their way back to Tucson now. 'We used to do this trip on motorbikes – not that long ago.' Henrietta widens her eyes and moves her tongue between her teeth. She's wearing a subtle lipstick and mascara.

I tell them – while shaking my head in, perhaps, false self-deprecation – that I marched against the Vietnam War in the late 1960s.

'Didn't make any difference,' John says with a laugh.

Henrietta is drinking gin or vodka with tonic. She takes a sip and says, 'The Vietnam vets were treated very badly, shunned, because everyone thought the war was a bad thing by the time it ended.'

'Yes. But they were doing their job,' I say. 'They were conscripted.'

'That's right,' she says. 'Now there's a lot of attention on veterans – almost as if people are making up for their guilt. We went to stay somewhere with two friends, and the whole stay for four of us was free once the hotel people realised that he was a Vietnam vet.'

'It's different in England. Ex-soldiers don't get that much respect. Falklands veterans weren't looked after very well – they still aren't.'

'We went to the Falklands,' Henrietta smiles. 'We are the only people we know who have been there.'

I don't find out why they went to the Falklands because we are interrupted by some people they met earlier. And then they leave – and I imagine them on a cruise, leaning on the rail, drinking gin and tonic and gazing at penguins.

On my way out I put twenty-five cents in a slot and push a button. Wheels whirl and stop. No line. I lose my quarter.

68

Trump After Breakfast

I'm sitting in a booth in the breakfast room reading *The Bristlecone: The Official Newspaper of Great Basin National Park* when John and Henrietta walk in. Lots of smiles and good mornings, and they sit down in a booth about four along from mine – which means we can't see each other and can concentrate on eating our breakfasts.

Fifteen minutes later, as I leave, we discuss accents in the USA and England. I mention a Congressman who was speaking on television last night; he had a very southern accent, but I can't remember his name.

'What was he talking about?' Henrietta asks.

'About Trump denying that three thousand people died when Hurricane Florence hit Puerto Rico.'

Henrietta smiles and shrugs her shoulders.

'Trump does seem to polarise opinion.'

'Yes. I think that's because his election was such a surprise.' She picks up a knife and puts it on her plate. 'Although if you travelled around the US during the campaign – Wisconsin, Indiana, my

361

state, Illinois, Ohio – you could see signs and stickers for Trump everywhere.' She says that Trump has very good people around him: General Mattis, Mike Pompeo and a couple of others. 'Hillary Clinton ran a very poor campaign, attacking Trump supporters as deplorables.' She drinks some coffee. John eats toast without looking up. 'And look at the economy,' she says. 'It's doing well.'

'I heard someone say that won't last – that it's a hangover from Obama.'

She laughs. 'Don't give me that. Obama was terrible for the economy. We know; we run a business.'

'So are you a Republican but a progressive one?'

'I'm a Republican, but also an independent. Trump has done some good things: with Iran, and freeing up business from regulations. I know that because we have a business, and small businesses are the basis of a good economy.'

I ask the big question. Why not? 'Did you vote for Trump?'

'I did. And I've got two master's degrees.' She chuckles. 'I've voted for every Republican since Jimmy Carter. I regretted voting for him. He said, "We must save energy. Turn the lights down." We were working in darkness in the office I was in. Then Reagan came in and said, "It's fine. You can turn the lights on." And it was fine.' She smiles and waves her hands.

John is smiling too, and spreading jam on toast. I feel I should leave and let him enjoy his breakfast.

But Henrietta is talking again. 'I certainly couldn't have voted for Clinton. Her policies, her manner, her disdain for the poorer people. She's not a great person. I know a lot of women who didn't vote for her; many women don't like her. Her husband is OK, a good old boy.'

Soon after that, I manage to escape and leave John in peace. Is it possible that he votes Democrat, but doesn't tell her?

I drive to Baker and stop at the Great Basin Visitor Center. Outside on warm, mown grass, black crickets with red wings are making a terrific racket, jumping, flying and drumming loudly as if they are

362

woodpeckers. Inside, I pick up a free map, and find that the Great Basin Desert covers almost all of Nevada – except for the southern spike around Las Vegas – as well as the western half of Utah. I've been driving across this desert since I came into the beautiful country around Scipio and will continue across it until I reach the border with California, 400 miles ahead. This desert is North America's largest and only *cold* desert – where sagebrush and a few other plants survive hot summers and freezing winters, while sucking up less than ten inches of rain each year.

I've come to get a ticket for the Lehman Caves, where the stalagmites and stalactites are. But I fail dismally. There are two guided tours each day. One has left already. The other is this evening and is fully booked . . . Idiot! What made me think I could pay my money and wander in when I felt like it?

However, I can drive up to Wheeler Peak and look at the view, and get close to the colourful trees. Once again, ignoring the fear that I know to be irrational, I set off to drive up a mountain on a narrow road. I can see that it's going to get hairy up there, but if I can't gawp at stalagmites, I have to do something else; otherwise why do I keep coming to this little village which is off my route?

It turns out to be another test of nerve in a decorative setting – not quite as terrifying as the Skyline Drive, but still I feel a little nauseous. The road is narrow, though two cars can squeeze past one another – but that means that half the time I am driving close to the edge of a precipice, with a steep mountain on my other side.

As I drive into a viewpoint called Mather Outlook, John and Henrietta are driving out. Henrietta lets her window down. 'Hello again.'

Startled, I joke feebly, 'We must stop meeting like this.'

John leans across and says, 'It's even better higher up, the colours, the fall colours, you know.'

I ask about the road. 'Is it OK? Is it the same as so far?'

'Yeah, it's the same,' he says.

'You just don't want to look down.' Henrietta chuckles.

They drive off. I look from behind a low wall – there's no danger here – just a long view over evergreens and yellowing aspens down to a golden meadow studded with grey rock. Above, a patchy forest of mixed trees peters out in channels of bare rock, flowing from a ridge that stands out like a blade against the sky.

I drive on and stop at the highest point of the road, where walkers set out on an eight-and-a-half-mile round trail to Wheeler Peak. A board warns of the dangers of altitude sickness. I am standing at 10,161 feet – no wonder, to misquote Bernie Taupin, I feel a little bit funny – but that's nothing compared with Wheeler Peak, which at 13,063 feet is the second-highest mountain in Nevada. Up here, there are three empty cars and no people – just birds and trees: tall, dark firs and spruces, and slim, silver-trunked aspens with leaves of lemon yellow and fiery orange. Down below, the shadows of the clouds move slowly across the plain.

69

Soft Shoulder

Back on 50, the road is empty for many miles, until a sign saying School Bus Stop, which seems strange, because I have seen no place where children – or anyone – might live.

The road climbs, bending up to Sacramento Pass. I stop at the top, stand in a cool breeze and look ahead at miles of sweeping sagebrush desert with green-purple mountains in the distance. I drive down from the pass and cross the desert below on a straight road. Then I climb another pass and come down into a space so empty and huge that I don't notice at first that sixty wind turbines, planted in rows like an orchard, are wheeling away. Thirty miles on, I get to Ely, a hard-boiled kind of town where the main street brims with casinos and old-style diners, and the side streets end in the desert. I take a short walk in suffocating heat and duck into a Subway to cool down – and eat a sandwich.

Aware that the Loneliest Road in America, in *Life* magazine's opinion, starts here, I set out from Ely with some trepidation – although I feel I've some experience of lonely roads already, since

50 has been low on traffic and signs of humanity since Scipio. The next town, Eureka, is seventy-seven miles – and several mountain passes – ahead. A pattern sets in: twisting climbs to high passes – brightened by yellow sagebrush flowers and small, long-lived pinyon pine trees – and winding descents to long, flat valleys where the road straightens.

On the plain below Little Antelope Summit, where the road crosses a stream called Fish Creek, three motorcyclists dressed in black roar past going east. Five minutes later I see something coming up fast in the rear-view mirror: three motorcyclists dressed in black. I am a little freaked. Have they turned round with a plan to mug me and make off with Harpo? They whoosh past and in a few seconds are half a mile ahead. It still feels a little spooky. They are the only people on the four-mile stretch of road in front and behind – and they could form a roadblock! In real life, they quickly disappear over the next mountain. And I don't see them again.

I pass a sign saying Soft Shoulder. I've seen it before; it sounds like a dance, but is, I think, indicating that the dead grass beside the road is concealing a bog in which a car could get stuck.

The Barr Brothers have been playing for a while; now they move into the mesmeric 'Please Let Me Let It Go'. And the road seems less lonely. I see two cows high on a mountain, behind a fence. And in a small field a woman and a man are trying to catch a couple of horses. A beautiful small, dark horse is wheeling and running away. The man holds a board, and uses it to coax the horse towards the woman.

Coming down from Pinto Mountain, almost unexpectedly, I'm in Eureka, a small town, named, of course, when some nineteenth-century roustabout found silver in the nearby hills and shouted that word across the valley to his mates. I park in front of an old building, once the office of *The Sentinel*, the local newspaper, and now a museum, mercifully closed. I walk around the few streets, passing lovely old buildings: some, including an opera house, well maintained and functioning; others heading for dereliction. I'd like to spend the night here, but the four motels are full.

As I leave the town, convoys of pickups and vans packed with men wearing high-vis jackets come towards me with green lights flashing on their roofs and curious flags sticking up on poles behind. On the plain, trucks and diggers rest in a sea of mud. It's 5.45 p.m. Whatever they've been doing out here, the workers are going back to Eureka. That's why the motels are full.

I drive on towards Austin, the next town on the loneliest road, seventy miles ahead. The road is straight and flat with no mountains to climb. Herds of black cattle graze on bleak land where grass survives among the brush. I see no buildings – but perhaps there's a ranch house among those shapely hills.

I'm busting for a pee; there's nothing to hide behind. But then, except for the driver of a truck in front travelling at the same speed as me, there's nobody around. No need for modesty.

I drive on into the sun along a long straight road; the sun stays behind the visor. Hills rise in silhouette in front of me, and the furthest hills seem to be cut from black paper. The road climbs up to a pass and comes down into Austin, a small town that straggles downhill.

I walk around and visit the three motels. They are all full. What to do? It's 7 p.m. I drive to the western edge of town and into a small gas station.

Its owner is chatting to a friend. He fills Harpo's tank – and I ask them if they know of anywhere that I might stay the night.

'Drive to Fallon.' The owner says. 'It's a big place. You'll get a room and something to eat. Just a hundred and ten miles.'

'So it has motels?'

'Oh yeah.' The friend, an older man, smiles. 'All of them – the chains. And all the fast-food places.'

'Why are the motels here so busy? It's the same in Eureka.'

'Gold,' the friend says and laughs.

'Three new gold mines. They have to build 'em and then mine 'em. Construction workers all over.'

367

I pay for the gas and thank them.

'It'll soon be dark, but you should be in Fallon by' – the owner looks at his watch – 'nine, nine-thirty. Just be careful.'

Soon after Austin, I join the open road again. And on it goes, straight and curvy, up and down – but not really mountainous or bendy as it was earlier today. Just the road in the headlights, a half-moon to the left and stars – one in particular bright and low in the sky in front. Sometimes I confuse that star with headlights approaching from miles away; and sometimes I think that headlights in the mirror, miles behind, are a star in front of me.

The drive isn't difficult, now that I'm into it, tootling along at sixty-five or seventy. Occasionally I meet a car or a truck going the other way, its headlights dipped. And rarely, I glimpse tail lights miles in front – it's impossible to judge how far, but I don't pass anyone. I watch the milometer: 663 back in Austin, so 773 will take me into Fallon.

Rows of orange and white lights appear to the left a long way ahead; for fifteen minutes they come closer until I'm level with them, though they are still a mile away across the darkness. Then a side road and a sign, United States Naval Air Station, Fallon Nevada. Those lights are marking a runway.

And ten miles on, darkness ends in a world I seemed to have forgotten: street lights, traffic lights, casinos with flashing lights, headlights, tail lights, Taco Bell, McDonald's, Arby's, Comfort Inn, Best Western ... Best Western is full. I check in next door at the Rodeway Inn. It's 9.30 p.m. The receptionist says I can get beer and a meal at Stockman's Casino – two blocks west and across the road.

I sit at the bar in an empty dining room drinking a delicious local beer called Great Basin Icky IPA. I'm waited on by a young white man with cheeks like a hamster, who tells me that the ichthyosaur, commonly known as Icky, is Nevada's state fossil.

'You want this beer? You just ask for an Icky.'

I eat fettuccine alfredo with chicken, study the road atlas and realise that I've driven 321 miles today, not counting the morning diversion up Wheeler Peak. It's a record on this trip – probably twice as far as on any other day – and I drove the whole of the Loneliest Road in America, by anyone's definition.

'Excuse me.'

'Yes sir.'

'Another Icky, please.'

70

Self-Harm and the Lizard

A man comes to my room at the Rodeway to fix the television. It's mid-morning. I've decided to stay another night, rather than rush ahead. I'll retrace some of the road that I drove over in the dark yesterday to see what I missed. The man fiddles with buttons, cables and the remote – and decides that a new cable is needed.

He goes away, comes back ten minutes later and resumes fiddling. He's a practical kind of man, middle-aged, white and he's happy to talk. We've discussed England and London – and that he has lived in Fallon for fifteen years and likes it. He installed this television not long ago, so he should be able to make it work, he says. And he points to a wall he put up in this room to provide a space for hanging clothes. 'I'm rebuilding this motel on my own,' he says.

'On your own? How many rooms are there?'

'Sixty.'

'Blimey! Are you doing them all?'

'Yep. It's my job: upgrading this hotel. I've been doing it for eighteen months.' He's pressing buttons on the remote, and staring up at the television. 'I'm renovating the passage out there. You probably saw.'

'Yes. I saw it was being repainted. It's going to look good.'

'I put in those rails, so luggage doesn't scrape the paint.'

'Dado rails. Do you call them that?'

'Dado' – he shakes his head – 'I've not heard that. Chair rails, we call them' – he reaches behind the television, pulls out a cable and pushes it in again – 'because they're at the height of a chair back. But I put them in a bit lower to buffer the cases.' He points the remote, clicks – and the television comes on: CNN. 'There you are.' He hands me the remote. 'Just use that.'

'Thanks. Fantastic.'

He's facing me now. 'I'm giving my life to this place. I lost a finger.' He holds up his left hand. It's missing the index finger. At the base of where it used to be, his palm has healed neatly.

'Oh God! I'm sorry. How did that happen? Did you get compensation?'

'No,' he looks at his hand and raises his eyebrows. 'It was my fault. I hit it with a hammer.'

'Oh, no.'

He looks at me with a grim smile. 'I've still got the hammer.'

'Really! ... Well, I guess it's useful.'

'Yeah, I use it. I take more care now.' He shrugs, picks up his box of tools, and goes to the door. 'You have a good trip.'

'Thanks. Bye.'

I drive east out of town and am surprised to find cattle grazing and fields of maize. Five minutes later, just a few miles on, the land has turned to sandy desert with a sprinkling of dry sagebrush.

I stop at Grimes Point Archaeological Area, a low hill – which I couldn't see last night – where the ancestors of the local Paiute Indians engraved pictures and shapes on rocks between 500 and 3,000 years ago.

Even though there are shaded picnic tables and what Americans call a 'bathroom', I am the only person here. I follow a trail and am

371

struck by the number of images and by their age. Many are patterns: spots, lines, circles, waves, zigzags; others show stick people and animals. No one seems to know what these images, or petroglyphs, represent. Perhaps something religious; the Paiute had shamans and sacred places. Or they have to do with hunting; this hill once looked down on a lake rather than a desert, and hunters hid among these rocks waiting for animals to come to the lake to drink.

I watch a small lizard rushing about, then stopping suddenly, then dashing off again. Then it sits still on a rock in the sun. At most, it is three inches long. I can see its four legs, and look hard to make out the features of its arrow-shaped head. It turns its head to the right. Is it looking for food or for predators, or both? I feel it is aware of me. Perhaps my size makes me a threat. It turns its head back and faces front, then it turns to the left. I speak to it – I don't know why. I've spoken to dogs, cats, horses, budgerigars – even an owl. Why not lizards?

'Hello, little chap,' I say. 'Are you having a nice life? Do you like living here? I guess you were born here. It's your place.'

I look at the lizard's four legs and feet, its body, its head – it looks like a tiny dinosaur. These creatures have been here longer than we have. I can't help thinking that they will be here when we are gone. They know how to survive. They live in a hot, barren landscape where the only shelter is ancient rock and sagebrush.

I can see, and hear, planes taking off across the desert at the Naval Air Station. I guess that the pilots are practising lifting off from aircraft carriers. 'Do you hear that roar, little chap? Can you see those flying machines? You and they are in the same world.'

I drive on east towards pink and purple mountains. The road is like a causeway with desert sitting low on both sides. And the desert is more barren than it is further west around Austin and Eureka. There is no shade, and white sand – or is it salt? – sits in pools to the right, beyond a line of telegraph poles. To the left, at the foot of the mountain, an expanse of yellow sand; a beach with a huge dune behind it. This is Sand Mountain, sacred to the Paiute, who

372

used to pray to it; nowadays it is a recreation area, popular with riders of quad bikes.

The road climbs gradually. I stop at the top by a green metal sign, pitted as if it has been shot at with a shotgun from close range: Sand Springs Pass: Elev 4644. I head down into the desert below. Here a lake of creamy sand is surrounded by scrub, and a line of mountains lit by sharp sunlight looks like stiff, crumpled paper. I came through here last night, and saw nothing except the road. I'm glad I came back, but I can't retrace 110 miles. If I did, I would have to drive into Fallon in the dark – again.

Turning back over the pass, I come to the pools of what looks like salt. A small sign says Huck Salt Company. So, it is salt – probably.

Back in Fallon, I go to Walmart to buy a new notebook and a banana. I find the notebook and head to the food end. I can't see any fruit at all, let alone a banana. A woman Walmart worker says, 'How you doing?'

'Fine thanks. You?'

'Oh, I'm OK.'

'Do you have any bananas?'

'Yeah. Just beyond the bread down there.' She points. 'Where you from?'

'England.'

'Oh, cool!'

'Are you from round here?'

'Yeah.'

'I like it round here. All the way from Colorado, it's beautiful. I've been on Route 50 – the loneliest road, you know?'

'Yeah. I know it. We go that way to Colorado Springs. It's kinda boring.'

71

The Misfits

Six miles west of Fallon the road forks – left to Carson City on 50, right to Reno. From Ely to this fork, 50 has been following the route of the Lincoln Highway, the first road to cross the United States. Completed in 1913, it connected New York's Times Square to San Francisco's Lincoln Park, and became known as the Main Street Across America. (I'm mentioning this because I have a paranoid sense that, if I don't, a history buff somewhere will say, 'He doesn't mention that US 50 follows the old Lincoln Highway for 258 miles!')

50 is still, according to the Nevada tourism authority, the loneliest road in America. There is a little more traffic, but it still feels wild and empty with sandy scrub either side of the road and mountains looming ahead.

At a junction in a small town called Silver Springs, an ad for a Chevron gas station shouts CLEAN BATHROOMS and, underneath in smaller lettering, 'food and beer left at stoplight'.

Now 50 is fairly flat, crossing a kind of moorland while curving between hills and mountains. I am just thirty-six miles from Carson City, the state capital, and fifty-seven from South Lake Tahoe, across the border in California.

I come to Dayton, a town divided by the Carson River: to the east, a modern town with schools, churches, shops, a library and a golf course; to the west, across the river, a historic old town where a small group of nineteenth-century buildings – some of them used as cafés, small hotels and shops – are maintained but not tarted up. This part of Dayton is like a film set, with wooden sidewalks, and freestanding buildings with false fronts, wooden verandas and first-floor balconies.

It's 12.30. I go into the Gold Canyon Café – in the mid-nineteenth century Dayton was a gold-mining town – and am greeted by a dark-haired man of about forty, who shows me to a seat at the bar. It's an attractive, old-style place with a touch of the speakeasy, dark wood and a long bar in front of a fine array of bottles. Less dandy is a stag's head that gazes down on the only other customers, a couple sitting at a high table in the corner. I ask for an orange juice with soda and look at the menu – and then notice that the words CLARK GABLE are printed in white letters on the further edge of the bar in front of me. And in front of the seat to my right, MONTGOMERY CLIFT. To my left, MARILYN MONROE. What is this?

The man brings the orange juice – and guesses what I am about to ask. 'This is where they drank in the evenings while they were filming *The Misfits*.'

'No! Really?'

'Yes. It's true – and some of the movie was filmed in here.'

'Really! Wow.'

'You know the bit where Marilyn is playing pat-a-ball and Gable and Clift look at her bum?' He grins. 'That was filmed right there, in that corner.' He points to the table where the couple are sitting.

I don't remember that scene, though I've seen the movie twice. 'That's amazing!'

'You know, I didn't know any of this when I bought the bar

three years ago. I found out slowly. Some locals mentioned it. Then an old man – he's about seventy – came in. His mother ran the bar then, around 1960, and he worked here as a teenager – moving bottles around and washing up. His mom asked him to come and meet Marilyn and Clark and Montgomery – they all shook his hand.' He points to the names printed in white. 'The old man had the idea to put those name labels there because there, he swore, is where they sat.'

'They sat right here! Amazing.'

'That's what I figured, but I haven't made too much of it. I put a couple of pictures of them on the mantelpiece over there – and that's it. I bought this place to serve good food, home cooking – my mother's recipes, her family's recipes. I got a steak marinade that comes from my great-grandfather.'

He shows me the menu and gets excited talking about the food. He and his wife do the cooking. I tell him that I don't want to eat a big meal – and he says he'll make me three tacos with different fillings. 'Not too much to eat. Just a lunchtime snack. Is that OK?'

'Yes. It sounds wonderful.'

'By the way, I'm Chris – Chris Martinez.'

I tell him my name, where I come from and why I'm there. And he tells me, with some pride, that he is Spanish and comes from an old family that came to America at the time of Cortés.

He goes off to make the tacos and I go over to the mantelpiece. Among other items – oil lamps, old black-and-white photos of the bar – a frame holds a promotional shot of the three stars of *The Misfits* leaning into the camera: Gable and Monroe are grinning with plenty of teeth; Clift has a can-we-get-this-over-with-quickly look. They stand under a blue sky, the men wearing cowboy hats and shirts, Monroe in a white dress printed with red cherries. In the same frame is a smaller picture of Monroe and a printed announcement of the première on 1 February 1961, with a list of credits. I'm reminded that Monroe's husband, Arthur Miller, wrote the screenplay, that the movie was directed by John Huston and that there was another great actor involved, Eli Wallach.

I go back to my seat. My head is filling up with memories. My father took me to see this movie soon after it came out. He was a fan of Clark Gable and, I expect, though he didn't say so, of Marilyn Monroe. I would have been twelve; my parents separated when I was ten, and after that my father often took me to the cinema on Saturday afternoons. He was old to be my father – fifty-six when I was born – and he often fell asleep during movies. We saw *The Misfits* in an old, smoke-filled Odeon, where the broken springs in the seats made my bum ache. My father nodded off near the beginning, and I sat beside him feeling confused by this curious story. When the lights went up, he woke with a jerk, turned to me and said, as he often did at the end of a movie, 'What was all that about?'

I don't remember, but I probably told him that these people went out to catch wild horses – and perhaps that they argued a lot.

Then we would have gone out into the dark and had something to eat at a cafeteria that my father liked. I feel sad – sitting here now, in Clark Gable's seat – remembering my father old and alone. Even though he asked for it. He was lovely to me, but horrible to my mother who, after years of mostly verbal abuse, left him.

Chris brings the three tacos – each with a different filling. People come into the bar, and he goes off to serve them.

The Misfits was both Gable's and Monroe's last movie. Gable died before it was released. Monroe the year after, and my dad died in 1969.

Chris collects my plate and asks if I liked the tacos.

And I tell him truthfully, 'Yes. Delicious. The perfect lunch.'

He's pleased, as people should be when their work is praised. And when I leave, he says, 'Please come back again. Please tell your friends that we do good food here.'

'I will.' And I hope I do – go back.

72

Banjo at the Bucket of Blood

I make a sixteen-mile detour – driving up, and later down, an excruciatingly steep hill with a perpendicular drop to one side – to visit Virginia City, a town that boomed in the 1860s and 1870s, after the most productive silver mine ever known, the Comstock Lode, was unearthed there.

Now the town exists for tourism. Many old buildings have been preserved and much tackiness has been added. Virginia City's main street, C Street, is vastly preferable to Dodge City's phoney Front Street. Old buildings from the boom years run for five blocks on both sides of C Street, oozing anachronisms and forged together with continuous stretches of creaky, uneven wooden sidewalk.

If you had all day and some companionship and felt like having a drink in every saloon – and visiting the Washoe Club Haunted Museum, the Wild West Gun Show, the Ponderosa Saloon and Mine Tour, the Mark Twain Saloon, the Historic Delta Café, the Courthouse Slammer, Piper's Opera House and the Red Dog Saloon and Pizza Parlour – this could be fun. I rush along the sidewalk, gawping – and am thrilled to see a picture of Hoss from *Bonanza*, the western series that was on TV throughout the 1960s. It turns out that the more than 400 episodes of *Bonanza* caused this town's second boom – a century after the first subsided – because Hoss Cartwright and his family lived nearby and frequently galloped in from their ranch, the Ponderosa.

After studying the competition I go into the Bucket of Blood Saloon for a lime and soda. The bar, chairs, tables, the jungle of dangling lamps, all of them different, and the high walls crammed with period paintings and prints, rifles, pistols and swords, reek of the town's boom years. The Wild West feel is dented only by the slots, the display of souvenir T-shirts, and the customers in their baseball caps and baggy shorts. A picture window looks down on the rest of the town and the sandy mountains beyond. I sit at a table, away from the hubbub, close to a grey-haired man who is playing popular tunes on a banjo. No one is listening except me. When I leave, I thank him and put a dollar in the bowl in front of him. He smiles, and mutters, 'Thanks'.

Within an hour I'm driving on Carson Street in Carson City, casing motels and bars. Here formality and vulgarity sit close together. The Capitol Building is old, beautiful and small, like an exquisite country house; close by is an excrescence, the Carson City Nugget, a massive bungalow of a casino built in the 1970s which, but for the awful lettering and flashing lights, might be a giant Walmart. I'm reminded of the plonking down of the Busch Stadium next to the Old Courthouse in St Louis.

I check into the Carson-Tahoe Hotel and am given a large room. It feels good; size does make a difference to a hotel room.

Later, three blocks away at a place called the Union, I sit at the bar and order a pale ale. The room is large and noisy, with people eating at tables. There's one other customer at the bar, two seats from me: a man with an academic air who is bending over a book opened flat and making notes as he reads. I talk to the bartender, a young white man who spent a week in England two years ago. He frequently breaks off our conversation to make drinks for the waiters to take to the tables, but he comes back when he is free.

I order tilapia with berruti, which Tyler, the bartender, says is 'kind of a long macaroni' – and our intermittent conversation moves on to Donald Trump.

'I can tell you something,' he says. 'I went to a Trump rally in Reno – not on my own – with others' – he gives a high-pitched laugh – 'it'd be scary on your own – because our professor said he would give us credits if we would go and observe. And you know, there wasn't a single minority there. All white: poor white, and rich white who are with him for the tax breaks. No middle classes.' He looks along the bar at one of the waitresses, and turns back. 'And he's a good speaker. At least, he knows how to work a room. He's a businessman. Excuse me.' The waitress needs him to fetch a bottle of wine and uncork it.

Meanwhile, a waiter brings my tilapia. Tyler returns.

'Do you think he'll win another election?' I ask.

He shrugs, then stretches his mouth in a grimace. 'What I can't believe is that he keeps *saying* these things, *doing* these things – I mean during that 2016 campaign especially, insulting women, Mexicans are rapists, thousands of Arabs in New Jersey cheered on 9/11 – and people aren't *"What?"'* – he's waving his arms now – 'They aren't *open-mouthed* in astonishment!'

He drops his arms and goes away again. I eat some tilapia; the berruti are good.

And then he's back, leaning on the bar and speaking quietly. 'I'm fed up with listening to Trump supporters in this bar.'

'You mean . . .' I look along the bar towards a waiter and a waitress standing together.

'No. The bar staff are fine. But some of the guests.' He's waving his arms again. 'I have to just keep quiet because they assume I support Trump. Carson City is an old-fashioned Republican place, though Nevada is Democrat because of Las Vegas.'

'Did your parents vote for Trump?'

'My mother's family voted Trump because they're Republicans, but now they don't approve of everything he does.' He looks side-ways. 'Sorry, I got to go again.'

When he comes back, I order a Black Butte porter.

'Good choice,' he says, and quickly puts it in front of me.

Tyler goes away for several minutes, mixing drinks and helping waiters with bills. The porter is good: cold and a little sweet. I finish eating. Along the bar, Academic Man is still reading and making notes in small letters with a black pen. He raises a finger towards Tyler and is given another beer.

Tyler comes back and tells me that what he really wants is to move to Amsterdam where his uncle – a Dutchman who is married to his biological aunt – runs four bars and develops property. 'I spent a year there, and I want to go back for another – or longer. I have to get a work visa. There's an idea that I can register as an *au pair*.' He looks at me wide-eyed.

'Really!'

'Yeah! It's Holland!' He shrugs and raises his hands. 'My uncle might somehow fix it.'

He goes away again – a crowd of people are ordering cocktails.

I drink the porter slowly. And get my bill from Tyler. 'Good luck.' He smiles. 'You're almost there! It's been great to talk.'

I walk down the street, blinking at the lights of the Carson City Nugget, and remember that he told me his full name: 'Tyler Valley – like Yosemite Valley.'

Back at the Carson-Tahoe Hotel, I go into the bathroom, where arrangements are immaculate and the best so far. A paper band, labelled Sani-Shield, SANITISED, FOR YOUR PROTECTION, is wrapped around the loo seat, and the loo roll is folded to a point.

73

Gondolas on Lake Tahoe

A few miles out of Carson City, 50 begins to climb, swaying round broad bends one way, then the other. This is the Carson Range of the Sierra Nevada; on the other side, a few miles away, are Lake Tahoe and California. It's an easy glide on a smooth, four-lane, divided highway through mountains covered in scrub. Pines and firs crowd in. The high point, the 7,000-foot Spooner Summit, goes by without my noticing, though I soon realise that I'm rolling downhill – and then, through a fold in the mountains, I see the blue of the lake below. I drop lower, shoot through a short tunnel and stop in a lay-by. As I open the car door, I am hit by the scent of hot pine needles. I dawdle among pines and firs, entranced by a sheet of glittering green–blue water, which darkens as it approaches mountains perhaps ten miles away.

I drive on down until I'm level with the lake and the road is surrounded by hotels, outdoor cafés and people in shorts and sun hats carrying towels. I turn in at a sign to Visitor Center and ask a loud white man with a black crew cut whether I'm in California.

'California? Half a mile that way.' He points west. 'Do you want somewhere to stay?'

I tell him I do, and he unfolds a glossy map and slaps it on the counter facing me.

'OK. Where we are now is Stateline, here.' He rings it in biro. 'And here, right next door, is South Lake Tahoe.' He draws another circle, creating a Venn diagram. 'There are plenty of motels here, between Route 50 and the beach. So you could choose there. Some are cheap, some are more expensive. You can go around these streets and take a look at what's there.' He draws a hasty circle. 'Or you can go up here. This is Emerald Bay' – another circle – 'it's wilder, not so many people – and not so many hotels. But it's beautiful up there. You should look over there anyway.'

'OK. Thanks.'

'Now. What do you want to do while you're here?' He looks up at me and back down at the map. 'We got the beach right here.' He points across the road and draws more circles on the map. 'You've got paddle-steamer rides. And you've got the gondolas—'

'What? Like in Venice?'

He glances up at me, puzzled. And I'm puzzled too – to me, gondolas mean Venice and a man in a white shirt and a red neckerchief making the thing move while a couple lie back and eat chocolates. And they might well have them here, in a ritzy holiday resort in America; they've got London Bridge, haven't they? He whips out a brochure, thumbs through it, flattens the page, and shows me pictures of a kind of ski lift, cable car, funicular. 'These are the gondolas.' He points.

And then I understand. The gondolas look like the pods on the London Eye.

'You get a great view up there.' He points again – at a gondola on the top of a mountain.

I leave with three maps and a fat brochure, and sit in traffic, crawling past casinos, bars, fast-food outlets – and the border with California. I know there's a beach a block or two away – and am tempted to go to it and hunker down under a tree if I can find one. But I keep going and turn off to Emerald Bay.

The road climbs easily for a few miles, then turns into another grit-your-teeth, don't-look-down, rollercoaster ride. For a short distance, it's Skyline Drive once again: a huge drop on both sides, no barriers, not even a bush. I pull into the next viewpoint and study the map. Is there another route back down to the bars and motels of South Lake Tahoe? Not unless I drive round the whole lake, which I can see is twenty-two miles long, north to south, and twelve miles wide.

I get out of the car and join a small crowd of fun-seekers who are staring down at Emerald Bay, a beautiful, slender bite out of the lake, enclosed by pines, firs and lofty, bare-topped mountains. A plaque tells me that this place was sacred to the Washoe Indians for thousands of years and that they used to gather here every summer, and 'The Washoe people continue to enjoy Lake Tahoe'.

Concentrating hard, I manage to drive back to South Lake Tahoe, where I get myself a room at a Rodeway Inn and head for the beach. It turns out that the beach is behind a chain-link fence, the entrance is locked with a numerical code and adults must pay $8 to get in. A sign says that the beach is private property, and dresses up the enterprise as necessary to maintain the quality of the beach. I have an almost innate objection to anyone claiming that they own a beach – I think the great Tecumseh would agree with me about this – so I walk slowly away, after wondering whether to slipstream someone else or to watch and remember as someone enters the sacred numbers.

I walk along the chain-link fence, looking through at the sand, the blue water and the few people sitting, strolling, lying in the sun. A voice calls out, 'Is this called State Beach?' A black man is sitting in a folding chair under an umbrella inside the fence. 'Do you know?'

'I don't know. Sorry.'

'OK,' he says.

'Do you have to pay to be in there?' I ask.

'No,' he says. 'Not today. Just turn the handle on the gate.'

So I do and, as I go in, I check the beach's name: 'Lakeside Beach'.

I take off my trainers, walk on the soft sand round to the man and tell him, 'It's called Lakeside Beach.'

A woman is sitting next to him; they both overwhelm me with

thanks and smiles. The man picks up his phone. I walk away – and hear him say, 'It's Lakeside Beach ... Yeah ... *Lakeside* ... Beach. Yep ... OK.'

There are benches here and a children's playground and plenty of space. A metal breakwater encloses a patch of lake, presumably for swimming, though no one is in the water. Beyond it, a few small boats are anchored and, far away, a white sail is raised. A man in swimming trunks lies on a towel, and a woman in a T-shirt and bikini bottom rests on her front, wearing a bicycle helmet. Others, wearing more clothes, sit on folding chairs, benches or on the sand, and a couple, arms around waists, wander by the water's edge.

I sit on a bench, eat a biscuit and drink some water. I read a Robert B. Parker novel that I began when I was in Cambridge, Maryland, weeks ago – I read in bed before going to sleep – and quickly finish it. I look across the bay and see the silhouettes of the mountains serrated by the pointed tops of the pines.

The tranquillity of the beach is interrupted by a thudding bass line coming from a passing car – and again, a few minutes later, by a phutting moped. I go to the water's edge and paddle. The water is cold and my feet sink into gritty sand. A few ducks and seagulls stand nearby. There's a slight breeze; for once, I'm outdoors and not too hot.

At about eight o'clock, I go to a bar called McP's, an Irish pub designed like a circus tent. As so often, I sit at the end of the bar on the only empty stool. McP's is noisy and crowded, but I'm here now and there's a choice of forty beers, listed and numbered on a blackboard. The bartender is attentive but I can't hear anything she says. 'Deschutes porter, please,' I shout.

She gives me a thumbs-up – and, when she brings the porter, I order Mulligan's Stew.

I don't think I'll stay long; there's no chance of any conversation, though I catch a little of the chat between my neighbours: a pale young man who looks weary and rinsed out, and a young woman who has a dark bob and her back to me. He is cross because he thought his course at Berkeley would take up three days a week, but it's turning out to be four. No wonder he looks tired! But at least he can recover here on the beach at weekends.

Mention of Berkeley, the university across the bay from San Francisco, reminds me that I have less than 200 miles left to drive. I hope to spend tomorrow night in Sacramento, and reach journey's end the next day.

The Mulligan's Stew arrives. It's a standard beef stew served inside a circular loaf of soda bread, the top of which has been sliced almost through so that it forms a hinged lid. It tastes OK, but I struggle to eat it with the knife and spoon that were stuck into it. After a while, I manage to get the bartender's attention and shout, 'Could I get a fork, please?'

The fork arrives. I eat and watch baseball highlights – and leave at 9.15.

It's cold out on the street, and I've just eaten a loaf of bread stuffed with meat and vegetables, but I still fancy an ice cream. I wander along Lake Tahoe Boulevard – the local name for Route 50 – and find nothing. I walk back and see a Starbucks on the corner of Stateline Avenue. I could probably get something in there – perhaps a piece of cake.

I go in and find a wall of flashing lights, plush carpet and noise. This isn't Starbucks! Rows of slot machines are booping, and people are standing around craps tables, shouting and catcalling as sweaty men throw dice. I walk past tables where roulette, blackjack, baccarat and poker are being played more quietly. The room is fifty yards long and contains several bars where punters can drink cocktails while gambling on a tablet computer. At the farther end, I turn into a wide corridor, lined with high-end shops, which leads to the reception area for Harrah's Lake Tahoe Hotel. And there in a corner is a very small Starbucks, hardly more than a kiosk. I look in and decide that I'm not hungry after all.

Downstairs, outside the restrooms, notices promote coming attractions. Eric Burdon and the Animals will be here in October. Blimey! Would that I might be here then. At school I sang in a band and tried to sound like the great Eric.

386

74

Luponic Distortion in Sacramento

West from South Lake Tahoe, I drive through thick woods of pine and fir as 50 again climbs into the Sierra Nevada. The bends are gentle, the slope gradual, the road is two-lane with three-lane stretches where faster drivers can overtake. There's a car close behind ... and then another ... and soon, in the mirror, I can see a line of cars stretching back to the previous bend. It's all right; they'll come past when the next passing lane appears. But they don't – not one of them. And the bends get tighter – hairpins, one after another. All right then, that's OK; they can follow me.

A notice says Echo Summit, 7,377 feet, the highest point on 50 in California: a steep drop to my left, and beyond it, mountains and sky; to my right tall evergreens and a track winding upwards. A few miles on a grey rock towers up sheer to my left: Lover's Leap, from which a pair of young Indian lovers, thwarted like Romeo and Juliet, are said to have jumped. The road has become a divided highway, swooping and swerving down and down. Now a few cars steam past. And soon I come to Placerville.

I park and walk in hot sun. American tourists and their kids wear shorts and shades as they wander along the pretty main street of a town that was at the heart of the 1849 Gold Rush. The buildings are old and crammed together: cafés, clothes boutiques, souvenir shops, convenience stores – and no chain fast-food outlets. Outside a small, dignified building, I think, almost aloud, 'There's a museum ... Oh ... It's closed ... Thank heaven.'

I hear a woman say, 'What was I gonna ask him?' And her friend replying, 'Who?'

I walk on, thinking about that answer.

Outside the Hangman's Tree Ice Cream Saloon a life-size dummy of a man, wearing a white shirt and red neckerchief, swings from a rope above the heads of passers-by. I go in, thinking this might be tacky, but I fancy an ice cream on a hot day. However, the place is dark, cool and delightful, recently restored to resemble the bar that stood here in the nineteenth century. Even the light switches are in period, and the furniture includes a bar built in the 1850s, at which John Sutter – founder of what became Sacramento – used to drink. Behind the bar, a mural shows the town as it was in 1849, when it was called Hangtown because of its reputation for hangings.

I buy a coffee ice cream and chat to the smiling mixed-race woman who serves it. She tells me that the dummy outside is named George and has been hanging there, with occasional changes of clothes, for seventy-five years.

I leave Placerville, and make a detour to Coloma, where, in January 1848, gold was discovered by James Marshall in the mill race at a sawmill owned by John Sutter. This was the gold that triggered the Gold Rush – which increased the white population of California from 14,000 to more than 200,000 in four years, and led to the building of the First Transcontinental Railroad, uniting a fragmented nation.

I drive on a narrow country road for eight miles, through a rustic landscape of gentle hills, deciduous woods and green meadows. Coloma is now a part of Marshall Gold Discovery State Historic

Park and comprises a picturesque sprinkling of old buildings, many of them functioning – a blacksmith, a post office, a gun shop – which survive from a town that boomed for less than ten years. I walk to Sutter's Mill, a recent reconstruction of the original, a barn-like structure with a ramp built of logs, up which tree trunks were rolled to be sawn into planks. Close by is the spot on the South Fork of the American River where Marshall saw gold; the river is clear and shallow, perfect for finding gold. Or trout.

Back in the outskirts of Placerville, a sign swings outside an elegant detached house: Aaron B. Dosh, Attorney at Law. I rejoin 50, and it soon becomes a six-lane freeway filled with traffic belting across California's flat Central Valley. In little more than half an hour I am in downtown Sacramento, the capital of California. Exploring a little, I find the Vagabond Inn, a motel for business people, close to the waterfront in Old Sacramento where someone told me there are bars and restaurants. I head that way and find a district of old brick buildings with arcades shading the pavements, grouped around the Sacramento River.

I turn into a short street, busy with people, and find that I'm behind two policewomen, one of whom is carrying a shiny steel hatchet with two sharp blades. It's a vicious-looking weapon that can't possibly be standard issue for the Sacramento police. A man walking in front of me asks them about it.

'We just took it off some guy.' Big smiles from both police-women. 'No, it's not our new weapon.'

'In England the police don't have weapons.' Why am I saying this? I haven't even had a beer yet.

'I know. That's great,' one of them says.

Then, for some reason – perhaps because they are so friendly – I say, 'You're like Cagney and Lacey.' Well, they are. They're both big and strong, and one is blonde and the other dark.

Then I start to cringe. Why did I say that? How could I be so crass? That was like the scene in *Father Ted* where Ted goes up to Richard Wilson (the actor who played Victor Meldrew in *One Foot in the Grave*) and yells Wilson's catchphrase, 'I don't believe it!'

389

But they don't react angrily, as Wilson does to Ted. They smile. And one of them says, 'Gee. Thanks.'

The man who first spoke to them, says, 'Thank you for looking after us' – which strikes me as a little saccharine – but then, like me, he's smaller than they are.

They thank him and say it's their job, and they're pleased to do it.

After wandering by the river and looking at boats which house clubs and restaurants, I go into a bar on a corner, a block away from the waterfront. Seats at the bar are all taken. I buy a pint of IPA, sit on a stool at a high circular table and watch baseball on a large screen: the LA Dodgers are playing the San Diego Padres. I feel myself unwinding.

The umpire has two huge pockets, like black saddlebags attached to his waist on either side. What has he got in there?

The bartender comes from behind the bar to hand me a menu. I find it hard to hear her because of the loud music, but I think she said to wave when I've decided what I'd like to eat.

A few feet away, by the bar, an American male voice is shouting, but all I can make out are several fucks and a couple of dudes.

It looks as if the hitter for the Padres has his phone and his wallet in his back pocket. He's swung his bat high in the air, ready for the pitch. What if his mother phones up?

I wave to the nice bartender. She's very busy – there's just her and another young woman who washes glasses and moves crates of bottles around – but she soon comes over. I order pastrami on rye. 'Shall I bring another IPA?' she says.

'Yes, please. Thanks.' Wonderful! She's saving me the trouble of elbowing my way to the bar.

IPA, I reckon, after some study now, is like pale ale used to be, but with much more flavour – and not just from hops.

The bar is emptier now. I've been watching this for more than an hour. The Padres were winning 2–1 when I sat down. Since then they have scored one more run, and the Dodgers haven't scored any. There's a new Padres hitter called Cory Spangenberg.

After much unrecognisable music, I suddenly hear 'Walk on the Wild Side'. But no. Horrors! It's rap. They've ripped off – sampled perhaps – Lou Reed's opening.

Why do some pitchers, such as the Padres' Craig Stammen, wear socks and knee britches? There's a Dodgers hitter now who has one arm covered in what looks like a leg from a pair of tights. The Dodgers just got a run! One of their guys made it in from third base. So it's now 3–2.

The bartender takes away my plate and offers me another pint. Blimey! Great service in here. It's fun just to watch a baseball game. The bar has filled up again. It's 10.25 p.m. When did I come in here? Sometime after 8 p.m.

The Padres' pitcher, Stammen in the knee britches, has made some kind of mistake, committed a foul – and the Dodgers all get to move on to the next base. Stammen looks angry.

Cody Bellinger is batting for the Dodgers, and there's a new pitcher called Kirby Yates. Stammen has been bumped out. It's the end of the eighth inning and it's still 3–2 to the Padres. The place has really filled up, and there are still just two bartenders, one of whom doesn't serve drinks.

It's 11 p.m. The place is emptying again, but not closing. I look for the restroom and a big white guy I've not seen before – he must be a bouncer – gives me a key attached to a huge slotted spoon, shows me through two doors and points down some stairs. I seem to be in a different building, next door to the bar.

When I get back, the bartender offers me another pint! Blimey again! Well, OK. I can celebrate. I'm nearly at the end of this journey – though not quite.

The key hitter for the Padres, I reckon, is Freddy Galvis; he is brown-skinned with dreadlocks and has black greasepaint slashed on his cheeks. The game ends. The Padres win 5–3. It's 11.30. I stand up to leave, pay the check and give the bartender a grateful tip in cash. Then I ask, 'What is that IPA I've been drinking?'

I don't catch her reply. She says it again. I hear something, but

I'm not sure I've got it right. She laughs, finds a piece of paper and writes, 'Luponic Distortion – 5.9%. Firestone Brewery.'

'Blimey,' I say. 'Well, thanks for a great evening.'

I walk towards the river. There are still people around, but not so many. It's cold now. Some of the lights have been turned out, and I can see the stars and a big sky; this is a low-rise district.

There's a small place called Willie's Burgers, where a few people are sitting at tables outside. I feel hungry. It's hours since I ate that pastrami sandwich. I go in and order a cheeseburger from a man whose name tag says Danny. Somehow, while he cooks the burger, we start talking about Donald Trump.

'Trump is a nightmare,' Danny says. 'If Joe Biden had stood, he'd have won. But he didn't because his son Beau Biden died of cancer just then.' He flips the burger and fills a glass with lime and soda for me. 'You know, Trump even talks about having a relationship with his own daughter, Ivanka.'

'No!'

'Yes. He did that.'

I take the burger and the drink outside and sit under the stars. Trump is temporary. Not like the stars – or San Francisco. Tomorrow or the next day, I'll go to the City Lights Bookshop, which has been owned since 1953 by Lawrence Ferlinghetti, whose poems I read in coin-op laundries – and who is now ninety-nine.

75

'You Think Too Much'

I get up a little late and linger over breakfast. I go online to look at hotels in San Francisco. This will be the first time I book a room on the whole trip. It will help to know where I'm trying to go when I reach this huge city. After much consideration, and finding that many hotels are fully booked, I get a room at the SOMA Park Inn, on the corner of 9th Street and Mission. (SOMA is an abbreviation for the South of Market district.)

I drive across Sacramento to visit Sutter's Fort. I have mixed feelings about John Sutter. He was Swiss and came to America from Germany in 1834 to escape his debts, leaving his wife and children behind. After adventures and perpetrating swindles all over the US and in Hawaii and Alaska, he settled here and became a Mexican citizen – California was then ruled by Mexico. The Mexicans gave him thousands of acres of land in return for his maintaining order among the Indians, and his help with defending their territory against the Americans and the British. Sutter began to build his fort in 1840 and, helped by men he'd recruited in Hawaii, coerced the local Nisenan and Miwok Indians into doing the work, treating them almost as slaves. He exploited the Indians again when he built his sawmill at Coloma a few years later.

Having built the fort and being, by then, a wealthy farmer and trader, he became famous for his generosity towards immigrants and settlers. He and his men helped to rescue the survivors of the Donner party from near starvation, and many who came to California in covered wagons saw Sutter's Fort as their goal, a place of safety. Sutter welcomed them, helped them and gave some of them jobs.

The fort is built around a patch of dun-coloured, baked earth about the size of a football pitch. Five or six people in nineteenth-century clothing stand around chatting to each other while, from beyond the walls, the glass, steel and concrete of twenty-first-century Sacramento peer down on this outpost of the past. I wander in and out of low buildings set against the outer walls and look inside a two-storey house in the middle. My recently acquired museum phobia quickly takes hold; most of the rooms have a purpose – blacksmith shop, bakery, kitchen – and contain old implements. The buildings themselves feel authentic, though the fort is a recon-struction built on the same site in the 1890s and is smaller than the original. I'm glad it is here, but I don't stay long.

Instead I go to the State Indian Museum next door. It's 2 p.m. Am I procrastinating, trying to delay the end of this momentous trip? Maybe. But San Francisco isn't far. And I'm interested in Indians, at least as much as in European and American settlers.

I go in and find a calming quiet – there is just one other vis-itor touring this subtly lit room – and much about the lives of Californian Indians. I look at photographs of an Indian man called Ishi, read about him – and am glad I came in. In 1911, Ishi appeared on the edge of a town called Oroville. He was fifty, a Yahi Indian and had lived his entire life hiding from white people and living in the wild in the traditional way of his people. It came to be under-stood that the last of his family had died three years earlier and that he had come out of hiding in search of food. Ishi was given a home by anthropologists at the University of Berkeley, who studied him, provided him with an apartment at the Museum of Anthropology and employed him as a janitor. He learned English and passed on a lot about the language, music and way of life of the Yahi. He was greatly liked and became famous throughout the United States as 'the last wild Indian' in America. He died of tuberculosis in 1916.

I eat a bit of lunch at a pavement café and finally set off for San Francisco. Following signs to US50 and I80 – which are now the same road – I rush around on expressways, kicking Harpo's accelerator to get him up to about 90 mph when I have to change lanes. Perhaps I've finally learned how to drive in American cities.

Streaky white clouds sit above mountains to the north, but otherwise the sky is blue as three lanes of traffic hammer downhill towards the Pacific. The road gradually flattens and, like a silver bullet, a train belts along beside the road.

A notice says I am thirty minutes from Berkeley. From there San Francisco is across the bay. The road has expanded to five lanes and everyone is tearing along. It's no fun driving like this, but I have to.

Now there are no trees, just brownish grass. A traffic jam and a distant view of the sun sparkling on water. Can that be the Pacific? Suddenly I'm on a concrete structure with about a million cars travelling very slowly, a misty cloud in front and blue sky everywhere else. The next three exits are to Berkeley; that's probably what's slowing the traffic.

Water and little sailing boats beside the road and a tremendous city skyline – pointed spires and skyscrapers – across the bay. San Francisco! And this must be the Bay Bridge. Exit to Treasure Island and Yerba Buena Island one mile ahead. Now a stunning sky, an early sunset with streaks over the sea.

We – all these cars – are going into a tunnel, five lanes of us. There doesn't seem to be any traffic going the other way. Where is it? Underneath us. A beautiful structure, this is a series of massive suspension bridges with a tunnel in the middle – through Yerba Buena Island. (Before it was San Francisco, the settlement here was called Yerba Buena – 'good herb' in Spanish.) Now the skyline is at

395

two o'clock, with cloud like cotton wool lying behind it: wonderful and spectacular. Below me to the right, I can see the sea.

I stick in the right-hand lane – and take an exit marked 9th Street. I end up in a one-way street full of traffic, and manage to stop to look at the San Francisco street map in my road atlas. I'm going the right way; Mission Street and the Soma Park Inn are four blocks ahead.

The receptionist gives me a room key and suggests I put a notice in my car's window saying 'Nothing of value in this car'. 'We try to keep the cars secure, but occasionally we get a break-in.'

The car park is on street level and open to Mission and 9th streets; the rooms are higher up. I tear a page out of my notebook, write in big capitals and beef them up by inking them over. When I put the sign on the dashboard, I see that other cars have similar notices.

It's 8 p.m. and dark by the time I go out. And it's cold. I get my jacket from Harpo's boot – I haven't worn it since I got off the plane at Dulles airport weeks ago – and walk up 9th Street towards Market Street. It's Saturday night but there aren't many people around, except homeless people lying in doorways under filthy duvets. I walk along Market, back down 10th and return to 9th – and a place I passed earlier. I go into the Cadillac Bar and Grill, a large, high-ceilinged space on the ground floor of an art-deco skyscraper. There's a long bar – perhaps twenty bar stools with no one sitting on them – scattered tables, where a few people are eating, and chefs, low down, behind a stainless-steel counter.

A bartender wearing a loud, floral shirt pours me a Lagunitas IPA. I look at the menu and see that the food is Mexican. In fact, the whole place is Mexican and descended from a bar and grill that opened in Nueva Laredo in 1926.

I drink the cold beer and think. I'm actually here. No more driving, or walking about in boiling sunshine, or searching for a town with a motel. No more sitting in bars alone or meeting people – a shame, that one. No more thinking what next, or planning. No more getting lost – remember Cincinnati and Cambridge, Maryland? And no more panic about how to get through this:

forty-six days, thirteen states, 3,000 miles. That had much to do with loneliness: I know now, at least, that I can endure days of it and that it gets me out there, talking to people.

I order prawn and red snapper brochette – and another IPA. The bartender is about thirty, good-looking, an expert, a man whose life is measured in other people's drinks. He stands beside numerous glasses, sparkling and ready – many primed with salt for margaritas.

No more missing people. Family, especially: wife, daughters, grandchildren. I'm lucky to have good relationships with five young children. When they see me, they either ignore me – which I take as a sign that I belong in their lives – or, sometimes, they seem pleased.

The food is good. The bartender, whose name, like my oldest grandson's, is Freddie, has been joined by an older man, also wearing a floral shirt, who I guess is the head honcho – perhaps the proprietor.

I tell him I like his shirt.

'I buy the shirts for the barmen in Mexico,' he says.

I've finished the fish. He takes away my plate. 'You like dessert? We have great ice cream.' He gives me the dessert menu. 'You know,' – he is smiling – 'you think too much.'

'Maybe,' I say. 'Maybe. I have a lot to think about.'

'Maybe, but I've seen you thinking very hard.' He's chuckling and shaking his head. 'It's good to stop for a while.'

'OK. I'll try.' I move down the bar so that I can see a screen. Someone is talking to Tiger Woods. I don't look at him. Instead I listen to the music; I've shut it out till now: brass and voices, Mexican probably. And I can't help thinking that, perhaps, out of the mouths of babes and restaurant proprietors . . .

Instead of an ice cream, I ask for a glass of Glenfiddich. Freddie begins pouring, down low, close to the glass, then keeps it flowing as he raises the bottle a foot in the air and lowers it again. It's quite a drink, generous, perhaps a quadruple. I ask for water and he gives it me in a glass.

I spend half an hour drinking scotch in a new way – neat with a water chaser – while trying not to think. Or thinking only: *Swill slowly. That tastes good. This is the life.* Tiger Woods has gone, replaced by American football. I watch Freddie pulling glasses out of a dish-washer and drying his hands on his trousers.

Four people come in and order Cadillac Margaritas. Freddie shovels ice into a shaker and, with a flip of both wrists, simultaneously upends bottles of tequila, Cointreau and Grand Marnier so that the three mix and splatter onto the ice. Then much shaking before he fills four ready-salted glasses.

Freddie and his boss salt more glasses. They rub each one on a wet circular sponge, shove it in a plate of salt and stand it upright to dry.

I take a final swig, pay my bill and thank them.

I walk down 9th Street marvelling that I've finished something that, at one time, I thought was beyond me – and then I remember the man saying, 'You think too much.'

76

On the Beach 2

Two men are cleaning the hotel's car park with mops. I caught the scent of urine last night. Several homeless-looking people linger at the junction of 9th and Mission: standing, sitting against walls, lying down. Many look miserable, raddled, ill-clothed; a few look like everyone else, like the people who are going somewhere, except that these people aren't – they seem stuck, perhaps newly homeless or not homeless, perhaps looking for drugs.

I walk up 9th Street past the Cadillac and the art-deco edifice above it. I round the corner on to Market Street, and walk along the longer side, the front of the building. At the further end, on the corner of 10th Street, this wonderful building has an enormity attached to it – a vertical plastic sign that says Twitter below a giant dicky-bird logo. I look in at the front door and there it is again – that logo.

I go inside and walk across a shiny marble floor to a reception desk. 'Excuse me. I just wondered: does this building have a name?'

'This is the Twitter Building.'

'Oh, OK. Just wondered. Thanks.'

'You're welcome.' The man smiles. It's Sunday. There's no one else in this huge space. He's probably a janitor, not a receptionist. I'm different today, too: a tourist, not a traveller – walking, not driving.

I walk back along Market in the direction of, I hope, Union Square. It would be good to have a map. I'm relying on my memory of the small map in my road atlas.

What am I actually doing, now I'm here? I'm going to have a squint at what I perceive to be the city centre, around Union Square. This is probably like arriving in London for the first time and heading for Piccadilly Circus. Well, why not? From there it's a short walk to all sorts of treasures. After that I must find a beach so that I can swim in the Pacific, take a look at the City Lights Bookstore and at Haight-Ashbury, a place I became aware of in 1967 when I worked in London on the underground magazine *Oz*. I was eighteen and believed that young people would – or at least could – change the world, and that the hippies in San Francisco had already made a start. It was a romantic notion: peace and love, boosted by Scott McKenzie's song 'San Francisco (Be Sure to Wear Flowers in Your Hair)'. I would have loved to have come here back then. I had the hair, but not the time or the money.

A part of me still cleaves to that kind of idealism; it's why I like Nick Lowe's song '(What's So Funny 'Bout) Peace, Love and Understanding?' And why I respect Greta Thunberg – and a friend's daughter who bunks off school to sit outside the offices of Exeter City Council on Paris Street.

Still on Market Street, I come to the farmers' market: noisy and jovial with street food and a black guy in a purple Lurex tail-coat singing and accompanying himself on an electric piano. Two young policemen look on, smiling. I ask one of them if this is Union Square. It isn't; it's quite a way further and he tells me how to get there.

I've known that this is a hilly city since I saw Steve McQueen driving a Ford Mustang and chasing villains in *Bullitt*. Now I see streets lined with tall buildings rising like canyons into the north.

400

Union Square is surrounded by old, elegant skyscrapers and filled with palm trees and artists sitting under umbrellas trying to sell their work.

I wander into other streets, Taylor, Mason and Geary, where there are shops, restaurants, hotels. Here are young couples, straight and gay, in shorts and sports gear; people heading for Bloomingdale's, Macy's and Prada; a couple in a flashy red open-top car; and dawdling tourists from all over the world.

Here too, though, the homeless seem to dominate, and I steer around them. Many are what a New York friend calls 'crazies', wandering, out of their minds. Some trail suitcases by those extendable handles; one man has hooked two together. Others have carts of various kinds filled with plastic bags and, perhaps, a duvet. People lie in the street, half-covered by filthy bedding. Many talk to themselves, some shout. I see homeless people in wheelchairs, pushing themselves along, their stuff hanging off the back – one man levers himself along backwards with his feet. A very fat man, bum crack on display, pushes, and seems to be held up by, a wheelchair carrying a thin man with grey hair. Many sit begging in a tired, hopeless way, holding out a plastic cup or a hand.

I follow a sign to a visitor information centre where I tell a young guy that I want to swim in the Pacific – and that six weeks ago I swam in the Atlantic. 'Where should I go?' I ask.

'Baker Beach if you want the ocean without going out of the city.' He produces a map and picks up a pen. 'But I don't think you should swim. The ocean's *very* cold right now. I don't think you'll find anyone swimming. Paddling, but not swimming.'

'Really? Do you think it's actually dangerous to go right in?'

'You'll get very cold very fast.' He gives me a stern look. 'Paddle. Won't that do?'

'It'll have to.' I'm both disappointed and relieved. I knew the water would be cold.

'Baker Beach is right by the Golden Gate Bridge. It's worth a visit anyway.'

He explains that I can get there by taking two buses. He marks the stops on the map. The trip might take about an hour. I should pay on the first bus – put quarters in a slot by the driver, take a receipt and show it on the second bus. There's a machine for changing dollar bills into quarters right outside the information centre.

This fine man tells me that he is going to London next week via Paris. He's never been before.

I feel like saying I'll meet him there and show him round. But, perhaps sensibly, I hold back. 'Great. You'll love it. Thanks for all your help.'

I walk up towards the bus stop on Geary Street, and pass a group of homeless people lying close together on the pavement in the sun. Some are asleep. Some look drugged and almost asleep. A woman, thin and haggard, with pink hair, bare arms and a bra strap down by her elbow, sits in the gutter holding six or seven syringes in one hand, while rifling through a bag with the other. A man stands looking on, as if waiting for her to give him something.

You think too much, the man said yesterday. What is there to think about this? It's beyond thought. A feeling. A tragedy. Anger. Sadness. This shouldn't happen. With or without drugs, homelessness mutilates humanity, all of us.

The 38 bus trundles along Geary past the ends of suburban streets. I get off a long way to the west and take another bus north, as far as it goes, to Baker Beach. As the bus stops I see blue sea through pine trees below. A couple get off in front of me, step over a low fence and scramble down a steep sandy slope, grabbing at trees to slow their descent. I follow them.

I cross a car park. And I'm there, on the sand, staring at the Golden Gate Bridge while the waves roll in with a lovely crashing rhythm. Journey's end. Ocean to ocean.

The beach lines a bay between two points and faces a sheet of open sea, which twinkles in the south. Out there are boats – sailing boats, a container ship – and a long horizon beneath a pale sky. The bridge is a wondrous structure: an upward curve, held up by steel hawsers that, from here, look like piano strings. It is painted a curious red colour, which some might call plum – and I call stewed rhubarb. People, enough but not many, sit and stroll on soft sand pitted with footmarks. Children run, dig holes and paddle. The sun shines but it's not warm. I'm in long trousers after weeks in shorts. Everyone – almost everyone – is wearing clothes.

I want to enjoy being on this beach, and not just paddle in the Pacific for a photograph, so I stretch out on the sand, lean against a dry, silvery log and read a few pages of *Joyland* by Stephen King, a book I bought in Moab, Utah.

I become aware that a large, naked black man is walking a few feet in front of me; he has wrapped his body in the yellow plastic tape that the police use to cordon off the scenes of crimes. The tape doesn't conceal anything. A few people are looking at him unobtrusively, but most are taking no notice. I look down the beach towards the Golden Gate Bridge and see a naked white man walking about; he isn't even wearing scene-of-crime tape. I, staid Englishman that I am, find it hard to imagine waking up on a Sunday morning and thinking – 'I know what I'll do today. I ll go to Baker Beach, take all my clothes off, and walk up and down in the nude.' But, of course, there are many things I can't imagine wanting to do on any day of the week: shooting a pheasant, for example, or sipping wine in a church.

A woman in bright green tights is standing on her head with her legs in the air, one forward and one back: yoga, I think. It's time for me to do something strange. I take off my shoes, roll my trousers up to my knees, walk down to the water and step in so it just about covers my toes. It's very cold. Two women are standing a little way up the beach chatting – one is wearing Bermuda shorts; the other has shorter shorts. They look easy-going, approachable – although you can never be sure.

'Excuse me. I'm from London, England.' I'm freaking them out. 'Could you possibly take a photo of me standing in the water with the Golden Gate in the background.' I hold out my phone.

'Oh sure,' Bermuda Shorts says. They're both relaxing.

'It's just to show my family that I actually got here.'

'Oh, great.' She laughs and takes my phone. 'I bet they'll love that.'

The three of us walk down the beach, and I step into the water with my back to the bridge. 'Is this the right place?'

She points the phone towards me. 'Yep.' She looks at the screen.

Shorter Shorts says, 'Smile.' She grins and crosses her eyes.

Bermudas chuckles as I try to look sane while putting on a smile. 'There you go. Six pictures.' She hands me the phone.

77

Another Day

I sit on the bus heading back into the city. That's it. I've done it. I've even got the photographs. And there's one more day. It's 5 p.m. I don't have to leave for the airport till this time tomorrow.

I stay on the bus beyond the junction with Geary Street and take it across Golden Gate Park. I get off on the south side, buy a salad in a gas station and walk back into the park. It's beautifully landscaped, wild in places, constrained in others; unexpected vistas open up – between clumps of trees, around a bend, at the top of a rise. People walk, sit on benches or on the grass, and there are a few joggers. But it's late in the day and cold, which may explain why there aren't more people. A winding path takes me to a boating lake, where I sit on a bench warmed by the sun and eat my salad. Seagulls swim on the lake and four white girls, about fourteen years old, cruise around on pedalos, screaming and splashing one another. Their clothes, hair and confidence somehow tell me that these are middle-class kids whose families send them to a good school.

I walk on and get lost – and it doesn't matter; the park is a maze of paths that curve and rise and fall. I come across well-hidden restrooms, a rose garden, and a dip where the sun streaks the shade inside a grove of cedars.

I come out on Nancy Pelosi Drive, where exotic trees grow out of cut grass. Two young men cycle past. One says, 'Oh shit! What time's the Notre Dame game?' Of course, he uses the American pronunciation of Notre Dame, which rhymes with 'voter name'.

An old VW Microbus, painted with flowers and the words San Francisco Love Tours, chugs past. I'm close to Hippie Hill, the broad, grassy slope where, more than fifty years ago, Jefferson Airplane, the Grateful Dead, Janis Joplin, George Harrison and others performed free for crowds of hippies. It's getting dark. I leave the park and take a bus east towards my hotel.

Later I walk south on 9th Street, away from the Cadillac, away from the city centre, in search of a neighbourhood bar or restaurant. I pass a bar that is closed and come to Kama Sushi, a small, snug-looking Japanese restaurant.

I sit among others at a counter; facing us, behind glass cabinets filled with sushi ingredients, two men chop and roll with the speed of long practice. The food is great – many of the customers are Japanese – while the conversation is limited to brief exchanges with the charming waitress who says, 'Thee-ank yo-woo.' When it comes to dessert, I make up for all the raw fish by ordering green tea ice cream fried in tempura with whipped cream and chocolate sauce – and the waitress says, 'Thee-ank yo-woo,' twice.

In the morning, I put my bags in Harpo's boot and cross the road for breakfast at the Allstar Café, where customers order and pay at a counter, then eat at formica tables while staring at a screen that hangs from the ceiling. I order the regular breakfast, asking for one egg instead of two. When I come to pay, the bill shows the price of a two-egg breakfast.

'I only asked for one egg.'

'It's the same price.'

'Isn't there a discount for the egg?'

'No. Sorry.'

'Oh.' I give the man a look ... but he doesn't flinch. 'Well, I'll have two eggs, then.'

I sit down and wait for the two-egg breakfast. Beside me, a middle-aged woman in a brown woolly hat is drinking a Diet Coke very slowly and staring up at the television; she has the air of someone who wants to sit here as long as possible while spending as little money as possible. By the window, an old man of East Asian origin sits on a stool; he has a Zimmer frame beside him and is filling in a form in tiny writing.

The two-egg breakfast arrives. I eat the first egg with bacon and tomato. I pause – and then eat the second one with sausage and home fries, while thinking I'm eating an egg I don't want because I can't bear to waste the price of an egg; or, to put it another way, this egg is a free egg and if I can get something for free I jolly well will. What does this say about me? That I'm an idiot. Despite my liberal pretensions, I'm a little money-hoarding twerp of a capitalist who will do anything to get his money's worth. I must *learn* from this – a little wisdom to take home: have one egg and eat it, however much it appears to cost.

I cross back over the road to the bus stop on Mission Street. I need to go east and then north to the City Lights Bookstore. I wait with four other people, including a woman in a wheelchair with bruises on her arms. Behind us, a variety of homeless people sit down, stand up, walk off and return. Facing us, is the Go Go Market & Deli and, next to it, the Re-Leaf Herbal Center, which sells cannabis; a big man, wearing a black T-shirt, calf-length shorts and green rubber gloves, stands on the pavement watching customers come and go.

Yesterday, the manager of the Go Go Market told me that he thinks cannabis is now legal throughout California. And then he said, with a tired shrug, that while the politicians have legalised cannabis, they are making menthol cigarettes and flavoured vapes illegal because they entice children into smoking.

Two fit, black-clad, East Asian-looking young policemen arrive

407

on black bikes marked POLICE. They dismount and approach a grey-haired, apparently sober man who is sitting on the pavement, leaning against the wall of the Soma Park Inn, with no trousers on. They seem to be telling him, politely, that he must put on some trousers. He gets up and sits down. It is apparent that, beneath a long-tailed shirt, he is wearing sports-style shorts. He mutters and shakes his head. Another apparently homeless man, a friend, speaks to him. He rummages in a plastic bag, pulls out some grey trousers and puts them on. The two policemen thank him and get on their bikes.

The bus arrives. The woman in the wheelchair stands up, pushes her wheelchair on to the bus and sits in it.

Several blocks to the east, I get off and walk north up Kearney Street, where the pavements are clean and sleek skyscrapers soar up behind stone plazas prettified with manicured box hedges and triangular beds of multicoloured stocks. This is the financial district, where men wear suits or tweed sports jackets and black, polished shoes, but not ties – and there's a Starbucks on every other block. Even the homeless look smarter and sit neatly behind their begging bowls.

I buy coffee in a Starbucks and sit in a comfortable chair by the window. Outside a young woman sits on the pavement leaning against a traffic light. She seems tired, sleepy, but otherwise all right. Her hands are a little dirty but her clothes are clean: a woolly hat, wrap, hoodie, trousers, good shoes; and she has a newish rucksack, a snakeskin-style bag, a nice-looking dog in a jacket, dark-rimmed glasses, a stainless-steel water container and a bag of dog biscuits. The dog is snuggled up to her and she is writing something on a small cardboard box, very slowly because she keeps falling asleep, and then nodding awake.

A woman stops, smiles and says something to her. An older man in sunglasses walks by slowly and looks. A dachshund trots past on a lead; the dog raises his eyes, but doesn't move. Otherwise people – perhaps fifty come by as I sip coffee and watch – don't seem to see her. And no one puts money in the cardboard box, on which she still struggles to write a message.

408

I walk on uphill, past Chinatown, and take a left fork onto Columbus Avenue. Another block – and there it is, on a sharp corner: the City Lights Bookstore, a wedge-shaped building that comes almost to a point – long and low and painted terracotta, two storeys with large, elegant windows. I come to the thin end of the wedge and a sign in a window: '3 Floors of Books, Open Every Day, 11 a.m. to Midnight'. I walk on – it seems dark inside – to the door. A notice, printed on white paper: 'We will be closed Monday September 24th for a staff function. Sorry for the inconvenience and please visit us again.'

No-oooo! 'For a staff function.' What an insult! Lawrence Ferlinghetti, the founder, owner and Beat poet, wouldn't use that sort of HR-speak. He'd say closed 'for waving and whispering to each other' or 'for tilting at ginmills'.

Oh well! I take a few photographs and notice that the street to the left of the wedge is called Jack Kerouac Alley. Plaques on the ground are engraved with quotes from Kerouac, Ferlinghetti and Maya Angelou – and with this spirited message from John Steinbeck: 'The free exploring mind of the individual human is the most valuable thing in the world.' I walk past the store and, to my right, a little way along Broadway, see a painting of Jack Kerouac and Neal Cassady with the words The Beat Museum written across their legs. I find myself thinking: *With a bit of luck, it'll be shut.*

But it isn't – and I go in. The man in charge is young, friendly and knows plenty about the Beat writers. From time to time he sees Ferlinghetti, who is physically fine and will be one hundred years old in March. 'A few eyesight problems, but that's all.' There are two floors of wonderful exhibits – and no fossils. I look at photographs, films, books, letters, manuscript pages and Jack Kerouac's jacket – cut like a jean jacket but tweed with large checks, and worn, it is suggested, on the mountain walks described in *The Dharma Bums.*

And I read short essays and biographies, from which I pick up the message that – though William Burroughs might be the father of the Beats because he was the eldest, and Jack Kerouac the best known because his novels, especially *On the Road*, were popular – the unifying figure was the gay poet Allen Ginsberg. He had many contacts and helped the others, including Burroughs and Kerouac, find publishers. And, while others, such as Kerouac, weren't supportive of the hippies, Ginsberg promoted them, appeared at their events and influenced musicians including Bob Dylan, John Lennon, Patti Smith and the Clash.

I want to spend more time here, but I have to collect Harpo from the Soma Park Inn; they gave me extra parking time but they have new guests arriving – and I'm already late. I rush back and am soon driving west along Hayes Street. It's half-past two and I'm hungry, so when I see at a café with tables outside on the pavement I stop. It turns out that I'm in a ritzy district called Hayes Valley, where sophisticates come to eat and to shop for designer gear. I go into an airy place called Boulangerie and order a smoked trout salad and a cup of tea.

A pleasant breeze comes from a ceiling fan as I wait for my trout at a large pine table. There aren't many customers but, of course, I gawp at those who come in. A large, bald man enters with a pretty woman, walks to a table at the back and beckons his woman friend, but she beckons him back; she wants to sit at the front and – hurray! – she gets her way. Three young women dressed in black sashay in. They might be models. Or rich men's wives. Or both. Or neither. Or orthopaedic surgeons in mufti. One has a fringe and her hair shaved at the sides; she seems to be in charge of the others, who have conventional, long glossy hair; she decides where they will sit and, probably, what they are going to eat.

I move on and drive a few blocks along Hayes to Alamo Park, where a grassy hill is topped by palm trees, cedars and assorted pines – and the houses in the surrounding streets are large and painted in pastel colours. Here people sit, arms around knees, on the grass in the sun and stare at the city below. I join them, smile at some children, and find that I can see the skyscrapers to the east and the ocean in the west. I read a little Stephen King and watch, beside some small awestruck children, as a tiny plane chugs over our heads, dragging a banner advertising Stella Rosa wine.

I drive west again – this time to my final stop, the district where it all happened in 1967, Haight-Ashbury. The heart of it is the junction that gives it its name, where Haight Street crosses Ashbury Street. I manage to park close to Ashbury and a block north of Haight. I walk along Ashbury, a disappointingly quiet street of terraced homes, uphill towards Haight, where I find people and shops. This is where the flower children gathered and made love, rather than war. Indeed, there are more flowers – some of them plastic – in, below and above shop windows than in most streets. There are a few young hippies, and one or two old ones. I catch the scent of patchouli, once beloved by hippie women. Some stores trade on the history – Sunchild's Parlor, Land of the Sun, Jimi Hendrix Red House – while many make no reference to it – gift and clothes shops, Indian restaurants and pizza parlours. Four blocks west of the junction with Ashbury, Haight faces Golden Gate Park and Hippie Hill, the scene of those magical free concerts and the hippie love-ins and be-ins, with the sex and drugs that so disturbed older people. Now, a branch of Whole Foods faces a store selling DVDs.

I drive away east. I must find my way out of the city now. I have to catch a plane. I sit back and pat Harpo on the steering wheel. Soon he and I will part. Soon I will be home in London. And I will write about all this. I might begin with a lifeguard dressed in red and a small boy with a plastic baseball bat . . .

Slow Road to San Francisco Discography

The Barr Brothers, *Sleeping Operator*

Antonin Dvořák, *Symphony No 9 'From the New World'*

The Eagles, *Their Greatest Hits 1971-1975*

Bill Evans, *The Paris Concert, edition one*

John Fogerty, *Wrote a Song for Everyone*

Charlie Haden and Pat Metheny, *Beyond the Missouri Sky*

Emmylou Harris, *Red Dirt Girl*

Keith Jarrett, Gary Peacock, Jack DeJohnette, *The Out-of-Towners*

Art Tatum, Ben Webster, Red Callender, Bill Douglass, *Tatum Group Masterpieces, Vol. 8*

Neil Young, *Harvest Moon*

Acknowledgements

I am thrilled to be published by a newly reinvigorated publisher, Muswell Press, essentially the creation of the wonderful sisters Sarah and Kate Beal, and to benefit from their energy, enthusiasm and fresh thinking. While working on *Slow Road to San Francisco*, I have drawn on their ideas, imagination and encouragement and I owe them huge thanks. I also want to thank Kate Quarry for her wise and whoops-saving editorial work, Roy Williams for his clear, contour-washed map of my journey across the United States, and the starry star-maker Fiona Brownlee for promoting the book with the brio and panache that are part of her nature.

Thanks to: Mike Davies for all the coffees, paninis and geeing up – 'but you were writing about St Louis *last* week!'; my Texan friend Brent Bratton for encouragement and for championing Larry McMurtry; my daughter Grace for being a good egg and lending me her study on Fridays; my other daughters, Martha and Rose, also for being good eggs and for oozing interest and merriment; Philippa Campbell for coffee and warm chat; Arthur Broome for cold Peronis; Chris Scott for excellent seats at the new White Hart Lane; Tommy Barnes for many varieties of his own creation, Braslou Bière; and my nephew Steve Roest for his insights and for MOTing the car. Friends who have provided beer and wisdom include Ben

Yarde-Buller, David Hunt, Mike Bailey, Stephen Powell, Bruce Mackay, Rob Sanders, Andy Jarman, Nick Cash, Miren Lopategui and Nigel Richardson. Encouragement has come from Nigel Phillips, Tony Peake, Sally Holloway, Louie Burghes, Ros Franey, Jennifer Potter, Sheena Phillips, Miranda Gudenian, Maggie Morris, Matthew Tomkinson, Fanny Blake and Louise Davies.

My wife, Penny Phillips, has endured this thing, read it relentlessly over and over, and, great editor that she is, has poured beer while accentuating the positive and, with great effect, suggesting removal of the 'onanistic', as the great William Styron once, so delicately, put it. My admiration for her knowledge and expertise, and my love of the tilt of her nose, are infinite.